# LEGAL AND POLITICAL OBLIGATION

## Classic and Contemporary Texts and Commentary

## R. George Wright
Professor of Law
Cumberland School of Law
Samford University

UNIVERSITY
PRESS OF
AMERICA

Lanham • New York • London

Copyright © 1992 by
**University Press of America®, Inc.**
4720 Boston Way
Lanham, Maryland 20706

3 Henrietta Street
London WC2E 8LU England

**Library of Congress Cataloging-in-Publication Data**

Wright, R. George.
Legal and political obligation : classic and contemporary texts
and commentary / R. George Wright.
p.    cm.
Includes bibliographical references and index.
1. Obedience (Law).    2. Law—Philosophy.
3. Political obligation.    4. Political science—
Philosophy.    I. Title.
K258.W75    1992    340'.1—dc20    91–47710 CIP

ISBN 0–8191–8595–7 (cloth : alk. paper)
ISBN 0–8191–8596–5 (pbk. : alk. paper)

The paper used in this publication meets the minimum requirements of
American National Standard for Information Sciences—Permanence
of Paper for Printed Library Materials, ANSI Z39.48–1984.

For a lifetime of insistence on holding the criminal justice system to exacting standards of fairness and respect for the disadvantaged and the outcast, this book is dedicated to Owen M. Mullin.

# Acknowledgments

For their encouragement, doubtless implicitly conditioned on this disclaimer of their responsibility for the finished product, the author wishes to thank Randy Barnett, Robby George, John Leslie, Judy McAlister, Irene Morissette, Robert Post, Charles Rice, Tom Shaffer, Steven D. Smith, Karen Walker, Lisa White, Dean Parham Williams and, preeminently, Mary Wright.

Acknowledgment is hereby gratefully extended to the respective copyright holders for permission to reprint excerpts from the following works:

Plato, EUTHYPHRO, APOLOGY, CRITO, AND PHAEDO, trans. Benjamin Jowett (Buffalo, N.Y.: Prometheus Books, 1988).

Thomas Hobbes, THE LEVIATHAN (Buffalo, N.Y.: Prometheus Books, 1988).

John Locke, THE SECOND TREATISE ON CIVIL GOVERNMENT (Buffalo, N.Y.: Prometheus Books, 1986).

Jean-Jacques Rousseau, THE SOCIAL CONTRACT, trans. G.D.H. Cole (Buffalo, N.Y.: Prometheus Books, 1988).

David Hume, A TREATISE OF HUMAN NATURE, E.C. Mossner ed. (London: Penguin Books, 1969, 1984).

Thomas Aquinas, Summa Theologica, in THE POLITICAL IDEAS OF ST. THOMAS AQUINAS, Dino Bigongiari ed. (New York: Hafner, 1953 & Mission Hills, Calif.: Benziger Publishing Co./Glenco/ McGraw-Hill).

Henry David Thoreau, On the Duty of Civil Disobedience, in CIVIL DISOBEDIENCE AND VIOLENCE, Jeffrie G. Murphy ed. (Belmont, Calif.: Wadsworth Publishing Co., 1971).

Kai Nielsen, State Authority and Legitimation, in ON POLITICAL OBLIGATION, Paul Harris ed. (London: Routledge, 1989).

Frances Olsen, Socrates on Legal Obligation: Legitimation Theory and Civil Disobedience, 18 GEORGIA LAW REVIEW 929-966 (1984).

Dr. Martin Luther King, Jr., Letter From Birmingham Jail, reprinted by permission of the Joan Daves Agency, copyright 1963 by Rev. Martin Luther King, Jr.

# Contents

# Introduction

This book is intended as an introduction to the problems of legal and political obligation. Unfortunately, writers differ among themselves as to what these terms mean. As a start, though, we may think of legal obligation as an alleged moral obligation to obey particular laws. By contrast, we may use the idea of political obligation as including a broader alleged moral obligation to obey a regime's laws in general.[1]

Most of the book consists of reproductions or excerpts from the works of writers whose influence has been broad and enduring. Some attention is also devoted to contemporary writers who make distinctive and valuable contributions to the ongoing discussion. What is unusual about this book, though, is its special emphasis upon contemporary critical reaction to classic arguments and ideas. Most of the notes follow an excerpt from a classic text; some stand alone. Of course, no pretense to thoroughness in this respect is possible. But it is fair to say that many of the most interesting contemporary scholarly responses to classic discussions of legal and political obligation are at least briefly referred to below. Full and plain citations are provided immediately to each such scholarly response, for the student's convenience in exploring particularly intriguing ideas or in developing paper topics.

The notes, comments, and questions following many of the classic texts are meant to be understandable, at least with the help of an instructor, but they do not patronize the student. Most of the questions do not have obvious answers easily confirmed merely by re-reading the preceding text. Instead, they normally involve genuinely controversial approaches to unsolved problems of interpretation and criticism. The student is asked to think about the same issues and problems that interest and divide the experts. Thus, even with the assistance of a course instructor, the answers to many of the questions will remain unclear. The book assumes, however, that most students would rather tackle real issues, even if inconclusively, than a series of mere workbook exercises that are pointless in themselves.

Many of the questions are, as the lawyers would say, "leading," in that their statement itself may suggest one answer rather than another. This technique, though, is intended to provoke, and not to endorse or indoctrinate. The book's aim is to assist the student in doing the best possible sustained critical thinking about the issues, rather than to create mere political partisans. While no selection of materials can be genuinely neutral, it is hoped that the book represents a wide and diverse range of political perspectives as accurately as possible within a limited space.

It is worth taking a moment to think about the relationship between the study of legal and political obligation, and the broader fields of legal and political philosophy in general. There is a good deal to be said for the idea of focusing on legal and political obligation as a manageable approach to the otherwise intimidatingly broad and complex subject of legal and political philosophy in general. Political and legal obligation is indeed central to the overall political thinking of some leading philosophers. It is, however, admittedly less central to the thinking of others.[2] Thus the number of pages allocated in this book to each of the writers represented below is not in every case proportional to the writer's overall importance to legal and political philosophy generally. The page allocation below is thus in a sense potentially misleading, but the student who is mainly interested in beginning to develop a broad understanding of legal and political philosophy in general may find that the narrower, coherently focused approach taken in this book has advantages and is surprisingly helpful.

It has occasionally been argued, though, that the question of a moral obligation of some sort to obey a government is not only of secondary importance, but practically meaningless. One writer suggests, for example, that "[w]e have not understood what it *means* to be a member of a political society if we suppose that political obligation is something we might not have had and that therefore needs to be *justified*."[3] It seems clear, though, that this approach is not particularly helpful. It simply pushes the issue back to whether we are, or ought to be, full members of the actual political society within which we geographically find ourselves. It is certainly not obvious, for example, that German citizens under the Nazi regime should have taken the question of political obligation as absurd or meaningless. This would have amounted to the most grave moral error.

As we will see below, however, certain complications are unavoidable. It is at least conceivable, for example, that under even the most clearly illegitimate, morally abominable regime, we may have a moral duty on some grounds to conform to a number of laws, such as, for example, typical anti-drunk driving statutes.[4] On the other hand, it is also at least conceivable that genuine political obligation may require not just faithful adherence to or observance of the laws, but active political participation, and in some cases the acceptance of risks and of the need for sacrifice beyond what the laws themselves may require.[5]

Further complicating matters for the student is the fact that the most prominent contemporary debates on legal and political obligation cannot be taken at face value. The introductory student may be surprised to learn that many, if not most, contemporary academic philosophers deny that there is any sort of morally binding general obligation to obey the law. As it turns out, though, there is less here than meets the eye. As we will see below, most such writers immediately qualify this claim in various ways that minimize its practical consequences. In contrast, contemporary writers who do accept some sort of morally binding general obligation to obey the law tend to recognize the tentativeness or weakness of such an obligation, and the broad range of exceptions to such an obligation. The practical differences between the two camps is thus minimal.

Equally misleading is much of the contemporary academic debate over civil disobedience. To a surprising degree, the debate tends to center on apparently definitional questions of what is or is not included within the very idea of civil disobedience. In reality, these debates are over matters of tactics, public perceptions, and substantive moral issues. Why the debates are typically conducted as disputes over the definition or meaning of the concept of civil disobedience itself is mysterious. One possible explanation is that at least within academic circles, the idea of civil disobedience has a much more favorable connotation than does generalized law violation. Narrowing or expanding the accepted definition of an idea with a permanent favorable connotation may advance or retard a wide range of particular political agendas.

These and other complications are explored below. While it will often be tempting to the student to bypass the complications, it remains true that no conclusion arrived at by sidestepping the difficult issues is really worth retaining.

Finally, it should be noted that most of the authors' footnotes associated with the classic texts reproduced below have been omitted. This has been done for the sake of readability. Those who miss such footnotes should appreciate that it would still be impossible to fully assess the works below without studying the remainder of the substantive texts concerned, as well as other related works by that particular author in question.

## NOTES TO INTRODUCTION

[1] By way of justification for this approach, one might point to George Klosko's observation that "[b]ecause modern states exercise their authority through the rule of law, questions of political obligation can be construed as questions about the obligation to obey the law." George Klosko, *The Moral Force of Political Obligations*, 84 AMERICAN POLITICAL SCIENCE REVIEW 1235, 1236 (1990).

[2] John Plamenatz has written, for example, that "Locke's political philosophy is above all else a theory of political obligation; but Rousseau's is so much less, and Hegel's even less than Rousseau's." JOHN P. PLAMENATZ, CONSENT, FREEDOM AND POLITICAL OBLIGATION 164 (2d ed. 1968). Roland Pennock has written similarly of political obligation that "[w]hile it has often been said that it constituted the heart of political theory or comprised its most fundamental category, a moment's reflection will point to a contrary view." J. Roland Pennock, *Introduction*, in 12 NOMOS: POLITICAL AND LEGAL OBLIGATION xiii (J. Roland Pennock & John W. Chapman eds. 1970). Pennock goes on to argue specifically that "[t]he *Crito* to the contrary notwithstanding, neither Plato nor Aristotle was primarily concerned with the problem of political obligation. The same can be said of many, perhaps most, other major figures in the history of political thought." *Id.*

[3] THOMAS MCPHERSON, POLITICAL OBLIGATION 64 (1967) (emphasis in the original).

[4] See Richard K. Dagger, *What is Political Obligation?*, 71 AMERICAN POLITICAL SCIENCE REVIEW 86, 93 (1977).

[5] See JOHN DUNN, POLITICAL OBLIGATION IN ITS HISTORICAL CONTEXT 290 (1980).

# Plato, Crito

| | |
|---|---|
| *Socrates.* | WHY have you come at this hour, Crito? It must be quite early. |
| *Crito.* | Yes, certainly. |
| *Soc.* | What is the exact time? |
| *Cr.* | The dawn is breaking. |
| *Soc.* | I wonder the keeper of the prison would let you in. |
| *Cr.* | He knows me because I often come, Socrates; moreover, I have done him a kindness. |
| *Soc.* | And are you only just come? |
| *Cr.* | No, I came some time ago. |
| *Soc.* | Then why did you sit and say nothing, instead of awakening me at once? |
| *Cr.* | Why, indeed, Socrates, I myself would rather not have all this sleeplessness and sorrow. But I have been wondering at your peaceful slumbers, and that was the reason why I did not awaken you, because I wanted you to be out of pain. I have always thought you happy in the calmness of your temperament; but never did I see the like of the easy, cheerful way in which you bear this calamity. |
| *Soc.* | Why, Crito, when a man has reached my age he ought not to be repining at the prospect of death. |
| *Cr.* | And yet other old men find themselves in similar misfortunes, and age does not prevent them from repining. |
| *Soc.* | That may be. But you have not told me why you come at this early hour. |
| *Cr.* | I come to bring you a message which is sad and painful; not, as I believe, to yourself, but to all of us who are your friends, and saddest of all to me. |
| *Soc.* | What! I suppose that the ship has come from Delos, on the arrival of which I am to die? |
| *Cr.* | No, the ship has not actually arrived, but she will probably be here to-day, as persons who have come from Sunium tell me that they have left her there; and therefore to-morrow, Socrates, will be the last day of your life. |
| *Soc.* | Very well, Crito; if such is the will of God, I am willing; but my belief is that there will be a delay of a day. |

*Cr.*    Why do you say this?

*Soc.*   I will tell you. I am to die on the day after the arrival of the ship?

*Cr.*    Yes; that is what the authorities say.

*Soc.*   But I do not think that the ship will be here until to-morrow; this I gather
from a vision which I had last night, or rather only just now, when you
fortunately allowed me to sleep.

*Cr.*    And what was the nature of the vision?

*Soc.*   There came to me the likeness of a woman, fair and comely, clothed in
white raiment, who called to me and said: O Socrates—
             "The third day hence, to Phthia shalt thou go."

*Cr.*    What a singular dream, Socrates!

*Soc.*   There can be no doubt about the meaning, Crito, I think.

*Cr.*    Yes: the meaning is only too clear. But, O! my beloved Socrates, let me
entreat you once more to take my advice and escape. For if you die I
shall not only lose a friend who can never be replaced, but there is
another evil: people who do not know you and me will believe that I
might have saved you if I had been willing to give money, but that I did
not care. Now, can there be a worse disgrace than this—that I should be
thought to value money more than the life of a friend? For the many will
not be persuaded that I wanted you to escape, and that you refused.

*Soc.*   But why, my dear Crito, should we care about the opinion of the many?
Good men, and they are the only persons who are worth considering, will
think of these things truly as they happen.

*Cr.*    But do you see, Socrates, that the opinion of the many must be regarded,
as is evident in your own case, because they can do the very greatest evil
to anyone who has lost their good opinion?

*Soc.*   I only wish, Crito, that they could; for then they could also do the
greatest good, and that would be well. But the truth is, that they can do
neither good nor evil: they cannot make a man wise or make him foolish;
and whatever they do is the result of chance.

*Cr.*    Well, I will not dispute about that; but please to tell me, Socrates,
whether you are not acting out of regard to me and your other friends:
are you not afraid that if you escape hence we may get into trouble with
the informers for having stolen you away, and lose either the whole or
a great part of our property; or that even a worse evil may happen to us?
Now, if this is your fear, be at ease; for in order to save you, we ought
surely to run this or even a greater risk; be persuaded, then, and do as I
say.

*Soc.*   Yes, Crito, that is one fear which you mention, but by no means the only
one.

*Cr.*    Fear not. There are persons who at no great cost are willing to save you
and bring you out of prison; and as for the informers, you may observe
that they are far from being exorbitant in their demands; a little money

will satisfy them. My means, which, as I am sure, are ample, are at your service, and if you have a scruple about spending all mine, here are strangers who will give you the use of theirs; and one of them, Simmias the Theban, has brought a sum of money for this very purpose; and Cebes and many others are willing to spend their money too. I say, therefore, do not on that account hesitate about making your escape, and do not say, as you did in the court, that you will have a difficulty in knowing what to do with yourself if you escape. For men will love you in other places to which you may go, and not in Athens only; there are friends of mine in Thessaly, if you like to go to them, who will value and protect you, and no Thessalian will give you any trouble. Nor can I think that you are justified, Socrates, in betraying your own life when you might be saved; this is playing into the hands of your enemies and destroyers; and moreover I should say that you were betraying your children; for you might bring them up and educate them; instead of which you go away and leave them, and they will have to take their chance; and if they do not meet with the usual fate of orphans, there will be small thanks to you. No man should bring children into the world who is unwilling to persevere to the end in their nurture and education. But you are choosing the easier part, as I think, not the better and manlier, which would rather have become one who professes virtue in all his actions, like yourself. And, indeed, I am ashamed not only of you, but of us who are your friends, when I reflect that this entire business of yours will be attributed to our want of courage. The trial need never have come on, or might have been brought to another issue; and the end of all, which is the crowning absurdity, will seem to have been permitted by us, through cowardice and baseness, who might have saved you, as you might have saved yourself, if we had been good for anything (for there was no difficulty in escaping); and we did not see how disgraceful, Socrates, and also miserable all this will be to us as well as to you. Make your mind up then, or rather have your mind already made up, for the time of deliberation is over, and there is only one thing to be done, which must be done, if at all, this very night, and which any delay will render all but impossible; I beseech you therefore, Socrates, to be persuaded by me, and to do as I say.

*Soc.*   Dear Crito, your zeal is invaluable, if a right one; but if wrong, the greater the zeal the greater the evil; and therefore we ought to consider whether these things shall be done or not. For I am and always have been one of those natures who must be guided by reason, whatever the reason may be which upon reflection appears to me to be the best; and now that this fortune has come upon me, I cannot put away the reasons which I have before given: the principles which I have hitherto honored and revered I still honor, and unless we can find other and better principles on the instant, I am certain not to agree with you; no, not even if the power of the multitude could inflict many more imprisonments, confiscations, deaths, frightening us like children with hobgoblin terrors. But what will be the fairest way of considering the question? Shall I return to your old argument about the opinions of men, some of which are to be regarded, and others, as we were saying, are not to be regarded? Now were we right in maintaining this before I was condemned? And has the argument which was once good now proved to be talk for the sake of talking; in fact an amusement only, and altogether vanity? That is what I want to consider with your help, Crito: whether, under my present circumstances, the argument appears to be in any way different or not; and is to be allowed by me or disallowed. That argument, which, as I believe, is maintained by many who assume to be authorities, was to the effect, as I was saying, that the opinions of some men are to be regarded, and of other men not to be regarded. Now you, Crito, are a disinterested person who are not going to die to-morrow—at least, there is no human probability of this, and you are therefore not liable to be deceived by the circumstances in which you are placed. Tell me, then, whether I am right in saying that some opinions, and the opinions of some men only, are to be valued, and other opinions, and the opinions of other men, are not to be valued. I ask you whether I was right in maintaining this?

*Cr.*      Certainly.

*Soc.*    The good are to be regarded, and not the bad?

*Cr.*      Yes.

*Soc.*    And the opinions of the wise are good, and the opinions of the unwise are evil?

*Cr.*      Certainly.

*Soc.*    And what was said about another matter? Was the disciple in gymnastics supposed to attend to the praise and blame and opinion of every man, or of one man only—his physician or trainer, whoever that was?

*Cr.*      Of one man only.

*Soc.*    And he ought to fear the censure and welcome the praise of that one only, and not of the many?

*Cr.*      That is clear.

*Soc.*    And he ought to live and train, and eat and drink in the way which seems good to his single master who has understanding, rather than according to the opinion of all other men put together?

*Cr.*      True.

*Soc.*    And if he disobeys and disregards the opinion and approval of the one, and regards the opinion of the many who have no understanding, will he not suffer evil?

*Cr.*      Certainly he will.

*Soc.*  And what will the evil be, whither tending and what affecting, in the disobedient person?

*Cr.*  Clearly, affecting the body; that is what is destroyed by the evil.

*Soc.*  Very good; and is not this true, Crito, of other things which we need not separately enumerate? In the matter of just and unjust, fair and foul, good and evil, which are the subjects of our present consultation, ought we to follow the opinion of the many and to fear them; or the opinion of the one man who has understanding, and whom we ought to fear and reverence more than all the rest of the world: and whom deserting we shall destroy and injure that principle in us which may be assumed to be improved by justice and deteriorated by injustice; is there not such a principle?

*Cr.*  Certainly there is, Socrates.

*Soc.*  Take a parallel instance; if, acting under the advice of men who have no understanding, we destroy that which is improvable by health and deteriorated by disease—when that has been destroyed, I say, would life be worth having? And that is—the body?

*Cr.*  Certainly not.

*Soc.*  More honored, then?

*Cr.*  Far more honored.

*Soc.*  Then, my friend, we must not regard what the many say of us: but what he, the one man who has understanding of just and unjust, will say, and what the truth will say. And therefore you begin in error when you suggest that we should regard the opinion of the many about just and unjust, good and evil, honorable and dishonorable. Well, someone will say, "But the many can kill us."

*Cr.*  Yes, Socrates; that will clearly be the answer.

*Soc.*  That is true; but still I find with surprise that the old argument is, as I conceive, unshaken as ever. And I should like to know whether I may say the same of another proposition—that not life, but a good life, is to be chiefly valued?

*Cr.*  Yes, that also remains.

*Soc.*  And a good life is equivalent to a just and honorable one—that holds also?

*Cr.*  Yes, that holds.

*Soc.*  From these premises I proceed to argue the question whether I ought or ought not to try to escape without the consent of the Athenians: and if I am clearly right in escaping, then I will make the attempt; but if not, I will abstain. The other considerations which you mention, of money and loss of character, and the duty of educating children, are as I hear, only the doctrines of the multitude, who would be as ready to call people to life, if they were able, as they are to put them to death—and with as little reason. But no, since the argument has thus far prevailed, the only question which remains to be considered is, whether we shall do rightly either in escaping or in suffering others to aid in our escape and paying them in money and thanks, or whether we shall not do rightly; and if the latter, then death or any other calamity which may ensue on my remaining here must not be allowed to enter into the calculation.

Cr.    I think that you are right, Socrates; how then shall we proceed?

Soc.   Let us consider the matter together, and do you either refute me if you can, and I will be convinced; or else cease, my dear friend, from repeating to me that I ought to escape against the wishes of the Athenians: for I am extremely desirous to be persuaded by you, but not against my own better judgment. And now please to consider my first position, and do your best to answer me.

Cr.    I will do my best.

Soc.   Are we to say that we are never intentionally to do wrong, or that in one way we ought and in another way we ought not to do wrong, or is doing wrong always evil and dishonorable, as I was just now saying, and as has been already acknowledged by us? Are all our former admissions which were made within a few days to be thrown away? And have we, at our age, been earnestly discoursing with one another all our life long only to discover that we are no better than children? Or are we to rest assured, in spite of the opinion of the many, and in spite of consequences whether better or worse, of the truth of what was then said, that injustice is always an evil and dishonor to him who acts unjustly? Shall we affirm that?

Cr.    Yes.

Soc.   Then we must do no wrong?

Cr.    Certainly not.

Soc.   Nor when injured injure in return, as the many imagine; for we must injure no one at all?

Cr.    Certainly not.

Soc.   Again, Crito, may we do evil?

Cr.    Surely not, Socrates.

Soc.   And what of doing evil in return for evil, which is the morality of the many—is that just or not?

Cr.    Not just.

Soc.   For doing evil to another is the same as injuring him?

Cr.    Very true.

Soc.   Then we ought not to retaliate or render evil for evil to anyone, whatever evil we may have suffered from him. But I would have you consider, Crito, whether you really mean what you are saying. For this opinion has never been held, and never will be held, by any considerable number of persons; and those who are agreed and those who are not agreed upon this point have no common ground, and can only despise one another, when they see how widely they differ. Tell me, then, whether you agree with and assent to my first principle, that neither injury nor retaliation nor warding off evil by evil is ever right. And shall that be the premise of our argument? Or do you decline and dissent from this? For this has been of old and is still my opinion; but, if you are of another opinion, let me hear what you have to say. If, however, you remain of the same mind as formerly, I will proceed to the next step.

*Cr.* You may proceed, for I have not changed my mind.

*Soc.* Then I will proceed to the next step, which may be put in the form of a question: Ought a man to do what he admits to be right, or ought he to betray the right?

*Cr.* He ought to do what he thinks right.

*Soc.* But if this is true, what is the application? In leaving the prison against the will of the Athenians, do I wrong any? Or rather do I not wrong those whom I ought least to wrong? Do I not desert the principles which were acknowledged by us to be just? What do you say?

*Cr.* I cannot tell, Socrates, for I do not know.

*Soc.* Then consider the matter in this way: Imagine that I am about to play truant (you may call the proceeding by any name which you like), and the laws and the government come and interrogate me: "Tell us, Socrates," they say; "what are you about? Are you going by an act of yours to overturn us—the laws and the whole State, as far as in you lies? Do you imagine that a State can subsist and not be overthrown, in which the decisions of law have no power, but are set aside and overthrown by individuals?" What will be our answer, Crito, to these and the like words? Anyone, and especially a clever rhetorician, will have a good deal to urge about the evil of setting aside the law which requires a sentence to be carried out; and we might reply, "Yes; but the State has injured us and given an unjust sentence." Suppose I say that?

*Cr.* Very good, Socrates.

*Soc.* "And was that our agreement with you?" the law would say; "or were you to abide by the sentence of the State?" And if I were to express astonishment at their saying this, the law would probably add:

Answer, Socrates, instead of opening your eyes: you are in the habit of asking and answering questions. Tell us what complaint you have to make against us which justifies you in attempting to destroy us and the State? In the first place did we not bring you into existence? Your father married your mother by our aid and begat you. Say whether you have any objection to urge against those of us who regulate marriage?

None, I should reply. "Or against those of us who regulate the system of nurture and education of children in which you were trained? Were not the laws, who have the charge of this, right in commanding your father to train you in music and gymnastic?" Right, I should reply.

Well, then, since you were brought into the world and nurtured and educated by us, can you deny in the first place that you are our child and slave, as your fathers were before you? And if this is true you are not on equal terms with us; nor can you think that you have a right to do to us what we are doing to you. Would you have any right to strike or revile or do any other evil to a father or to your master, if you had one, when you have been struck or reviled by him, or received some other evil at his hands?—you would not say this? And because we think right to destroy you, do you think that you have any right to destroy us in return, and your country as far as in you lies? And will you, O professor of true virtue, say that you are justified in this? Has a philosopher like you failed to discover that our country is more to be valued and higher and holier far than mother or father or any ancestor, and more to be regarded in the eyes of the gods and of men of understanding? Also to be soothed, and gently and reverently entreated when angry, even more than a father, and if not persuaded, obeyed? And when we are punished by her, whether with imprisonment or stripes, the punishment is to be endured in silence; and if she leads us to wounds or death in battle, thither we follow as is right; neither may anyone yield or retreat or leave his rank, but whether in battle or in a court of law, or in any other place, he must do what his city and his country order him; or he must change their view of what is just: and if he may do no violence to his father or mother, much less may he do violence to his country.

What answer shall we make to this, Crito? Do the laws speak truly, or do they not?

*Cr.*     I think that they do.

*Soc.*    Then the laws will say:

Consider, Socrates, if this is true, that in your present attempt you are going to do us wrong. For, after having brought you into the world, and nurtured and educated you, and given you and every other citizen a share in every good that we had to give, we further proclaim and give the right to every Athenian, that if he does not like us when he has come of age and has seen the ways of the city, and made our acquaintance, he may go where he pleases and take his goods with him; and none of us laws will forbid him or interfere with him. Any of you who does not like us and the city, and who wants to go to a colony or to any other city, may go where he likes, and take his goods with him. But he who has experience of the manner in which we order justice and administer the State, and still remains, has entered into an implied contract that he will do as we command him. And he who disobeys us is, as we maintain, thrice wrong; first, because in disobeying us he is disobeying his parents; secondly, because we are the authors of his education; thirdly, because he has made an agreement with us that he will duly obey our commands; and he neither obeys them nor convinces us that our commands are wrong; and we do not rudely impose them, but give him the alternative of obeying or convincing us; that is what we offer, and he does neither. These are the sort of accusations to which, as we were saying, you, Socrates, will be exposed if you accomplish your intentions; you, above all other Athenians.

Suppose I ask, why is this? They will justly retort upon me that I above all other men have acknowledged the agreement.

There is clear proof, they will say, Socrates, that we and the city were not displeasing to you. Of all Athenians you have been the most constant resident in the city, which, as you never leave, you may be supposed to love. For you never went out of the city either to see the games, except once when you went to the Isthmus, or to any other place unless when you were on military service; nor did you travel as other men do. Nor had you any curiosity to know other States or their laws: your affections did not go beyond us and our State; we were your especial favorites, and you acquiesced in our government of you; and this is the State in which you begat your children, which is a proof of your satisfaction. Moreover, you might, if you had liked, have fixed the penalty at banishment in the course of the trial—the State which refuses to let you go now would have let you go then. But you pretended that you preferred death to exile, and that you were not grieved at death. And now you have forgotten these fine sentiments, and pay no respect to us, the laws, of whom you are the destroyer; and are doing what only a miserable slave would do, running away and turning your back upon the compacts and agreements which you made as a citizen. And first of all answer this very question: Are we right in saying that you agreed to be governed according to us in deed, and not in word only: Is that true or not?

How shall we answer that, Crito? Must we not agree?

*Cr.* There is no help, Socrates.

*Soc.* Then will they not say:

You, Socrates, are breaking the covenants and agreements which you made with us at your leisure, not in any haste or under any compulsion or deception, but having had seventy years to think of them, during which time you were at liberty to leave the city if we were not to your mind, or if our covenants appeared to you to be unfair. You had your choice, and might have gone either to

Lacedæmon or Crete, which you often praise for their good government, or to some other Hellenic or foreign State. Whereas you, above all other Athenians, seemed to be so fond of the State, or, in other words, of us her laws (for who would like a State that has no laws?), that you never stirred out of her: the halt, the blind, the maimed, were not more stationary in her than you were. And now you run away and forsake your agreements. Not so, Socrates, if you will take our advice; do not make yourself ridiculous by escaping out of the city.

For just consider, if you transgress and err in this sort of way, what good will you do, either to yourself or to your friends? That your friends will be driven into exile and deprived of citizenship, or will lose their property, is tolerably certain; and you yourself, if you fly to one of the neighboring cities, as, for example, Thebes or Megara, both of which are well-governed cities, will come to them as an enemy, Socrates, and their government will be against you, and all patriotic citizens will cast an evil eye upon you as a subverter of the laws, and you will confirm in the minds of the judges the justice of their own condemnation of you. For he who is a corrupter of the laws is more than likely to be corrupter of the young and foolish portion of mankind. Will you then flee from well-ordered cities and virtuous men? And is existence worth having on these terms? Or will you go to them without shame, and talk to them, Socrates? And what will you say to them? What you say here about virtue and justice and institutions and laws being the best things among men? Would that be decent of you? Surely not. But if you go away from well-governed States to Crito's friends in Thessaly, where there is great disorder and license, they will be charmed to have the tale of your escape from prison, set off with ludicrous particulars of the manner in which you were wrapped in a goatskin or some other disguise, and metamorphosed as the fashion of runaways is—that is very likely; but will there be no one to remind you that in your old age you violated the most sacred laws from a miserable desire of a little more life? Perhaps not, if you keep them in a good temper; but if they are out of temper you will hear many degrading things; you will live, but how?—as the flatterer of all men, and the servant of all men; and doing what?—eating and drinking in Thessaly, having gone abroad in order that you may get a dinner. And where will be your fine sentiments about justice and virtue then? Say that you wish to live for the sake of your children, that you may bring them up and educate them—will you take them into Thessaly and deprive them of Athenian citizenship? Is that the benefit which you would confer upon them? Or are you under the impression that they will be better cared for and educated here if you are still alive, although absent from them; for that your friends will take care of them? Do you fancy that if you are an inhabitant of Thessaly they will take care of them, and if you are an inhabitant of the other world they will not take care of them? Nay; but if they who call themselves friends are truly friends, they surely will.

Listen, then, Socrates, to us who have brought you up. Think not of life and children first, and of justice afterwards, but of justice first, that you may be justified before the princes of the world below. For neither will you nor any that belong to you be happier or holier or juster in this life, or happier in another, if you do as Crito bids. Now you depart in innocence, a sufferer and not a doer of evil; a victim, not of the laws, but of men. But if you go forth, returning evil for evil, and injury for injury, breaking the covenants and agreements which you have made with us, and wronging those whom you ought least to wrong, that is to say, yourself, your friends, your country, and us, we shall be angry with you while you live, and our brethren, the laws in the world below, will receive you as an enemy; for they will know that you have done your best to destroy us. Listen, then, to us and not to Crito.

This is the voice which I seem to hear murmuring in my ears, like the sound of the flute in the ears of the mystic; that voice, I say, is humming in my ears, and prevents me from hearing any other. And I know that anything more which you will say will be in vain. Yet speak, if you have anything to say.

Cr.  I have nothing to say, Socrates.

Soc.  Then let me follow the intimations of the will of God.

**2**

# Notes on the Crito

1. Socrates, whose death sentence is the subject of Plato's dialogue *Crito* and whose death itself is movingly recounted by Plato in his dialogue *Phaedo*, produced no written work of his own. His student, Plato, is thus mainly responsible for Socrates's enormous historical importance. Plato is the author of a number of dialogic works dealing with justice and politics, most notably the *Republic*. Plato, in turn, was the teacher of Aristotle. Together, these writers set the agenda for much of medieval and modern scholarship.

2. Are the speeches of the Laws consistent with what Socrates has said earlier in the Dialogue? Are the speeches made by the Laws themselves really intended to be philosophically convincing, or merely to somehow persuade Socrates's unphilosophical friend Crito? See Ernest J. Weinrib, *Obedience to the Law in Plato's* Crito, 27 AMERICAN JOURNAL OF JURISPRUDENCE 85 (1982).

3. Should we read the *Crito* as claiming that it is always immoral to disobey the law and that unjust laws should therefore always be obeyed? See Daniel M. Farrell, *Illegal Actions, Universal Maxims, and the Duty to Obey the Law*, 6 POLITICAL THEORY 173, 179 (1978); Rex Martin, *Socrates on Disobedience to Law*, 24 REVIEW OF METAPHYSICS 21, 38 (1970).

4. Does Socrates develop in the *Crito* an early version of a consent or agreement-based theory of an obligation to obey? Does his consent theory depend crucially upon whether that which is consented to is, independently, just or not? See Bruce Wardhaugh, *Socratic Civil Disobedience: Some Reflections on* Morgentaler, 2 CANADIAN JOURNAL OF LAW AND JURISPRUDENCE 91, 93 (1989). If people have not consented to unjust laws, does that open the door to justified disobedience of those laws? See RICHARD KRAUT, SOCRATES AND THE STATE 36 (1984). For criticism of Kraut's argument on this point, see T.H. Irwin, *Socratic Inquiry and Politics*, 96 ETHICS 400, 404 (1986).

Is .there any conflict between the argument based on consent or agreement to obey, and the argument that the Laws and Socrates stand to one another in a relationship akin to master and slave? Can an enslaved person give binding consent? See Rex Martin, *Socrates on Disobedience to Law*, 24 REVIEW OF METAPHYSICS 21, 36 (1970).

6. Note that among the arguments against disobedience raised by the Laws are early forms of the argument based on gratitude to those who have helped us and of the argument based on acting fairly in a cooperative venture. See Ernest J. Weinrib, *Obedience to the Law in Plato's* Crito, 27 AMERICAN JOURNAL OF JURISPRUDENCE 85, 99 (1982). Each of these forms of argument in general receives some attention in separate commentary below.

7. Could Socrates have argued that he has fully repaid any obligation of gratitude for what the Laws have done for him not by obeying unjust laws along with the just, but by nurturing and educating his children as the Laws nurtured and educated him? See Anthony D'Amato, *Obligation to Obey the Law: A Study of the Death of Socrates*, 49 SOUTHERN CALIFORNIA LAW REVIEW 1079, 1091 (1976).

8. Could gratitude for what one's political society has done for oneself permit disobedience to a law that happens to be unworthy of that society, or of a law inconsistent either with that society's moral progress or with what has led one to be grateful to that society? See RICHARD E. FLATHMAN, POLITICAL OBLIGATION 279 (1972); J. Peter Euben, *Philosophy and Politics in Plato's* Crito, 6 POLITICAL THEORY 149, 153 (1978).

9. Note that in the course of the preceding Platonic Dialogue, the *Apology*, in which Socrates is tried and condemned for impiety and corrupting the young, Socrates has said at Stephanus page 29D that regardless of what the law commands, he will go on philosophizing as long as he is able. See Richard Kraut, *Plato's* Apology *and* Crito: *Two Recent Studies*, 91 ETHICS 651, 651, 657-58 (1981).

10. Would it be fair to say that those who advocate civil disobedience in the case of a more or less broad range of unjust laws cannot draw support from Socrates, on the grounds that Socrates rejected only the command not to philosophize, but urged obedience in all other matters? See Gary Young, *Socrates and Obedience*, 19 PHRONESIS 1, 29 (1974).

11. Do Socrates's conclusions make more sense if the question is confined to whether he should escape now, under his own particular circumstances, rather than a broad, general inquiry into the possibility of justified civil disobedience

or conscientious refusal under any circumstances? See Gregory Vlastos, *Socrates on Political Obedience and Disobedience*, 63 YALE REVIEW 517, 534 (1974).

12. Would the kind of law violation urged upon Socrates by Crito be an example of what we would today call "civil disobedience?" See Gregory Vlastos, *Socrates on Political Obedience and Disobedience*, 63 YALE REVIEW 517, 531 (1974).

13. Could it be said that Socrates refuses to escape in part for reasons of personal dignity? See Frederick Rosen, *Obligation and Friendship in Plato's* Crito, 1 POLITICAL THEORY 307, 316 (1973). Could Socrates have simply wanted most to display the virtues of steadfastness and resistance in the way most likely to leave a lasting impact? See HANS-GEORG GADAMER, THE IDEA OF THE GOOD IN PLATONIC-ARISTOTELIAN PHILOSOPHY 96-97 (P. Christopher Smith trans. 1986).

14. Anthony Woozley asks rhetorically whether Socrates would "have to agree that in breaking the law which determined the execution of his sentence he was manifesting his character as a destroyer of law." ANTHONY D. WOOZLEY, LAW AND OBEDIENCE: THE ARGUMENTS OF PLATO'S *Crito* 134 (1979). What would disobedience to the legal command of his sentence have really said about Socrates's character?

15. Does an intention to defy the law in a particular case necessarily involve an intention to damage or destroy the laws in general as far as may be within one's power? For background, see Andrew Barker, *Why Did Socrates Refuse to Escape?*, 22 PHRONESIS 13, 17 (1977).

16. In arguing that by escaping, Socrates will be doing his best to destroy all the laws, do the Laws ignore the distinction between, on the one hand, intending or desiring a particular result, as a means or an end, and merely foreseeing some large or small risk of a bad unintended side effect of one's action on the other? For extended discussion of this distinction in other contexts, see RICHARD A. McCORMICK & PAUL RAMSEY, DOING EVIL TO ACHIEVE GOOD: MORAL CHOICE IN CONFLICT SITUATIONS (1978).

17. Is it possible that Socrates's decision not to escape is based upon the foreseeable misuse and misapplication by others of the example of Socrates's disobedience? See R.E. Allen, *Law and Justice in Plato's* Crito, 69 JOURNAL OF PHILOSOPHY 557, 563 (1972); Ann Congleton, *Two Kinds of Lawlessness: Plato's* Crito, 2 POLITICAL THEORY 432, 442 (1974). Is part of the problem simply the idea that many people will sincerely, but mistakenly, consider their own criminal conviction or sentencing to have been unfair or unjustly harsh?

18. Would Socrates have been more likely to have chosen exile rather than
    obedience if his action in choosing exile had been less open to misinterpreta-
    tion? Suppose in this regard that Socrates's sentence had been only to pay a
    readily affordable fine. See, for background, Anthony D'Amato, *Obligation
    to Obey the Law: A Study of the Death of Socrates*, 49 SOUTHERN CALIFORNIA
    LAW REVIEW 1079, 1103 (1976) and the *Apology*, Stephanus pages 36C to
    38D.

19. George Klosko argues that "[t]o the Laws' question 'What if everyone did the
    same?' there is an obvious response: there is virtually no chance that
    everyone will do so." George Klosko, *The Moral Force of Political
    Obligations*, 84 AMERICAN POLITICAL SCIENCE REVIEW 1235, 1242 (1990). Is this
    in fact what the Laws ask? Should it have been?

20. Do the Laws argue that breaking the law will lead, inevitably, to harm to the
    system of laws, and to the public in general? Or that breaking the law is
    somehow in and of itself harm to the laws? See Andrew Barker, *Why Did
    Socrates Refuse to Escape?*, 22 PHRONESIS 13, 18 (1977).

21. Is it possible that Socrates believes that we may be morally required, and not
    just permitted, to disobey a law requiring us to really harm others, but that his
    accepting his own execution does not harm others, and really does not even
    harm himself morally? And that while it might be morally permissible for
    Socrates to disobey the law requiring his own death under some circum-
    stances, Socrates has good moral reasons for preferring death to exile? For
    background, see Gene G. James, *Socrates on Civil Disobedience and
    Rebellion*, 11 SOUTHERN JOURNAL OF PHILOSOPHY 119, 124-24 (1973).

22. Does Socrates's obedience in the *Crito* show "what the good man does when
    he himself is treated unjustly but is not required to treat others unjustly?"
    Francis C. Wade, *In Defense of Socrates*, 25 REVIEW OF METAPHYSICS 311, 320
    (1971). What if a law required all members of some unpopular minority to
    forfeit their lives or property? Should they obey, on the grounds that their
    obedience treats no one else unjustly? What if, on the other hand, the law
    requires one to treat others in a clearly unjust way?

23. Would Socrates's obedience to his death sentence perhaps involve him not
    only in suffering injustice himself, but in actually committing injustice, in the
    form of abandoning his uniquely socially valuable role of philosopher? See
    Robert J. McLaughlin, *Socrates on Political Disobedience: A Reply to Gary
    Young*, 21 PHRONESIS 185, 191 & 191 n.15 (1976). But could Socrates have
    philosophized in any socially valuable way after having escaped into exile?
    See J. Peter Euben, *Philosophy and Politics in Plato's* Crito, 6 POLITICAL

THEORY 149, 156 (1978).

24. For Socrates, what counts as genuine harm to a person? Only what "impairs his capacity for moral excellence?" Andrew Barker, *Why Did Socrates Refuse to Escape?*, 22 PHRONESIS 13, 20 (1977).

25. Is Socrates's decision to obey dependent upon his belief that there is no genuine evil, for the morally good person, in the death of that person? See R.E. Allen, *Law and Justice in Plato's* Crito, 69 JOURNAL OF PHILOSOPHY 557, 559 (1972).

26. If Socrates's position is that we are never to harm or do evil to anyone, what are we to do if both obeying and disobeying the law would harm other persons? For background, see Francis C. Wade, *In Defense of Socrates*, 24 REVIEW OF METAPHYSICS 311, 312 (1971).

27. Could Socrates argue that while there was real moral wrong in unjustly accusing and sentencing him, that moral wrong, as embodied in the judgment and intentions of his accusers, has already occurred and already had its effects on the character of his accusers, and that Socrates's escaping now would not undo that harm, while his accepting the death sentence would not cooperate with or promote the genuine moral evil involved? For background, see Anthony D'Amato, *Obligation to Obey the Law: A Study of the Death of Socrates*, 49 SOUTHERN CALIFORNIA LAW REVIEW 1079, 1087-88 (1976).

28. Could Socrates have argued that there is a crucial difference between a generally or facially valid law on piety or corruption of the youth, and the unjust application of that generally just law in his case? See Jerome Hall, *Plato's Legal Philosophy*, 31 INDIANA LAW JOURNAL 171, 173 (1956); Rex Martin, *Socrates on Disobedience to Law*, 24 REVIEW OF METAPHYSICS 21, 33 (1970). Would this argument have simply re-raised the problem of the possible future abuse of Socrates's example?

29. Robert Rodes, Jr. argues, in the context of discussing Socrates, that "[a] human being has rights that the community did not bestow, and cannot abrogate, whether for edification or for public order. Among these, surely, is the right not to be punished when one has done nothing wrong." ROBERT E. RODES, JR., THE LEGAL ENTERPRISE 56 (1976). How far, in practice, should the moral right to actively resist what one deems an unjustly imposed penalty extend? Note that while persons just convicted of a crime are likely to be exceptionally knowledgeable of many morally relevant facts, they may not be in the best position to dispassionately weigh the merits of their own case.

30. Richard Flathman argues that "for Socrates the ground of the obligation to obey is the argument that the state or political society is potentially of great value . . . supplemented by the . . . rule (which gives the content of most political obligations) that political societies would be impossible without general obedience to law and other authoritative commands." RICHARD E. FLATHMAN, POLITICAL OBLIGATION 256 (1972). Does this fairly summarize Socrates's argument? Is it a potentially convincing argument? Arguments for political obligation based upon "necessity" for a functioning political society are briefly considered below.

31. Can Socrates be read as suggesting that one must inevitably be a slave either to the laws or to other persons, and that it is better to be a slave to the laws? See Gary Young, *Socrates and Obedience*, 19 PHRONESIS 1, 18 (1974). Is this really the choice we face?

32. Is it helpful to assume that Socrates believed that laws, because they must be simple and general, can never really embody what is right or best for all those persons affected? See Ann Congleton, *Two Kinds of Lawlessness: Plato's* Crito, 2 POLITICAL THEORY 432, 438 (1974).

33. What, if anything, should we make of the fact that the personified Laws of Athens do not precisely claim that law violation involves treating any actual living people unjustly? See ANTHONY D. WOOZLEY, LAW AND OBEDIENCE: THE ARGUMENTS OF PLATO'S *Crito* 135 (1979).

34. For further discussion of Plato's approach to the framing and value of concrete general laws as "second best" to rule by the wise and virtuous, see Glenn R. Morrow, *Plato and the Rule of Law*, in 2 PLATO: ETHICS, POLITICS, AND PHILOSOPHY OF RELIGION 144-65 (Gregory Vlastos ed. 1971).

35. For the analogous Confucian judgment that the uniform observance of legal principle is second best, for reasons with which Socrates would have been sympathetic, see RAYMOND DAWSON, CONFUCIUS 72 (1981). The classical Chinese Legalist school, however, took up the theme of the value of authoritarian centralized rule of law. See FUNG YU-LAN, 1 A HISTORY OF CHINESE PHILOSOPHY 312-17 (Derk Bodde trans. 1952); HARRLEE G. GREEN, CHINESE THOUGHT FROM CONFUCIUS TO MAO TSE-TUNG 135-40 (1953).

36. For discussion of the crucial Confucian emphasis on governmental leadership by means of virtuous example, see THE WISDOM OF CHINA AND INDIA 838-39 (Lin Yutang ed. 1942). Confucius himself famously holds that "[h]e who rules by moral force . . . is like the pole-star, which remains in its place while all the lesser stars do homage to it." THE ANALECTS OF CONFUCIUS book II, I at 88

(Arthur Waley trans. 1938). For the general agreement of the classical Chinese philosopher Mo Tzu, see HARRLEE G. GREEN, CHINESE THOUGHT FROM CONFUCIUS TO MAO TSE-TUNG 48 (1953), and for that of Mencius, see FUNG YU-LAN, 1 A HISTORY OF CHINESE PHILOSOPHY 112, 115 (Derk Bodde trans. 1952). Confucius's "pole star" metaphor is briefly discussed in DAVID L. HALL & ROGER T. AMES, THINKING THROUGH CONFUCIUS 168 (1987).

37. For Socrates's great successor Aristotle, political society in the form of the greek polis or city-state was natural and appropriate for and completive of human beings. Aristotle writes that "the polis belongs to the class of things that exist by nature, and . . . man is by nature an animal intended to live in a polis." ARISTOTLE, THE POLITICS 1253a (Ernest Barker trans. 1958).

38. With Aristotle's understanding of the relationship between the individual citizen and the city-state, compare that of Confucius as depicted in DAVID L. HALL & ROGER T. AMES, THINKING THROUGH CONFUCIUS 164 (1987) ("[p]ersonal ordering can only take place in the context of social and political participation, and social and political station are only justifiable as attendant upon the achievements of personal cultivation").

39. Ultimately the state must, according to Aristotle, aim at the good for human beings, which turns out to be happiness. Happiness in turn involves, in light of our natures, action or contemplation in accordance with reason and virtue. See ARISTOTLE, ETHICS book I, chs. 1-7 (J.A.K. Thomson trans. 1955).

40. Aristotle thus finds unsatisfactory any merely contractarian view of government limited to the collective defense of life and property. For Aristotle, "[t]he State is no mere society for mutual assurance against assault or robbery, but a moral community, formed for the ends of virtue. The rules by which that community lives are not negative prohibitions of offenses, but positive counsels of moral perfection." ERNEST BARKER, THE POLITICAL THOUGHT OF PLATO AND ARISTOTLE 326 (1959). Note the development of this idea in Aquinas, as discussed below, and contrast this approach with that of Thomas Hobbes, also discussed below. Consider at that point whether Hobbes would disagree with Aristotle's approach, or would merely differ on emphasis.

41. As Ernest Barker notes, Aristotle assumed, in a way not unlike that later idealized by Rousseau, a small, intimate, face-to-face society that "makes no distinction between the province of the state and that of society; it is, in a word, an integrated system of social ethics, which realizes to the full the capacity of its members, and therefore claims their full allegiance." Ernest Barker, *Introduction* to THE POLITICS OF ARISTOTLE xlvii (Ernest Barker trans. 1946). Could we develop an "Aristotelian" critique of the polis, or of any

modern government, based on the government's failure to permit or maximally promote the development of the distinctive capacities of each of its members? Are modern democracies immune to such a charge?

# 3

# Notes on the Argument from Gratitude

1. Consider gratitude-based arguments for an obligation to obey the law, as presented first in the *Crito*. Isn't gratitude most appropriate when benefits have been provided without demanding or expecting any return or reciprocity on the part of the beneficiary? If so, isn't it difficult to tie gratitude to any particular form of response, such as generally obeying the law? To the extent that our benefactors really expect us to obey the law in return for their sacrifices, this seems to suggest what might be called a reciprocity or fairness-based approach rather than a gratitude-based approach to obligation. *But see* GREGORY S. KAVKA, HOBBESIAN MORAL AND POLITICAL THEORY 413-14 (1986).

2. Typically, we feel obligations of gratitude most clearly toward people who provide us more than the minimum they are morally and legally obliged to provide. But mere law obedience by others, and the sacrifices involved therein, are plainly morally and legally required on gratitude-based theories of legal obligation. So why should law obedience by others inspire gratitude? For background, see Fred Berger, *Gratitude*, 85 ETHICS 298, 299 (1975).

3. George Klosko has criticized gratitude-based arguments on the grounds that "though obligations of gratitude undoubtedly exist, they are generally weak and diffuse, too weak to function as prime facie political obligations in the usual sense. Such obligations would be overridden frequently, not just in unusual circumstances. They would not appear generally to require compliance with onerous or burdensome laws." George Klosko, *Political Obligation and Gratitude*, 18 PHILOSOPHY & PUBLIC AFFAIRS 352 (1989). For a brief reply by A.D.M. Walker, see *id.* at 359-64.

4. It has been observed that "the sense of obligation associated with gratitude has its . . . particularities: although it often brings out the debtor in us, it fails to make clear the nature of the debt or how we are to pay it." Claudia Card, *Gratitude and Obligation*, 25 AMERICAN PHILOSOPHICAL QUARTERLY 115,

116 (1988). Note that we normally do not express our gratitude by returning or paying back what we have been given freely by our benefactor. Is the obligation of gratitude simply too indeterminate to ground a general obligation to obey the law?

5.  Fred Berger notes similarly that "there is rarely a *particular* act which *must* be done if we are to show gratitude; there are no acts which the benevolent person may *demand* as a grateful return for his largess. . . ." Fred Berger, *Gratitude*, 85 ETHICS 298, 306 (1975) (emphasis in the original). Of course, some expressions of gratitude may, under the circumstances, seem insufficient. But won't obedience to one or all laws often seem either excessive, inappropriate, or merely one of several roughly equally appropriate ways of showing gratitude?

6.  Roslyn Weiss has argued that the moral element of gratitude is exhausted in having the proper attitude or feeling toward one's benefactor, and that expressions or acts of gratitude may be social requirements, but not moral obligations. See Roslyn Weiss, *The Moral and Social Dimensions of Gratitude*, 23 SOUTHERN JOURNAL OF PHILOSOPHY 491, 492, 498-99 (1985). Is it possible, though, that one's failure to undertake any positive act of gratitude could render one's claim to entertain the proper feelings of gratitude implausible? If so, could one's failure to obey a particular law, or the laws in general, ever constitute strong evidence that one did not in fact harbor an appropriately grateful attitude toward one's state or society?

7.  Fred Berger notes that we rarely say that the obligation of gratitude is such that the benefactor has a legal or moral right to demand any sort of recompense or acknowledgment for the benefactor's special generosity. Fred Berger, *Gratitude*, 85 ETHICS 298, 300 (1975). Is it possible that gratitude-based theories could help explain why some persons have a moral obligation to obey without providing a satisfactory account of why the government has a moral right to command or coerce anyone's obedience?

8.  A.D.M. Walker argues that "the interests of the state may sometimes be advanced if bad legislation is opposed or disregarded, and in these circumstances the argument from gratitude will demand not compliance, but noncompliance with the law." A.D.M. Walker, *Political Obligation and the Argument from Gratitude*, 17 PHILOSOPHY & PUBLIC AFFAIRS 191, 204 (1988). Note that by analogy, we might feel that our sense of gratitude obligates us to make some effort to save a benefactor from a choice the benefactor makes which the benefactor falsely imagines will promote the benefactor's own interests.

9. For further discussion of the gratitude model of political obligation, see PHILIP ABBOTT, THE SHOTGUN BEHIND THE DOOR: LIBERALISM AND THE PROBLEM OF POLITICAL OBLIGATION ch. 4 (1976).

# 4

# Henry David Thoreau, On the Duty of Civil Disobedience

I heartily accept the motto,—"That government is best which governs least;" and I should like to see it acted up to more rapidly and systematically. Carried out, it finally amounts to this, which also I believe,—"That government is best which governs not at all," and when men are prepared for it, that will be the kind of government which they will have. Government is at best but an expedient; but most governments are usually, and all governments are sometimes, inexpedient. The objections which have been brought against a standing army, and they are many and weighty, and deserve to prevail, may also at last be brought against a standing government. The standing army is only an arm of the standing government. The government itself, which is only the mode which the people have chosen to execute their will, is equally liable to be abused and perverted before the people can act through it. Witness the present Mexican war, the work of comparatively a few individuals using the standing government as their tool; for, in the outset, the people would not have consented to this measure.

This American government,—what is it but a tradition, though a recent one, endeavoring to transmit itself unimpaired to posterity, but each instant losing some of its integrity? It has not the vitality and force of a single living man; for a single man can bend it to his will. It is a sort of wooden gun to the people themselves. But it is not the less necessary for this; for the people must have some complicated machinery or other, and hear its din, to satisfy that idea of government which they have. Governments show thus how successfully men can be imposed on, even impose on themselves, for their own advantage. It is excellent, we must all allow. Yet this government never of itself furthered any enterprise, but by the alacrity with which it got out of its way. It does not keep the country free. It does not settle the West. It does not educate. The character inherent in the American People has done all that has been accomplished; and it would have done somewhat more, if the government had not sometimes got in its way. For government is an expedient by which men would fain succeed in letting one another alone; and, as has been said, when it is most expedient, the governed are most let alone by it.

Trade and commerce, if they were not made of India-rubber, would never manage to bounce over the obstacles which legislators are continually putting in their way; and, if one were to judge these men wholly by the effects of their actions and not partly by their intentions, they would deserve to be classed and punished with those mischievous persons who put obstructions on the railroads.

But, to speak practically and as a citizen, unlike those who call themselves no-government men, I ask for, not at once no government, but at once a better government. Let every man make known what kind of government would command his respect, and that will be one step toward obtaining it.

After all, the practical reason why, when the power is once in the hands of the people, a majority are permitted, and for a long period continue, to rule is not because they are most likely to be in the right, nor because this seems fairest to the minority, but because they are physically the strongest. But a government in which the majority rule in all cases cannot be based on justice, even as far as men understand it. Can there not be a government in which majorities do not virtually decide right and wrong, but conscience?—in which majorities decide only those questions to which the rule of expediency is applicable? Must the citizen ever for a moment, or in the least degree, resign his conscience to the legislator? Why has every man a conscience, then? I think that we should be men first, and subjects afterward. It is not desirable to cultivate a respect for the law, so much as for the right. The only obligation which I have a right to assume is to do at any time what I think right. It is truly enough said, that a corporation has no conscience; but a corporation of conscientious men is a corporation *with* a conscience. Law never made men a whit more just; and, by means of their respect for it, even the well-disposed are daily made the agents of injustice. A common and natural result of an undue respect for law is, that you may see a file of soldiers, marching in admirable order over hill and dale to the wars, against their wills, ay, against their common sense and consciences, which makes it very steep marching indeed, and produces a palpitation of the heart. They have no doubt that it is a damnable business in which they are concerned; they are all peaceably inclined. Now, what are they? Men at all? Or small movable forts and magazines, at the service of some unscrupulous man in power? Visit the Navy-Yard, and behold a marine, such a man as an American government can make, or such as it can make a man with its black arts,—a mere shadow and reminiscence of humanity, a man laid out alive and standing, and already, as one may say, buried under arms with funeral accompaniments, though it may be,—

> Not a drum was heard, not a funeral note,
>     As his corse to the rampart we hurried;
> Not a soldier discharged his farewell shot
>     O'er the grave where our hero we buried.

The mass of men serve the state thus, not as men mainly, but as machines, with their bodies. They are the standing army, and the militia, jailors, constables, posse comitatus, etc. In most cases there is no free exercise whatever of the judgment or of the moral sense; but they put themselves on a level with wood and earth and stones; and wooden men can perhaps be manufactured that will serve the purpose as well. Such command no more respect than men of straw or a lump of dirt. They have the same sort of worth only as horses and dogs. Yet such as these even are commonly esteemed good citizens. Others—as most legislators, politicians, lawyers, ministers, and office-holders—serve the state chiefly with their heads; and, as they rarely make any moral distinctions, they are as likely to serve the Devil, without *intending* it, as God. A very few, as heroes, patriots, martyrs, reformers in the great sense, and men, serve the state with their consciences also, and so necessarily resist it for the most part; and they are commonly treated as enemies by it. A wise man will only be useful as a man, and will not submit to be "clay," and "stop a hole to keep the wind away," but leave that office to his dust at least:—

*I am too high-born to be propertied,*
*To be a secondary at control,*
*Or useful serving-man and instrument*
*To any sovereign state throughout the world.*

He who gives himself entirely to his fellow-men appears to them useless and selfish; but he who gives himself partially to them is pronounced a benefactor and philanthropist.

How does it become a man to behave toward this American government to-day? I answer, that he cannot without disgrace be associated with it. I cannot for an instant recognize that political organization as *my* government which is the slave's government also.

All men recognize the right of revolution; that is, the right to refuse allegiance to, and to resist, the government, when its tyranny or its inefficiency are great and unendurable. But almost all say that such is not the case now. But such was the case, they think, in the Revolution of '75. If one were to tell me that this was a bad government because it taxed certain foreign commodities brought to its ports, it is most probable that I should not make an ado about it, for I can do without them. All machines have their friction; and possibly this does enough good to counterbalance the evil. At any rate, it is a great evil to make a stir about it. But when the friction comes to have its machine, and oppression and robbery are organized, I say, let us not have such a machine any longer. In other words, when a sixth of the population of a nation which has undertaken to be the refuge of liberty are slaves, and a whole country is unjustly overrun and conquered by a foreign army, and subjected to military law, I think that it is not too soon for honest men to rebel and revolutionize. What makes this duty the more urgent is the fact that the country so overrun is not our own, but ours is the invading army.

Paley, a common authority with many on moral questions, in his chapter on the "Duty of Submission to Civil Government," resolves all civil obligation into expediency; and he proceeds to say, "that so long as the interest of the whole society requires it, that is, so long as the established government cannot be resisted or changed without public inconveniency, it is the will of God that the established government be obeyed, and no longer. . . . This principle being admitted, the justice of every particular case of resistance is reduced to a computation of the quantity of the danger and grievance on the one side, and of the probability and expense of redressing it on the other." Of this, he says, every man shall judge for himself. But Paley appears never to have contemplated those cases to which the rule of expediency does not apply, in which a people, as well as an individual, must do justice, cost what it may. If I have unjustly wrested a plank from a drowning man, I must restore it to him though I drown myself. This, according to Paley, would be inconvenient. But he that would save his life, in such a case, shall lose it. This people must cease to hold slaves, and to make war on Mexico, though it cost them their existence as a people.

In their practice, nations agree with Paley; but does any one think that Massachusetts does exactly what is right at the present crisis?

*A drab of state, a cloth-o'-silver slut,*
*To have her train borne up, and her soul trail in the dirt.*

Practically speaking, the opponents to a reform in Massachusetts are not a hundred thousand politicians at the South, but a hundred thousand merchants and farmers here, who are more interested in commerce and agriculture than they are in humanity, and are not prepared to do justice to the slave and to Mexico, *cost what it may.* I quarrel not with far-off foes, but with those who, near at home, coöperate with, and do the bidding of, those far away, and without whom the latter would be harmless. We are accustomed to say, that the mass of men are unprepared; but improvement is slow, because the few are not materially wiser or better than the many. It is not so important that many should be as good as you, as that there be some absolute goodness somewhere; for that will leaven the whole lump. There are thousands who are in opinion opposed to slavery and to the war, who yet in effect do nothing to put an end to them; who, esteeming themselves children of Washington and Franklin, sit down with their hands in their pockets, and say that they know not what to do, and do nothing; who even postpone the question of freedom to the question of free-trade, and quietly read the prices-current along with the latest advices from Mexico, after dinner, and, it may be, fall asleep over them both. What is the price-current of an honest man and patriot to-day? They hesitate, and they regret, and sometimes they petition; but they do nothing in earnest and with effect. They will wait, well disposed, for others to remedy the evil, that they may no longer have it to regret. At most, they give only a cheap vote, and a feeble countenance and Godspeed, to the right, as it goes by them. There are nine hundred and ninety-nine patrons of virtue to one virtuous man. But it is easier to deal with the real possessor of a thing than with the temporary guardian of it.

All voting is a sort of gaming, like checkers or backgammon, with a slight moral tinge to it, a playing with right and wrong, with moral questions; and betting naturally accompanies it. The character of the voters is not staked. I cast my vote, perchance, as I think right; but I am not vitally concerned that that right should prevail. I am willing to leave it to the majority. Its obligation, therefore, never exceeds that of expediency. Even voting *for the right* is *doing* nothing for it. It is only expressing to men feebly your desire that it should prevail. A wise man will not leave the right to the mercy of chance, nor wish it to prevail through the power of the majority. There is but little virtue in the action of masses of men. When the majority shall at length vote for the abolition of slavery, it will be because they are indifferent to slavery, or because there is but little slavery left to be abolished by their vote. *They* will then be the only slaves. Only *his* vote can hasten the abolition of slavery who asserts his own freedom by his vote.

I hear of a convention to be held at Baltimore, or elsewhere, for the selection of a candidate for the Presidency, made up chiefly of editors, and men who are politicians by profession; but I think, what is it to any independent, intelligent, and respectable man what decision they may come to? Shall we not have the advantage of his wisdom and honesty, nevertheless? Can we not count upon some independent votes? Are there not many individuals in the country who do not attend conventions? But no: I find that the respectable man, so called, has immediately drifted from his position, and despairs of his country, when his country has more reason to despair of him. He forthwith adopts one of the candidates thus selected as the only available one, thus proving that he is himself available for any purposes of the demagogue. His vote is of no more worth than that of any unprincipled foreigner or hireling native, who may have been bought. O for a man who is a *man*, and, as my neighbor says, has a bone in his back which you cannot pass your hand through! Our statistics are at fault: the population has been returned too large. How many *men* are there to a square thousand miles in this country? Hardly one. Does not America offer any inducement for men to settle here? The American has dwindled into an Odd Fellow,—one who may be known by the development of his organ of gregarious-ness, and a manifest lack of intellect and cheerful self-reliance; whose first and chief concern, on coming into the world, is to see that the Almshouses are in good repair; and, before yet he has lawfully donned the virile garb, to collect a fund for the support of the widows and orphans that may be; who, in short, ventures to live only by the aid of the Mutual Insurance company, which has promised to bury him decently.

It is not a man's duty, as a matter of course, to devote himself to the eradication of any, even the most enormous wrong; he may still properly have other concerns to engage him; but it is his duty, at least, to wash his hands of it, and, if he gives it no thought longer, not to give it practically his support. If I devote myself to other pursuits and contemplations, I must first see, at least, that I do not pursue them sitting upon another man's shoulders. I must get off him first, that he may pursue his contemplations too. See what gross inconsistency is tolerated. I have heard some of my townsmen say, "I should like to have them order me out to help put down an insurrection of the slaves, or to march to

Mexico;—see if I would go;" and yet these very men have each, directly by their allegiance, and so indirectly, at least, by their money, furnished a substitute. The soldier is applauded who refuses to serve in an unjust war by those who do not refuse to sustain the unjust government which makes the war; is applauded by those whose own act and authority he disregards and sets at naught; as if the state were penitent to that degree that it hired one to scourge it while it sinned, but not to that degree that it left off sinning for a moment. Thus, under the name of Order and Civil Government, we are all made at last to pay homage to and support our own meanness. After the first blush of sin comes its indifference; and from immoral it becomes, as it were, *un*moral, and not quite unnecessary to that life which we have made.

The broadest and most prevalent error requires the most disinterested virtue to sustain it. The slight reproach to which the virtue of patriotism is commonly liable, the noble are most likely to incur. Those who, while they disapprove of the character and measures of a government, yield to it their allegiance and support are undoubtedly its most conscientious supporters, and so frequently the most serious obstacles to reform. Some are petitioning the state to dissolve the Union, to disregard the requisitions of the President. Why do they not dissolve it themselves,—the union between themselves and the state,—and refuse to pay their quota into its treasury? Do not they stand in the same relation to the state that the state does to the Union? And have not the same reasons prevented the state from resisting the Union which have prevented them from resisting the state?

How can a man be satisfied to entertain an opinion merely, and enjoy *it*? Is there any enjoyment in it, if his opinion is that he is aggrieved? If you are cheated out of a single dollar by our neighbor, you do not rest satisfied with knowing that you are cheated, or with saying that you are cheated, or even with petitioning him to pay you your due; but you take effectual steps at once to obtain the full amount, and see that you are never cheated again. Action from principle, the perception and the performance of right, changes things and relations; it is essentially revolutionary, and does not consist wholly with anything which was. It not only divides states and churches, it divides families; ay, it divides the *individual*, separating the diabolical in him from the divine.

Unjust laws exist; shall we be content to obey them, or shall we endeavor to amend them, and obey them until we have succeeded, or shall we transgress them at once? Men generally, under such a government as this, think that they ought to wait until they have persuaded the majority to alter them. They think that, if they should resist, the remedy would be worse than the evil. But it is the fault of the government itself that the remedy *is* worse than the evil. *It* makes it worse. Why is it not more apt to anticipate and provide for reform? Why does it not cherish its wise minority? Why does it cry and resist before it is hurt? Why does it not encourage its citizens to be on the alert to point out its faults and *do* better than it would have them? Why does it always crucify Christ, and excommunicate Copernicus and Luther, and pronounce Washington and Franklin rebels?

One would think, that a deliberate and practical denial of its authority was the only offense never contemplated by government; else, why has it not assigned its definite, its suitable and proportionate penalty? If a man who has no property refuses but once to earn nine shillings for the state, he is put in prison for a period unlimited by any law that I know, and determined only by the discretion of those who placed him there; but if he should steal ninety times nine shillings from the state, he is soon permitted to go at large again.

If the injustice is part of the necessary friction of the machine of government, let it go, let it go: perchance it will wear smooth,—certainly the machine will wear out. If the injustice has a spring, or a pulley, or a rope, or a crank, exclusively for itself, then perhaps you may consider whether the remedy will not be worse than the evil; but if it is of such a nature that it requires you to be the agent of injustice to another, then, I say, break the law. Let your life be a counter friction to stop the machine. What I have to do is to see, at any rate, that I do not lend myself to the wrong which I condemn.

As for adopting the ways which the state has provided for remedying the evil, I know not of such ways. They take too much time, and a man's life will be gone. I have other affairs to attend to. I came into this world, not chiefly to make this a good place to live in, but to live in it, be it good or bad. A man has not everything to do, but something; and because he cannot do *everything*, it is not necessary that he should do *something* wrong. It is not my business to be petitioning the Governor or the Legislature any more than it is theirs to petition me; and if they should not hear my petition, what should I do then? But in this case the state has provided no way: its very Constitution is the evil. This may seem to be harsh and stubborn and unconciliatory; but it is to treat with the utmost kindness and consideration the only spirit that can appreciate or deserves it. So is all change for the better, like birth and death, which convulse the body.

I do not hesitate to say, that those who call themselves Abolitionists should at once effectually withdraw their support, both in person and property, from the government of Massachusetts and not wait till they constitute a majority of one, before they suffer the right to prevail through them. I think that it is enough if they have God on their side, without waiting for that other one. Moreover, any man more right than his neighbors constitutes a majority of one already.

I meet this American government, or its representative, the state government, directly, and face to face, once a year—no more—in the person of its tax gatherer; this is the only mode in which a man situated as I am necessarily meets it; and it then says distinctly, Recognize me; and the simplest, most effectual, and, in the present posture of affairs, the indispensablest mode of treating with it on this head, of expressing your little satisfaction with and love for it, is to deny it then. My civil neighbor, the tax-gatherer, is the very man I have to deal with,—for it is, after all, with men and not with parchment that I quarrel,—and he has voluntarily chosen to be an agent of the government. How shall he ever know well what he is and does as an officer of the government, or as a man, until he is obliged to consider whether he shall treat me, his neighbor, for whom he has respect, as a neighbor and well-disposed man, or as a maniac and disturber of the peace, and see if he can get over this obstruction to his neighborliness without a ruder and more impetuous thought or speech corresponding with his action. I know this well, that if one thousand, if one hundred, if ten men whom I could name,—if ten *honest* men only,—ay, if *one honest* man, in this State of Massachusetts, *ceasing to hold slaves*, were actually to withdraw from this copartnership, and be locked up in the county jail therefor, it would be the abolition of slavery in America. For it matters not how small the beginning may seem to be: what is once well done is done forever. But we love better to talk about it: that we say is our mission. Reform keeps many scores of newspapers in its service, but not one man. If my esteemed neighbor, the State's ambassador, who will devote his days to the settlement of the question of human rights in the Council Chamber, instead of being threatened with the prisons of Carolina, were to sit down the prisoner of Massachusetts, that State which is so anxious to foist the sin of slavery upon her sister,—though at present she can discover only an act of inhospitality to be the ground of a quarrel with her,—the Legislature would not wholly waive the subject the following winter.

Under a government which imprisons any unjustly, the true place for a just man is also a prison. The proper place to-day, the only place which Massachusetts has provided for her freer and less desponding spirits, is in her prisons, to be put out and locked out of the State by her own act, as they have already put themselves out by their principles. It is there that the fugitive slave, and the Mexican prisoner on parole, and the Indian come to plead the wrongs of his race should find them; on that separate, but more free and honorable ground, where the State places those who are not *with* her, but *against* her,—the only house in a slave State in which a free man can abide with honor. If any think that their influence would be lost there, and their voices no longer afflict the ear of the State, that they would not be as an enemy within its walls, they do not know by how much truth is stronger than error, nor how much more eloquently and effectively he can combat injustice who has experienced a little in his own person. Cast your whole vote, not a strip of paper merely, but your whole influence. A minority is powerless while it conforms to the majority; it is not even a minority then; but it is irresistible when it clogs by its whole weight. If the alternative is to keep all just men in prison, or give up war and slavery, the State will not hesitate which to choose. If a thousand men were not to pay their tax-bills this year, that would not be a violent and bloody measure, as it would be to pay them, and enable the state to commit violence and shed innocent blood. This is, in fact, the definition of a peaceable revolution, if any such is possible. If the tax-gatherer, or any other public officer, asks me, as one has done, "But what shall I do?" my answer is, "If you really wish to do anything, resign your office." When the subject has refused allegiance, and the officer has resigned his office, then the revolution is accomplished. But even suppose blood should flow. Is there not a sort of blood shed when the conscience is wounded? Through this wound a man's real manhood and immortality flow out, and he bleeds to an everlasting death. I see this blood flowing now.

I have contemplated the imprisonment of the offender, rather than the seizure of his goods,—though both will serve the same purpose,—because they who assert the purest right, and consequently are most dangerous to a corrupt State, commonly have not spent much time in accumulating property. To such the State renders comparatively small service, and a slight tax is wont to appear exorbitant, particularly if they are obliged to earn it by special labor with their hands. If there were one who lived wholly without the use of money, the State itself would hesitate to demand it of him. But the rich man—not to make any invidious comparison—is always sold to the institution which makes him rich. Absolutely speaking, the more money, the less virtue; for money comes between a man and his objects, and obtains them for him; and it was certainly no great virtue to obtain it. It puts to rest many questions which he would otherwise be taxed to answer; while the only new question which it puts is the hard but superfluous one, how to spend it. Thus, his moral ground is taken from under his feet. The opportunities of living are diminished in proportion as what are called the "means" are increased. The best thing a man can do for his culture when he is rich is to endeavor to carry out those schemes which he entertained when he was poor. Christ answered the Herodians according to their condition. "Show me the tribute-money," said he;—and one took a penny out of his pocket;—if you use money which has the image of Cæsar on it and which he has made current and valuable, that is, *if you are men of the State*, and gladly enjoy the advantages of Cæsar's government, then pay him back some of his own when he demands it: "Render therefore to Cæsar that which is Cæsar's, and to God those things which are God's,"—leaving them no wiser than before as to which was which; for they did not wish to know.

When I converse with the freest of my neighbors, I perceive that, whatever they may say about the magnitude and seriousness of the question, and their regard for the public tranquility, the long and the short of the matter is, that they cannot spare the protection of the existing government, and they dread the consequences to their property and families of disobedience to it. For my own part, I should not like to think that I ever rely on the protection of the State. But, if I deny the authority of the State when it presents its tax-bill, it will soon take and waste all my property, and so harass me and my children without end. This is hard. This makes it impossible for a man to live honestly, and at the same time comfortably, in outward respects. It will not be worth the while to accumulate property; that would be sure to go again. You must hire or squat somewhere, and raise but a small crop, and eat that soon. You must live within yourself, and depend upon yourself always tucked up and ready for a start, and not have many affairs. A man may grow rich in Turkey even, if he will be in all respects a good subject of the Turkish government. Confucius said: "If a state is governed by the principles of reason, poverty and misery are subjects of shame; if a state is not governed by the principles of reason, riches and honors are the subjects of shame." No: until I want the protection of Massachusetts to be extended to me in some distant Southern port, where my liberty is endangered, or until I am bent solely on building up an estate at home by peaceful enterprise, I can afford to refuse allegiance to Massachusetts, and her right to my property and life. It costs me less in every sense to incur the penalty of disobedience to the State than it would to obey. I should feel as if I were worth less in that case.

Some years ago, the State met me in behalf of the Church, and commanded me to pay a certain sum toward the support of a clergyman whose preaching my father attended, but never I myself. "Pay," it said, "or be locked up in the jail." I declined to pay. But, unfortunately, another man saw fit to pay it. I did not see why the schoolmaster should be taxed to support the priest, and not the priest the schoolmaster; for I was not the State's schoolmaster, but I supported myself by voluntary subscription. I did not see why the lyceum should not present its tax-bill, and have the State to back its demand, as well as the Church. However, at the request of the selectmen, I condescended to make some such statement as this in writing:—"Know all men by these presents, that I, Henry Thoreau, do not wish to be regarded as a member of any incorporated society which I have not joined." This I gave to the town clerk; and he has it. The State, having thus learned that I did not wish to be regarded as a member of that church, has never made a like demand on me since; though it said that it must adhere to its original presumption that time. If I had known how to name them, I should then have signed off in detail from all the societies which I never signed on to; but I did not know where to find a complete list.

I have paid no poll-tax for six years. I was put into a jail once on this account, for one night; and, as I stood considering the walls of solid stone, two or three feet thick, the door of wood and iron, a foot thick, and the iron grating which strained the light, I could not help being struck with the foolishness of that institution which treated me as if I were mere flesh and blood and bones, to be locked up. I wondered that it should have concluded at length that this was the best use it could put me to, and had never thought to avail itself of my services in some way. I saw that, if there was a wall of stone between me and my townsmen, there was a still more difficult one to climb or break through before they could get to be as free as I was. I did not for a moment feel confined, and the walls seemed a great waste of stone and mortar. I felt as if I alone of all my townsmen had paid my tax. They plainly did not know how to treat me, but behaved like persons who are underbred. In every threat and in every compliment there was a blunder; for they thought that my chief desire was to stand the other side of that stone wall. I could not but smile to see how industriously they locked the door on my meditations, which followed them out again without let or hinderance, and *they* were really all that was dangerous. As they could not reach me, they had resolved to punish my body; just as boys, if they cannot come at some person against whom they have a spite, will abuse his dog. I say that the State was half-witted, that it was timid as a lone woman with her silver spoons, and that it did not know its friends from its foes, and I lost all my remaining respect for it, and pitied it.

Thus the State never intentionally confronts a man's sense, intellectual or moral, but only his body, his senses. It is not armed with superior wit or honesty, but with superior physical strength. I was not born to be forced. I will breathe after my own fashion. Let us see who is the strongest. What force has a multitude? They only can force me who obey a higher law than I. They force me to become like themselves. I do not hear of men being forced to live this way or that by masses of men. What sort of life were that to live? When I meet a government which says to me, "Your money or your life," why should I be in haste to give it my money? It may be in a great strait, and not know what to do: I cannot help that. It must help itself; do as I do. It is not worth the while to snivel about it. I am not responsible for the successful working of the machinery of society. I am not the son of the engineer. I perceive that, when an acorn and a chestnut fall side by side, the one does not remain inert to make way for the other, but both obey their own laws, and spring and grow and flourish as best they can, till one, perchance, overshadows and destroys the other. If a plant cannot live according to its nature, it dies; and so a man.

The night in prison was novel and interesting enough. The prisoners in their shirt-sleeves were enjoying a chat and the evening air in the doorway, when I entered. But the jailer said, "Come, boys, it is time to lock up;" and so they dispersed, and I heard the sound of their steps returning into the hollow apartments. My room-mate was introduced to me by the jailer as "a first rate fellow and a clever man." When the door was locked, he showed me where to hang my hat, and how he managed matters there. The rooms were white-washed once a month; and this one, at least, was the whitest, most simply furnished, and probably the neatest apartment in the town. He naturally wanted to know where I came from, and what brought me there; and, when I had told him, I asked him in my turn how he came there, presuming him to be an honest man, of course; and, as the world goes, I believe he was. "Why," said he, "they accuse me of burning a barn; but I never did it." As near as I could discover, he had probably gone to bed in a barn when drunk, and smoked his pipe there; and so a barn was burnt. He had the reputation of being a clever man, had been there some three months waiting for his trial to come on, and would have to wait as much longer; but he was quite domesticated and contented, since he got his board for nothing, and thought that he was well treated.

He occupied one window, and I the other; and I saw that if one stayed there long, his principal business would be to look out the window. I had soon read all the tracts that were left there, and examined where former prisoners had broken out, and where a grate had been sawed off, and heard the history of the various occupants of that room; for I found that even here there was a history and a gossip which never circulated beyond the walls of the jail. Probably this is the only house in the town where verses are composed, which are afterward printed in a circular form, but not published. I was shown quite a long list of verses which were composed by some young men who had been detected in an attempt to escape, who avenged themselves by singing them.

I pumped my fellow-prisoner as dry as I could, for fear I should never see him again; but at length he showed me which was my bed, and left me to blow out the lamp.

It was like traveling into a far country, such as I had never expected to behold, to lie there for one night. It seemed to me that I never had heard the town-clock strike before, nor the evening sounds of the village; for we slept with the windows open, which were inside the grating. It was to see my native village in the light of the Middle Ages, and our Concord was turned into a Rhine stream, and visions of knights and castles passed before me. They were the voices of old burghers that I heard in the streets. I was an involuntary spectator and auditor of whatever was done and said in the kitchen of the adjacent village-inn,—a wholly new and rare experience to me. It was a closer view of my native town. I was fairly inside of it. I never had seen its institutions before. This is one of its peculiar institutions; for it is a shire town. I began to comprehend what its inhabitants were about.

In the morning, our breakfasts were put through the hole in the door, in small oblong-square tin pans, made to fit, and holding a pint of chocolate, with brown bread, and an iron spoon. When they called for the vessels again, I was green enough to return what bread I had left; but my comrade seized it and said that I should lay that up for lunch or dinner. Soon after he was let out to work at haying in a neighboring field, whither he went every day, and would not be back till noon; so he bade me good-day, saying that he doubted if he should see me again.

When I came out of prison,—for some one interfered, and paid that tax,—I did not perceive that great changes had taken place on the common, such as he observed who went in a youth and emerged a tottering and gray headed man; and yet a change had to my eyes come over the scene,—the town, and State, and country,—greater than any that mere time could effect. I saw yet more distinctly the State in which I lived. I saw to what extent the people among whom I lived could be trusted as good neighbors and friends; that their friendship was for summer weather only; that they did not greatly propose to do right; that they were a distinct race from me by their prejudices and superstitions, as the Chinamen and Malays are; that in their sacrifices to humanity they ran no risks, not even to their property; that after all they were not so noble but they treated the thief as he had treated them, and hoped, by a certain outward observance and a few prayers, and by walking in a particular straight though useless path from time to time, to save their souls. This may be to judge my neighbors harshly; for I believe that many of them are not aware that they have such an institution as the jail in their village.

It was formerly the custom in our village, when a poor debtor came out of jail, for his acquaintances to salute him, looking through their fingers, which were crossed to represent the grating of a jail window, "How do ye do?" My neighbors did not thus salute me, but first looked at me, and then at one another, as if I had returned from a long journey. I was put into jail as I was going to the shoemaker's to get a shoe which was mended. When I was let out the next morning, I proceeded to finish my errand, and, having put on my mended shoe, joined a huckleberry party, who were impatient to put themselves under my conduct; and in half an hour,—for the horse was soon tackled,—was in the midst of a huckleberry field, one of our highest hills, two miles off, and then the State was nowhere to be seen.

This is the whole history of "My Prisons."

I have never declined paying the highway tax, because I am as desirous of being a good neighbor as I am of being a bad subject; and as for supporting schools, I am doing my part to educate my fellow-countrymen now. It is for no particular item in the tax-bill that I refuse to pay it. I simply wish to refuse allegiance to the State, to withdraw and stand aloof from it effectually. I do not care to trace the course of my dollar, if I could, till it buys a man or musket to shoot with,—the dollar is innocent,—but I am concerned to trace the effects of my allegiance. In fact, I quietly declare war with the State, after my fashion, though I will still make what use and get what advantage of her I can, as is usual in such cases.

If others pay the tax which is demanded of me, from a sympathy with the State, they do but what they have already done in their own case, or rather they abet injustice to a greater extent than the State requires. If they pay the tax from a mistaken interest in the individual taxed, to save his property, or prevent his going to jail, it is because they have not considered wisely how far they let their private feelings interfere with the public good.

This, then, is my position at present. But one cannot be too much on his guard in such a case, lest his action be biased by obstinacy or an undue regard for the opinions of men. Let him see that he does only what belongs to himself and to the hour.

I think sometimes, Why, this people mean well, they are only ignorant; they would do better if they knew how; why give your neighbors this pain to treat you as they are not inclined to? But I think again, This is no reason why I should do as they do, or permit others to suffer much greater pain of a different kind. Again, I sometimes say to myself, When many millions of men, without heat, without ill will, without personal feeling of any kind, demand of you a few shillings only, without the possibility, such is their constitution, of retracting or altering their present demand, and without the possibility, on your side, of appeal to any other millions, why expose yourself to this overwhelming brute force? You do not resist cold and hunger, the winds and the waves, thus obstinately; you quietly submit to a thousand similar necessities. You do not put your head into the fire. But just in proportion as I regard this as not wholly a brute force, but partly a human force, and consider that I have relations to those millions as to so many millions of men, and not of mere brute or inanimate things, I see that appeal is possible, first and instantaneously, from them to the Maker of them, and secondly, from them to themselves. But if I put my head deliberately into the fire, there is no appeal to fire or to the Maker of fire, and I have only myself to blame. If I could convince myself that I have any right to be satisfied with men as they are, and to treat them accordingly, and not according, in some respects, to my requisitions and expectations of what they and I ought to be, then, like a good Mussulman and fatalist, I should endeavor to be satisfied with things as they are, and say it is the will of God. And, above all, there is this difference between resisting this and a purely brute or natural force, that I can resist this with some effect; but I cannot expect, like Orpheus, to change the nature of the rocks and trees and beasts.

I do not wish to quarrel with any man or nation. I do not wish to split hairs, to make fine distinctions, or set myself up as better than my neighbors. I seek rather, I may say, even an excuse for conforming to the laws of the land. I am but too ready to conform to them. Indeed, I have reason to suspect myself on this head; and each year, as the tax-gatherer comes round, I find myself disposed to review the acts and position of the general and State governments, and the spirit of the people, to discover a pretext for conformity.

> *We must affect our country as our parents,*
> *And if any time we alienate*
> *Our love or industry from doing it honor,*
> *We must respect effects and teach the soul*
> *Matter of conscience and religion,*
> *And not desire of rule or benefit.*

I believe that the State will soon be able to take all my work of this sort out of my hands, and then I shall be no better a patriot than my fellow-countrymen. Seen from a lower point of view, the Constitution, with all its faults, is very good; the law and the courts are very respectable; even this State and this American government are, in many respects, very admirable, and rare things, to be thankful for, such as a great many have described them; but seen from a point of view a little higher, they are what I have described them; seen from a higher still, and the highest, who shall say what they are, or that they are worth looking at or thinking of at all?

However, the government does not concern me much, and I shall bestow the fewest possible thoughts on it. It is not many moments that I live under a government, even in this world. If a man is thought-free, fancy-free, imagination-free, that which *is not* never for a long time appearing *to be* to him, unwise rulers or reformers cannot fatally interrupt him.

I know that most men think differently from myself; but those whose lives are by profession devoted to the study of these or kindred subjects content me as little as any. Statesmen and legislators, standing so completely within the institution, never distinctly and nakedly behold it. They speak of moving society, but have no resting-place without it. They may be men of a certain experience and discrimination, and have no doubt invented ingenious and even useful systems, for which we sincerely thank them; but all their wit and usefulness lie within certain not very wide limits. They are wont to forget that the world is not governed by policy and expediency. Webster never goes behind government, and so cannot speak with authority about it. His words are wisdom to those legislators who contemplate no essential reform in the existing government; but for thinkers, and those who legislate for all time, he never once glances at the subject. I know of those whose serene and wise speculations on this theme would soon reveal the limits of his mind's range and hospitality. Yet, compared with the cheap professions of most reformers, and the still cheaper wisdom and eloquence of politicians in general, his are almost the only sensible and valuable words, and we thank Heaven for him. Comparatively, he is always strong, original, and, above all, practical. Still, his quality is not wisdom, but prudence. The lawyer's truth is not Truth, but consistency or a consistent expediency. Truth is always in harmony with herself, and is not concerned chiefly to reveal the justice that may consist with wrongdoing. He well deserves to be called, as he has been called, the Defender of the Constitution. There are really no blows to be given by him but defensive ones. He is not a leader, but a follower. His leaders are the men of '87. "I have never made an effort," he says, "and never propose to make an effort; I have never countenanced an effort, and never mean to countenance an effort, to disturb the arrangement as originally made, by which the various States came into the Union." Still thinking of the sanction which the Constitution gives to slavery, he says, "Because it was a part of the original compact,—let it stand." Notwithstanding his special acuteness and ability, he is unable to take a fact out of its merely political relations, and behold it as it lies absolutely to be disposed of by the intellect,—what, for instance, it behooves a man to do here in America to-day with regard to slavery,—but ventures, or is driven to make some such desperate answer as the following, while professing to speak absolutely, and as a private man,—from which what new and singular code of social duties might be inferred? "The manner," says he, "in which the governments of those States where slavery exists are to regulate it is for their own consideration, under their responsibility to their constituents, to the general laws of propriety, humanity, and justice, and to God. Associations formed elsewhere, springing from a feeling of humanity, or other cause, have nothing whatever to do with it. They have never received any encouragement from me, and they never will."

They who know of no purer sources of truth, who have traced up its stream no higher, stand, and wisely stand, by the Bible and the Constitution, and drink at it there with reverence and humility; but they who behold where it comes trickling into this lake or that pool, gird up their loins once more, and continue their pilgrimage toward its fountainhead.

No man with a genius for legislation has appeared in America. They are rare in the history of the world. There are orators, politicians, and eloquent men, by the thousand; but the speaker has not yet opened his mouth to speak who is capable of settling the much-vexed questions of the day. We love eloquence for its own sake, and not for any truth which it may utter, or any heroism it may inspire. Our legislators have not yet learned the comparative value of free-trade and of freedom, of union, and of rectitude, to a nation. They have no genius or talent for comparatively humble questions of taxation and finance, commerce and manufactures and agriculture. If we were left solely to the wordy wit of legislators in Congress for our guidance, uncorrected by the seasonable experience and the effectual complaints of the people, America would not long retain her rank among the nations. For eighteen hundred years, though perchance I have no right to say it, the New Testament has been written; yet where is the legislator who has wisdom and practical talent enough to avail himself of the light which it sheds on the science of legislation?

The authority of government, even such as I am willing to submit to,—for I will cheerfully obey those who know and can do better than I, and in many things even those who neither know nor can do as well,—is still an impure one: to be strictly just, it must have the sanction and consent of the governed. It can have no pure right over my person and property but what I concede to it. The progress from an absolute to a limited monarchy, from a limited monarchy to a democracy, is a progress toward a true respect for the individual. Even the Chinese philosopher was wise enough to regard the individual as the basis of the empire. Is a democracy, such as we know it, the last improvement possible in government? Is it not possible to take a step further towards recognizing and organizing the rights of man? There will never be a really free and enlightened State until the State comes to recognize the individual as a higher and independent power, from which all its own power and authority are derived, and treats him accordingly. I please myself with imagining a State at last which can afford to be just to all men, and to treat the individual with respect as a neighbor; which even would not think it inconsistent with its own repose if a few were to live aloof from it, not meddling with it, nor embraced by it, who fulfilled all the duties of neighbors and fellowmen. A State which bore this kind of fruit, and suffered it to drop off as fast as it ripened, would prepare the way for a still more perfect and glorious State, which also I have imagined, but not yet anywhere seen.

# 5

# Reverend Martin Luther King, Jr., Letter from Birmingham Jail

April 16, 1963

MY DEAR FELLOW CLERGYMEN:

While confined here in Birmingham city jail, I came across your recent statement calling my present activities "unwise and untimely." Seldom do I pause to answer criticism of my work and ideas. If I sought to answer all the criticisms that cross my desk, my secretaries would have little time for anything other than such correspondence in the course of the day, and I would have no time for constructive work. But since I feel that you are men of genuine good will and that your criticisms are sincerely set forth, I want to try to answer your statement in what I hope will be patient and reasonable terms.

I think I should indicate why I am here in Birmingham, since you have been influenced by the view which argues against "outsiders coming in." I have the honor of serving as president of the Southern Christian Leadership Conference, an organization operating in every southern state, with headquarters in Atlanta, Georgia. We have some eighty-five affiliated organizations across the South, and one of them is the Alabama Christian Movement for Human Rights. Frequently we share staff, educational and financial resources with our affiliates. Several months ago the affiliate here in Birmingham asked us to be on call to engage in a nonviolent direct-action program if such were deemed necessary. We readily consented, and when the hour came we lived up to our promise. So I, along with several members of my staff, am here because I was invited here. I am here because I have organizational ties here.

But more basically, I am in Birmingham because injustice is here. Just as the prophets of the eighth century B.C. left their villages and carried their "thus saith the Lord" far beyond the boundaries of their home towns, and just as the Apostle Paul left his village of Tarsus and carried the gospel of Jesus Christ to the far corners of the Greco-Roman world, so am I compelled to carry the gospel of freedom beyond my own home town. Like Paul, I must constantly respond to the

Macedonian call for aid.

Moreover, I am cognizant of the interrelatedness of all communities and states. I cannot sit idly by in Atlanta and not be concerned about what happens in Birmingham. Injustice anywhere is a threat to justice everywhere. We are caught in an inescapable network of mutuality, tied in a single garment of destiny. Whatever affects one directly, affects all indirectly. Never again can we afford to live with the narrow, provincial "outside agitator" idea. Anyone who lives inside the United States can never be considered an outsider anywhere within its bounds.

You deplore the demonstrations taking place in Birmingham. But your statement, I am sorry to say, fails to express a similar concern for the conditions that brought about the demonstrations. I am sure that none of you would want to rest content with the superficial kind of social analysis that deals merely with effects and does not grapple with underlying causes. It is unfortunate that demonstrations are taking place in Birmingham, but it is even more unfortunate that the city's white power structure left the Negro community with no alternative.

In any nonviolent campaign there are four basic steps: collection of the facts to determine whether injustices exist; negotiation; self-purification; and direct action. We have gone through all these steps in Birmingham. There can be no gainsaying the fact that racial injustice engulfs this community. Birmingham is probably the most thoroughly segregated city in the United States. Its ugly record of brutality is widely known. Negroes have experienced grossly unjust treatment in the courts. There have been more unsolved bombings of Negro homes and churches in Birmingham than in any other city in the nation. These are the hard, brutal facts of the case. On the basis of these conditions, Negro leaders sought to negotiate with the city fathers. But the latter consistently refused to engage in good-faith negotiation.

Then, last September, came the opportunity to talk with leaders of Birmingham's economic community. In the course of the negotiations, certain promises were made by the merchants—for example, to remove the stores' humiliating racial signs. On the basis of these promises, the Reverend Fred Shuttlesworth and the leaders of the Alabama Christian Movement for Human Rights agreed to a moratorium on all demonstrations. As the weeks and months went by, we realized that we were the victims of a broken promise. A few signs, briefly removed, returned; the others remained.

As in so many past experiences, our hopes had been blasted, and the shadow of deep disappointment settled upon us. We had no alternative except to prepare for direct action, whereby we would present our very bodies as a means of laying our case before the conscience of the local and the national community. Mindful of the difficulties involved, we decided to undertake a process of self-purification. We began a series of workshops on nonviolence, and we repeatedly asked ourselves: "Are you able to accept blows without retaliating?" "Are you able to endure the ordeal of jail?" We decided to schedule our direct-action program for the Easter season, realizing that except for Christmas, this is the main shopping period of the year. Knowing that a strong economic-withdrawal program would be the by-product of direct action, we felt that this would be the best time to bring pressure to bear on the merchants for the needed change.

Then it occurred to us that Birmingham's mayoral election was coming up in March, and we speedily decided to postpone action until after election day. When we discovered that the Commissioner of Public Safety, Eugene "Bull" Connor, had piled up enough votes to be in the runoff, we decided again to postpone action until the day after the run-off so that the demonstrations could not be used to cloud the issues. Like many others, we waited to see Mr. Connor defeated, and to this end we endured postponement after postponement. Having aided in this community need, we felt that our direct-action program could be delayed no longer.

You may well ask: "Why direct action? Why sit-ins, marches and so forth? Isn't negotiation a better path?" You are quite right in calling for negotiation. Indeed, this is the very purpose of direct action. Nonviolent direct action seeks to create such a crisis and foster such a tension that a community which has constantly refused to negotiate is forced to confront the issue. It seeks so to dramatize the issue that it can no longer be ignored. My citing the creation of tension as part of the work of the nonviolent-resister may sound rather shocking. But I must confess that I am not afraid of the word "tension." I have earnestly opposed violent tension, but there is a type of constructive, non-violent tension which is necessary for growth. Just as Socrates felt that it was necessary to create a tension in the mind so that individuals could rise from the bondage of myths and half-truths to the unfettered realm of creative analysis and objective appraisal, so must we see the need for nonviolent gadflies to create the kind of tension in society that will help men rise from the dark depths of prejudice and racism to the majestic heights of understanding and brotherhood.

The purpose of our direct-action program is to create a situation so crisis-packed that it will inevitably open the door to negotiation. I therefore concur with you in your call for negotiation. Too long has our beloved Southland been bogged down in a tragic effort to live in monologue rather than dialogue.

One of the basic points in your statement is that the action that I and my associates have taken in Birmingham is untimely. Some have asked: "Why didn't you give the new city administration time to act?" The only answer that I can give to this query is that the new Birmingham administration must be prodded about as much as the outgoing one, before it will act. We are sadly mistaken if we feel that the election of Albert Boutwell as mayor will bring the millennium to Birmingham. While Mr. Boutwell is a much more gentle person than Mr. Connor, they are both segregationists, dedicated to maintenance of the status quo. I have hope that Mr. Boutwell will be reasonable enough to see the futility of massive resistance to desegregation. But he will not see this without pressure from devotees of civil rights. My friends, I must say to you that we have not made a single gain in civil rights without determined legal and nonviolent pressure.

Lamentably, it is an historical fact that privileged groups seldom give up their privileges voluntarily. Individuals may see the moral light and voluntarily give up their unjust posture; but, as Reinhold Niebuhr has reminded us, groups tend to be more immoral than individuals.

We know through painful experience that freedom is never voluntarily given by the oppressor; it must be demanded by the oppressed. Frankly, I have yet to engage in a direct-action campaign that was "well timed" in the view of those who have not suffered unduly from the disease of segregation. For years now I have heard the word "Wait!" It rings in the ear of every Negro with piercing familiarity. This "Wait" has almost always meant "Never." We must come to see, with one of our distinguished jurists, that "justice too long delayed is justice denied."

We have waited for more than 340 years for our constitutional and God-given rights. The nations of Asia and Africa are moving with jetlike speed toward gaining political independence, but we still creep at horse-and-buggy pace toward gaining a cup of coffee at a lunch counter. Perhaps it is easy for those who have never felt the stinging darts of segregation to say, "Wait." But when you have seen vicious mobs lynch your mothers and fathers at will and drown your sisters and brothers at whim; when you have seen hate-filled policemen curse, kick and even kill your black brothers and sisters; when you see the vast majority of your twenty million Negro brothers smothering in an airtight cage of poverty in the midst of an affluent society; when you suddenly find your tongue twisted and your speech stammering as you seek to explain to your six-year-old daughter why she can't go to the public amusement park that has just been advertised on television, and see tears welling up in her eyes when she is told that Funtown is closed to colored children, and see ominous clouds of inferiority beginning to form in her little mental sky, and see her beginning to distort her personality by developing an unconscious bitterness toward white people; when you have to concoct an answer for a five-year-old son who is asking: "Daddy, why do white people treat colored people so mean?"; when you take a cross-country drive and find it necessary to sleep night after night in the uncomfortable corners of your automobile because no motel will accept you; when you are humiliated day in and day out by nagging signs reading "white" and "colored"; when your first name becomes "nigger," your middle name becomes "boy" (however old you are) and your last name becomes "John," and your wife and mother are never given the respected title "Mrs."; when you are harried by day and haunted by night by the fact that you are a Negro, living constantly at tiptoe stance, never quite knowing what to expect next, and are plagued with inner fears and outer resentments; when you are forever fighting a degenerating sense of "nobodiness"—then you will understand why we find it difficult to wait. There comes a time when the cup of endurance runs over, and men are no longer willing to be plunged into the abyss of despair. I hope, sirs, you can understand our legitimate and unavoidable impatience.

You express a great deal of anxiety over our willingness to break laws. This is certainly a legitimate concern. Since we do diligently urge people to obey the

Supreme Court's decision of 1954 outlawing segregation in the public schools, at first glance it may seem rather paradoxical for us consciously to break laws. One may well ask: "How can you advocate breaking some laws and obeying others?" The answer lies in the fact that there are two types of laws: just and unjust. I would be the first to advocate obeying just laws. One has not only a legal but a moral responsibility to obey just laws. Conversely, one has a moral responsibility to disobey unjust laws. I would agree with St. Augustine that "an unjust law is no law at all."

Now, what is the difference between the two? How does one determine whether a law is just or unjust? A just law is a man-made code that squares with the moral law or the law of God. An unjust law is a code that is out of harmony with the moral law. To put it in the terms of St. Thomas Aquinas: An unjust law is a human law that is not rooted in eternal law and natural law. Any law that uplifts human personality is just. Any law that degrades human personality is unjust. All segregation statutes are unjust because segregation distorts the soul and damages the personality. It gives the segregator a false sense of superiority and the segregated a false sense of inferiority. Segregation, to use the terminology of the Jewish philosopher Martin Buber, substitutes an "I-it" relationship for an "I-thou" relationship and ends up relegating persons to the status of things. Hence segregation is not only politically, economically and sociologically unsound, it is morally wrong and sinful. Paul Tillich has said that sin is separation. Is not segregation an existential expression of man's tragic separation, his awful estrangement, his terrible sinfulness? Thus it is that I can urge men to obey the 1954 decision of the Supreme Court, for it is morally right; and I can urge them to disobey segregation ordinances, for they are morally wrong.

Let us consider a more concrete example of just and unjust laws. An unjust law is a code that a numerical or power majority group compels a minority group to obey but does not make binding on itself. This is *difference* made legal. By the same token, a just law is a code that a majority compels a minority to follow and that it is willing to follow itself. This is *sameness* made legal.

Let me give another explanation. A law is unjust if it is inflicted on a minority that, as a result of being denied the right to vote, had no part in enacting or devising the law. Who can say that the legislature of Alabama which set up the state's segregation laws was democratically elected? Throughout Alabama all sorts of devious methods are used to prevent Negroes from becoming registered voters, and there are some counties in which, even though Negroes constitute a majority of the population, not a single Negro is registered. Can any law enacted under such circumstances be considered democratically structured?

Sometimes a law is just on its face and unjust in its application. For instance, I have been arrested on a charge of parading without a permit. Now, there is nothing wrong in having an ordinance which requires a permit for a parade. But such an ordinance becomes unjust when it is used to maintain segregation and to deny citizens the First-Amendment privilege of peaceful assembly and protest.

I hope you are able to see the distinction I am trying to point out. In no sense do I advocate evading or defying the law, as would the rabid segregationist. That would lead to anarchy. One who breaks an unjust law must do so openly, lovingly, and with a willingness to accept the penalty. I submit that an individual who breaks a law that conscience tells him is unjust, and who willingly accepts the penalty of imprisonment in order to arouse the conscience of the community over its injustice, is in reality expressing the highest respect for law.

Of course, there is nothing new about this kind of civil disobedience. It was evidenced sublimely in the refusal of Shadrach, Meshach and Abednego to obey the laws of Nebuchadnezzar, on the ground that a higher moral law was at stake. It was practiced superbly by the early Christians, who were willing to face hungry lions and the excruciating pain of chopping blocks rather than submit to certain unjust laws of the Roman Empire. To a degree, academic freedom is a reality today because Socrates practiced civil disobedience. In our own nation, the Boston Tea Party represented a massive act of civil disobedience.

We should never forget that everything Adolf Hitler did in Germany was "legal" and everything the Hungarian freedom fighters did in Hungary was "illegal." It was "illegal" to aid and comfort a Jew in Hitler's Germany. Even so, I am sure that, had I lived in Germany at the time, I would have aided and comforted my Jewish brothers. If today I lived in a Communist country where certain principles dear to the Christian faith are suppressed, I would openly advocate disobeying that country's antireligious laws.

I must make two honest confessions to you, my Christian and Jewish brothers. First, I must confess that over the past few years I have been gravely disappointed with the white moderate. I have almost reached the regrettable conclusion that the Negro's great stumbling block in his stride toward freedom is not the White Citizen's Counciler or the Ku Klux Klanner, but the white moderate, who is more devoted to "order" than to justice; who prefers a negative peace which is the absence of tension to a positive peace which is the presence of justice; who constantly says: "I agree with you in the goal you seek, but I cannot agree with your methods of direct action"; who paternalistically believes he can set the timetable for another man's freedom; who lives by a mythical concept of time and who constantly advises the Negro to wait for a "more convenient season." Shallow understanding from people of good will is more frustrating than absolute misunderstanding from people of ill will. Lukewarm acceptance is much more bewildering than outright rejection.

I had hoped that the white moderate would understand that law and order exist for the purpose of establishing justice and that when they fail in this purpose they become the dangerously structured dams that block the flow of social progress. I had hoped that the white moderate would understand that the present tension in the South is a necessary phase of the transition from an obnoxious negative peace, in which the Negro passively accepted his unjust plight, to a substantive and positive peace, in which all men will respect the dignity and worth of human personality. Actually, we who engage in nonviolent direct action are not the creators of tension. We merely bring to the surface the hidden tension that is already alive. We bring it out in the open, where it can be seen and dealt with. Like a boil that can never be cured so long as it is covered up but must be opened with all its ugliness to the natural medicines of air and light, injustice must be exposed, with all the tension its exposure creates, to the light of human conscience and the air of national opinion before it can be cured.

In your statement you assert that our actions, even though peaceful, must be condemned because they precipitate violence. But is this a logical assertion? Isn't this like condemning a robbed man because his possession of money precipitated the evil act of robbery? Isn't this like condemning Socrates because his unswerving commitment to truth and his philosophical inquiries precipitated the act by the misguided populace in which they made him drink hemlock? Isn't this like condemning Jesus because his unique God-consciousness and never-ceasing devotion to God's will precipitated the evil act of crucifixion? We must come to see that, as the federal courts have consistently affirmed, it is wrong to urge an individual to cease his efforts to gain his basic constitutional rights because the quest may precipitate violence. Society must protect the robbed and punish the robber.

I had also hoped that the white moderate would reject the myth concerning time in relation to the struggle for freedom. I have just received a letter from a white brother in Texas. He writes: "All Christians know that the colored people will receive equal rights eventually, but it is possible that you are in too great a religious hurry. It has taken Christianity almost two thousand years to accomplish what it has. The teachings of Christ take time to come to earth." Such an attitude stems from a tragic misconception of time, from the strangely irrational notion that there is something in the very flow of time that will inevitably cure all ills. Actually, time itself is neutral; it can be used either destructively or constructively. More and more I feel that the people of ill will have used time much more effectively than have the people of good will. We will have to repent in this generation not merely for the hateful words and actions of the bad people but for the appalling silence of the good people. Human progress never rolls in on wheels of inevitability; it comes through the tireless efforts of men willing to be co-workers with God, and without this hard work, time itself becomes an ally of the forces of social stagnation. We must use time creatively, in the knowledge that the time is always ripe to do right. Now is the time to make real the promise of democracy and transform our pending national elegy into a creative psalm of brotherhood. Now is the time to lift our national policy from the quicksand of racial injustice to the solid rock of human dignity.

You speak of our activity in Birmingham as extreme. At first I was rather disappointed that fellow clergymen would see my nonviolent efforts as those of an extremist. I began thinking about the fact that I stand in the middle of two opposing forces in the Negro community. One is a force of complacency, made up in part of Negroes who, as a result of long years of oppression, are so drained of self-respect and a sense of "somebodiness" that they have adjusted to segregation; and in part of a few middle-class Negroes who, because of a degree of academic and economic security and because in some ways they profit by segregation, have become insensitive to the problems of the masses. The other force is one of bitterness and hatred, and it comes perilously close to advocating violence. It is expressed in the various black nationalist groups that are springing up across the nation, the largest and best-known being Elijah Muhammad's Muslim movement. Nourished by the Negro's frustration over the continued existence of racial discrimination, this movement is made up of people who have lost faith in America, who have absolutely repudiated Christianity, and who have concluded that the white man is an incorrigible "devil."

I have tried to stand between these two forces, saying that we need emulate neither the "do-nothingism" of the complacent nor the hatred and despair of the black nationalist. For there is the more excellent way of love and non-violent protest. I am grateful to God that, through the influence of the Negro church, the way of nonviolence became an integral part of our struggle.

If this philosophy had not emerged, by now many streets of the South would, I am convinced, be flowing with blood. And I am further convinced that if our white brothers dismiss as "rabble-rousers" and "outside agitators" those of us who employ nonviolent direct action, and if they refuse to support our nonviolent efforts, millions of Negroes will, out of frustration and despair, seek solace and security in black-nationalist ideologies—a development that would inevitably lead to a frightening racial nightmare.

Oppressed people cannot remain oppressed forever. The yearning for freedom eventually manifests itself, and that is what has happened to the American Negro. Something within has reminded him of his birthright of freedom, and something without has reminded him that it can be gained. Consciously or unconsciously, he has been caught up by the *Zeitgeist*, and with his black brothers of Africa and his brown and yellow brothers of Asia, South America and the Caribbean, the United States Negro is moving with a sense of great urgency toward the promised land of racial justice. If one recognizes this vital urge that has engulfed the Negro community, one should readily understand why public demonstrations are taking place. The Negro has many pent-up resentments and latent frustrations, and he must release them. So let him march; let him make prayer pilgrimages to the city hall; let him go on freedom rides—and try to understand why he must do so. If his repressed emotions are not released to nonviolent ways, they will seek expression through violence; this is not a threat but a fact of history. So I have not said to my people: "Get rid of your discontent." Rather, I have tried to say that this normal and healthy discontent can be channeled into the creative outlet of nonviolent direct action. And now this approach is being termed extremist.

But though I was initially disappointed at being categorized as an extremist, as I continued to think about the matter I gradually gained a measure of satisfaction from the label. Was not Jesus an extremist for love: "Love your enemies, bless them that curse you, do good to them that hate you, and pray for them which despitefully use you, and persecute you." Was not Amos an extremist for justice: "Let justice roll down like waters and righteousness like an ever-flowing stream." Was not Paul an extremist for the Christian gospel: "I bear in my body the marks of the Lord Jesus." Was not Martin Luther an extremist: "Here I stand, I cannot do otherwise, so help me God." And John Bunyan: "I will stay in jail to the end of my days before I make a butchery of my conscience." And Abraham Lincoln: "This nation cannot survive half slave and half free." And Thomas Jefferson: "We hold these truths to be self-evident, that all men are created equal . . ." So the question is not whether we will be extremists, but what kind of extremists we will be. Will we be extremists for hate or for love? Will we be extremists for the preservation of injustice or for the extension of justice? In that dramatic scene on Calvary's hill three men were crucified. We must never forget that all three were crucified for the same crime—the crime of extremism. Two were extremists for immorality, and thus fell below their environment. The other, Jesus Christ, was an extremist for love, truth and goodness, and thereby rose above his environment. Perhaps the South, the nation and the world are in dire need of creative extremists.

I had hoped that the white moderate would see this need. Perhaps I was too optimistic; perhaps I expected too much. I suppose I should have realized that few members of the oppressor race can understand the deep groans and passionate yearnings of the oppressed race, and still fewer have the vision to see that injustice must be rooted out by strong, persistent and determined action. I am thankful, however, that some of our white brothers in the South have grasped the meaning of this social revolution and committed themselves to it. They are still all too few in quantity, but they are big in quality. Some—such as Ralph McGill, Lillian Smith, Harry Golden, James McBride Dabbs, Ann Braden and Sarah Patton Boyle—have written about our struggle in eloquent and prophetic terms. Others have marched with us down nameless streets of the South. They have languished in filthy, roach-infested jails, suffering the abuse and brutality of policemen who view them as "dirty nigger-lovers." Unlike so many of their moderate brothers and sisters, they have recognized the urgency of the moment and sensed the need for powerful "action" antidotes to combat the disease of segregation.

Let me take note of my other major disappointment. I have been so greatly disappointed with the white church and its leadership. Of course, there are some notable exceptions. I am not unmindful of the fact that each of you has taken some significant stands on this issue. I commend you, Reverend Stallings, for your Christian stand on this past Sunday, in welcoming Negroes to your worship service on a nonsegregated basis. I commend the Catholic leaders of this state for integrating Spring Hill College several years ago.

But despite these notable exceptions, I must honestly reiterate that I have been disappointed with the church. I do not say this as one of those negative critics who can always find something wrong with the church. I say this as a minister of the gospel, who loves the church; who was nurtured in its bosom; who has been sustained by its spiritual blessings and who will remain true to it as long as the cord of life shall lengthen.

When I was suddenly catapulted into the leadership of the bus protest in Montgomery, Alabama, a few years ago, I felt we would be supported by the white church. I felt that the white ministers, priests and rabbis of the South would be among our strongest allies. Instead, some have been outright opponents, refusing to understand the freedom movement and misrepresenting its leaders; all too many others have been more cautious than courageous and have remained silent behind the anesthetizing security of stained-glass windows.

In spite of my shattered dreams, I came to Birmingham with the hope that the white religious leadership of this community would see the justice of our cause and, with deep moral concern, would serve as the channel through which our just grievances could reach the power structure. I had hoped that each of you would understand. But again I have been disappointed.

I have heard numerous southern religious leaders admonish their worshipers to comply with a desegregation decision because it is the law, but I have longed to hear white ministers declare: "Follow this decree because integration is morally right and because the Negro is your brother." In the midst of blatant injustices inflicted upon the Negro, I have watched white churchmen stand on the sideline and mouth pious irrelevancies and sanctimonious trivialities. In the midst of a mighty struggle to rid our nation of racial and economic injustice, I have heard many ministers say: "Those are social issues, with which the gospel has no real concern." And I have watched many churches commit themselves to a completely otherworldly religion which makes a strange, un-Biblical distinction between body and soul, between the sacred and the secular.

I have traveled the length and breadth of Alabama, Mississippi and all the other southern states. On sweltering summer days and crisp autumn mornings I have looked at the South's beautiful churches with their lofty spires pointing heavenward. I have beheld the impressive outlines of her massive religious-education buildings. Over and over I have found myself asking: "What kind of people worship here? Who is their God? Where were their voices when the lips of Governor Barnett dripped with words of interposition and nullification? Where were they when Governor Wallace gave a clarion call for defiance and hatred? Where were their voices of support when bruised and weary Negro men and women decided to rise from the dark dungeons of complacency to the bright hills of creative protest?"

Yes, these questions are still in my mind. In deep disappointment I have wept over the laxity of the church. But be assured that my tears have been tears of love. There can be no deep disappointment where there is not deep love. Yes, I love the church. How could I do otherwise? I am in the rather unique position of being the son, the grandson and the great-grandson of preachers. Yes, I see the church as the body of Christ. But, oh! How we have blemished and scarred that body through social neglect and through fear of being nonconformists.

There was a time when the church was very powerful—in the time when the early Christians rejoiced at being deemed worthy to suffer for what they believed. In those days the church was not merely a thermometer that recorded the ideas and principles of popular opinion; it was a thermostat that transformed the mores of society. Whenever the early Christians entered a town, the people in power became disturbed and immediately sought to convict the Christians for being "disturbers of the peace" and "outside agitators." But the Christians pressed on, in the conviction that they were "a colony of heaven," called to obey God rather than man. Small in number, they were big in commitment. They were too God-intoxicated to be "astronomically intimidated." By their effort and example they brought an end to such ancient evils as infanticide and gladiatorial contests.

Things are different now. So often the contemporary church is a weak, ineffectual voice with an uncertain sound. So often it is an archdefender of the status quo. Far from being disturbed by the presence of the church, the power structure of the average community is consoled by the church's silent—and often even vocal—sanction of things as they are.

But the judgment of God is upon the church as never before. If today's church does not recapture the sacrificial spirit of the early church, it will lose its authenticity, forfeit the loyalty of millions, and be dismissed as an irrelevant social club with no meaning for the twentieth century. Every day I meet young people whose disappointment with the church has turned into outright disgust.

Perhaps I have once again been too optimistic. Is organized religion too inextricably bound to the status quo to save our nation and the world? Perhaps I must turn my faith to the inner spiritual church, the church within the church, as the true *ekklesia* and the hope of the world. But again I am thankful to God that some noble souls from the ranks of organized religion have broken loose from the paralyzing chains of conformity and joined us as active partners in the struggle for freedom. They have left their secure congregations and walked the streets of Albany, Georgia, with us. They have gone down the highways of the South on tortuous rides for freedom. Yes, they have gone to jail with us. Some have been dismissed from their churches, have lost the support of their bishops and fellow ministers. But they have acted in the faith that right defeated is stronger than evil triumphant. Their witness has been the spiritual salt that has preserved the true meaning of the gospel in these troubled times. They have carved a tunnel of hope through the dark mountain of disappointment.

I hope the church as a whole will meet the challenge of this decisive hour. But even if the church does not come to the aid of justice, I have no despair about the future. I have no fear about the outcome of our struggle in Birmingham, even if our motives are at present misunderstood. We will reach the goal of freedom in Birmingham and all over the nation, because the goal of America is freedom. Abused and scorned though we may be, our destiny is tied up with America's destiny. Before the pilgrims landed at Plymouth, we were here. Before the pen of Jefferson etched the majestic words of the Declaration of Independence across the pages of history, we were here. For more than two centuries our forebears labored in this country without wages; they made cotton king; they built the homes of their masters while suffering gross injustice and shameful humiliation—and yet out of a bottomless vitality they continued to thrive and develop. If the inexpressible cruelties of slavery could not stop us, the opposition we now face will surely fail. We will win our freedom because the sacred heritage of our nation and the eternal will of God are embodied in our echoing demands.

Before closing I feel impelled to mention one other point in your statement that has troubled me profoundly. You warmly commended the Birmingham police force for keeping "order" and "preventing violence." I doubt that you would have so warmly commended the police force if you had seen its dogs sinking their teeth into unarmed, nonviolent Negroes. I doubt that you would so quickly commend the policemen if you were to observe their ugly and inhumane treatment of Negroes here in the city jail; if you were to watch them push and curse old Negro women and young Negro girls; if you were to see them slap and kick old Negro men and young boys; if you were to observe them, as they did on two occasions, refuse to give us food because we wanted to sing our grace together. I cannot join you in your praise of the Birmingham police department.

It is true that the police have exercised a degree of discipline in handling the demonstrators. In this sense they have conducted themselves rather "nonviolently" in public. But for what purpose? To preserve the evil system of segregation. Over the past few years I have consistently preached that nonviolence demands that the means we use must be as pure as the ends we seek. I have tried to make clear that it is wrong to use immoral means to attain moral ends. But now I must affirm that it is just as wrong, or perhaps even more so, to use moral means to preserve immoral ends. Perhaps Mr. Connor and his policemen have been rather nonviolent in public, as was Chief Pritchett in Albany, Georgia, but they have used the moral means of nonviolence to maintain the immoral end of racial injustice. As T. S. Eliot has said: "The last temptation is the greatest treason: To do the right deed for the wrong reason."

I wish you had commended the Negro sit-inners and demonstrators of Birmingham for their sublime courage, their willingness to suffer and their amazing discipline in the midst of great provocation. One day the South will recognize its real heroes. They will be the James Merediths, with the noble sense of purpose that enables them to face jeering and hostile mobs, and with the agonizing loneliness that characterizes the life of the pioneer. They will be old, oppressed, battered Negro women, symbolized in a seventy-two-year-old woman in Montgomery, Alabama, who rose up with a sense of dignity and with her people decided not to ride segregated buses, and who responded with ungrammatical profundity to one who inquired about her weariness: "My feets is tired, but my soul is at rest." They will be the young high school and college students, the young ministers of the gospel and a host of their elders, courageously and nonviolently sitting in at lunch counters and willingly going to jail for conscience' sake. One day the South will know that when these disinherited children of God sat down at lunch counters, they were in reality standing up for what is best in the American dream and for the most sacred values in our Judaeo-Christian heritage, thereby bringing our nation back to those great wells of democracy which were dug deep by the founding fathers in their formulation of the Constitution and the Declaration of Independence.

Never before have I written so long a letter. I'm afraid it is much too long to take your precious time. I can assure you that it would have been much shorter if I had been writing from a comfortable desk, but what else can one do when he is alone in a narrow jail cell, other than write long letters, think long thoughts and pray long prayers?

If I have said anything in this letter that overstates the truth and indicates an unreasonable impatience, I beg you to forgive me. If I have said anything that understates the truth and indicates my having a patience that allows me to settle for anything less than brotherhood, I beg God to forgive me.

I hope this letter finds you strong in the faith. I also hope that circumstances will soon make it possible for me to meet each of you, not as an integrationist or a civil-rights leader but as a fellow clergyman and a Christian brother. Let us all hope that the dark clouds of racial prejudice will soon pass away and the deep fog of misunderstanding will be lifted from our fear-drenched communities, and in some not too distant tomorrow the radiant stars of love and brotherhood will shine over our great nation with all their scintillating beauty.

Yours for the cause of Peace and Brotherhood,
MARTIN LUTHER KING, JR.

# 6

# Cases on Obligation and Obedience

**United States v. Schwimmer**
279 U.S. 644 (1929)

MR. JUSTICE BUTLER delivered the opinion of the Court.

Respondent filed a petition for naturalization in the District Court for the Northern District of Illinois. The court found her unable, without mental reservation, to take the prescribed oath of allegiance and not attached to the principles of the Constitution of the United States and not well disposed to the good order and happiness of the same; and it denied her application. The Circuit Court of Appeals reversed the decree and directed the District Court to grant respondent's petition. 27 F.(2d) 742.

The Naturalization Act of June 29, 1906 required:

"He [the applicant for naturalization] shall, before he is admitted to citizenship, declare on oath in open court . . . that he will support and defend the Constitution and laws of the United States against all enemies, foreign and domestic, and bear true faith and allegiance to the same." U.S.C., Tit. 8, § 381.

"It shall be made to appear to the satisfaction of the court . . . that during that time [at least 5 years preceding the application] he has behaved as a man of good moral character, attached to the principles of the Constitution of the United States, and well disposed to the good order and happiness of the same. . . ." § 382.

Respondent was born in Hungary in 1877 and is a citizen of that country. She came to the United States in August, 1921, to visit and lecture, has resided in Illinois since the latter part of that month, declared her intention to become a citizen the following November, and filed petition for naturalization in September, 1926. On a preliminary form, she stated that she understood the principles of and fully believed in our form of government and that she had read, and in becoming a citizen was willing to take, the oath of allegiance. Question 22 was this: "If necessary, are you willing to take up arms in defense of this country?" She answered: "I would not take up arms personally."

She testified that she did not want to remain subject to Hungary, found the United States nearest her ideals of a democratic republic, and that she could whole-heartedly take the oath of allegiance. She said: "I cannot see that a woman's refusal to take up arms is a contradiction to the oath of allegiance." For the fulfillment of the duty to support and defend the Constitution and laws, she had in mind other ways and means. She referred to her interest in civic life, to her wide reading and attendance at lectures and meetings, mentioned her knowledge of foreign languages and that she occasionally glanced through Hungarian, French, German, Dutch, Scandinavian, and Italian publications and said that she could imagine finding in meetings and publications attacks on the American form of government and she would conceive it her duty to uphold it against such attacks. She expressed steadfast opposition to any undemocratic form of government like proletariat, fascist, white terror, or military dictatorships. "All my past work proves that I have always served democratic ideals and fought—though not with arms—against undemocratic institutions." She stated that before coming to this country she had defended American ideals and had defended America in 1924 during an international pacifist congress in Washington.

She also testified:

If . . . the United States can compel its women citizens to take up arms in the defense of the country—something that no other civilized government has ever attempted—I would not be able to comply with this requirement of American citizenship. In this case I would recognize the right of the Government to deal with me as it is dealing with its male citizens who for conscientious reasons refuse to take up arms.

The district director of naturalization by letter called her attention to a statement made by her in private correspondence: "I am an uncompromising pacifist. . . . I have no sense of nationalism, only a cosmic consciousness of belonging to the human family." She answered that the statement in her petition demonstrated that she was an uncompromising pacifist.

Highly as I prize the privilege of American citizenship I could not compromise my way into it by giving an untrue answer to question 22, though for all practical purposes I might have done so, as even men of my age—I was 49 years old last September—are not called to take up arms. . . . That 'I have no nationalistic feeling' is evident from the fact that I wish to give up the nationality of my birth and to adopt a country which is based on principles and institutions more in harmony with my ideals. My 'cosmic consciousness of belonging to the human family' is shared by all those who believe that all human beings are the children of God.

And at the hearing she reiterated her ability and willingness to take the oath of allegiance without reservation and added:

I am willing to do everything that an American citizen has to do except fighting. If American women would be compelled to do that, I would not do that. I am an uncompromising pacifist. . . . I do not care how many other women fight, because I consider it a question of conscience. I am not willing to bear arms. In every other single way I am ready to follow the law and do everything that the law compels American citizens to do. That is why I can take the oath of allegiance, because, as far as I can find out there is nothing that I could be compelled to do that I can not do. . . . With reference to spreading propaganda among women throughout the country about my being an uncompromising pacifist and not willing to fight, I am always ready to tell anyone who wants to hear it that I am an uncompromising pacifist and will not fight. In my writings and in my lectures I take up the question of war and pacifism if I am asked for that.

Except for eligibility to the Presidency, naturalized citizens stand on the same footing as do native born citizens. All alike owe allegiance to the Government, and the Government owes to them the duty of protection. These are reciprocal obligations and each is a consideration for the other. *Luria v. United States*, 231 U.S. 9, 22. But aliens can acquire such equality only by naturalization according to the uniform rules prescribed by the Congress. They have no natural right to become citizens, but only that which is by statute conferred upon them. Because of the great value of the privileges conferred by naturalization, the statutes prescribing qualifications and governing procedure for admission are to be construed with definite purpose to favor and support the Government. . . .

That it is the duty of citizens by force of arms to defend our government against all enemies whenever necessity arises is a fundamental principle of the Constitution.

The common defense was one of the purposes for which the people ordained and established the Constitution. It empowers Congress to provide for such defense, to declare war, to raise and support armies, to maintain a navy, to make rules for the government and regulation of the land and naval forces, to provide for organizing, arming and disciplining the militia, and for calling it forth to execute the laws of the Union, suppress insurrections and repel invasions; it makes the President commander in chief of the army and navy and of the militia of the several States when called into the service of the United States; it declares that a well regulated militia, being necessary to the security of a free State, the right of the people to keep and bear arms, shall not be infringed. We need not refer to the numerous statutes that contemplate defense of the United States, its Constitution and laws by armed citizens. This Court, in the *Selective Draft Law Cases*, 245 U.S. 366, speaking through Chief Justice White, said (p. 378) that "the very conception of a just government and its duty to the citizen includes the reciprocal obligation of the citizen to render military service in case of need. . . ."

Whatever tends to lessen the willingness of citizens to discharge their duty to bear arms in the country's defense detracts from the strength and safety of the Government. And their opinions and beliefs as well as their behavior indicating a disposition to hinder in the performance of that duty are subjects of inquiry under the statutory provisions governing naturalization and are of vital importance, for if all or a large number of citizens oppose such defense the "good order and happiness" of the United States can not long endure. And it is evident that the views of applicants for naturalization in respect of such matters may not be disregarded. The influence of conscientious objectors against the use of military force in defense of the principles of our Government is apt to be more detrimental than their mere refusal to bear arms. The fact that, by reason of sex, age or other cause, they may be unfit to serve does not lessen their purpose or power to influence others. It is clear from her own statements that the declared opinions of respondent as to armed defense by citizens against enemies of the country were directly pertinent to the investigation of her application.

The record shows that respondent strongly desires to become a citizen. She is a linguist, lecturer and writer; she is well educated and accustomed to discuss governments and civic affairs. Her testimony should be considered having regard to her interest and disclosed ability correctly to express herself. Her claim at the hearing that she possessed the required qualifications and was willing to take the oath was much impaired by other parts of her testimony. Taken as a whole it shows that her objection to military service rests on reasons other than mere inability because of her sex and age personally to bear arms. Her expressed willingness to be treated as the Government dealt with conscientious objectors who refused to take up arms in the recent war indicates that she deemed herself to belong to that class. The fact that she is an uncompromising pacifist with no sense of nationalism but only a cosmic sense of belonging to the human family justifies belief that she may be opposed to the use of military force as contemplated by our Constitution and laws. And her testimony clearly suggests that she is disposed to exert her power to influence others to such opposition.

A pacifist in the general sense of the word is one who seeks to maintain peace and to abolish war. Such purposes are in harmony with the Constitution and policy of our Government. But the word is also used and understood to mean one who refuses or is unwilling for any purpose to bear arms because of conscientious considerations and who is disposed to encourage others in such refusal. And one who is without any sense of nationalism is not well bound or held by the ties of affection to any nation or government. Such persons are liable to be incapable of the attachment for and devotion to the principles of our Constitution that is required of aliens seeking naturalization.

It is shown by official records and everywhere well known that during the recent war there were found among those who described themselves as pacifists and conscientious objectors many citizens—though happily a minute part of all—who were unwilling to bear arms in that crisis and who refused to obey the laws of the United States and the lawful commands of its officers and encouraged such disobedience in others. Local boards found it necessary to issue a great number of noncombatant certificates, and several thousand who were called to camp made claim because of conscience for exemption from any form of military service. Several hundred were convicted and sentenced to imprisonment for offenses involving disobedience, desertion, propaganda and sedition. It is obvious that the acts of such offenders evidence a want of that attachment to the principles of the Constitution of which the applicant is required to give affirmative evidence by the Naturalization Act.

The language used by respondent to describe her attitude in respect of the principles of the Constitution was vague and ambiguous; the burden was upon her to show what she meant and that her pacifism and lack of nationalistic sense did not oppose the principle that it is a duty of citizenship by force of arms when necessary to defend the country against all enemies, and that her opinions and beliefs would not prevent or impair the true faith and allegiance required by the Act. She failed to do so. The District Court was bound by the law to deny her application. . . .

MR. JUSTICE HOLMES, dissenting.

The applicant seems to be a woman of superior character and intelligence, obviously more than ordinarily desirable as a citizen of the United States. It is agreed that she is qualified for citizenship except so far as the views set forth in a statement of facts "may show that the applicant is not attached to the principles of the Constitution of the United States and well disposed to the good order and happiness of the same, and except in so far as the same may show that she cannot take the oath of allegiance without a mental reservation." The views referred to are an extreme opinion in favor of pacifism and a statement that she would not bear arms to defend the Constitution. So far as the adequacy of her oath is concerned I hardly can see how that is affected by the statement, inasmuch as she is a woman over fifty years of age, and would not be allowed to bear arms if she wanted to. And as to the opinion, the whole examination of the applicant shows that she holds none of the now-dreaded creeds but thoroughly believes in organized government and prefers that of the United States to any other in the world. Surely it cannot show lack of attachment to the principles of the Constitution that she thinks that it can be improved. I suppose that most intelligent people think that it might be. Her particular improvement looking to the abolition of war seems to me not materially different in its bearing on this case from a wish to establish cabinet government as in England, or a single house, or one term of seven years for the President. To touch a more burning question, only a judge mad with partisanship would exclude because the applicant thought that the Eighteenth Amendment should be repealed.

Of course the fear is that if a war came the applicant would exert activities such as were dealt with in *Schenck v. United States*, 249 U.S. 47. But that seems to me unfounded. Her position and motives are wholly different from those of Schenck. She is an optimist and states in strong and, I do not doubt, sincere words her belief that war will disappear and that the impending destiny of mankind is to unite in peaceful leagues. I do not share that optimism nor do I think that a philosophic view of the world would regard war as absurd. But most people who have known it regard it with horror, as a last resort, and even if not yet ready for cosmopolitan efforts, would welcome any practicable combinations that would increase the power on the side of peace. The notion that the applicant's optimistic anticipations would make her a worse citizen is sufficiently answered by her examination, which seems to me a better argument for her admission than any that I can offer. Some of her answers might excite popular prejudice, but if there is any principle of the Constitution that more imperatively calls for attachment than any other it is the principle of free thought—not free thought for those who agree with us but freedom for the thought that we hate. I think that we should adhere to that principle with regard to admission into, as well as to life within this country. And recurring to the opinion that bars this applicant's way, I would suggest that the Quakers have done their share to make the country what it is, that many citizens agree with the applicant's belief and that I had not supposed hitherto that we regretted our inability to expel them because they believe more than some of us do in the teachings of the Sermon on the Mount.

MR. JUSTICE BRANDEIS concurs in this opinion.

\* \* \* \* \* \* \* \* \* \*

### Girouard v. United States
#### 328 U.S. 61 (1946)

MR. JUSTICE DOUGLAS delivered the opinion of the Court.

In 1943 petitioner, a native of Canada, filed his petition for naturalization in the District Court of Massachusetts. He stated in his application that he understood the principles of the government of the United States, believed in its form of government, and was willing to take the oath of allegiance (54 Stat. 1157, 8 U.S.C. § 735 (b)) which reads as follows:

I hereby declare, on oath, that I absolutely and entirely renounce and abjure all allegiance and fidelity to any foreign prince, potentate, state, or sovereignty of whom or which I have heretofore been a subject or citizen; that I will support and defend the Constitution and laws of the United States of America against all enemies, foreign and domestic; that I will bear true faith and allegiance to the same; and that I take this obligation freely without any mental reservation or purpose of evasion: So help me God.

To the question in the application "If necessary, are you willing to take up arms in defense of this country?" he replied, "No (Non-combatant) Seventh Day Adventist." He explained that answer before the examiner by saying "it is a purely religious matter with me, I have no political or personal reasons other than that." He did not claim before his Selective Service board exemption from all military service, but only from combatant military duty. At the hearing in the District Court petitioner testified that he was a member of the Seventh Day Adventist denomination, of whom approximately 10,000 were then serving in the armed forces of the United States as non-combatants, especially in the medical corps; and that he was willing to serve in the army but would not bear arms. The District Court admitted him to citizenship. The Circuit Court of Appeals reversed, one judge dissenting. 149 F.2d 760. It took that action on the authority of *United States v. Schwimmer*, 279 U.S. 644; *United States v. Macintosh*, 283 U.S. 605, and *United States v. Bland*, 283 U.S. 636, saying that the facts of the present case brought it squarely within the principle of those cases. The case is here on a petition for a writ of certiorari which we granted so that those authorities might be re-examined.

The *Schwimmer*, *Macintosh* and *Bland* cases involved, as does the present one, a question of statutory construction. At the time of those cases, Congress required an alien, before admission to citizenship, to declare on oath in open court that "he will support and defend the Constitution and laws of the United States against all enemies, foreign and domestic, and bear true faith and allegiance to the same." It also required the court to be satisfied that the alien had during the five-year period immediately preceding the date of his application "behaved as a man of good moral character, attached to the principles of the Constitution of the United States, and well disposed to the good order and happiness of the same." Those provisions were reenacted into the present law in substantially the same form.

While there are some distinctions between this case and the *Schwimmer* and *Macintosh* cases, the *Bland* case on its facts is indistinguishable. But the principle emerging from the three cases obliterates any factual distinction among them. As we recognized in *In re Summers*, 325 U.S. 561, 572, 577, they stand for the same general rule—that an alien who refuses to bear arms will not be admitted to citizenship. As an original proposition, we could not agree with that rule. The fallacies underlying it were, we think, demonstrated in the dissents of Mr. Justice Holmes in the *Schwimmer* case and of Mr. Chief Justice Hughes in the *Macintosh* case.

The oath required of aliens does not in terms require that they promise to bear arms. Nor has Congress expressly made any such finding a prerequisite to citizenship. To hold that it is required is to read it into the Act by implication. But we could not assume that Congress intended to make such an abrupt and radical departure from our traditions unless it spoke in unequivocal terms.

The bearing of arms, important as it is, is not the only way in which our institutions may be supported and defended, even in times of great peril. Total war in its modern form dramatizes as never before the great cooperative effort necessary for victory. The nuclear physicists who developed the atomic bomb, the worker at his lathe, the seamen on cargo vessels, construction battalions, nurses, engineers, litter bearers, doctors, chaplains—these, too, made essential contributions. And many of them made the supreme sacrifice. Mr. Justice Holmes stated in the *Schwimmer* case (279 U.S. p. 655) that "the Quakers have done their share to make the country what it is." And the annals of the recent war show that many whose religious scruples prevented them from bearing arms, nevertheless were unselfish participants in the war effort. Refusal to bear arms is not necessarily a sign of disloyalty or a lack of attachment to our institutions. One may serve his country faithfully and devotedly, though his religious scruples make it impossible for him to shoulder a rifle. Devotion to one's country can be as real and as enduring among non-combatants as among combatants. One may adhere to what he deems to be his obligation to God and yet assume all military risks to secure victory. The effort of war is indivisible; and those whose religious scruples prevent them from killing are no less patriots than those whose special traits or handicaps result in their assignment to duties far behind the fighting front. Each is making the utmost contribution according to his capacity. The fact that his role may be limited by religious convictions rather than by physical characteristics has no necessary bearing on his attachment to his country or on his willingness to support and defend it to his utmost.

Petitioner's religious scruples would not disqualify him from becoming a member of Congress or holding other public offices. While Article VI, Clause 3 of the Constitution provides that such officials, both of the United States and the several States, "shall be bound by Oath or Affirmation, to support this Constitution," it significantly adds that "no religious Test shall ever be required as a Qualification to any Office or public Trust under the United States." The oath required is in no material respect different from that prescribed for aliens under the Nationality Act. It has long contained the provision "that I will support and defend the Constitution of the United States against all enemies, foreign and domestic; that I will bear true faith and allegiance to the same; that I take this obligation freely, without any mental reservation or purpose of evasion . . ." R.S. § 1757, 5 U.S.C. § 16. As Mr. Chief Justice Hughes stated in his dissent in the *Macintosh* case (283 U.S. p. 631), "the history of the struggle for religious liberty, the large number of citizens of our country, from the very beginning, who have been unwilling to sacrifice their religious convictions, and in particular, those who have been conscientiously opposed to war and who would not yield what they sincerely believed to be their allegiance to the will of God"—these considerations make it impossible to conclude "that such persons are to be deemed disqualified for public office in this country because of the requirement of the oath which must be taken before they enter upon their duties."

There is not the slightest suggestion that Congress set a stricter standard for aliens seeking admission to citizenship than it did for officials who make and enforce the laws of the nation and administer its affairs. It is hard to believe that one need forsake his religious scruples to become a citizen but not to sit in the high councils of state. . . .

We conclude that the *Schwimmer*, *Macintosh* and *Bland* cases do not state the correct rule of law. . . .

*Reversed.*

\* \* \* \* \* \* \* \* \*

**United States v. Moylan**
417 F.2d 1002 (4th Cir. 1969), *cert. denied*,
397 U.S. 910 (1970)

SOBELOFF, Circuit Judge:

The defendants appeal their conviction in the United States District Court for the District of Maryland for violation of three federal statutes proscribing the mutilation of Government property and interference with the administration of the Selective Service System. The facts are uncontroverted. At 12:50 P.M. on May 17, 1968, the appellants entered the office of Local Board No. 33 in Catonsville, Maryland and removed approximately 378 I-A, I-Y and II-A files to an adjacent parking lot where they burned the files with homemade napalm. The appellants, men and women with sincere and strong commitments, readily admit the commission of these acts as a protest against the war in Vietnam.

. . . As an undercurrent throughout the trial and interwoven with appellants' assertions of error is an appeal to morality as justification for their conduct. The argument consists of two closely related strands. They argue that the motivation for their action was moral in the sense that they intended to protest a war which is outrageous to their individual standards of humanity. Therefore, their actions are said to be not punishable regardless of the literal violation of a statute. Moreover, appellants argue that apart from their motivation, which is subjective, the war in Vietnam is in fact illegal and immoral and hence their acts in protest of this war were themselves moral acts for which they must be similarly immunized from punishment. In effect, the appellants focus upon the means by which an organized society treats those citizens who choose to commit an act of civil disobedience in the name of justice.

From the earliest times when man chose to guide his relations with fellow men by allegiance to the rule of law rather than force, he has been faced with the problem how best to deal with the individual in society who through moral conviction concluded that a law with which he was confronted was unjust and therefore must not be followed. Faced with the stark reality of injustice, men of sensitive conscience and great intellect have sometimes found only one morally justified path, and that path led them inevitably into conflict with established authority and its laws. Among philosophers and religionists throughout the ages there has been an incessant stream of discussion as to when, if at all, civil disobedience, whether by passive refusal to obey a law or by its active breach, is morally justified. However, they have been in general agreement that while in restricted circumstances a morally motivated act contrary to law may be ethically justified, the action must be non-violent and the actor must accept the penalty for his action. In other words, it is commonly conceded that the exercise of a moral judgment based upon individual standards does not carry with it legal justification or immunity from punishment for breach of the law.

The defendants' motivation in the instant case—the fact that they engaged in a protest in the sincere belief that they were breaking the law in a good cause—cannot be acceptable legal defense or justification. Their sincerity is beyond question. It implies no disparagement of their idealism to say that society will not tolerate the means they chose to register their opposition to the war. If these defendants were to be absolved from guilt because of their moral certainty that the war in Vietnam is wrong, would not others who might commit breaches of the law to demonstrate their sincere belief that the country is not prosecuting the war vigorously enough be entitled to acquittal? Both must answer for their acts.

We are not called upon in this case to establish guidelines for determining in what extreme circumstances, if any, governmental acts may be resisted. We confine ourselves to this case and hold only that the law does not allow the seizure of public records and their mutilation or destruction, even when this is done as an act of conscience to dramatize the protest of a presumed evil. The acts of these appellants are not as extreme as some committed by other dissenters. Nevertheless, this publicly exploited action cannot be dismissed as *de minimis*. To encourage individuals to make their own determinations as to which laws they will obey and which they will permit themselves as a matter of conscience to disobey is to invite chaos. No legal system could long survive if it gave every individual the option of disregarding with impunity any law which by his personal standard was judged morally untenable. Toleration of such conduct would not be democratic, as appellants claim, but inevitably anarchic.

The judgment below is
Affirmed.

\* \* \* \* \* \* \* \* \* \*

**State v. Marley**
54 Haw. 450, 509 P.2d 1095 (1973)

ABE, Justice.

The defendants-appellants in this case were convicted of criminal trespass on the premises of the Honolulu office of the Honeywell Corporation. The convictions, following a jury trial in Circuit Court . . . resulted in sentences of fine (in all instances partially suspended) and of jail (in all instances suspended).

The significant facts are as follows: On May 14, 1971, at approximately 2:00 o'clock p.m., the defendants entered on the premises which served as the Honolulu office of the Honeywell Corporation. One of the defendants, Rodney J. Marley, who was then A.W.O.L. from the United States Navy, read to the Honeywell staff a statement concerning the corporation's participation in the Indochina war. The other defendants established a "sanctuary" in the Honeywell office for the A.W.O.L. sailor and hoped, thereby, to stop the alleged "war crimes" being committed by Honeywell. Defendants hung pictures on the office walls, and engaged in other activities including singing and talking among themselves. The activities of the defendants were disruptive of the normal business operations of the corporation, but were completely nonviolent. After approximately three hours, at about 5:00 o'clock p.m., Mr. Paulk, Honeywell's local office manager, read a statement to the defendants asking them to leave at closing time or face the charge of trespass. Since the defendants chose to remain and not depart as requested, the police were summoned, and defendants were arrested.

At their trial, the defendants and the state introduced a considerable amount of factual testimony about the Honeywell Corporation and its Honolulu office. Throughout the trial defendants contended that they were justified (under several theories, *infra*) in being on the premises of the Honolulu office, because, as was stipulated at trial, Honeywell manufactured "anti-personnel" weapons used in Indochina. Evidence was undisputed that none of these weapons was produced at the Honolulu office, but rather that the Honolulu office dealt chiefly with the computer business of the Honeywell Corporation. However, evidence was conflicting about the extent to which these computers actually played a part in the hostilities in Indochina. It was undisputed that the Honeywell Corporation was a major defense contractor doing an annual business of many millions of dollars with the United States Government.

. . . Reasonable action, even if technically a violation of criminal statutes, if taken to prevent or terminate the commission of a crime by another, is, in certain circumstances, completely defensible. Such action is immune from criminal punishment as one of the "justification" defenses for otherwise criminal conduct. One of the requirements for the particular justification defense on which defendants rely has always been that the criminal act that defendants seek to prevent or terminate must be committed in defendant's presence. LaFave and Scott, Criminal Law (1972), p. 406. The basis of the general rule is firmly founded on case law, chiefly presenting problems of the use of force. Defendants' nonviolent conduct presents us with essentially undecided questions of law, *i.e.*, whether the absence of force in the defendants' acts, or, indeed, the disparity in seriousness between the defendants' conduct and Honeywell's alleged crime, are distinctions of sufficiently significant importance to merit a deviation from the general rule that the criminal act sought to be prevented or terminated must occur in the presence of defendants.

Prevention or termination of the commission of a crime is only one of several "justification" defenses. Some of the others are self-defense, defense of another, and defense of property. Each of these justification defenses obviously and inevitably requires that the criminal act to be counteracted occur in the presence of the actor. A presence requirement is the concomitant of the "immediate harm" requirement. The inevitable requirement of presence stands, even where the criminal acts done to prevent harm to self, others, or property do *not* involve force. Failure of the courts to require presence would license persons to violate the criminal statutes far more frequently. Such license is to be given only in exceptional cases, and even when given is to be severely limited to matters of intimate personal concern. Where the limiting factor of intimate personal concern is absent from the surrounding circumstances, as here, we see no reason to expand the scope of the justification defense. To rule that a full justification defense to the prosecution for commission of crime is established even absent a presence requirement would be to create a very dangerous precedent, for it would make each citizen a judge of the criminality of all the acts of every other citizen, with power to mete out sentence.

The only limitation that defendants can suggest as a control of such untoward consequences is that the acts to be exonerated be nonviolent and/or less serious than those allegedly to be prevented or terminated. It is evident that these new limiting requirements to replace "presence" are insufficient to prevent the development, under the new suggested rules, of a vigilante society.

Defendants alternatively contend, however, that even if "presence" be required for the justification defense of prevention or termination of crime, sufficient "presence" is shown by the fact that radio and television broadcasts, as well as newspaper stories and news films, daily present defendants with evidence of Honeywell's alleged crimes. To find the presence requirement met by the uncertainties of the news media dissemination of information varies precious little in consequences from a total abolition of the presence requirement. As we have rejected the latter, we must reject the former. Both are prescriptions for government by vigilantes.

Defendants appear to argue that they should be exonerated for criminal trespass for another reason. They claim that the "necessity defense" applies to their actions. It is evident that defendants misunderstand the defense.

The "necessity defense", which is another of the justification defenses, has sometimes been called the "choice of evils" defense. The latter phrase is very descriptive of the defense, yet fails to include, even by implication, all of its elements. Several of the crucial elements of the "necessity" or "choice of evils" defense are absent from this case, and thus it is impossible for defendants to rely on the defense to exonerate them.

In essence, the "necessity" defense exonerates persons who commit a crime under the "pressure of circumstances", if the harm that would have resulted from compliance with the law would have significantly exceeded the harm actually resulting from the defendants' breach of the law. The defense is not effective in the following situations:

(1) Where there is a third alternative available to defendants that does not involve violation of the law, defendants are not justified in violating the law. LaFave and Scott, Criminal Law, p. 387; Bice v. State, 109 Ga. 117, 120, 34 S.E. 202, 203 (1899); United States v. Holmes, 26 F. Cas. 360, 367 (No. 15,383) (C.C.Pa. 1842). Other forms of noncriminal protest were and are available to defendants to enable them to dramatize, and hence hopefully terminate, conduct which they may view are harmful.

(2) A closely related required element is that the harm to be prevented be imminent. Where, as here, the harmful acts to be prevented by defendants' actions were, at best, only tenuously connected with the situs of the crime, and would be only tenuously affected by defendants' acts, we cannot find any real "necessity" for defendants to act.

(3) Thirdly, and most importantly, even assuming *arguendo* that alternative courses of action were "unavailable" (perhaps because ineffective) or that there

was some strong connection between the Honeywell office in Honolulu and the allegedly criminal acts that defendants sought to prevent, such connection being significant enough to establish the requisite degree of immediacy or imminence of the greater harm to be prevented, defendants remain unentitled to the defense of "necessity" because their actions were not reasonably designed to actually prevent the threatened greater harm. In United States v. Simpson, 460 F.2d 515, 518 (9th Cir. 1972), the court stated: "An essential element of the so-called justification defenses is that a direct causal relationship be reasonably anticipated to exist between the defender's action and the avoidance of harm". Under any possible set of hypotheses, defendants could foresee that their actions would fail to halt Honeywell's production of the war material, the production of which defendants assert to be a war crime. Since no reasonable man could find otherwise, it was not error for the judge to have omitted an instruction on the "necessity defense".

Defendants make one other major contention. They urge that it was error for the court to fail to give an instruction to the effect that their failure to attempt to stop the allegedly criminal acts of Honeywell would render them liable under American treaty law to prosecution, and that avoiding this potential liability was a justification for their criminal trespass. As a basis for the asserted defense, defendants attempted to show that Honeywell's acts were in fact criminal under American treaty law; for this reason defendants insisted that the criminality of Honeywell's acts was itself a major issue. The state asserted that the exonerating belief required of defendants was that *the defendants'* own action in sitting-in at Honeywell was honestly and reasonably seen to be legal, and that the absence of any reasonable basis for defendants to believe that *their own* action was legal deprived them of this justification defense. We agree with the state. We find it unnecessary to consider whether the Honeywell Corporation is, or is not, a war criminal. Even assuming that Honeywell is a war criminal, the applicable law does not give these defendants either a right or a duty to be present without invitation on the Honeywell premises.

. . . The Nuremberg defenses have been raised in several instances recently in American courts as proffered excuses for alleged criminal acts. In cases in which the defendants had a status similar to the defendants in this case, it has been consistently held that defendants lacked standing to raise arguments that the statute under which they were indicted was inconsistent with international law or that any inconsistency permitted them to violate statutory provisions with impunity.

It is true that an American citizen can sometimes be tried in American courts for violations of the law of war. Ex parte Quirin, 317 U.S. 1, 27-28, 63 S.Ct. 1, 87 L.Ed. 3 (1942). It has also been said that individuals can be punished for violations of international law. The Nuremberg Trial, 7 F.R.D. 69, 110. Two justices of the United States Supreme Court have stated that at some point members of the Armed Forces sent for combat duty in Vietnam should be permitted to raise issues involving international treaty obligations. Dissents of Stewart and Douglas, JJ., Mora v. McNamara, 389 U.S. 934-939, 88 S.Ct. 282, 19 L.Ed.2d 287 (1967).

But the courts have not permitted the raising of treaty obligation issues by a soldier, in an action for injunction after being ordered to Vietnam. Mora v. McNamara, 128 U.S.App.D.C. 297, 387 F.2d 862 (1967), cert. denied, 389 U.S. 934, 88 S.Ct. 282. 19 L.Ed.2d 287 (1967). Nor have treaty obligations been a defense to criminal prosecution for failure to submit to induction. United States v. Valentine, 288 F.Supp. 957 (D.P.R. 1968). As a basis for an action for injunction after induction, treaty obligations were again declared beyond the purview of legal principles assertable by the movant party. Luftig v. McNamara, 126 U.S.App.D.C. 4, 373 F.2d 664 (1967), cert. denied, 387 U.S. 945, 87 S.Ct. 2078, 18 L.Ed.2d 1332 (1967). And in United States v. Berrigan, 283 F.Supp. 336 (D.Md.1968), cert. denied, 397 U.S. 909, 90 S.Ct. 907, 25 L.Ed.2d 90 (1970), it was held that since the defendants were not in the military service in Indochina, they did not have the necessary status to raise, as a defense to a criminal prosecution, legal principles of treaty law similar to those relied on by defendants in this case.

The most commonly given reason for the above holdings is that it is generally improper for the judiciary to decide "political questions" of the sort presented by reliance on a theory that one's own government violates its own treaty obligations. In addition, it would seem that mere membership in the Armed Forces does not, under any circumstances, create criminal liability under the treaty law on which defendants here rely; nor do conspiracy doctrines reach individual members of the Armed Forces not in Indochina so as to give rise to criminal liability. United States v. Valentine, 288 F.Supp. 957, 987 (D.P.R. 1968). The Nuremberg Military Tribunals established nothing to the contrary. *Id.*

With regard to seven of the eight defendants here, we find frivolous any contention that they were legally obligated to act to avoid criminal liability. The case of the eighth defendant, the A.W.O.L. sailor, is more difficult. But in light of the *Mora, Valentine,* and *Luftig* cases, we hold that, *in this situation*, he has no standing to raise, as a defense, alleged violations, by Honeywell, of American treaty law. In light of our holding, we find that, since defendants had no valid defenses arising from treaty law that are assertable by them against the operation of a valid state statute reasonably regulating conduct, it was not error for the court to omit to charge the jury concerning this claimed "justification defense." It is essential *for the rights of the parties before the court to be violated before the defense becomes assertable.* United States v. Berrigan, 283 F.Supp. 336, 341 (D.Md.1968), cert. denied, 397 U.S. 909, 90 S.Ct. 907, 25 L.Ed.2d 90 (1970). .
. .

Affirmed.

# 7

# Frances Olsen,*
# Socrates On Legal Obligation:
# Legitimation Theory and Civil Disobedience

The question whether one has a moral obligation to obey the law becomes increasingly important during periods of immoral legislation and unjust court decisions.[1] If the United States military involvement in Central America continues to grow and if the draft registration law[2] becomes a military conscription, we can expect a great many men and women[3] to struggle over issues of draft refusal and civil disobedience that have lain relatively dormant since the Vietnam War.[4] One moral position often adopted or advocated during the Vietnam War condoned the violation of a law that one believed to be seriously unjust, but only if the violator gracefully accepted whatever punishment the law prescribed. Draft refusers should peacefully go to jail, it was argued, just as Socrates peacefully drank the poison as required by the laws of Athens.[5]

This article takes a fresh look at Socrates's attitude toward law and examines the significance of this attitude to contemporary civil disobedience. I challenge the interpretation accepted by many that Socrates opposed conscientious disobedience or that he would require a person who violated the law, for however moral a reason, to "patiently submit to any punishment"[6] that the laws might impose. The main source for this conventional view is the *Crito*, the Platonic dialogue between Socrates and his friend Crito who is urging him to escape from jail before he is put to death.[7] Many lawyers and others understand Socrates to argue that one must obey the law, regardless of the consequences. I present an alternative interpretation of this dialogue and of the choice that Socrates made.

Instead of focusing on Socrates's obedience to the laws of Athens, I focus on his defiance of the customs of Athens. In Athens, I argue, one threatened with death, as Socrates was, would customarily escape into exile. After a few years, or even less time, the person might be allowed to return to Athens without penalty. By the popular norms and values of his day, Socrates's act of turning down an escape and remaining in Athens to be put to death was scandalous.[8] I present this perspective simply to raise doubts for those people who appeal to Socrates as authority for imposing strict, formal limits upon what conscientiously disobedient behavior shall be morally acceptable. Although one can interpret Socrates to advocate obedience to law or a graceful acceptance of whatever punishment the law prescribes, Socrates provides equal or greater authority for radically more provocative behavior, including, I shall argue, the choice by the American Indian Movement to arm themselves militarily at Wounded Knee in 1973.

## I. SOCRATES ON THE DUTY TO OBEY THE LAW

### A. Arguments for Obedience in the Crito

Strong arguments in favor of obeying the law can be found in the *Crito*, in which Socrates explains his refusal to escape jail to his wealthy Athenian friend. He asks Crito to suppose that while the two of them were preparing his escape the constitution and laws of Athens were to come and confront him: "Now Socrates, what are you proposing to do?"[9] Socrates proceeds to have a discussion with the laws of Athens, periodically checking his answers to the laws' accusations with Crito. "What shall we say to this, Crito?" he asks. "What are we to say to that, Crito? Are we not bound to admit it?"[10]

Socrates imagines the laws of Athens to carry out what George Grote has called "a rhetorical harangue forcible and impressive."[11] The laws argue that if Socrates escapes, he will be attempting to destroy the laws and the city, as far as he has the power to do so. How, ask the laws rhetorically, can a city continue to exist if the acts of private persons can nullify the legal judgments it pronounces?[12] Nor does the wrong that the state imposed upon Socrates by passing a faulty judgment justify his escape. It was through the laws that Socrates was born and raised and, they continue, Socrates owes the laws even more obedience than one owes one's parents. To retaliate against the laws and the city would be worse than to retaliate against a parent. The laws then make their strongest condemnation of disobedience, in a passage worth quoting at length:

> Do you not realize that you are even more bound to respect and placate the anger of your country than your father's anger? That if you cannot persuade your country you must do whatever it orders, and patiently submit to any punishment that it imposes, whether it be flogging or imprisonment? And if it leads you out to war, to be wounded or killed, you must comply, and it is right that you should do so. You must not give way or retreat or abandon your position. Both in war and in the law courts and everywhere else you must do whatever your city and your country command, or else persuade them in accordance with universal justice, but violence[13] is a sin even against your parents, and it is a far greater sin against your country.[14]

The laws assert that they do not savagely command, but give people "the choice of either persuading us or doing what we say."[15] In addition, because Athenians were free to emigrate without forfeiting their property, anyone who did not leave "has in fact undertaken to do anything"[16] that the laws require.

The laws argue that Socrates, by not traveling abroad as others have done, has evinced exceptional satisfaction with Athens.[17] Moreover, he begat children—"crowning proof" that he was satisfied with the city.[18] Socrates undertook in deed if not in word to obey the laws. Were Socrates to leave jail without permission, he would be breaking his agreement with the laws, an agreement he made without compulsion and fully understanding what it entailed. "Who," ask the laws, "would care for a city without laws?"[19]

B. *The* Apology *and Disobedience: Three Representative Theories*

Many authors who have looked to the *Crito* to decide when, if ever, it is morally right to disobey an unjust law, have difficulty reconciling their conclusion, that Socrates counsels unquestioning obedience, with the *Apology*, Socrates's speech to the court a month earlier.[20] In this dialogue Socrates seems committed to obey his conscience or God and to disobey unjust orders. The *Apology* seems to many readers to present a very different Socrates from the Socrates of the *Crito* and a very different answer to the question of when one should disobey an unjust law than the answer they believe they find in the *Crito*. Over the years commentators have devised a variety of theories to reconcile the formulae they glean from the *Crito* with the sense of Socrates they get from the other classical sources, especially the *Apology*. Three of these theories will illustrate their range and their limitations.

*1. Socrates Changes.* George Grote, an important nineteenth-century writer,[21] characterizes the doctrine set forth by the laws as one "which every Athenian audience would warmly applaud"—"almost an Athenian commonplace."[22] Grote reads the *Crito* to be Socrates's straight-forward endorsement of this doctrine, and therefore concludes that the dialogue presents "a very different picture"[23] of Socrates and his relations with Athens than Plato's other dialogues.[24] The *Apology*[25] and the *Gorgias*,[26] for example, represent Socrates to be "an isolated and eccentric individual, a dissenter, not only departing altogether from the character and purposes general among his fellow-citizens, but also certain to incur dangerous antipathy, in so far as he publicly proclaimed what he was."[27]

Grote has two explanations for this marked difference: first, Socrates changed after his trial and, second, Plato wanted to convey in the *Crito* a different side of Socrates—a side that would begin to "restor[e] Sokrates to harmony with his fellow citizens."[28] Grote understands the *Crito* to be Socrates's compromise of his long-standing dissent with the reigning orthodoxy, just before his death"[29]—an attempt "to make peace with the Athenian authorities after the opposition which had been declared in his Apology."[30]

*2. Obedience in the* Apology. Professor A.D. Woozley finds a "discrepancy"[31] between the *Apology* and the *Crito* and presents a solution sharply different from Grote's. According to Woozley, one "could hardly get a more emphatic and unequivocal statement of the citizen's obligation to abide by a court finding than that made in the *Crito*."[32] Yet in the *Apology* Socrates "both expresses some pride in his own defiance [of the law] and maintains that there can be a higher call than the call of human law."[33] Woozley rejects Grote's solution because he doubts that there could "have been such a discrepancy between his attitude at the trial and his attitude in the death cell a few weeks later, and yet that [Socrates] never noticed it nor pointed it out himself."[34] Woozley adds that "although men do have death-bed changes of view, Socrates in the *Crito* emphatically denies that he has."[35]

Woozley adheres to his interpretation that the *Crito* supports obedience and attempts to show that the *Apology* does not really support or justify disobedience to the law. There are two strong suggestions in the *Apology* that Socrates would break a law he considered wrong, and Woozley attempts to dispose of both.

First, in the *Apology* Socrates cites two instances in which he defied authority at personal risk to himself. During a brief period in public office, Socrates tried to frustrate a popular effort to hold a joint trial en bloc of ten commanders accused of failing to rescue survivors or recover bodies after a naval battle.[36] Members of the assembly who opposed Socrates "were ready to indict him and bring him to trial."[37] Because such an en bloc trial of the naval commanders would violate the constitution of Athens,[38] Socrates characterized the effort to try the ten together as "illegal, as you all recognized later."[39]

The other instance Socrates cites occurred during the brief, unpopular rule of the Thirty Tyrants.[40] The Thirty ordered Socrates and four other men to bring one Leon of Salamis to be summarily executed.[41] The other four men complied, presumably out of fear, but Socrates went home instead, demonstrating, as he said, "not by my words but by my actions"[42] that he would risk his own death rather than commit a wrongful act. Socrates does not characterize the order of the Thirty as "illegal," as he had characterized the en bloc trial of the naval commanders.[43] Woozley argues, however, that it "would have been impossible for Socrates to believe that in disobeying [the order of the Thirty Tyrants] he was disobeying the law."[44] Socrates did not have to say in court that the order was illegal because, according to Woozley, everyone knew it was.[45]

Second, Socrates argues to his judges that he will never change his behavior to please them—"not even if I have to die a hundred deaths."[46] Suppose you were to acquit me, he argues, on condition that I stop philosophizing: "If we catch you going on in the same way, you shall be put to death."[47] Socrates claimed that the god at Delphi had directed him to do as he did, and "I owe a greater obedience to God than to you, and . . . I shall never stop practicing philosophy."[48]

This second example of apparent defiance in the *Apology* presents a greater problem. Recognizing that he is perhaps raising a "technical point,"[49] Woozley argues that the only thing Socrates actually states in the *Apology* is that he would refuse to stop philosophizing as a condition for release, even with death the only alternative.[50] But "he does not declare that he would disobey [an order of] the court, because he does not represent the court as giving him an order."[51] Woozley admits that the "notion that the Socrates of the *Apology* would have said to the court that, if they were giving him an *order* to stop philosophizing, that made all the difference, does take some swallowing,"[52] but argues that we "cannot tell" whether "as in the *Crito*, the fact that it was a court order, and as such had the backing of a νομοσ [*nomos*, law], would have made the difference."[53] Woozley sees this to be the best solution to an otherwise vexing inconsistency.[54]

*3. Qualified Disobedience in the* Crito. Professor Reginald Allen presents a third method for resolving the question of consistency between the *Crito* and the *Apology*, based on a slightly different interpretation of the *Crito*.[55] Allen accepts the implications from the *Apology* that Socrates would choose the moral or just over the legal and agrees with other commentators that, "[p]lainly, Socrates would disobey a law that required him to do an unjust thing."[56] Professor Allen qualifies or clarifies this statement somewhat: Socrates would disobey a law that required him to commit injustice, but he would not disobey a law that required him to *suffer* injustice.[57] The *Crito* is thus consistent with the *Apology*.[58] Allen interprets the *Crito* to say that even bad laws "bind to obedience up to the point where they require the doing of injustice."[59]

Allen also suggests another formulation. The argument in the *Crito* "shows . . . that there is a duty *either* to obey all laws, *or* to accept the legal consequences of disobedience when imposed by a court and even, as in Socrates' case, to accept those consequences when there has in fact been no disobedience."[60] "Law and sanction," argues Allen, "are detachable."[61]

This line of argument suggests that a person may violate the law—and should disobey any particular law that would require her to commit injustice—but should also accept the legal consequences of this disobedience, even if she suffers injustice as a result. It seems to me that the strength of this formulation is that it resembles Socrates's actual behavior—behavior that strikes most of us as admirable. Allen's distinction is appealing as long as it appears to favor moral behavior and oppose expediency. His formula loses its appeal, however, whenever this linkage is missing. For example, merely accepting the legal consequences of breaking a law seems inadequate in those cases in which the violator, despite these consequences, has still benefitted at the expense of another. Similarly, a defendant should not obey an injunction requiring immoral behavior simply because the court issued the injunction as a legal consequence of the defendant's violation of some law. Finally, the concept of accepting legal consequences has limited meaning. Crito was quite willing for Socrates and others to accept the legal consequences of Socrates's escape, if only Socrates would agree to do it.[62]

*4. Conclusions Regarding the Theories.* Each of these three attempts to deal with the question of consistency between the *Apology* and the *Crito* illuminates some aspect of Plato's many dimensions, and I draw on them in my subsequent discussion. From Grote I accept the idea that the arguments presented by the laws of Athens were neither novel nor controversial. I do not agree with Grote, however, that Plato was trying to restore Socrates to harmony with Athens or that Socrates changed in the month following his trial. Woozley, it seems to me, correctly discounts this possibility. Like Allen, I conclude from the *Apology* that Socrates would disobey a law rather than commit injustice. I find no problem of consistency between the two dialogues, however, because the *Crito* does not speak to the relationship between formal legality and justice or between legality and morality. I understand it to address initially the relationship between legality and expediency and then only indirectly to inform questions of an individual's relationship to unjust laws. Thus interpreted, the *Crito* does not result in any formula for determining when it is morally justifiable to violate the law, nor do I believe the question should be reduced to any simple precept.

## C. Values at Stake in the Crito

To understand the *Crito*, it is important to consider the values that were at stake in the argument. An examination of the arguments urged upon Socrates by Crito suggests that the *Crito* concerns the conflict between two different moralities, not between legality and morality. Crito's arguments to Socrates are not based on the unfairness of Socrates's trial or verdict, but on the popular "success morality" of fifth-century Greece. A man's honor could in some instances require behavior that we might today criticize as mere expediency. Crito argues simply that Socrates should accept the help of his friends to avoid being killed; Socrates opposes this system of values in favor of a morality based on personal responsibility and a concern with "quiet" virtues, such as justice and self-control.[63]

*1. Crito's Argument to Socrates.* Crito first argues to Socrates that his death would be a great personal loss to Crito and that if Socrates does not escape, many[64] citizens of Athens will blame Crito and Socrates's other friends. The Athenians will not believe that Socrates refused to escape but will think instead that his friends were too stingy, cowardly, or incompetent to manage it.[65] Crito assures Socrates that several friends have offered more than enough money to finance the escape, including friends from outside Athens (and thus in relatively little danger from Socrates's enemies in Athens), and that Socrates can choose among many Greek city-states that would welcome him. If Socrates remains in Athens, he will be advancing the efforts of his enemies and helping to bring about his own death—the very thing for which these enemies strove.[66] Finally, Socrates has two young sons he would leave orphaned.[67] One ought not bring children into this world, argues Crito, unless one is willing to stay around and see to their education.[68] Recognizing that Socrates is disinclined to leave Athens, Crito accuses him of taking the line of least resistance instead of making the choice of the admirable (*agathos*) and brave man; the failure to escape would be a disgrace to Socrates and his friends."[69]

Crito's arguments to Socrates are not based on the claim that his trial was unfair or the verdict unjust. The only indication that Crito believed Socrates to have been unjustly condemned is suggested by Crito's ready approval when Socrates asks whether they should respond to the laws' accusations as follows:

> Socrates: . . . Shall we say, Yes, I do intend to destroy the laws, because the state wronged me by passing a faulty judgment at my trial? Is this to be our answer, or what?
>
> Crito: What you have just said, by all means, Socrates.[70]

It seems fair to say, as Professor Adkins does in his study of Greek morals, that it is "irrelevant" that Socrates was unjustly condemned.[71] Crito's arguments, according to Adkins, are based instead on the popular morality of the day, a "success morality."[72] The successful and admirable man (*agathos*) was supposed to be "a self-sufficient unit, able to defend both himself and his friends, and harm his enemies; . . . able to protect his children, his property, and his wife; and when it is threatened by an external enemy, able to defend his city."[73] Crito speaks as a decent Athenian citizen, promoting ordinary Greek values when he urges Socrates to break the law to protect himself.[74] Adkins argues that when the city is not jeopardized, there is nothing in conventional values "to prevent the *agathos polites* [good citizen] from attempting to thwart the laws of the city on behalf of his family and friends, with whom he has closer ties."[75] Whenever "the prosperity of the family depends directly on being disobedient to the laws, to be disobedient to the laws is simply to act in accordance with the generally accepted scale of values."[76]

Crito considers Socrates's refusal to accept the planned escape from jail to be an act of self-betrayal. Rather than helping his friends, hurting his enemies, and protecting his household, Socrates is doing the opposite. He hurts his friends by depriving them of their friend Socrates and, by refusing help, giving them the reputation of people unable or unwilling to help a friend.[77] He helps his enemies by bringing about his own death, exactly the result sought by the enemies. Finally, instead of protecting his household, he is leaving his children fatherless and unprotected. What could be more shameful?

*2. Socrates's Response to Crito.* Socrates responds that he cannot abandon his principles just to save his life. He proposes that he and Crito examine the matter together and decide what is right.[78]

Socrates quickly redefines the question by arguing that what matters is not what most[79] people believe but what really is just or unjust. Even if the people have power to put him to death, this does not affect principles. The point is to live justly, not simply to stay alive at any cost.[80] Socrates dismisses the concerns of Crito about expense, reputation, and raising children. If escape is just, they must make the attempt; if it is not just, then they must not. "[T]he question whether we are sure to die or to suffer any other ill effect for that matter, if we stand our ground and take no action, ought not to weigh with us at all in comparison with the risk of doing what is [unjust]."[81]

Crito agrees with what Socrates says but still wants him to escape.[82] Socrates replies that if Crito can challenge his arguments, he will listen to him, but otherwise Crito should "be a good fellow and stop telling me over and over again that I ought to leave this place without official permission."[83] He continues, "I am very anxious to obtain your approval before I adopt the course which I have in mind. I don't want to act against your convictions."[84]

Socrates goes on to argue, and Crito agrees, that one ought not to return harm or injustice in retaliation for being harmed or treated unjustly. Here Socrates pauses to let Crito consider whether he really does abide by this claim, since many do not. Socrates warns Crito against admitting to a belief he does not really hold.[85] Crito affirms that he does truly believe all these things, and he further agrees with Socrates that one should keep the agreements one makes, if they are just agreements.[86] Socrates then asks whether he would not be committing a wrong if he were to flee jail and whether such action would be abiding by or failing to abide by his just agreements. At this point Crito balks: I don't know.[87] As one commentator puts it, "Crito seems afraid of understanding what is meant; the consequences alarm him."[88]

It is here in the discussion that Socrates introduces the laws of Athens. If Grote is correct, the laws present a conventional, patriotic argument that Crito is bound to agree with in theory, but would be unlikely to follow in practice.

Socrates, speaking on behalf of the laws, also answers Crito's arguments more directly. If Socrates escapes, his friends may be banished, lose their citizenship, or have their property confiscated. The laws claim that Socrates will be ridiculed. Any well-governed state will shun you, Socrates—a destroyer of laws. And won't you feel foolish trying to talk to people about justice and integrity? "Incidentally, you will confirm the opinion of the jurors who tried you that they gave a correct verdict; a destroyer of laws might very well be supposed to have a destructive influence upon young and foolish human beings."[89]

The laws suggest to Socrates that perhaps the Greek city-state of Thessaly is lax and undisciplined enough to be amused to hear stories of how he sneaked away from jail in disguise. But if you irritate anyone, you will hear many humiliating comments.[90] And do you think you will benefit your children by taking them to Thessaly? If you take them with you, you will deprive them of Athens and force them to live as exiles. If you let them stay in Athens without you, your friends will have to care for them; these friends will care for them as well if you are dead as if you are alive.[91]

No one will benefit from your escape. But if you remain in Athens you will leave this world an innocent victim, not of the laws but of your fellow men. This is far better than leaving "in that dishonorable way, returning wrong for wrong and evil for evil, breaking your agreements and covenants with us, and injuring those whom you least ought to injure—yourself, your friends, your country and us."[92]

## II. TAKING CRITO SERIOUSLY: AN ALTERNATIVE READING OF THE *Crito*

One of Crito's arguments to Socrates was that if he refused to escape, the people of Athens would blame Socrates's friends for having failed him.[93] This extraordinary statement has received surprisingly little attention. Crito claims that the people of Athens will belittle as misers or cowards a group of fellow citizens if this group fails to subvert its laws.[94] And these are the same citizens who, according to George Grote, would "warmly applaud"[95] the sentiments expressed by the laws in their dialogue with Socrates!

Professor Woozley, one of the few scholars to comment upon this argument in the *Crito*, concludes simply that Crito was wrong.[96] As an empirical matter, Crito is mistaken: the people of Athens would not have accused Socrates's friends of "stinginess or cowardice because they had not snatched him out of gaol."[97] Woozley asserts that Socrates was not a popular hero and there would have been no "public clamour" for his release.[98]

Woozley is surely correct that many people of Athens were not fond of Socrates.[99] Indeed, only one month before he had been condemned to die by the majority of the 500 judges or "dikasts" who composed the popular courts of Athens.[100] An Englishman today would need to be considerably more popular than Socrates was in Athens before Woozley and his countrymen would criticize the "stinginess or cowardice" of those who failed to rescue him from jail. This fact about Woozley's society does not, however, convince me that Crito was mistaken.

It seems quite possible that Crito's evaluation of Greek attitudes would be more accurate than Woozley's. Crito's own devotion to Socrates might be supposed to have blinded him to the antipathy felt by other Athenians, but, as Woozley points out, "Crito himself insisted that it was public clamour that landed Socrates"[101] in jail. A more plausible explanation comes to mind if we recall Professor Adkins's study of Greek popular values.[102] The successful and admirable men (*agathoi*) were those able to protect and benefit their friends, and by the generally accepted scale of values it was *agathon* to thwart the laws to benefit one's family or friends.[103] Thus, the people of Athens expected Socrates's friends to smuggle him out of jail, not because he was popular or because he was unjustly condemned, but because he was their friend.

I propose that we take Crito's statement seriously as an evaluation of popular attitudes and think about the implications. Crito goes further than saying just that people would not blame him for rescuing Socrates; he says that his reputation will suffer if he does not do so. I suggest that we misunderstand this argument by overlooking how customary it was to flee from Athens to avoid death. Crito's statement supports the hypothesis that there may have been a settled custom for wealthy and influential Athenians to avoid jail or death for themselves and their friends. Such a custom would help explain Crito's frustration at Socrates's refusal to accept the escape offered by his friends.[104]

A custom of escaping to exile also gives new meaning to Socrates's choice to remain in Athens. His refusal to accept escape was not the reconciliation of Socrates with the people of Athens—as Grote would have it.[105] Rather, it was his final act of defiance. Grote refers to Socrates's behavior in the *Crito* as "an ostentatious deference to the law."[106] I would agree that it was ostentatious, but I would add that it was also ironic and contentious. I believe Socrates did not intend "to make peace with the Athenian authorities" but instead wanted to put maximum pressure on them to reconsider their unjust ways. Rather than a compromise of his longstanding dissent, Socrates's behavior was an even more radical and eccentric departure from the "character and purposes general among his fellow-citizens."[107]

This is not like a draft refuser politely spending two years in jail but more like a militant saying, "over my dead body!"

Several authors have suggested that an escape by Socrates would have been greeted with relief by many of the people of Athens.[108] Probably no one, except his most thoughtless enemies, really wanted to kill Socrates. Socrates was seventy years old, and the Athenians had already suffered through many years of his incessant questioning. As Socrates pointed out, before long nature would take its course[109] and Athens would be freed of its gadfly without the embarrassment of having put him to death. Moreover, if he fled jail, he would go into exile in some other Greek city-state, not remain in town to vex Athenians.

I am arguing that there was a conflict between law and custom—or between what the law *said* and what people really meant. There was also a conflict—a sharp conflict—between the virtuous sentiments that the people of Athens claimed to believe and the behavior that they actually practiced. This inconsistency is neatly expressed by Crito when he tells Socrates, "I agree with what you say, Socrates, but I wish you would consider what we ought to *do*."[110] The people of Athens might well applaud what the laws said to Socrates, but most, if called upon to act, would take the expedient route endorsed by popular morality, not the high road Socrates chose.

Once he limited himself to a straightforward reading of the *Crito*, it is no wonder Grote considered it a complete capitulation to the reigning orthodoxy.[111] A man often accused of breeding disrespect for parents among youth and of putting himself above the law—thus breeding disrespect for the laws among the citizens—suddenly uses the parent-state analogy[112] to argue that he must submit to the law and die. And he does this in "the precise circumstances in which many others, generally patriotic, might be disposed to recede" from their patriotism.[113]

Moreover, Socrates, the master of dialectic who has been known to insult and belittle rhetoric,[114] seems suddenly to embrace or fall victim to a conventional rhetorical harangue. Socrates initially invites Crito to engage in a dialectical discussion and seems convinced that through reason the two of them can agree on what is right for Socrates to do.[115] Then the laws come and shut off discussion with their rhetorical harangue. In Grote's opinion, no attempt is made to bring out and examine the difficulties attendant to the laws' arguments. Rather, the laws appeal to "pre-established and widespread emotions, veneration for parents, love of country, respect for covenants."[116] Grote charges the laws with "working up these sentiments into fervour, but neglecting all difficulties, limits and counter-considerations: assuming that the familiar phrases of ethics and politics are perfectly understood and indisputable."[117] Finally, at the end of the laws' harangue, Socrates invites Crito to respond, but warns him that "the sound of [the laws'] arguments rings so loudly in my head that I cannot hear the other side."[118]

If I am right that Socrates flouted the values and customs of Athens when he refused to escape, his use of conventional rhetoric to justify his behavior would add further offense. Rather than a capitulation to rhetoric, the speech by the laws can be more accurately characterized as an ironic satire of rhetoric.

I recognize that it is too easy and always dangerous to dismiss (or rather embrace) something one disagrees with as irony or satire.[119] Even Professor Allen, who has suggested that Socrates uses rhetoric in the *Apology* to satirize rhetoric,[120] takes at face value the rhetoric of the laws in the *Crito*.[121] Allen explains that the speech of the laws is "both rhetoric and dialectic" or "philosophical rhetoric, aimed at persuasion based on truth."[122] Yet Grote's description of the speech as a forceful and impressive statement of the patriotic platitudes of the day[123] is more convincing than Allen's attempt to find truth or deep philosophical meaning in it.[124] I do agree with Allen, however, that commentators make a mistake if they simply dismiss the speech by the laws as "a merely biographical document."[125] The speech takes on a radically different—but consistent and, I believe, convincing—meaning if we consider that Socrates's refusal to escape was an aggressive provocation. Socrates was not constructing a new argument to provide moral or theoretical justification for obeying the law, but instead employing a "discourse of venerated common-place"[126] to justify a radical departure from the expedient practices of his day.

This leads us to the important question of why Socrates would choose to behave this way. Xenophon suggested that Socrates was ready to die and considered an unjust execution the neatest way to end his life.[127] Indeed, sometimes Crito does sound like a man trying to dissuade a friend from suicide. To modern readers this explanation may seem quite unsatisfactory. We prefer to put Socrates on a pedestal, respecting him but also putting him out of reach, and thus out of our lives.[128]

If Socrates did not simply take advantage of a good opportunity for a timely exit, neither did he accept death just to tease or outrage his fellow citizens. Obviously irony is not something to die for. If Socrates had not believed that he should remain in jail unless the authorities in Athens freed him, we should hardly believe that he would have done so as a mere ironic statement about the contrast between popular rhetoric and common practice.

This analysis leaves open the question of motivation. If the people of Athens did not want to kill Socrates, why did they do so? And if fleeing the city was an established custom, why did Socrates refuse to follow the custom? To begin to answer these questions, and to consider what values were at stake in this struggle, it will be useful to examine legitimation theory.

## III. LEGITIMATION THEORY

"Legitimation" is the process by which actions that one group of persons engages in to the apparent detriment of another group come to seem morally justified. In the context of law, it is the process by which laws and the coercion exercised in their name come to seem fair. "Legitimation theory" refers to a collection of different analyses or hypotheses that attempt to explain human actions—especially those of judges, legislators, and other state officials—by reference to their effect upon the perceived legitimacy of law or of some aspect of law or society. For example, legitimation theorists argue that anti-discrimination law not only forbids particular instances of overt discrimination, but also makes the racism and sexism that it does not eliminate seem legitimate.[129] Thus, laws against discrimination can serve to reduce the moral condemnation that properly should fall upon the practices of institutional racism and sexism.[130]

In its simplest form, legitimation theory focuses upon the way that legal practices serve to reconcile the oppressed to their oppression. More sophisticated theorists expand this concept in two ways. First, they sometimes examine a broader collection of behaviors, including actions that would not be considered legal practices, such as the bribery of judges or the exercise of police discretion. The second important expansion of simple legitimation theory recognizes that legitimation involves the acceptance of particular actions by all groups, not just by those who are harmed. The oppressed have more reason than other groups to revolt, but the oppressors can rule most effectively if they and their functionaries can believe that they are fair people dispensing justice.

Legitimation theory provides a non-apologetic explanation of the stake that rulers have in behaving in a manner that they perceive to be just. It also suggests that the refusal to let rulers avoid the consequences of their unfair behavior may contribute substantially to a more just society. Thus, legitimation theory provides a set of justice-related motives for the socially concerned disobedient to forego certain forms of leniency or of escape from punishment.

A. *Legitimation Theory in* Albion's Fatal Tree

One of the most useful developments of legitimation theory has been presented in a study of early English criminal law.[131] In eighteenth-century England, capital punishment was the prescribed penalty for a wide variety of offenses, ranging from minor theft to aggravated murder. Hangings, however, were quite rare. Judges routinely refused to enforce the penalties prescribed by Parliament; they dismissed capital indictments for minor procedural irregularities and often acquiesced to pleas of leniency. In addition to the judiciary's efforts, the executive would often grant pardons and reprieves.[132]

In a brilliant essay,[133] Douglas Hay characterizes as "unsatisfactory" the conclusion of some scholars that this behavior resulted from a disagreement between Parliament and the other branches of government.[134] He propounds instead a theory that the strictness of the legislation, the formal justice and compassionate mercy of the judges, and the leniency of the executive were all part of an effective unified system.[135] In Hay's essay, legitimation theory becomes a way of understanding how disparate elements can function together to make potentially unpopular policies seem fairer than they would appear in a simpler system.[136]

Specifically, Hay argues that the extension of the death penalty terrorized the poorer classes of Britain and directly protected the property of the wealthy.[137]

Strict judicial recognition of technical defenses reduced the carnage from the laws and provided the illusion that courts would protect the rights of Englishmen.[138] To borrow a phrase from Anatole France, even the poor who "sleep under bridges" might escape prosecution on a technicality, further demonstrating the law's "majestic equality."[139] Judicial leniency can make every actor, including the victim, feel better about his or her role in the system. Moreover, executive pardons could, and when necessary did, protect the wealthy and influential from the brutality of the law[140] as well as provide an opportunity for the wealthy and influential to grant favors to the poor by securing a pardon for them, their family, or their friends. Bonds of gratitude tied those who received favors to their higher-class benefactors who dispensed them.[141] Thus there was a system in which people could easily find their lives in legal jeopardy but in which there were also a variety of escapes from punishment. These escapes helped to legitimate the whole system.

## B. Legitimation Theory and Individual Choice

One can recognize the legitimating function of law and yet, as an individual, be unable to respond effectively. Imagine a socially-conscious lawyer living in eighteenth-century England. Would the insight that criminal law tends to legitimate the exploitative property system of England help his practice? To get a suit dismissed on a technicality would promote the illusion of justice, and to obtain a pardon could create bonds of obligation and thus contribute to a politically debilitating paternalism. The only way to avoid legitimating the legal system or supporting the patronage system might be to allow his client to hang, and even this choice could contribute to the terror upon which the property system was also based.

An individual defendant may have to choose between either legitimating the system or suffering imprisonment or death. Now, if we examine the choices available to Socrates from this perspective, we see that he was willing to die rather than to legitimate the system. Before, during, and after his trial, Socrates refused to make compromises that would have saved his life but that would also have tended to legitimate the actions taken against him. He would not return injustice for injustice, but neither would he mitigate the injustice condoned by the Athenians by escaping into exile. If they were going to behave that way, *they* were going to have to realize the consequences, even if it cost Socrates his life.

## C. The Legitimating System of Law (Nomos) and Custom (Nomos)

In Athens, as in eighteenth-century England, private parties rather than public prosecutors conducted criminal prosecutions.[142] Defendants in both countries were often able to buy off prosecutors,[143] and prosecutions were sometimes begun to extort money.[144] At an Athenian trial, depending upon the particular crime charged, a convicted defendant would be asked to propose what was called a counterpenalty. The judges would then vote between the penalty proposed by the private prosecutor and the counterpenalty proposed by the defendant. The charges brought against Socrates—corrupting the youth and religious heresy—were such crimes, and after his conviction Socrates was called upon to propose a counter-penalty. In the *Apology*, Socrates is reluctant to propose a counterpenalty because he does not consider himself guilty of any wrong.[145] To propose a counterpenalty would add legitimacy to the verdict against him.

Socrates raises a similar argument in the *Crito*. If he were to flee Athens, he would be compromising his position and legitimating the behavior of his enemies. As the laws argue, if Socrates does leave jail he will "confirm the opinion of the [judges] . . . that they gave a correct verdict; a destroyer of laws might very well be supposed to have a destructive influence upon young and foolish human beings."[146] Socrates's refusal to escape jail was a continuation of his refusal to flee Athens instead of facing trial and of his refusal to propose exile as a counter-penalty during his trial. For Socrates to have accepted exile—before, during, or after trial—would have tended to legitimate the unjust behavior of his accusers.

Just as in eighteenth-century England where legal technicalities, judicial leniency, and pardons legitimated an unjust system,[147] so too in fifth-century Athens pre-trial exile, counterpenalties and escape could legitimate unjust prosecutions. The law (*nomos*) prescribed death, but both the law and custom (also *nomos* in Greek) provided exceptions.[148] First, according to Professor A.E. Taylor, it was customary for an accused to leave Athens before trial if there were any doubt about an acquittal.[149] In addition, the law provided that in many cases—including homicide—a citizen could voluntarily exile himself as an alternative to standing trial.[150] After conviction, the accused could often save his life by proposing a counterpenalty. Finally, I argue, the accused might be able to choose exile, even after he was sentenced to die, if he paid bribe money and suffered the indignity of adopting a disguise and being smuggled out of jail.[151] Allowing people to escape jail legitimates the system in many of the same ways a pardon system would, and perhaps even more effectively.[152]

Moreover, if Socrates was right that the common people of Athens "put people to death, and would bring them back to life if they could,"[153] the custom of exile would seem to have much to recommend it.[154] Indeed, Greek histories refer to many people who escape to exile for a few years and then return. Had Socrates been younger, we may suppose Athens would have sought his return after he had spent some time in exile.

The existence of an established custom permitting escape into exile would provide Socrates with good reason not to follow the custom. Socrates was engaged in an ongoing struggle about human values.[155] In the particular circumstances in which he found or placed himself, he could promote the values he supported by obeying the law and violating the custom. In other circumstances, other behavior might have promoted these values more effectively, and Socrates might then have acted differently.[156]

What Socrates, or rather the laws of Athens, said in the *Crito* was a commonplace.[157] That Socrates *acted* on this commonplace was shocking and perhaps revolutionary.[158] It is indeed ironic that so much of our focus should be on what the laws said, as though that were controversial.[159] Certainly it is possible to read the *Crito* to mean that a person should never violate the law—or never except under very limited circumstances. My claim is simply that a very different reading of the dialogue is also possible. The further questions of which reading is preferable or by what criterion one chooses I will leave to be decided on a case-by-case basis by people to whom the choice becomes important.

## IV. CIVIL DISOBEDIENCE

Judge Simon Sobeloff of the Fourth Circuit appealed to Socrates as authority for upholding the criminal convictions of the "Catonsville Nine."[160] The Berrigan brothers and seven others had raided a draft board in Maryland in 1968 and burned draft files with napalm—the same substance that was being dropped on the people of Vietnam. The Catonsville Nine characterized their behavior as "doing a very tiny bit" to stop the illegal and immoral war in Vietnam.[161] They burned the draft files, one of the defendants said, "to hinder this effort in . . . an actual, physical, literal way, by preventing these . . . young men, from being taken by the war effort and then put to killing people unnecessarily."[162] They were charged with and convicted of destroying government property, mutilating government records, and interfering with the administration of the Selective Service system.[163] On appeal, Judge Sobeloff refused to consider the substance of the defendants' claim—whether the war was immoral and whether the defendants' conduct was justified under the circumstances. He found it unnecessary to "establish guidelines for determining in what extreme circumstances, if any, governmental acts may be resisted."[164] In the case before him, the defendants had engaged in civil disobedience and they had to accept the legal penalty. Otherwise, asked the judge, "would not others who might commit breaches of the law to demonstrate their sincere belief that the country is not prosecuting the war vigorously enough be entitled to acquittal?"[165]

Judge Sobeloff maintained that throughout the ages philosophers have debated the overall legitimacy of civil disobedience, but that "they have been in general agreement that while in restricted circumstances a morally motivated act contrary to law may be ethically justified, the action must be non-violent and the actor must accept the penalty for his action."[166] This position is supported, he said, by the actions of innumerable adherents and practitioners of civil disobedience, including Socrates.[167]

I argue that, properly understood, Socrates does not support this effort to limit civil disobedience. Because the *Crito* is concerned with issues of consistency between theory and practice rather than with the resolution of a conflict between what is legal and what is good, I believe that the conventional use of the *Crito* as an argument against any deviant form of civil disobedience is misguided.[168] The example set by Socrates is quite consistent with a defendant's choosing to resist a state-imposed penalty and consistent even with behavior that would generally not be considered nonviolent.

Rather than offering a narrow set of rules of behavior for those claiming moral justification in violating a law, the *Crito* supports broadening our conventional notion of justified disobedience. I argue first that we should not impose stifling and unnecessary restrictions upon civil disobedience. Then, I suggest that even behavior such as the 1973 armed resistance of the Indians at Wounded Knee bears a close kinship to the behavior of Socrates. Finally I advocate what I refer to as ad hoc disobedience to the law.

A. *Expanding Civil Disobedience*

The only kind of civil disobedience generally recognized by the legal system is the violation of a law to test its constitutionality. Abe Fortas, for example, supports civil disobedience that is limited to the "peaceful, nonviolent disobedience of laws which themselves are unjust and which the protester challenges as unconstitutional."[169] If the challenged law is struck down, the violator is vindicated; but if it is upheld, the objector "must accept the penalty imposed by law."[170]

A slightly broader concept of civil disobedience treats it as an urgent and emphatic appeal to others to reconsider a policy or action that the violator strongly opposes. John Rawls, for example, refers to civil disobedience as speech designed to change the judgment of the electorate, to "address the sense of justice of the majority."[171] Rawls would require the people engaged in civil disobedience to be willing to "accept the legal consequences" of their conduct in order to keep civil disobedience "within the limits of fidelity to the law."[172]

In such civil disobedience the protester uses the legitimacy of law in general to give added weight to his voice. Breaking the law and subjecting himself to punishment could be important to communicating his message. The impact of such civil disobedience might be lost if defendants were routinely let off. Thus the law contributes to this form of civil disobedience in the process of refusing to recognize it or grant an exception.

David Daube supports a still broader concept of civil disobedience. He rejects the requirement that the defendant accept the penalty prescribed by law.[173] He would include as civilly disobedient the person "who, having performed his act of defiance, attempts the very best defence in court, maybe exploits procedural loopholes, or even . . . runs away to a neighboring country."[174] One good reason, according to Daube, for expanding the concept of civil disobedience is that restricting the concept supports the status quo. He suggests that one motive

> behind the restriction of the term [civil disobedience] to the takers-of-the-consequences has to do with the honourable overtone nowadays attaching to it in a wide section of the public. Those who avoid or evade punishment are to be debarred from this honourable category, with effects which are obviously welcome to the authorities. If you joyfully or at least resignedly accept the legal penalty, you indicate your basic recognition of the regime in power.[175]

Legal authorities have used the "accept the consequences" argument as an excuse for evading the substance of issues raised by acts of civil disobedience. They draw a sharp distinction between the moral and the legal and characterize a defendant's behavior as a strictly individual act of conscience. The justification asserted by the law violator is dismissed as legally irrelevant. As Judge Soboloff expressed the idea in the Catonsville Nine case, "the exercise of a moral judgment based upon individual standards does not carry with it legal justification."[176]

This statement includes two important claims about civil disobedience; it is moral, not legal, and it is individual and merely subjective, not political and capable of resolution. As it becomes clear that law is not a science and that legal reasoning is not actually distinguishable from other forms of reasoning, this analysis of civil disobedience loses the power it once enjoyed.

The growing recognition that law is not autonomous from politics or morals and that legal reasoning is essentially the same as political reasoning and moral reasoning[177] suggests also that legal choices necessarily implicate political and moral commitments. When judges refuse to consider the substance behind the moral claims of the civilly disobedient, they are making an important political and moral choice—a choice that usually favors those with power.

Socrates, in refusing to escape Athens, stood his ground and struggled to promote the values he supported. Many people engaged in conventional civil disobedience are following Socrates's example. So too, however, are many people engaged in more provocative behavior, including armed resistance.

B. Socrates and Wounded Knee

In February, 1973, a group of Indians dissatisfied with alleged corruption within the tribal government on the Pine Ridge reservation formed the Oglala Sioux Civil Rights Organization and filed impeachment proceedings against the tribal chairman.[178] The Bureau of Indian Affairs, in a burst of support for the tribal chairman, sent a contingent of sixty-five United States marshalls to the Pine Ridge reservation, followed by an FBI contingent, which established a separate command post.[179] The Indian civil rights group protested this action and asked for help from American Indian Movement members throughout the country.[180] Matters escalated. The Pentagon supplied aircraft to the marshals, and army colonels maintained telephone contact with the federal agents in Pine Ridge.[181] On February 27, 1973, members· of the Oglala Sioux Civil Rights Organization, the American Indian Movement members they had invited, and other sympathizers seized control of the historic town of Wounded Knee, South Dakota.[182] By the next day, the federal force reached 250 men armed with M-16 machine guns and tanks (technically "Armed Personnel Carriers").[183] The Indians stood their ground with an assortment of rifles and makeshift weapons. What began as a local dispute over unpopular rule escalated into a confrontation lasting seventy-one days.[184]

The Indians at Wounded Knee were opposing meekness and resignation. Like Socrates, they were enacting within their struggle the values for which they were striving. There is also a more complicated parallel with Socrates.

When one of the negotiators sent to Wounded Knee by then-President Richard Nixon asserted that the United States government would not negotiate with a gun to its head, Russell Means answered for the Indians that the guns of the American Indian Movement were not aimed at the government's head.[185] The Indians had no illusion that they could defeat the military might of the United States.[186] Means explained that the only thing the Indians were doing with their guns was telling the United States that if they wanted to suppress Indians again, they could not do it quietly but would have to kill the Indians who were there.[187]

The similarities between Socrates and Wounded Knee are striking. Like Socrates, the Indians intended to put their lives on the line. A willingness to die was in both cases the last defense against government threats and intimidation. The Indians at Wounded Knee were an embarrassment and nuisance to the government not wholly unlike the embarrassment and nuisance Socrates was to many in Athens.[189]

Both cases also have an ironic twist. Socrates seemed on the surface meekly to acquiesce, yet this acquiescence might also be seen as an act of aggressive rebellion against the expectation of his day. The Indians seemed aggressively to rebel against the constituted authority; yet their primary message was like Socrates's statement in the *Apology*, reaffirmed in the *Crito*: if you really want to stop me from doing what is right, you may have to kill me.

Finally, Socrates and the Indians both seemed to fail in some ways but may well have succeeded in the long run. In the short run, the government allowed Socrates to be put to death, and philosophy in Athens may have been set back many years. Plato and others went into exile.[190] The Indians eventually allowed the government to spare their lives, and the government returned to its less controversial policy of gradual destruction of the indigenous people of America.

In the long run, the philosophical method of Socrates has become enormously influential, and the values Socrates promoted have become widely accepted, even if not often acted upon. It is difficult to say whether in the long run the struggles of the Indians will be successful. If they are, Wounded Knee may have made an important contribution. For now, however, the only Indians whose treatment seems to concern the United States government are the Mesquitos of Nicaragua.

## C. Ad Hoc Disobedience

The choice to obey or to violate a law depends upon the entire context surrounding the decision. Sometimes a law should be disobeyed in order to get a court to overturn it as unconstitutional. At other times, the best way to encourage a reevaluation of the unjustness of an offensive law may be to break it and go to jail. Sometimes disobeying a law and getting away with it will help demystify legality as such and encourage a clearer understanding of a people's true interests. At other times, to undermine legality might be a mistake and it may be appropriate to grit one's teeth and obey an unfair law. The shared sense that laws should be obeyed is sometimes helpful and sometimes destructive. It depends upon the particular context.

If asked, most of us would say that we support resistance to tyranny. A sufficiently oppressive government should be resisted in any of a variety of ways. If Nazis had required Jews in Denmark to wear yellow stars of David, a non-Jewish King of Denmark could have offered effective opposition by wearing one himself. But what about the Jews who were ordered to wear the yellow star? Very few people would argue that they had any obligation to comply, or if they chose to disobey, that they had to do so in any particular prescribed manner. At the time, the German Nazis disagreed.

Many Americans would condone any form of resistance to the laws of Nazi Germany but condemn any violation of democratically enacted laws in the United States. Neither position is fully justified. The anti-Nazi resistance movement had to calculate carefully which laws to resist and in what ways. There were semblances of justice that could sometimes be used to reduce the terror and destruction Nazism caused.[191]

Socrates cites in the *Apology* two examples of his defiance: resistance to a tyrannical government and resistance to a democratic government. Democracies make mistakes. If there is a war in Central America, it may be popular, however unjust it is, as long as the United States seems to be winning. Democratic support for an unjust war does not make it any less unjust or reduce the need to resist it. In the event of war in Central America, especially if it is supported by a democratic majority of Americans, war resisters should feel free to violate any law that is appropriate and to fill up jails, argue for acquittal, or avoid trial or sentence by a variety of different means.[192]

The concern is sometimes expressed that if these acts of defiance are celebrated and approved, it is not clear where it will all stop. If we allow civil rights activists to violate the law with impunity, how can we condemn the defiance by racists of anti-discrimination laws. If we allow war resisters to burn draft cards or draft files, how can we condemn the destruction of medical facilities by anti-vivisection or anti-abortion groups. Indeed some would ask, how can we condemn lynching if we support other forms of illegality. To me the more interesting question is how could anyone confuse these sets of activities.

Judges who wish to follow the tradition of Socrates rather than that of his accusers should take seriously acts of civil disobedience. Obviously judges need not acquit a person of a crime just because the violator felt justified. But just as obviously a judge should not dodge responsibility for evaluating whether the violator *was* justified. The fault is not simply that judges convict some people they should not convict, but that they refuse to accept responsibility for their own actions. Sobeloff might have sustained the convictions of the Catonsville Nine anyway, but he should have tried to consider the substance of the issues raised by the morality of the Vietnam War. He was not being neutral when he analogized the defendants to people supporting increased destruction.

## V. Conclusion

Socrates disobeyed unjust orders and stood his ground against government threats. He was put to death by people who probably did not want to kill him but lacked the courage and initiative to do otherwise. The substance of his teachings has long outlived the memory of his opponents.

Today, people who stand up against violence and oppression are following the tradition of Socrates. Their resistance may take many forms. The decision to obey or disobey particular laws and to seek or avoid legal sanctions depends upon the particular government being confronted, the wrong being resisted, and the likely effect of the tactic chosen. Instead of prescribing procedural rules for those engaged in civil disobedience, let us attend to the substance of their claims.

## NOTES TO SOCRATES ON LEGAL OBLIGATION

\* Professor of Law, University of California at Los Angeles. Goddard College, B.A., 1968; University of Colorado, J.D., 1971; Harvard University, S.J.D., 1984. Several friends and colleagues read earlier drafts of this essay and shared their insights and criticisms with me. I would like especially to thank Nick Pappas, Lilian Furst, Harold Porter, and Joe Singer.

[1] War, whether declared or undeclared, also increases popular concern with issues of principled disobedience. The first major American essay on civil disobedience was written in response to the United States' invasion of Mexico, which Henry David Thoreau considered immoral and resisted by refusing to pay taxes. See H. THOREAU, *On Civil Disobedience*, in WALDEN AND CIVIL DISOBEDIENCE 224 (1966). See generally J. REID, IN A DEFIANT STANCE (1977) (examining the elaborate efforts of the American colonists to justify their violations of British laws); The Declaration of Independence (U.S. 1776) (propounding a long list of British injustices in order to justify American rebellion).

[2] See Department of Defense Authorization Act of 1981, Pub. L. No. 97-86, 95 Stat. 1129 (1981) (to be codified at 50 U.S.C. app. § 453).

[3] Although the United States Supreme Court has suggested that a male-only military conscription would be constitutional, see Rostker v. Goldberg, 453 U.S. 57, 75-79 (1981), nothing would prevent Congress from choosing to include women. Moreover, women (and men) may feel morally opposed to a variety of other laws that may be employed in support of a Central American war or may in the future be enacted to further such a war.

[4] But see R. DWORKIN, TAKING RIGHTS SERIOUSLY 1 (1977) in which he argues that "[j]ust now . . . the question of whether men have a moral obligation to obey the law figures prominently in jurisprudence courses throughout the country." By "now" he originally meant 1969, when he wrote the chapter, see id. at xv, but he did not revise what he said for publication in 1977. For criticisms of Dworkin's theories and his response, see *Jurisprudence Symposium*, 11 GA. L. REV. 969-1267 (1977).

[5] See supra pp. 83-84 & note 62.

[6] PLATO, *Crito*, in THE COLLECTED DIALOGUES 51b (E. Hamilton & H. Cairns eds. 1961) [hereinafter cited as *Crito*]. For citations to Plato, I am using Stephanus's standard pagination system, devised in 1578. See R. PFEIFFER, HISTORY OF CLASSICAL SCHOLARSHIP FROM 1300 TO 1850, at 109 (1976).

[7] See id. at 43a-54e.

[8] See supra pp. 85-86. From the evidence available, it might be safer to assert that we have

reason to believe that the conventional values and norms of Athens would have required Socrates to accept his friend Crito's offer to smuggle him out of jail and into exile, but we cannot know for sure.

[9] *Crito, supra* note 6, at 50a.

[10] *Id.* at 51c, 52d.

[11] 1 G. GROTE, PLATO, AND THE OTHER COMPANIONS OF SOKRATES 430 (1888 & reprint 1974).

[12] *See Crito, supra* note 6, at 50b.

[13] *Biazesthai*: to use force.

[14] *Crito, supra* note 6, at 51b-c.

[15] *Id.* at 52a.

[16] *Id.* at 51e.

[17] *See id.* at 52b.

[18] *Id.* at 52c.

[19] *Id.* at 53a.

[20] *See* PLATO, *Apology*, in THE COLLECTED DIALOGUES, *supra* note 6, at 17a-42a [hereinafter cited as *Apology*]. This dialogue purports to be the speech made by Socrates in his own defense at the trial in which he was condemned. It is an "apology" in the sense of justification, not in the sense of atonement or expression of regret. Xenophon wrote his own version of Socrates's speech to the Court, similar to Plato's in some respects and different in others. *See* XENOPHON, *Apology of Socrates*, in XENOPHON'S MINOR WORKS 192-201 (J. Watson trans. 1898).

[21] *See* M. CLARK, GEORGE GROTE (1962). Grote's *Plato, supra* note 11, was originally published in 1875.

[22] 1 G. GROTE, *supra* note 11, at 430.

[23] *Id.* at 431.

[24] *See id.* at 428-29.

[25] *Apology, supra* note 20.

[26] PLATO, *Gorgias*, in THE COLLECTED DIALOGUES, *supra* note 6, at 447a-527e.

[27] 1 G. GROTE, *supra* note 11, at 431.

[28] *Id.* at 430. Grote placed importance on the transliteration of Greek to English and insisted on using "k" rather than "c" for kappa. *See* R. JENKYNS, THE VICTORIANS AND ANCIENT GREECE 160 (1980). In quotations from Grote, I retain his spelling.

[29] G. GROTE, *supra* note 11, at 431.

[30] *Id.* at 430 n.3.

[31] A. WOOZLEY, LAW AND OBEDIENCE: THE ARGUMENTS OF PLATO'S *Crito* 56 (1979); *see also id.* at 28 ("seeming discrepancy"), *passim*.

[32] *Id.* at 44.

[33] *Id.* at 28.

[34] *Id.* at 56.

[35] *Id.* at 41 (citing *Crito, supra* note 6, at 46b). Socrates's emphatic denial of a death-bed change of view deserves greater attention. From Woozley's statement we could assume that Socrates meant that he was always as obedient and respectful to authority as Woozley believes he is on the eve of his death. In context, Socrates's claim is that he cannot recede from the principled defiance he has expressed throughout his life. The clear implication is that for Socrates to accede to Crito's wishes and save his life would require a change of attitude that Socrates refuses to make.

[36] *See Apology, supra* note 20, at 32b.

[37] A. WOOZLEY, *supra* note 31, at 50.

[38] *See id.*

[39] *Apology, supra* note 20, at 32b. *Paranomos*: contrary to law. *See also* K. DOVER, GREEK

POPULAR MORALITY IN THE TIME OF PLATO AND ARISTOTLE 158 n.17 (1974).

[40] The Thirty Tyrants were appointed as part of a reorganization of the government of Athens under the domination of Sparta, who had just soundly defeated Athens in war. The Thirty were supposed to act as a provisional government while they drafted a new code of laws, including a new constitution. *See* C. HIGNETT, A HISTORY OF THE ATHENIAN CONSTITUTION 287 (1952). Instead of drafting laws, the Thirty kept governmental power and became increasingly despotic, arbitrarily executing people and confiscating their property. To secure their unpopular rule, the Thirty obtained a garrison of 700 troops from Sparta. The cost of the troops drove the Thirty to further executions and confiscations. *See id.* at 289. Eventually, after months of increasing brutality by the Thirty Tyrants, Sparta allowed their overthrow. *See id.* at 292.

[41] *See Apology, supra* note 20, at 32c; *see also* A. WOOZLEY, *supra* note 31, at 54. The reason for sending five men, according to Socrates, was that the Thirty wanted to "implicate as many people as possible in their wickedness." *Apology, supra* note 20, at 32c. Socrates's accuser Meletus may have been one of the four who complied with the order. *See* A. TAYLOR, PLATO, THE MAN AND HIS WORK 159 (1956).

[42] *Apology, supra* note 20, at 32c-d.

[43] *See supra* p. 82 & note 39.

[44] A. WOOZLEY, *supra* note 31, at 54.

[45] *See id.* at 54-55. For an opposing view, see A. ADKINS, MERIT AND RESPONSIBILITY 279 n.4 (1960).

[46] *Apology, supra* note 20, at 30c.

[47] *Id.* at 29c.

[48] *Id.* at 29d.

[49] A. WOOZLEY, *supra* note 31, at 55.

[50] *See id.* at 44-46, 54-55.

[51] *Id.* at 55.

[52] *Id.* at 56. According to Grote, the Thirty Tyrants did order Socrates to stop practicing philosophy and he continuously disobeyed the order. *See* 1 G. GROTE, *supra* note 11, at 394. This order could perhaps be distinguished as also obviously illegal and hence not binding. On the other hand, it does seem that the Thirty Tyrants came to power legally, and it is not easy to see why their order should be less binding than that of any other government.

[53] A. WOOZLEY, *supra* note 31, at 55.

[54] The solution offered by Woozley is, he claims, the refinement of a solution he worked out some eight years earlier in Woozley, *Socrates on Disobeying the Law,* in THE PHILOSOPHY OF SOCRATES 299-318 (G. Vlastos ed. 1971). *See* A. WOOZLEY, *supra* note 31, at 46 & n.1.

[55] *See* R. ALLEN, SOCRATES AND LEGAL OBLIGATION 109-10 (1980).

[56] Spitz, *Democracy and the Problem of Civil Disobedience,* 48 AM. POL. SCI. REV. 386, 386 n.1 (1954).

[57] *See* R. ALLEN, *supra* note 55, at 109-10; *see also* Allen, *Law and Justice in Plato's Crito,* 69 J. PHIL. 562-66 (1972); Wade, *In Defense of Socrates,* 25 REV. OF METAPHYSICS 311-25 (1971). Woozley criticizes these positions in A. WOOZLEY, *supra* note 31, at 56-61.

[58] *See* R. ALLEN, *supra* note 55, at 109.

[59] *Id.* at 111.

[60] *Id.* at 86 (emphasis in original).

[61] *Id.* at 110.

[62] The concept "to accept the legal consequences" has no single meaning. To illustrate, consider what it might mean to *violate* the prescription that if one chooses to break the law, one must accept the legal consequences. Suppose a violator argues jury nullification and succeeds. Then the legal consequence of her act is just that she must suffer a trial before she is acquitted. What

if a law violator flees to Canada and obtains landed immigrant status? The legal consequences of his action would seem to be landed immigrant status in Canada. Surely that cannot be what is meant by the prescription that one must accept the consequences of violating the law. Nor would the prescription seem to require a person to seek and obtain the longest jail term available for whatever law she has violated. Perhaps it means only that she must seek or cooperate in conviction for the most serious crime she violated or may have intended to violate. Even if we can agree on one of these definitions, we are left with the question of why this counts as accepting the legal consequences of one's behavior, and why it should be thought to be a good thing.

[63] *See* A. ADKINS, *supra* note 45. Most of what I say here about ancient Greek values is based on Adkins. *See also* K. DOVER, *supra* note 39.

[64] *Pollois*: many, most, the masses.

[65] *See Crito, supra* note 6, at 44b-c, 453-46.

[66] *See id.* at 45c.

[67] *See id.* at 45c-d. The children will not be orphans in our sense of the word, since their mother will remain alive. The position of women in fifth-century Greece was, however, very poor, and Socrates's widow might indeed be unable to raise the children properly without the support of Socrates's (male) friends.

[68] *See id.* at 45d.

[69] *See id.* at 45d-e.

[70] *Id.* at 50b-c.

[71] *See* A. ADKINS, *supra* note 45, at 231.

[72] Adkins does not generally use this term, but other scholars do. *See, e.g.,* R. ALLEN, *supra* note 55, at 68.

[73] A. ADKINS, *supra* note 45, at 231.

[74] This position sharply differs from that of Professor Woozley. *See* A. WOOZLEY, *supra* note 31. In order to fit them into his concept of moral argument, Woozley recharacterizes Crito's third and fourth arguments. He makes Crito's "helping your enemies" claim parasitic upon the assertion that the behavior of Socrates's enemies was morally wrong. *See id.* at 8. Nowhere, however, does Crito argue that it was morally wrong for Socrates's enemies to have acted as they did. Moreover, as Woozley himself points out, even if it was wrong for Socrates's enemies to try to bring about his death, it does not follow that it would have to be wrong for Socrates to do so. *See id.*

Woozley similarly refocuses Crito's argument about protecting one's household into a modern concern with the rights of children. *See id.* at 9. This leads Woozley to characterize Socrates as "callous" and hardhearted, for "dismissing [as] popular nonsense" Crito's assertion that fathers have a duty to their children. *See id.* at 9-10.

What Socrates dismisses as "popular nonsense" is the conventional view that expediency should govern moral decisions and that protecting one's household is more important than doing what is just.

[75] A. ADKINS, *supra* note 45, at 231. Adkins's analysis suggests that the question of whether one should obey the law when it caused inconvenience or a kind of failure was a more significant question for many Greeks than whether one should obey the law when it violated one's sense of moral duty. This second question is presented most vividly to modern Americans by the play *Antigone*. 3 SOPHOCLES, THE PLAYS AND FRAGMENTS (R. Jebb trans. 3d ed. 1900); *see also* A. FUGARD, *The Island,* in STATEMENTS: THREE PLAYS (1974) (adapting *Antigone* to the situation of black political prisoners in South Africa). The question seems to have been answered in the negative in the *Apology* and not to have been dealt with in the *Crito*. *But see* A. WOOZLEY, *supra* note 31, at 9 (suggesting Crito was asserting to Socrates a moral duty to raise his children, which would be thwarted if he obeyed the law and died).

[76] A. ADKINS, *supra* note 45, at 231-32.

[77] Within this context, it makes sense that Crito would be particularly concerned, as he

Crito's arguments in favor of escape is that for Socrates not to escape *would* hurt his friends. *See Crito, supra* note 6, at 44b-46.

[78] *See id.* at 46c.

[79] *Pollois*: many, most, the masses.

[80] *See Crito, supra* note 6, at 48a-b.

[81] *Id.* at 48d. Hugh Tredennick used the word "wrong" here for his translation of the Greek word *adikein*. For consistency, I will use "unjust" for *adikon* and "just" for *dikaion*.

[82] *See id.*

[83] *Id.* at 48e.

[84] *Id.*

[85] *See id.* at 49d.

[86] *See id.* at 49e.

[87] "I can't answer your question, Socrates. I am not clear in my mind." *Id.* at 50a.

[88] PLATO, APOLOGY AND CRITO 135 n.5 (L. Dyer ed. 1885 & T. Seymour rev. ed. & reprint 1981).

[89] *Crito, supra* note 6, at 53b-c.

[90] *See id.* at 53d-e.

[91] *See id.* at 54a-b.

[92] *Id.* at 54c. Crito cannot believe both what the laws tell Socrates *and* that Socrates should escape. This does not mean that what the laws say is correct any more than it means that if the laws' speech were wrong, Socrates should escape. Just as it is a mistake to assume that what characters say in a play represents the sentiments of the playwright, so too it is a mistake to assume Socrates agrees with the laws. All he says is that as long as he and Crito have not refuted the claims made by the laws Crito has not provided a good reason that Socrates should escape. The claims of Crito are inconsistent and Socrates himself points up the inconsistency. This is *not* to say the laws' arguments are "not what Socrates himself accepts, but are what he believes a man of Crito's limited intellectual capacity will accept." A. WOOZLEY, *supra* note 31, at 29 (characterizing the argument in Young, *Socrates and Obedience*, 19 PHRONESIS 1-29 (1974)). The issue is not intelligence but values. The arguments of the laws *are* a refutation of Crito's arguments. It is a different issue whether from some third perspective the arguments of the laws can themselves be refuted. Socrates is critiquing Crito's system of belief, not directly asserting or constructing his own.

[93] *See Crito, supra* note 6, at 44b-c, 45e-46a. For a statement of this argument, *see supra* p. 85.

[94] *See Crito, supra* note 6, at 44b-c, 45e-46a. At 44b-c Crito expresses concern that people will think he, Crito, refused to spend the money to rescue Socrates; at 45a-46b he expresses the more general concern that Socrates and all of his friends have managed the whole affair badly. He blames them for *kakia* (evil, cowardice) and *anandria* (unmanliness, which carries the same kinds of sexist implications the word does in English). The failure to escape would be the final cowardice and incompetence.

[95] G. GROTE, *supra* note 11, at 430; *see also supra* p. 81.

[96] *See* A. WOOLZEY, *supra* note 31, at 15-16.

[97] *Id.* at 16.

[98] *See id.* at 15. Woozley's evaluation may follow from his determined attempt to make Crito's assertion about his own reputation into what Woozley can consider a *moral* argument, instead of viewing it as a statement about the popular values of Athens, as I do. A drawback of Woozley's approach is that it cannot explain why Socrates would so "cavalierly" dismiss his friend's argument. *See id.* at 7. Woozley suggests simply, "Socrates does not emerge from [the] exchange too well." *Id.*

[99] Indeed, George Grote suggests that Socrates was feared and hated by a wide variety of eminent citizens of Athens. 1 G. GROTE, *supra* note 11, at 412. Socrates suggests in the *Apology* that he is unpopular with many of his countrymen. *See Apology, supra* note 20, at 18a-19b.

[100] *See* R. ALLEN, *supra* note 55, at 23-24, John Lofberg aptly describes the courts as "really popular mass meetings in character." J. LOFBERG, SYCOPHANCY IN ATHENS 10 (1979). Authorities differ whether the number of dikasts was 500 or 501 and whether they should be considered judges or jurors.

[101] A. WOOZLEY, *supra* note 31, at 15.

[102] *See supra* pp. 85-86.

[103] *See* A. ADKINS, *supra* note 55, at 231. Although arguments of the following kind can certainly go astray, it nevertheless seems worth considering that Plato chose to advertise the fact (or assertion) that Socrates's friends wanted to rescue him from jail and actually made at least preliminary arrangements for doing so. This need not imply that jailbreaks were socially approved at the time that Plato wrote, but it does seem unlikely Plato would want to present one of Socrates's (and his own) circle making a blatantly mistaken claim about what Athenians thought.

[104] A number of crimes, including homicide, explicitly provided that exile was an alternative open to a defendant. Even after a trial and conviction, the defendant in many crimes was allowed to propose a "counterpenalty," and the jury would then choose between the penalty and counterpenalty. Had Socrates proposed banishment as a counterpenalty, no one doubts the judges would have chosen that instead of death.

[105] *See supra* pp. 81-82. If I am correct in my reading of the *Crito*, Socrates is not compromising his "long standing dissent" from the "reigning orthodoxy," 1 G. GROTE, *supra* note 11, at 431, but instead escalating that dissent and throwing into the face of the reigning orthodoxy the inconsistency of its own claims. This analysis puts a new complexion also on Socrates's implicit suggestion that well-traveled Athenians are unpatriotic. Remember the statement by the laws that Socrates must have been even more satisfied than others with Athens, since he rarely left the city. *See supra* p. 81. In the absence of any evidence that residence abroad was ever a popular form of expressing dissatisfaction with Athens, this comment by the laws has been taken at face value but passed over quickly, because it appears to have little meaning. I would suggest that Socrates is poking fun at fashionable, well-traveled Athenians by impugning their patriotism. (The Greek term *xenos* refers to a foreign friend who protects you when you travel to another city. Wealthy Athenians like Crito would cultivate *xenous* and be able to travel abroad safely, whereas many other Athenians might not be able to do so.) When I was in college, my classmates who had been several times to Europe were considered debonair and sophisticated, not un-American. My strong suspicion is that Socrates was being ironic.

Another possibility is that Socrates had in mind the democrats who fled Athens during the reign of the Thirty Tyrants. The laws' argument would then be an ironic defense of Socrates's choice to remain in Athens during that period. *See generally* Seymour, *Introduction to* PLATO, APOLOGY AND CRITO, *supra* note 88, at 15 (asserting that Socrates's failure to flee Athens during the rule of the Thirty Tyrants was "doubtless" used against him at his trial to show his anti-democratic sentiments).

[106] 1 G. GROTE, *supra* note 11, at 430 n.3.

[107] *Id.* at 431. Let us suppose, with Grote, that most Athenians would warmly endorse the sentiments that the laws expressed to Socrates, but also suppose, with Adkins, that, if they were actually put to the test, Athenians would *act* in accordance with the wishes of Crito. It was the law (*nomos*) that Socrates stay and die, but it was the custom (*nomos*) that he escape. Socrates caught the laws (*nomoi*) in a lie, and he called them on it. This is not unlike the behavior of the delightful, if bratty, character Nicholas in stories by Saki. For instance, in one story Nicholas refuses to rescue his aunt from a rain-water tank and insists that she must be a clever-talking imposter. The aunt lied to Nicholas, and Nicholas called her on it by pretending to believe steadfastly what she had said.

*See* H.H. MUNRO, *The Lumber-Room,* in THE COMPLETE STORIES OF SAKI 416, 421-22 (1930). If the patriotic platitudes of the Athenians are true—if they really mean what they say—then Socrates must stay in jail and be killed, no matter how shocking it may be to the Athenians. Socrates referred to it as "stand[ing] our ground." *Crito, supra* note 6, at 48d, quoted *supra* p. 86.

[108] *See, e.g.,* H. GADAMER, DIALOGUE AND DIALECTIC 3 (1980); R. ALLEN, *supra* note 55, at 84; A. TAYLOR, SOCRATES 129-30 (1932).

[109] *Apology, supra* note 20, at 38c.

[110] *Crito, supra* note 6, at 48d. In the *Apology* Socrates also distinguishes between words and actions and emphasizes that his *actions* demonstrated that he would risk death instead of committing injustice. *Apology, supra* note 20, at 32c-d.

[111] It should be pointed out that Grote claims less than complete capitulation by Socrates to popular democratic sentiment; because Socrates adopts such sentiment "on a ground peculiar to himself," Socrates's "individuality is thus upheld." 1 G. GROTE, *supra* note 11, at 431. The *Crito* "embodies, and tries to reconcile, both the two distinct elements—constitutional allegiance, and Sokratic individuality." *Id.* at 432.

[112] *See Crito, supra* note 6, at 50e.

[113] *See* 1 G. GROTE, *supra* note 11, at 431.

[114] *See, e.g.,* R. ALLEN, *supra* note 55, at 10-11; 1 G. GROTE, *supra* note 11, at 433.

[115] *See supra* pp. 86, 87.

[116] 1 G. GROTE, *supra* note 11, at 433.

[117] *Id.* According to Grote,

> these . . . elements . . . would have been brought into the foreground had Sokrates pursued the dialectical path, which (as we know both from Xenophon and Plato) was his real habit and genius. He was perpetually engaged (says Xenophon) in dialectic enquiry. "What is the Holy, what is the Unholy? What is the Honourable and the Base? What is the Just and the Unjust? [etc.]" Now in the rhetorical appeal embodied in the Kriton, the important question, What is the Just and the Unjust? (*i.e.* Justice and Injustice in general), is assumed to be already determined and out of the reach of dispute. We are called upon to determine what is just and unjust in a particular case, as if we already knew what justice and injustice meant generally: to inquire about modifications of justice, before we have ascertained its essence. This is the fundamental assumption involved in the rhetorical process; which assumption we shall find Plato often deprecating as unphilosophical and preposterous.

*Id.* at 433-34 (notes omitted).

[118] *Crito, supra* note 6, at 54d. This seems to me more like a description of the effect of rock music than of truth.

[119] However foolish it might be to do so in some cases, it is always possible to argue that anyone espousing a belief you wish she did not have is being ironic and thus is stating indirectly exactly what you want her to say. "Unstable" or "romantic" irony has this risk; it must be watched, but cannot be helped. *See generally* L. FURST, FICTIONS OF ROMANTIC IRONY (1984); W. BOOTH, A RHETORIC OF IRONY 240-77 (1974). A reader who took this entire article to be ironic, for example, would be making exactly this mistake. *But see, e.g., supra* p. 88.

[120] *See* R. ALLEN, *supra* note 55, at 5; *see also* PLATO, PLATO'S EUTHYPHRO, APOLOGY OF SOCRATES AND CRITO 67 (J. Burnet ed. 1924).

[121] *See* R. ALLEN, *supra* note 55, at 81-96. The *Crito,* writes Allen, "lacks the superb irony of the speech of defense in the *Apology.*" *Id.* at 82. Professor Allen may be right that the *Apology* is superbly ironic. So, too, I believe is the *Crito.*

[122] *Id.*

[122] *Id.*

[123] *See* 1 G. GROTE, *supra* note 11, at 430-33.

[124] *See* R. ALLEN, *supra* note 55, at 65-113.

[125] *Id.* at 83. By considering statements out of context, one can easily misunderstand them. For example, Socrates states that "in war . . . you must do whatever your city and your country command, or else persuade them in accordance with universal justice." *Crito, supra* note 6, at 51b-c. Also, in the *Apology* Socrates says that when one is assigned to a military post he must remain in it and face danger, even death, and not desert the post. *See Apology, supra* note 20, at 28d-e. These statements should not be seen as renunciations of war resistance. Rather, Socrates is critical of the wishy-washy manner in which people slip out of commitments. His statements should be understood as a rejection not of pacifism but rather of cowardice.

[126] 1 G. GROTE, *supra* note 11, at 430.

[127] XENOPHON, *Memorabilia of Socrates,* in XENOPHON'S WORKS 349, 504-07 (J. Watson trans. 1912).

[128] A.E. Taylor considers Xenophon's explanation "absurd." A. TAYLOR, *supra* note 41, at 166. Taylor, however, argues that Socrates intentionally martyred himself. *See id.* at 160. For Taylor's view of the significance of Socrates's age, *see id.* at 168.

[129] *See* Freeman, *Legitimizing Racial Discrimination Through Anti-Discrimination Law: A Critical Review of Supreme Court Doctrine,* 62 MINN. L. REV. 1049 (1978); Olsen, *The Politics of Family Law,* 2 LAW & INEQUALITY 1, 1-4 (1984); Taub & Schneider, *Perspectives on Women's Subordination and the Role of Law,* in THE POLITICS OF LAW 117, 126-35 (D. Kairys ed. 1982).

[130] Labor law also provides particularly fertile ground for legitimation theory because of the way it mediates or domesticates workers' struggles. Although labor law may protect employees, it does so in such a way that in the process it legitimates capitalist exploitation of workers. *See* Klare, *Judicial Deradicalization of the Wagner Act and the Origins of Modern Legal Consciousness, 1937-1941,* 62 MINN. L. REV. 265 (1978). Many NLRB decisions, for example, tend to make employer actions that unfairly harm workers seem legitimate.

[131] *See* ALBION'S FATAL TREE: CRIME AND SOCIETY IN EIGHTEENTH-CENTURY ENGLAND (D. Hay, P. Linebaugh, J. Rule, E. Thompson & C. Winslow eds. 1975) [hereinafter cited as ALBION'S FATAL TREE]; E. THOMPSON, WHIGS AND HUNTERS (1975).

[132] *See* Hay, *Property, Authority and the Criminal Law* in ALBION'S FATAL TREE, *supra* note 131, at 18-23.

[133] *See id.* at 17-63.

[134] *See id.* at 23. "A conflict of such magnitude between Parliament and the judiciary would have disrupted eighteenth-century politics, and nothing of the sort happened." *Id.* Moreover, it was the same men who controlled Parliament and facilitated the granting of pardons.

[135] *See id.* at 25.

[136] *See id.*

[137] *See id.* at 28.

[138] *See id.* at 32-33.

[139] "The law in its majestic equality, forbids the rich as well as the poor to sleep under bridges, to beg in the streets, and to steal bread." A. FRANCE, LE LYS ROUGE 117-18 (1894).

[140] *See* Hay, *supra* note 132, at 42-43.

[141] *See id.* at 43-48.

[142] *See* J. LOFBERG, *supra* note 100. Criminal cases were thus conducted something like civil cases in the United States.

[143] *See* D. MACDOWELL, THE LAW IN CLASSICAL ATHENS 62 (1978). This practice may have been what Crito had in mind when he bemoaned the mismanagement of Socrates's defense and argued that Socrates's friends should have prevented him from having to go to court. *See* J.

LOFBERG, *supra* note 100, at 40 (discussing *Crito, supra* note 6, at 45e).

[144] *See* J. LOFBERG, *supra* note 100. According to Xenophon, Crito hired an agent to protect himself from lawsuits intended as blackmail. *Id.* at 57 (citing XENOPHON, II MEMORABILIA 9). When a blackmailer charged Crito with a crime, Crito's agent would bring an action, better founded, against the accuser. *See id.* at 58.

For an interesting English case in which Lord Mansfield suspected a private prosecutor of a motive of blackmail, see Rex v. Delaval, 3 Burr 1434, 97 Eng. Rep. 913 (K.B. 1763).

[145] Initially Socrates proposes as a counterpenalty that he be awarded a kind of pension traditionally given to athletes who won particularly important Olympic events. *See Apology, supra* note 20, at 36d. Under pressure from friends, according to Plato, Socrates offers 30 minas, a considerable sum put up by his friends. *Id.* at 38b.

There is come confusion regarding the counterpenalty that Socrates offered. Diogenes Laertius writes that Socrates proposed to pay 25 drachmae, but that Eubulides says it was 100 drachmae, and that it was after this proposal of such a tiny fine caused an uproar among the judges that Socrates proposed he be awarded a pension. 1 D. LAERTIUS, *Socrates*, in LIVES OF EMINENT PHILOSOPHERS II.39-42 (Loeb Libr. ed. 1925). Xenophon asserts that Socrates refused to propose a counterpenalty or allow his friends to do so. *See* XENOPHON, *The Defense of Socrates*, in THE WHOLE WORKS OF XENOPHON 511, 514 (1855).

[146] *Crito, supra* note 6, at 53b-c.

[147] *See supra* pp. 82.

[148] *See* D. MACDOWELL, *supra* note 143, at 44 (citing M. OSTWALD, NOMOS AND THE BEGINNING OF THE ATHENIAN DEMOCRACY 137-73 (1969)); J. JONES, THE LAW AND LEGAL THEORY OF THE GREEKS 34-35 (1956).

[149] *See* A. TAYLOR, *supra* note 41, at 159.

[150] In homicide cases the defendant was allowed to exile himself as late as the middle of the trial, after his first speech to the court. *See* D. MACDOWELL, *supra* note 143, at 119. Modern lawyers might consider this rule similar to our plea bargaining system. Exile was an admission of guilt, at least of sorts, and the departure of the violator restored the breached community in many ways that punishment does. The provision in many Athenian laws that after conviction the violator could propose a counterpenalty (which, if exile, might well be accepted in lieu of death) restored society in a similar manner.

[151] Socrates expresses his distaste for such undignified behavior when he has the laws sarcastically suggest that Thessaly might be unruly enough to take pleasure in the funny story of how Socrates escaped from jail in some disguise, altering his appearance. *See Crito, supra* note 6, at 53d. For a nearly opposite view (or, ironically, the same view), *see* K. GRAHAME, THE WIND IN THE WILLOWS (1940), in which Toad disguises himself as a washerwoman to sneak out of jail in a *most* undignified manner—all the while delighted with himself. *Id.* at 108-11.

[152] In eighteenth-century England, a condemned man could often get a pardon by humbling himself and becoming obligated to a wealthy or influential person. *See* Hay, *supra* note 132. In Athens, such a condemned man could escape jail—becoming indebted to wealthy friends and suffering the indignity of adopting a disguise and engaging in other subterfuge. The accused would still have an incentive to choose exile at an earlier point, before condemnation (especially if the risk of a failed escape is considered), and the society would still be restored following breach.

[153] *Crito, supra* note 6, at 48c.

[154] People can be brought back from exile considerably more successfully than from death. Many might doubt that it could really have been the custom for the *agathos* to break out of jail, because no city could exist that openly countenanced such regular defiance of the laws. I argue, however, that such a custom could help legitimate the status quo.

Crito and Socrates both imply, from their talk of bribe money and disguises, that escape from jail occurred often enough to be standardized. But it is unlikely that escapes were especially common. First, more people who were able to flee would already have left the city before they were condemned. *See* A. TAYLOR, *supra* note 41, at 159. In addition, executions were usually carried out immediately, *see* D. MACDOWELL, *supra* note 143, at 254, and friends would ordinarily not have time to arrange an escape. In Socrates's case execution was delayed a month because the annual religious mission to Delos, during which no executions could be carried out, took an unusually long time.

[155] *See* A. ADKINS, *supra* note 45. Adkins's study on Greek morals is discussed *supra* pp. 85-86.

[156] *See* A. TAYLOR, *supra* note 41, at 168.

[157] *See supra* p. 81.

[158] *See supra* pp. 88-91. The term "Socratic Revolution" has been used by many authors.

[159] *See infra* p. 95.

[160] *See* United States v. Moylan, 417 F.2d 1002, 1008 n.21 (4th Cir. 1969).

[161] *Id.* at 1008 n.19 (quoting trial testimony of defendant James Darst, at 401-02).

[162] *Id.*

[163] The defendants were accused of violating 18 U.S.C. §§ 1361, 2071(a) (1976) and 50 U.S.C. app. § 462(a) (1976). *Moylan*, 417 F.2d at 1003 n.1.

[164] *Moylan*, 417 F.2d at 1009.

[165] *Id.*

[166] *Id.* at 1008.

[167] *Id.* at 1008 n.21.

[168] The *Moylan* defendants' effort to gain an acquittal was not a retreat or compromise and thus was not inconsistent with the behavior of Socrates. The Catonsville Nine were promoting values they supported when they urged the judge to consider—and to instruct the jury to consider—the substance of their opposition to the war in Vietnam.

[169] A. FORTAS, CONCERNING DISSENT AND CIVIL DISOBEDIENCE 67 (1968). This section of my article has been influenced by the ideas of Nathaniel Berman who shared with me his essay *Leopards and Lawyers* written for Professor Günther Frankenberg's seminar on Comparative Constitutional Law at Harvard Law School, Spring 1984.

[170] A. FORTAS, *supra* note 169, at 80.

[171] J. RAWLS, A THEORY OF JUSTICE 382-83 (1971). *But see* A. FORTAS, *supra* note 169, at 62 (civil disobedience should not be used as "a technique of warfare in a social and political conflict over other issues" or "to make propaganda").

[172] J. RAWLS, *supra* note 171, at 366. Many people who wish to limit civil disobedience in America seem to support no end of defiance that is more distant, geographically or historically. President Reagan condemned the strike by federal air traffic controllers ostensibly because, in order to obtain or keep their jobs, they had signed a no-strike pledge. He approved, however, the strike by Solidarity in Poland; its illegality contributed to, rather than detracted from, its attractiveness. Similarly, many Americans approve the efforts by the White Rose in Nazi Germany as heroic—and rightly so—although Sophie and Hans Scholl would rather not have been caught distributing their anti-government literature. They took a great risk and died bravely. *See* I. SCHOLL, THE WHITE ROSE (1983). Americans also laud the historically and geographically distant midwives who systematically violated the edict from the Pharaoh to kill all male Hebrew babies immediately on delivery. These midwives not only acted clandestinely but also lied and denied their guilt when questioned by the authorities. *See* D. DAUBE, CIVIL DISOBEDIENCE IN ANTIQUITY 5-10 (1972).

[173] *See* D. DAUBE, *supra* note 172, at 3.

[174] *Id.* at 4.

[175] *Id.*

[176] United States v. Moylan, 417 F.2d 1002, 1008 (4th Cir. 1969).

[177] See Kennedy, *Form and Substance in Private Law Adjudication*, 89 HARV. L. REV. 1685, 1771-78 (1976); Kennedy, *The Structure of Blackstone's Commentaries*, 28 BUFFALO L. REV. 209 (1979); Singer, *The Player and the Cards: Nihilism and Legal Theory*, 94 YALE L.J. 1 (1984).

[178] See VOICES FROM WOUNDED KNEE, 1973, at 22-25 (R. Anderson, J. Brown, J. Lerner & B. Shafer eds. 1975).

[179] See *id.* at 22, 24-25. The number of marshalls was between 65 and 75. See *id.* at 14-32. For further background to this government reaction, see *id.* at 121.

[180] See *id.* at 22, 23, 31.

[181] See *id.* at 28.

[182] See *id.* at 31-32.

[183] See *id.* at 41.

[184] See *id.* Other examples could be used; I am more familiar with this example because I represented the Indians and was present at Wounded Knee during much of the occupation.

[185] See *id.* at 142.

[186] See *id.* at 56.

[187] See *id.* at 142.

[188] *Id.* As in Grenada, the government banned newspeople from Wounded Knee and tried to manage the news through daily press briefings. At Wounded Knee, the reporters refused to capitulate. Several walked circuitously through government lines and brought back videotapes that disproved statements made at the official press briefings. On March 5, after two CBS newsmen entered Wounded Knee and scooped major network coverage, the government lifted its press ban. I believe that this responsible behavior by the newspeople may have prevented a second massacre at Wounded Knee. See also *id.* at 45. The Ghost Dance Massacre occurred at Wounded Knee on December 29, 1890.

[189] In both cases there was reason to believe that those in authority would prefer not to kill anyone.

It has been suggested to me that the Indians may have been "pointing" their guns at their own heads, but they were aimed at the government troops and many shots were exchanged. True, but two things should be noted. First, shooting at the government's tanks may well have been the only way the Indians could effectively put their lives on the line. Moreover, there is some evidence that Indians did follow the advice of Reverend John Adams of the National Council of Churches that they should "use [your guns] as non-violently as possible." VOICES FROM WOUNDED KNEE, *supra* note 178, at 53. Second, Socrates's refusal to leave Athens, although appearing to jeopardize only his own life, may have resulted directly in the death of his chief accuser. Some authorities claim, though others dispute it, that the Athenians, remorseful after Socrates's death, put Meletus to death and exiled the other two chief accusers. See D. LAERTIUS, *supra* note 145, at II.42-45.

[190] A.E. Taylor distinguishes Socrates's choice to remain in Athens from the choice to escape that Plato might justly have made in the same situation. Plato was a young man, under 30, who had never really had the option to live elsewhere; therefore, he cannot be said to have agreed to live by the laws of Athens. See A. TAYLOR, *supra* note 41, at 168-69. Obviously, this rationale would apply to the young Americans who fled to Canada to avoid being drafted or jailed, and the example of Socrates should not be used to criticize their choice.

I would go further. The authorities wanted Socrates to flee Athens and his refusal to flee was a refusal to compromise. See *supra* pp. 88-89. Although the authorities in America might indeed have felt pressured if each American who fled to Canada instead stood his ground and forced them to jail him, these American authorities did not want draft-age men to flee to Canada and the choice of those who did was not the same kind of compromise that it would have been for Socrates to flee. A comparison could possibly be drawn to a convicted draft refuser accepting an offer to enlist in the Army instead of going to jail (or Canada). Such behavior might be seen as a kind of retreat or compromise that Socrates refused to make.

[191] *See* M. FOOT, RESISTANCE: EUROPEAN RESISTANCE TO NAZISM 1940-45 (1977).

[192] When I advocate ad hoc disobedience, I run the risk, of course, of having ad hoc disobedience used against me—against laws I support. This is unavoidable and, in fact, occurs also with the most restricted form of civil disobedience. The employers who violated protective labor legislation around the turn of the century and got the courts to support them probably believed in what they were doing. And certainly they were prepared to pay their fines had the courts disagreed with them.4c

# 8

# Notes on Civil Disobedience

1. The contemporary philosopher Joseph Raz endorses a division of the conscientious violation of law into three categories. In addition to civil disobedience itself, which is intended either to change, protest, or dissociate oneself from a law, Raz also lists revolutionary disobedience, which is aimed at broadly changing the government or constitution, and conscientious objection, which is undertaken from the belief that the actor is morally prohibited from obeying or cooperating with the law. See JOSEPH RAZ, THE AUTHORITY OF LAW 263 (1979).

2. Michael Perry finds no moral obligation to obey all laws in even a truly democratic society, but notes the realism of "a healthy sense of the fallibility of one's judgment that disobeying a particular law is justified. . . ." MICHAEL J. PERRY, MORALITY, POLITICS, AND LAW 113 (1988). Perry's theory of legitimate civil disobedience makes allowances, in certain cases, for non-public civil disobedience and non-acceptance of the specified legal punishment. *Id.* at 117. Perry cites as examples of such cases, respectively, operators of the Underground Railroad during the American slavery era, and those Germans who helped Jews escape from Nazi Germany. *Id.* at 118.

3. As a matter of definition, must a civilly disobedient person have reasonably exhausted, within the limits of her capacities, any practical legal means to change the objectionable law in question before resorting to civil disobedience? See Hugo A. Bedau, *On Civil Disobedience*, 58 JOURNAL OF PHILOSOPHY 653, 661 (1961). Or is this a matter that goes only to tactics, or the apparent sincerity, justifiability, popular appeal or morality of the act of civil disobedience? Does the news media's greater attention to illegal protests than to legal protests make the question of an "exhaustion" requirement more difficult?

4. Joseph Raz has argued that in certain instances, civil disobedience may be morally justified even where those who engage in the civil disobedience

conceal their identities, resist or seek to avoid legal punishment, engage in violence, or choose civil disobedience in preference to potentially effective legal protest. See JOSEPH RAZ, THE AUTHORITY OF LAW 265, 267, 275 (1979). As to the final point, Raz cites a choice between a campaign of civil disobedience on the one hand and the suffering involved in a long, disruptive legal strike in a crucial industry on the other. See *id.* at 275.

5. John Rawls adopts the controversial requirements that civil disobedience be non-violent, that lesser remedies be exhausted, and that the civilly disobedient actor accept the legal consequences of the act. See JOHN RAWLS, A THEORY OF JUSTICE 366, 373 (1971). Rawls adds as well the condition that the disobedience be targeted at "substantial and clear injustice," *id.* at 372. If all the other requirements for civil disobedience are met, is it likely that the typical civil disobedient actor will concede that the targeted injustice is insubstantial or unclear? Is there a certain lack of realism about this requirement, or in Rawls' further suggestion, *id.* at 374-75, that civilly disobedient groups should cooperate in ensuring that the overall level of civil disobedience does not become excessive?

6. Hugo Bedau, among others, has similarly argued that to qualify as civil disobedience, the action must involve neither the threat of violence nor actual violence, in the act of disobedience or in the course of any arrest. See Hugo A. Bedau, *On Civil Disobedience*, 58 JOURNAL OF PHILOSOPHY 653, 656 (1961). How should violence be defined here? Does it matter whether we classify a violent act as civil disobedience or not? Could the answer depend upon whether the idea of civil disobedience has a favorable connotation in some circles? Why does there seem to be so much unresolved dispute focusing, supposedly, on the definition or meaning of civil disobedience as a concept?

7. For Mahatma Gandhi's insistence upon non-violence and acceptance of legal punishment as a matter not merely of tactics, but of essential principle, see MOHANDAS K. GANDHI, NON-VIOLENT RESISTANCE 6-7, 9-15, 79 (Bharatan Kumarappa ed. 1961). Note as well Gandhi's emphasis on civil disobedience as an act or campaign of suffering, *id.* at 67, 112-15, and especially on the need for extensive, broad-ranging preparatory training for genuine civil disobedience, *id.* at 77, 88, 91-98. Are these and other Gandhian principles, such as having and displaying genuine love and respect for one's opponents, impractical or naive? What role should be given to other considerations such as the attraction of media attention in campaigns of contemporary civil disobedience?

8. For a sensitive, carefully argued discussion of issues such as the possible role

of violence, the variety of possible aims of civil disobedience, the role of publicity and communication, and the problem of respect or disrespect for the law, see Gerald C. MacCallum, *Some Truths and Untruths About Civil Disobedience*, in 12 NOMOS: POLITICAL AND LEGAL OBLIGATION 370-400 (J. Roland Pennock & John Chapman eds. 1970).

9. What does it mean to say that civil disobedience normally involves a rejection of even nonviolent resistance to the legal consequences of one's illegal act? See Hugo A. Bedau, *On Civil Disobedience*, 58 JOURNAL OF PHILOSOPHY 653, 659 (1961). Does entering a general not guilty plea involve non-violent resistance to the legal consequences of one's civil disobedience?

10. Note that there may be important reasons, such as practical impossibility, or the severity of the legal penalty, for a civilly disobedient actor to violate not the morally objectionable law in question itself, but some other loosely related law instead. Thus it may seem more sensible to violate a general trespass law at a military installation than to somehow "violate" a provision of the defense budget, or an unduly broad treason statute. For relevant discussion, see Hugo A. Bedau, *On Civil Disobedience* 58 JOURNAL OF PHILOSOPHY 653, 657 (1961).

11. As a matter of definition, should the idea of civil disobedience require a "willingness to act in public and to offer explanations to other people. . . .?" MICHAEL WALZER, OBLIGATIONS: ESSAYS ON DISOBEDIENCE, WAR, AND CITIZENSHIP 20 (1970). Could a regime be so repressive and punitive that it would be appropriate to defy the law in a public way, but without allowing oneself to be identified or trying to explain one's actions, the point of which may be clear anyway?

12. Howard Zinn has noted that "[a] common argument is that disobedience even of bad laws is wrong because that fosters a general disrespect for all laws, including good laws, which we need. But this is like arguing that children should be made to eat rotten fruit along with the good, lest they get the idea that *all* fruit should be thrown away." HOWARD ZINN, DISOBEDIENCE AND DEMOCRACY 12 (1968) (emphasis in the original). Does this analogy depend upon an ability to easily and uncontroversially recognize "bad" laws?

13. As for the scope of legitimate civil disobedience, Mahatma Gandhi writes that "[w]e must tolerate many laws of the State, even when they are inconvenient. A son may not approve of some of the orders of the Father and yet he obeys them. It is only when they are unworthy of obedience and immoral that he disobeys them." MOHANDAS K. GANDHI, NON-VIOLENT RESISTANCE 67 (Bharatan Kumarappa ed. 1961). Gandhi argues that a non-violent civil

resister "obeys the laws of society intelligently and of his own free will because he considers it his sacred duty to do so. It is only when a person has thus obeyed the laws of society scrupulously that he is in a position to judge as to which particular rules are good and just and which are unjust and iniquitous." *Id.* at 75.

14. Ronald Dworkin argues that the degree of tolerance for civil disobedience should vary according to whether the rule of law being challenged is officially justified in terms of a supposed "moral right to be free from some harm," as opposed to a law that seeks merely to promote the general welfare without upholding any such rights. See RONALD DWORKIN, TAKING RIGHTS SERIOUSLY 217-19 (1978). Note, though, that almost any conceivable law regarding matters such as racially-based civil rights statutes or the military draft, is likely to be based not only on the general welfare, but on some conception of someone's moral rights to be free from some harm, such as invasion by a foreign power. For Dworkin's argument to the contrary, see *id.* at 218-19.

15. Should a society nevertheless make greater efforts to accommodate civil disobedience to laws that merely give effect to social and economic policy than to laws intended to protect rights? Can a clear distinction between these two kinds of laws normally be drawn in an uncontroversial way? Won't the laws that inspire the most passionate civil disobedience tend to be laws that, at least in part, grant rights to some social groups, while denying them to others? See Eugene Schlossberger, *Civil Disobedience* 49 ANALYSIS 148, 149-50 (1989) (critiquing the views of Professor Ronald Dworkin).

16. Must civil disobedience be targeted against laws that, regardless of their basis or aim, allegedly violate someone's rights? Eugene Schlossberger offers the counterexample of someone's standing between a wrecking ball and an historic building in order to protect the local architectural heritage. See Eugene Schlossberger, *Civil Disobedience* 49 ANALYSIS 148, 151 (1989). No doubt any act of civil disobedience can be linked to some sort of alleged rights violation, but it also seems possible for those protecting the historic building to grant that demolition of the historic building, however morally objectionable, would not violate anyone's rights.

17. Are there any special moral problems with civil disobedience regarding issues in which a potentially decisive question is highly technical in nature, and where the uncertainty regarding such technical questions is genuine, and not the result of government secrecy? Could issues of nuclear power, space-based defense systems, and global warming ever fall within such a category?

18. Peter Singer argues that "there are two special reasons for obedience which are peculiar to a democracy. The first is based on the fact that a democratic society, in which all have equal power and there is no tendency for the majority to treat the minority with less than equal consideration, is a fair compromise between competing, otherwise irresolvable, claims to power. The second stems from the fact that participating in a decision-procedure, alongside others participating in good faith, gives rise to an obligation to act as if one had consented to be bound by the results of the decision-procedure." PETER SINGER, DEMOCRACY AND DISOBEDIENCE 133 (1974). Is Singer's first reason of only limited relevance to less fair and egalitarian democracies? Is his second reason plausible? For the views of other participants in this dispute, see JOHN P. PLAMENATZ, CONSENT, FREEDOM AND POLITICAL OBLIGATION 144-56 (2d ed. 1968); John J. Jenkins, *Political Consent*, 20 PHILOSOPHICAL QUARTERLY 60 (1970); Frederick Siegler, *Plamenatz On Consent and Obligation*, 18 PHILOSOPHICAL QUARTERLY 256 (1968) (arguing, as against Plamenatz and Jenkins, that voluntarily and understandingly voting in an election does not necessarily involve giving consent, even if voting is widely taken as a sign of consent, and even if the voter knows this); Albert Weale, *Consent*, 26 POLITICAL STUDIES 65, 71-72 (1978). Does voting with even the greatest awareness of how one's vote is likely to be interpreted count as consent if the voter's sole motive in voting is to try desperately to fend off the slightly lesser of two serious evils?

19. According to Robert Rodes, Jr., "the justification of any particular act of civil disobedience is a matter of balance. It involves weighing in every case the quantum of disruption against the quantum of good to be achieved." ROBERT E. RODES, JR., THE LEGAL ENTERPRISE 58 (1976). Could this approach be technically right, yet call for powers to perceive, envision, weigh, predict, calculate, and restrain emotion beyond our capacities, even if we adopt some simplifying rules of thumb? Compare this approach with some of the accounts and criticisms of utilitarian calculation discussed below.

20. What should be said about the idea that increasing the legitimacy or moral prestige of civil disobedience will unavoidably tend to promote the civil disobedience of "bad" groups and "bad" causes? See HOWARD ZINN, DIS-OBEDIENCE AND DEMOCRACY 14 (1968). For a recent, vivid restatement of Zinn's views, see Howard Zinn, *Law, Justice, and Disobedience*, 5 NOTRE DAME JOURNAL OF LAW, ETHICS & PUBLIC POLICY 899 (1991). Are all sorts of groups and interests equally inclined to rely on civil disobedience?

21. Could one argue that at least in some cases, civil disobedience tends to promote the overall responsiveness of the government to the public, and therefore the legitimacy of that government? See DON HERZOG, HAPPY

SLAVES: A CRITIQUE OF CONSENT THEORY 207 (1989).

22. Robert Rodes, Jr. writes that "small acts of civil disobedience to protest small wrongs are as justified as great acts to protest great wrongs." ROBERT E. RODES, JR., THE LEGAL ENTERPRISE 58 (1976). Could one argue instead that violating the law for a relatively trivial reason cannot be justified, as all intentional law violation contributes to the erosion of the institution of the rule of law, a consequence which should not lightly be disregarded? Or could one argue that the negative consequences, even over the long-term, of a pattern of law violation for only modest reasons will likely be small?

23. Are persons considering an act of civil disobedience morally or logically bound to consider what bad things would happen if everyone in a similar position also chose to violate the targeted law? How can we know who is in a similar position? Is it relevant that most people will probably not in fact choose to violate that law? For a discussion of some related issues, see Richard A. Wasserstrom, *Disobeying the Law*, 58 JOURNAL OF PHILOSOPHY 641, 650 (1961).

24. If civil disobedience is morally justified in a particular case, does that mean only that someone has a moral right to engage in civil disobedience if they wish to, or else that someone has a moral duty or obligation to engage in civil disobedience, whether they wish to or not? See MICHAEL WALZER, OBLIGA-TIONS: ESSAYS ON DISOBEDIENCE, WAR AND CITIZENSHIP 3-4 (1970). Might the answer depend upon whether the potential civil disobedient herself is a direct, special victim of the laws that are being protested? Consider the difference between someone bound by moral or religious principle to protest, as opposed to someone personally denied access, unfairly, to some right or benefit. Could there be a moral obligation to disobey in the first case, but not in the second?

25. Could civil disobedience be aimed not at thwarting the application of a law, even in one particular case, but merely at making a public "statement" or expression of one's deeply principled disagreement with a law one recognizes one is powerless to change? For a narrower focus on the aim of "thwarting" of the law, see Hugo A. Bedau, *On Civil Disobedience*, 58 JOURNAL OF PHILOSOPHY 653, 658-59 (1961).

26. Is civil disobedience in practice usually engaged in by those who could be called politically powerless or subordinated? Is civil disobedience in fact normally associated with either the political left or right wings? Does the term 'civil disobedience' usually have a positive or a negative connotation? If we want to promote social change, is it tactically better to define civil dis-

obedience broadly or restrictively? Is it possible that morally questionable tactics may tend to promote the most rapid favorable political change?

27. In United States v. O'Brien, 391 U.S. 367 (1968), the United States Supreme Court majority upheld the defendant O'Brien's conviction under a statute prohibiting the intentional destruction of one's draft card, despite the public, conscientious, and symbolic or communicative nature of O'Brien's action in burning his draft card. The Supreme Court held that in the context at issue, "a government regulation is sufficiently justified if it is within the constitutional power of government; if it furthers an important or substantial governmental interest; if the governmental interest is unrelated to the suppression of free expression; and if the incidental restriction on alleged First Amendment freedom is no greater than is essential to the furtherance of that interest." *Id.* at 377. Is the Court's first condition a useful part of the test? How do we tell whether a governmental interest is substantial or not? Won't it always be possible to imagine a workable statute that serves the government interest as well, or almost as well, with a slightly less restrictive impact on freedom of speech?

# 9

# From Thomas Aquinas, The Summa Theologica, First Part of the Second Part

QUESTION 91
## OF THE VARIOUS KINDS OF LAW
*(In Six Articles)*

WE must now consider the various kinds of law, under which head there are six points of inquiry: (1) Whether there is an eternal law? (2) Whether there is a natural law? (3) Whether there is a human law? (4) Whether there is a divine law? (5) Whether there is one divine law or several? (6) Whether there is a law of sin?

FIRST ARTICLE
## WHETHER THERE IS AN ETERNAL LAW?

*We proceed thus to the First Article:*

*Objection 1.* It would seem that there is no eternal law. Because every law is imposed on someone. But there was not someone from eternity on whom a law could be imposed, since God alone was from eternity. Therefore no law is eternal.

*Obj. 2.* Further, promulgation is essential to law. But promulgation could not be from eternity, because there was no one to whom it could be promulgated from eternity. Therefore no law can be eternal.

*Obj. 3.* Further, a law implies order to an end. But nothing ordained to an end is eternal, for the last end alone is eternal. Therefore no law is eternal.

*On the contrary,* Augustine says: "That Law which is the Supreme Reason cannot be understood to be otherwise than unchangeable and eternal."

*I answer that,* As stated above (Q. 90, A. 1 *ad* 2; AA. 3, 4), a law is nothing else but a dictate of practical reason emanating from the ruler who governs a perfect community. Now it is evident, granted that the world is ruled by divine providence, as was stated in the First Part, that the whole community of the universe is governed by divine reason. Wherefore the very Idea of the government of things in God the Ruler of the universe has the nature of a law. And since the divine reason's conception of things is not subject to time but is eternal, according to Proverbs viii. 23, therefore it is that this kind of law must be called eternal.

*Reply Obj. 1.* Those things that are not in themselves exist with God, inasmuch as they are foreknown and preordained by Him, according to Romans iv. 17, "Who calls those things that are not, as those that are." Accordingly the eternal concept of the divine law bears the character of an eternal law in so far as it is ordained by God to the government of things foreknown by Him.

*Reply Obj. 2.* Promulgation is made by word of mouth or in writing; and in both ways the eternal law is promulgated, because both the divine word and the writing of the Book of Life are eternal. But the promulgation cannot be from eternity on the part of the creature that hears or reads.

*Reply Obj. 3.* The law implies order to the end actively, in so far as it directs certain things to the end, but not passively—that is to say, the law itself is not ordained to the end—except accidentally, in a governor whose end is extrinsic to him, and to which end his law must needs be ordained. But the end of the divine government is God Himself, and His law is not distinct from Himself. Wherefore the eternal law is not ordained to another end.

SECOND ARTICLE
## WHETHER THERE IS IN US A NATURAL LAW?

*We proceed thus to the Second Article:*

*Objection 1.* It would seem that there is no natural law in us. Because man is governed sufficiently by the eternal law; for Augustine says that "the eternal law is that by which it is right that all things should be most orderly." But nature does not abound in superfluities, as neither does she fail in necessaries. Therefore no law is natural to man.

*Obj. 2.* Further, by the law man is directed in his acts to the end, as stated above (Q. 90, A. 2). But the directing of human acts to their end is not a function of nature, as is the case in irrational creatures, which act for an end solely by their natural appetite; whereas man acts for an end by his reason and will. Therefore no law is natural to man.

*Obj. 3.* Further, the more a man is free, the less is he under the law. But man is freer than all the animals, on account of his free will, with which he is endowed above all other animals. Since therefore other animals are not subject to a natural law, neither is man subject to a natural law.

*On the contrary,* A gloss on Romans ii. 14: "When the Gentiles, who have not the law, do by nature those things that are of the law," comments as follows: "Although they have no written law, yet they have the natural law, whereby each one knows, and is conscious of, what is good and what is evil."

*I answer that,* As stated above (Q. 90, A. 1 *ad* 1), law, being a rule and measure, can be in a person in two ways: in one way, as in him that rules and measures; in another way, as in that which is ruled and measured, since a thing is ruled and measured in so far as it partakes of the rule or measure. Wherefore, since all things subject to divine providence are ruled and measured by the eternal law, as was stated above (A. 1), it is evident that all things partake somewhat of the eternal law, in so far as, namely, from its being imprinted on them, they derive their respective inclinations to their proper acts and ends. Now among all others the rational creature is subject to divine providence in the most excellent way, in so far as it partakes of a share of providence, by being provident both for itself and for others. Wherefore it has a share of the eternal reason, whereby it has a natural inclination to its proper act and end: and this participation of the eternal law in the rational creature is called the natural law. Hence the Psalmist after saying: "Offer up the sacrifice of justice," as though someone asked what the works of justice are, adds: "Many say, Who showeth us good things?" in answer to which question he says: "The light of Thy countenance, O Lord, is signed upon us"; thus implying that the light of natural reason, whereby we discern what is good and what is evil, which is the function of the natural law, is nothing else than an imprint on us of the divine light. It is therefore evident that the natural law is nothing else than the rational creature's participation of the eternal law.

*Reply Obj. 1.* This argument would hold if the natural law were something different from the eternal law, whereas it is nothing but a participation thereof, as stated above.

*Reply Obj. 2.* Every act of reason and will in us is based on that which is according to nature, as stated above; for every act of reasoning is based on principles that are known naturally, and every act of appetite in respect of the means is derived from the natural appetite in respect of the last end. Accordingly the first direction of our acts to their end must needs be in virtue of the natural law.

*Reply Obj. 3.* Even irrational animals partake in their own way of the eternal reason, just as the rational creature does. But because the rational creature partakes thereof in an intellectual and rational manner, therefore the participation of the eternal law in the rational creature is properly called a law, since a law is something pertaining to reason, as stated above (Q. 90, A. 1). Irrational creatures, however, do not partake thereof in a rational manner, wherefore there is no participation of the eternal law in them, except by way of similitude.

### THIRD ARTICLE
### WHETHER THERE IS A HUMAN LAW?

*We proceed thus to the Third Article:*

*Objection 1.* It would seem that there is not a human law. For the natural law is a participation of the eternal law, as stated above (A. 2). Now through the eternal law "all things are most orderly," as Augustine states. Therefore the natural law suffices for the ordering of all human affairs. Consequently there is no need for a human law.

*Obj. 2.* Further, a law bears the character of a measure, as stated above (Q. 90, A. 1). But human reason is not a measure of things, but vice versa, as stated in *Metaphysics* x. text. 5. Therefore no law can emanate from human reason.

*Obj. 3.* Further, a measure should be most certain, as stated in *Metaphysics* x. text. 3. But the dictates of human reason in matters of conduct are uncertain, according to Wisdom ix. 14: "The thoughts of mortal men are fearful, and our counsels uncertain." Therefore no law can emanate from human reason.

*On the contrary,* Augustine distinguishes two kinds of law—the one eternal; the other temporal, which he calls human.

*I answer that,* As stated above (Q. 90, A. 1 *ad* 2), a law is a dictate of the practical reason. Now it is to be observed that the same procedure takes place in the practical and in the speculative reason, for each proceeds from principles to conclusions, as stated above (*ibid.*). Accordingly we conclude that just as, in the speculative reason, from naturally known indemonstrable principles we draw the conclusions of the various sciences, the knowledge of which is not imparted to us by nature, but acquired by the efforts of reason; so, too, it is from the precepts of the natural law, as from general and indemonstrable principles, that the human reason needs to proceed to the more particular determination of certain matters. These particular determinations, devised by human reason, are called human laws, provided the other essential conditions of law be observed, as stated above (Q. 90, AA. 2, 3, 4). Wherefore Cicero says in his *Rhetoric* that "justice has its source in nature; thence certain things came into custom by reason of their utility; afterward these things which emanated from nature and were approved by custom were sanctioned by fear and reverence for the law."

*Reply Obj. 1.* The human reason cannot have a full participation of the dictate of the divine reason but according to its own mode, and imperfectly. Consequently, as on the part of the speculative reason, by a natural participation of divine wisdom, there is in us the knowledge of certain general principles, but not proper knowledge of each single truth, such as that contained in the divine wisdom; so, too, on the part of the practical reason man has a natural participation of the eternal law, according to certain general principles, but not as regards the particular determinations of individual cases, which are, however, contained in the eternal law. Hence the necessity that human reason proceed to certain particular sanctions of law.

*Reply Obj. 2.* Human reason is not of itself the rule of things, but the principles impressed on it by nature are general rules and measures of all things relating to human conduct, whereof the natural reason is the rule and measure, although it is not the measure of things that are from nature.

*Reply Obj. 3.* The practical reason is concerned with practical matters, which are singular and contingent, but not with necessary things, with which the speculative reason is concerned. Wherefore human laws cannot have that inerrancy that belongs to the demonstrated conclusions of sciences. Nor is it necessary for every measure to be altogether unerring and certain, but according as it is possible in its own particular genus. . . .

### QUESTION 94
### OF THE NATURAL LAW
#### (*In Six Articles*)

WE must now consider the natural law, concerning which there are six points of inquiry: (1) What is the natural law? (2) What are the precepts of the natural law? (3) Whether all acts of virtue are prescribed by the natural law? (4) Whether the natural law is the same in all? (5) Whether it is changeable? (6) Whether it can be abolished from the heart of man?

FIRST ARTICLE

## WHETHER THE NATURAL LAW IS A HABIT?

*We proceed thus to the First Article*:

*Objection 1*. It would seem that the natural law is a habit. Because, as the Philosopher says, "there are three things in the soul: power, habit, and passion." But the natural law is not one of the soul's powers, nor is it one of the passions, as we may see by going through them one by one. Therefore the natural law is a habit.

*Obj. 2*. Further, Basil says that the conscience or "*synderesis* is the law of our mind," which can only apply to the natural law. But the *synderesis* is a habit, as was shown in the First Part. Therefore the natural law is habit.

*Obj. 3*. Further, the natural law abides in man always, as will be shown further on (A. 6). But man's reason, which is involved in law, does not always think about the natural law. Therefore the natural law is not an act, but a habit.

*On the contrary*, Augustine says that "a habit is that whereby something is done when necessary." But such is not the natural law, since it is in infants and in the damned who cannot act by it. Therefore the natural law is not a habit.

*I answer that*, A thing may be called a habit in two ways. First, properly and essentially: and thus the natural law is not a habit. For it has been stated above (Q. 90, A. 1 *ad* 2) that the natural law is something appointed by reason, just as a proposition is a work of reason. Now that which a man does is not the same as that whereby he does it, for he makes a becoming speech by the habit of grammar. Since, then, a habit is that by which we act, a law cannot be a habit, properly and essentially.

Secondly, the term "habit" may be applied to that which we hold by a habit: thus faith may mean that which we hold by faith. And accordingly, since the precepts of the natural law are sometimes considered by reason actually, while sometimes they are in the reason only habitually, in this way the natural law may be called a habit, Thus, in speculative matters, the indemonstrable principles are not the habit itself whereby we hold these principles, but are the principles the habit of which we possess.

*Reply Obj. 1*. The Philosopher proposes there to discover the genus of virtue; and since it is evident that virtue is a principle of action, he mentions only those things which are principles of human acts, viz., powers, habits and passions. But there are other things in the soul besides these three: there are acts; thus to will is in the one that wills; again, things known are in the knower; moreover its own natural properties are in the soul, such as immortality and the like.

*Reply Obj. 2. Synderesis* is said to be the law of our mind, because it is a habit containing the precepts of the natural law, which are the first principles of human actions.

*Reply Obj. 3*. This argument proves that the natural law is held habitually; and this is granted.

*To the argument advanced in the contrary sense* we reply that sometimes a man is unable to make use of that which is in him habitually, on account of some impediment: thus, on account of sleep, a man is unable to use the habit of science. In like manner, through the deficiency of his age, a child cannot use the habit of understanding of principles, or the natural law, which is in him habitually.

SECOND ARTICLE

WHETHER THE NATURAL LAW CONTAINS SEVERAL PRECEPTS, OR ONE ONLY?

*We proceed thus to the Second Article*:

*Objection 1.* It would seem that the natural law contains, not several precepts, but one only. For law is a kind of precept, as stated above (Q. 92, A. 2). If therefore there were many precepts of the natural law, it would follow that there are also many natural laws.

*Obj. 2.* Further, the natural law is consequent to human nature. But human nature, as a whole, is one, though, as to its parts, it is manifold. Therefore, either there is but one precept of the law of nature, on account of the unity of nature as a whole, or there are many, by reason of the number of parts of human nature. The result would be that even things relating to the inclination of the concupiscible faculty belong to the natural law.

*Obj. 3.* Further, law is something pertaining to reason, as stated above (Q. 90, A. 1). Now reason is but one in man. Therefore there is only one precept of the natural law.

*On the contrary,* The precepts of the natural law in man stand in relation to practical matters, as the first principles to matters of demonstration. But there are several first indemonstrable principles. Therefore there are also several precepts of the natural law.

*I answer that,* As stated above (Q. 91, A. 3), the precepts of the natural law are to the practical reason what the first principles of demonstrations are to the speculative reason, because both are self-evident principles. Now a thing is said to be self-evident in two ways: first, in itself; secondly, in relation to us. Any proposition is said to be self-evident in itself if its predicate is contained in the notion of the subject, although to one who knows not the definition of the subject it happens that such a proposition is not self-evident. For instance, this proposition, "Man is a rational being," is, in its very nature, self-evident, since who says "man" says "a rational being"; and yet to one who knows not what a man is, this proposition is not self-evident. Hence it is that, as Boethius says, certain axioms or propositions are universally self-evident to all; and such are those propositions whose terms are known to all, as, "Every whole is greater than its part," and, "Things equal to one and the same are equal to one another." But some propositions are self-evident only to the wise who understand the meaning of the terms of such propositions; thus to one who understands that an angel is not a body, it is self-evident that an angel is not circumspectively in a place; but this is not evident to the unlearned, for they cannot grasp it.

Now a certain order is to be found in those things that are apprehended universally. For that which, before aught else, falls under apprehension, is "being," the notion of which is included in all things whatsoever a man apprehends. Wherefore the first indemonstrable principle is that *the same thing cannot be affirmed and denied at the same time*, which is based on the notion of "being" and "not-being"; and on this principle all others are based, as it is stated in *Metaphysics* iv. text. 9. Now as "being" is the first thing that falls under the apprehension simply, so "good" is the first thing that falls under the apprehension of the practical reason, which is directed to action, since every agent acts for an end under the aspect of good. Consequently the first principle in the practical reason is one founded on the notion of good, viz., that *good is that which all things seek after*. Hence this is the first precept of law, that *good is to be done and ensued, and evil is to be avoided*. All other precepts of the natural law are based upon this, so that whatever the practical reason naturally apprehends as man's good (or evil) belongs to the precepts of the natural law as something to be done or avoided.

Since, however, good has the nature of an end, and evil the nature of a contrary, hence it is that all those things to which man has a natural inclination are naturally apprehended by reason as being good and, consequently, as objects of pursuit, and their contraries as evil and objects of avoidance. Wherefore the order of the precepts of the natural law is according to the order of natural inclinations. Because in man there is first of all an inclination to good in accordance with the nature which he has in common with all substances, inasmuch as every substance seeks the preservation of its own being, according to its nature; and by reason of this inclination, whatever is a means of preserving human life and of warding off its obstacles belongs to the natural law. Secondly, there is in man an inclination to things that pertain to him more specially, according to that nature which he has in common with other animals; and in virtue of this inclination, those things are said to belong to the natural law "which nature has taught to all animals," such as sexual intercourse, education of offspring, and so forth. Thirdly, there is in man an inclination to good, according to the nature of his reason, which nature is proper to him: thus man has a natural inclination to know the truth about God and to live in society; and in this respect, whatever pertains to this inclination belongs to the natural law, for instance, to shun ignorance, to avoid offending those among whom one has to live, and other such things regarding the above inclination.

*Reply Obj. 1.* All these precepts of the law of nature have the character of one natural law, inasmuch as they flow from one first precept.

*Reply Obj. 2.* All the inclinations of any parts whatsoever of human nature, e.g., of the concupiscible and irascible parts, in so far as they are ruled by reason, belong to the natural law and are reduced to one first precept, as stated above, so that the precepts of the natural law are many in themselves, but are based on one common foundation.

*Reply Obj. 3.* Although reason is one in itself, yet it directs all things regarding man, so that whatever can be ruled by reason is contained under the law of reason.

### THIRD ARTICLE
### WHETHER ALL ACTS OF VIRTUE ARE PRESCRIBED BY THE NATURAL LAW?

*We proceed thus to the Third Article*:

*Objection 1.* It would seem that not all acts of virtue are prescribed by the natural law. Because, as stated above (Q. 90, A. 2), it is essential to a law that it be ordained to the common good. But some acts of virtue are ordained to the private good of the individual, as is evident especially in regard to acts of temperance. Therefore not all acts of virtue are the subject of natural law.

*Obj. 2.* Further, every sin is opposed to some virtuous act. If therefore all acts of virtue are prescribed by the natural law, it seems to follow that all sins are against nature, whereas this applies to certain special sins.

*Obj. 3.* Further, those things which are according to nature are common to all. But acts of virtue are not common to all, since a thing is virtuous in one, and vicious in another. Therefore not all acts of virtue are prescribed by the natural law.

*On the contrary,* Damascene says that "virtues are natural." Therefore virtuous acts also are a subject of the natural law.

*I answer that,* We may speak of virtuous acts in two ways: first, under the aspect of virtuous; secondly, as such and such acts considered in their proper species. If then we speak of acts of virtue considered as virtuous, thus all virtuous acts belong to the natural law. For it has been stated (A. 2) that to the natural law belongs everything to which a man is inclined according to his nature. Now each thing is inclined naturally to an operation that is suitable to it according to its form: thus fire is inclined to give heat. Wherefore, since the rational soul is the proper form of man, there is in every man a natural inclination to act according to reason; and this is to act according to virtue. Consequently, considered thus, all acts of virtue are prescribed by the natural law, since each one's reason naturally dictates to him to act virtuously. But if we speak of virtuous acts considered in themselves, i.e., in their proper species, thus not all virtuous acts are prescribed by the natural law, the many things are done virtuously to which nature does not incline at first, but which, through the inquiry of reason, have been found by men to be conducive to well-living.

*Reply Obj. 1.* Temperance is about the natural concupiscences of food, drink, and sexual matters, which are indeed ordained to the natural common good, just as other matters of law are ordained to the moral common good.

*Reply Obj. 2.* By human nature we may mean either that which is proper to man—and in this sense all sins, as being against reason, are also against nature, as Damascene states—or we may mean that nature which is common to man and other animals; and in this sense, certain special sins are said to be against nature: thus contrary to sexual intercourse, which is natural to all animals, is unisexual lust, which has received the special name of the unnatural crime.

*Reply Obj. 3.* This argument considers acts in themselves. For it is owing to the various conditions of men that certain acts are virtuous for some, as being proportionate and becoming to them, while they are vicious for others, as being out of proportion to them.

FOURTH ARTICLE
### WHETHER THE NATURAL LAW IS THE SAME IN ALL MEN?

*We proceed thus to the Fourth Article:*

*Objection 1.* It would seem that the natural law is not the same in all. For it is stated in the *Decretals* that "the natural law is that which is contained in the Law and the Gospel." But this is not common to all men because, as it is written, "all do not obey the gospel." Therefore the natural law is not the same in all men.

*Obj. 2.* Further, "Things which are according to the law are said to be just," as stated in *Ethics* v. But it is stated in the same book that nothing is so universally just as not to be subject to change in regard to some men. Therefore, even the natural law is not the same in all men.

*Obj. 3.* Further, as stated above (AA. 2, 3), to the natural law belongs everything to which a man is inclined according to his nature. Now different men are naturally inclined to different things, some to the desire of pleasures, others to the desire of honors, and other men to other things. Therefore, there is not one natural law for all.

*On the contrary* Isidore says: "The natural law is common to all nations."

*I answer that,* As stated above (AA. 2, 3), to the natural law belong those things to which a man is inclined naturally; and among these it is a special property of man to be inclined to act according to reason. Now reason proceeds from what is common, or general, to what is proper, or special, as stated in *Physics* i. But there is a difference in this regard between the speculative reason and practical reason. The speculative reason is concerned primarily with what is necessary, that is, with those things which cannot be other than they are; and therefore, in the case of speculative reason, both the common principles and the special conclusions are necessarily true. In the case of the practical reason, on the other hand, which is concerned with contingent matters, such as human actions, even though there be some necessary truth in the common principles, yet the more we descend to what is proper and peculiar, the more deviations we find. Therefore in speculative matters the same truth holds among all men both as to principles and as to conclusions, even though all men do not discern this truth in the conclusions but only in those principles which are called axiomatic notions. In active matters, on the other hand, all men do not hold to the same truth or practical rectitude in what is peculiar and proper, but only in what is common. And even among those who hold to the same line of rectitude in proper and peculiar matters, such rectitude is not equally known to all. It is clear, therefore, that as far as common principles are concerned in the case of speculative as well as of practical reason the same truth and the same rectitude exists among all and is equally known to all. In the case, however, of the proper or peculiar conclusions of speculative reason, the same truth obtains among all, even though it is not known equally to all. For it is true among all men that the three angles of a triangle are equal to two right angles, even though not all men know this. But in the case of the proper or peculiar conclusions of the practical reason there is neither the same truth and rectitude among all men, nor, where it does exist, is it equally known to all. Thus it is true and right among all men that action proceed in accordance with reason. From this principle there follows as a proper conclusion that deposits should be restored to the owner. This conclusion is indeed true in the majority of cases. But a case must possibly arise in which such restitution is harmful and consequently contrary to reason; so, for example, if things deposited were claimed so that they might be used against the fatherland. This uncertainty increases the more particular the cases become: as, for example, if it were laid down that the restitution should take place in a certain way, with certain *definite* precautions; for as the limiting particular conditions become more numerous, so do the possibilities decrease that render the principle normally applicable, with the result that neither the restitution nor the failure to do so can be rigorously presented as right.

It follows therefore that natural law in its first common principles is the same among all men, both as to validity and recognition (something is right for all and is so by all recognized). But as to certain proper or derived norms, which are, as it were, conclusions of these common principles, they are valid and are so recognized by all men only in the majority of cases. For in special cases they may prove defective both as to validity because of certain particular impediments (just as things of nature in the sphere of generation and corruption prove to be defective because of impediments) and also as to recognition. And this because some men have a reason that has been distorted by passion, or by evil habits, or by bad natural relations. Such was the case among the ancient Germans, who failed to recognize theft as contrary to justice, as Julius Caesar relates, even though it is an explicit violation of natural law.

*Reply Obj. 1.* The meaning of the sentence quoted is not that whatever is contained in the Law and the Gospel belongs to the natural law, since they contain many things that are above nature, but that whatever belongs to the natural law is fully contained in them. Wherefore Gratian, after saying that "the natural law is what is contained in the Law and the Gospel," adds at once, by way of example, "by which everyone is commanded to do to others as he would be done by."

*Reply Obj. 2.* The saying of the Philosopher is to be understood of things that are naturally just, not as general principles, but as conclusions drawn from them, having rectitude in the majority of cases, but failing in a few.

*Reply Obj. 3.* As, in man, reason rules and commands the other powers, so all the natural inclinations belonging to the other powers must needs be directed according to reason. Wherefore it is universally right for all men that all their inclinations should be directed according to reason.

## FIFTH ARTICLE
### WHETHER THE NATURAL LAW CAN BE CHANGED?

*We proceed thus to the Fifth Article:*

*Objection 1.* It would seem that the natural law can be changed. Because on Ecclesiasticus xvii. 9, "He gave them instructions, and the law of life," the gloss says: "He wished the law of the letter to be written, in order to correct the law of nature." But that which is corrected is changed. Therefore the natural law can be changed.

*Obj. 2.* Further, the slaying of the innocent, adultery, and theft are against the natural law. But we find these things changed by God: as when God commanded Abraham to slay his innocent son; and when He ordered the Jews to borrow and purloin the vessels of the Egyptians; and when He commanded Osee to take to himself "a wife of fornications." Therefore the natural law can be changed.

*Obj. 3.* Further, Isidore says that "the possession of all things in common and universal freedom are matters of natural law." But these things are seen to be changed by human laws. Therefore it seems that the natural law is subject to change.

*On the contrary,* It is said in the *Decretals*: "The natural law dates from the creation of the rational creature. It does not vary according to time, but remains unchangeable."

*I answer that,* A change in the natural law may be understood in two ways. First, by way of addition. In this sense nothing hinders the natural law from being changed, since many things, for the benefit of human life, have been added over and above the natural law, both by the divine law and by human laws.

Secondly, a change in the natural law may be understood by way of subtraction, so that what previously was according to the natural law ceases to be so. In this sense the natural law is altogether unchangeable in its first principles, but in its secondary principles, which, as we have said (A. 4), are certain special conclusions drawn from the first principles, the natural law is not changed so that what it prescribes be not right in most cases. But it may be changed in some particular cases of rare occurrence, through some special causes hindering the observance of such precepts, as stated above (A. 4).

*Reply Obj. 1.* The written law is said to be given for the correction of the natural law, either because it supplies what was wanting to the natural law or because the natural law was perverted in the hearts of some men, as to certain matters, so that they esteemed those things good which are naturally evil; which perversion stood in need of correction.

*Reply Obj. 2.* All men alike, both guilty and innocent, die the death of nature; which death of nature is inflicted by the power of God on account of original sin,

according to 1 Kings ii. 6: "The Lord killeth and maketh alive." Consequently, by
the command of God, death can be inflicted on any man, guilty or innocent,
without any injustice whatever.—In like manner adultery is intercourse with
another's wife, who is allotted to him by the law emanating from God. Consequently intercourse with any woman, by the command of God, is neither adultery
nor fornication.—The same applies to theft, which is the taking of another's
property. For whatever is taken by the command of God, to Whom all things
belong, is not taken against the will of its owner, whereas it is in this that theft
consists. Nor is it only in human things that whatever is commanded by God is
right, but also in natural things—whatever is done by God is, in some way,
natural, as stated in the First Part.

*Reply Obj. 3.* A thing is said to belong to the natural law in two ways. First,
because nature inclines thereto: e.g., that one should not do harm to another.
Secondly, because nature did not bring in the contrary: thus we might say that for
man to be naked is of the natural law because nature did not give him clothes, but
art invented them. In this sense, "the possession of all things in common and
universal freedom" are said to be of the natural law because, to wit, the distinction
of possessions and slavery were not brought in by nature, but devised by human
reason for the benefit of human life. Accordingly the law of nature was not
changed in this respect, except by addition.

SIXTH ARTICLE
WHETHER THE LAW OF NATURE CAN BE ABOLISHED
FROM THE HEART OF MAN?

*We proceed thus to the Sixth Article:*

*Objection 1.* It would seem that the natural law can be abolished from the
heart of man. Because of Romans ii. 14, "When the Gentiles who have not the
law," etc., a gloss says that "the law of righteousness, which sin had blotted out,
is graven on the heart of man when he is restored by grace." But the law of
righteousness is the law of nature. Therefore the law of nature can be blotted out.

*Obj. 2.* Further, the law of grace is more efficacious than the law of nature.
But the law of grace is blotted out by sin. Much more therefore can the law of
nature be blotted out.

*Obj. 2.* Further, that which is established by law is made just. But many
things are established by law which are contrary to the law of nature. Therefore
the law of nature can be abolished from the heart of man.

*On the contrary,* Augustine says: "Thy law is written in the hearts of men,
which iniquity itself effaces not." But the law which is written in men's hearts is
the natural law. Therefore the natural law cannot be blotted out.

*I answer that,* As stated above (AA. 4, 5), there belong to the natural law,
first, certain most general precepts, that are known to all; and secondly, certain
secondary and more detailed precepts, which are, as it were, conclusions following
closely from first principles. As to those general principles, the natural law, in the
abstract, can nowise be blotted out from men's hearts. But it is blotted out in the

case of a particular action, in so far as reason is hindered from applying the general principle to a particular point of practice, on account of concupiscence or some other passion, as stated above. But as to the other, i.e., the secondary precepts, the natural law can be blotted out from the human heart either by evil persuasions, just as in speculative matters errors occur in respect of necessary conclusions, or by vicious customs and corrupt habits, as among some men theft and even unnatural vices, as the Apostle states, were not esteemed sinful.

*Reply Obj. 1.* Sin blots out the law of nature in particular cases, not universally, except perchance in regard to the secondary precepts of the natural law, in the way stated above.

*Reply Obj. 2.* Although grace is more efficacious than nature, yet nature is more essential to man and therefore more enduring.

*Reply Obj. 3.* The argument is true of the secondary precepts of the natural law, against which some legislators have framed certain enactments which are unjust.

## QUESTION 95
## OF HUMAN LAW
### (In Four Articles)

WE must now consider human law, and (1) this law considered in itself, (2) its power, (3) its mutability. Under the first head there are four points of inquiry: (1) its utility; (2) its origin; (3) its quality; (4) its division.

### FIRST ARTICLE
### WHETHER IT WAS USEFUL FOR LAWS TO BE FRAMED BY MEN?

*We proceed thus to the First Article:*

*Objection 1.* It would seem that it was not useful for laws to be framed by men. Because the purpose of every law is that man be made good thereby, as stated above (Q. 92, A. 1). But men are more to be induced to be good willingly, by means of admonitions, than against their will, by means of laws. Therefore there was no need to frame laws.

*Obj. 2.* Further, as the Philosopher says, "men have recourse to a judge as to animate justice." But animate justice is better than inanimate justice, which is contained in laws. Therefore it would have been better for the execution of justice to be entrusted to the decision of judges than to frame laws in addition.

*Obj. 3.* Further, every law is framed for the direction of human actions, as is evident from what has been stated above (Q. 90, AA. 1, 2). But since human actions are about singulars, which are infinite in number, matters pertaining to the direction of human actions cannot be taken into sufficient consideration except by a wise man, who looks into each one of them. Therefore it would have been better for human acts to be directed by the judgment of wise men than by the framing of laws. Therefore there was no need of human laws.

*On the contrary,* Isidore says: "Laws were made that in fear thereof human audacity might be held in check, that innocence might be safeguarded in the midst of wickedness, and that the dread of punishment might prevent the wicked from doing harm." But these things are most necessary to mankind. Therefore it was necessary that human laws should be made.

*I answer that*, As stated above (Q. 63, A. 1; Q. 94, A. 3), man has a natural aptitude for virtue, but the perfection of virtue must be acquired by man by means of some kind of training. Thus we observe that man is helped by industry in his necessities, for instance, in food and clothing. Certain beginnings of these he has from nature, viz., his reason and his hands, but he has not the full complement, as other animals have to whom nature has given sufficiency of clothing and food. Now it is difficult to see how man could suffice for himself in the matter of this training, since the perfection of virtue consists chiefly in withdrawing man from undue pleasures, to which above all man is inclined, and especially the young, who are more capable of being trained. Consequently a man needs to receive this training from another, whereby to arrive at the perfection of virtue. And as to those young people who are inclined to acts of virtue, by their good natural disposition, or by custom, or rather by the gift of God, paternal training suffices, which is by admonitions. But since some are found to be depraved and prone to vice, and not easily amenable to words, it was necessary for such to be restrained from evil by force and fear, in order that, at least, they might desist from evil-doing and leave others in peace, and that they themselves, by being habituated in this way, might be brought to do willingly what hitherto they did from fear, and thus become virtuous. Now this kind of training which compels through fear of punishment is the discipline of laws. Therefore, in order that man might have peace and virtue, it was necessary for laws to be framed, for, as the Philosopher says, "as man is the most noble of animals if he be perfect in virtue, so is he the lowest of all if he be severed from law and righteousness"; because man can use his reason to devise means of satisfying his lusts and evil passions, which other animals are unable to do.

*Reply Obj. 1.* Men who are well disposed are led willingly to virtue by being admonished better than by coercion, but men who are evilly disposed are not led to virtue unless they are compelled.

*Reply Obj. 2.* As the Philosopher says, "It is better that all things be regulated by law than left to be decided by judges"; and this for three reasons. First, because it is easier to find a few wise men competent to frame right laws than to find the many who would be necessary to judge aright of each single case. Secondly, because those who make laws consider long beforehand what laws to make, whereas judgment on each single case has to be pronounced as soon as it arises; and it is easier for man to see what is right by taking many instances into consideration than by considering one solitary fact. Thirdly, because lawgivers judge in the abstract and of future events, whereas those who sit in judgment judge of things present, toward which they are affected by love, hatred, or some kind of cupidity; wherefore their judgment is perverted.

Since then the animated justice of the judge is not found in every man, and since it can be deflected, therefore it was necessary, whenever possible, for the law to determine how to judge, and for very few matters to be left to the decision of men.

*Reply Obj. 3.* Certain individual facts which cannot be covered by the law "have necessarily to be committed to judges," as the Philosopher says in the same passage; for instance, "concerning something that has happened or not happened," and the like.

SECOND ARTICLE

WHETHER EVERY HUMAN LAW IS DERIVED FROM THE
NATURAL LAW?

*We proceed thus to the Second Article*:

*Objection 1.* It would seem that not every human law is derived from the natural law. For the Philosopher says that "the legal just is that which originally was a matter of indifference." But those things which arise from the natural law are not matters of indifference. Therefore the enactments of human laws are not all derived from the natural law.

*Obj. 2.* Further, positive law is contrasted with natural law, as stated by Isidore and the Philosopher. But those things which flow as conclusions from the general principles of the natural law belong to the natural law, as stated above (Q. 84, A. 4). Therefore that which is established by human law does not belong to the natural law.

*Obj. 3.* Further, the law of nature is the same for all, since the Philosopher says that "the natural just is that which is equally valid everywhere." If, therefore, human laws were derived from the natural law, it would follow that they too are the same for all, which is clearly false.

*Obj. 4.* Further, it is possible to give a reason for things which are derived from the natural law. But "it is not possible to give the reason for all the legal enactments of the lawgivers," as the Jurist says. Therefore not all human laws are derived from the natural law.

*On the contrary*, Cicero says: "Things which emanated from nature and were approved by custom were sanctioned by fear and reverence for the laws."

*I answer that*, As Augustine says, "that which is not just seems to be no law at all"; wherefore the force of a law depends on the extent of its justice. Now in human affairs a thing is said to be just from being right according to the rule of reason. But the first rule of reason is the law of nature, as is clear from what has been stated above (Q. 91, A. 2 *ad* 2). Consequently, every human law has just so much of the nature of law as it is derived from the law of nature. But if in any point it deflects from the law of nature, it is no longer a law but a perversion of law.

But it must be noted that something may be derived from the natural law in two ways: first, as a conclusion from premises; secondly, by way of determination of certain generalities. The first way is like to that by which, in the sciences, demonstrated conclusions are drawn from the principles, while the second mode is likened to that whereby, in the arts, general forms are particularized as to details: thus the craftsman needs to determine the general form of a house to some particular shape. Some things are therefore derived from the general principles of the natural law by way of conclusions, e.g., that "one must not kill" may be derived as a conclusion from the principle that "one should do harm to no man"; while some are derived therefrom by way of determination, e.g., the law of nature has it that the evildoer should be punished; but that he be punished in this or that way is not directly by natural law but is a derived determination of it.

Accordingly, both modes of derivation are found in the human law. But those things which are derived in the first way are contained in human law, not as emanating therefrom exclusively, but having some force from the natural law also. But those things which are derived in the second way have no other force than that of human law.

*Reply Obj. 1.* The Philosopher is speaking of those enactments which are by way of determination or specification of the precepts of the natural law.

*Reply Obj. 2.* This argument avails for those things that are derived from the natural law, by way of conclusions.

*Reply Obj. 3.* The general principles of the natural law cannot be applied to all men in the same way, on account of the great variety of human affairs, and hence arises the diversity of positive laws among various people.

*Reply Obj. 4.* These words of the Jurist are to be understood as referring to decisions of rulers in determining particular points of the natural law, on which determinations the judgment of expert and prudent men is based as on its principles, in so far, to wit, as they see at once what is the best thing to decide.

Hence the Philosopher says that in such matters "we ought to pay as much attention to the undemonstrated sayings and opinions of persons who surpass us in experience, age, and prudence as to their demonstrations."

### THIRD ARTICLE
### WHETHER ISIDORE'S DESCRIPTION OF THE QUALITY OF POSITIVE LAW IS APPROPRIATE?

*We proceed thus to the Third Article:*

*Objection 1.* It would seem that Isidore's description of the quality of positive law is not appropriate, when he says: "Law shall be virtuous, just, possible, in agreement with nature, and in agreement with the customs of the country, suitable to place and time, necessary, useful; clearly expressed, lest by its obscurity it lead to misunderstanding; framed for no private benefit, but for the common good." Because he had previously expressed the quality of law in three conditions, saying that "law is anything founded on reason provided that it foster religion, be helpful to discipline, and further the common weal." Therefore it was needless to add any further conditions to these.

*Obj. 2.* Further, justice is included in virtue, as Cicero says. Therefore after saying "virtuous" it was superfluous to add "just."

*Obj. 3.* Further, written law is contrasted to custom, according to Isidore. Therefore it should not be stated in the definition of law that it is "in agreement with the customs of the country."

*Obj. 4.* Further, a thing may be necessary in two ways. It may be necessary simply because it cannot be otherwise; and that which is necessary in this way is not subject to human judgment, wherefore human law is not concerned with necessity of this kind. Again a thing may be necessary for an end, and this necessity is the same as usefulness. Therefore it is superfluous to say both "necessary" and "useful."

*On the contrary* stands the authority of Isidore.

*I answer that,* Whenever a thing is for an end, its form must be determined proportionately to that end, as the form of a saw is such as to be suitable for cutting (*Physics* ii. text. 88). Again, everything that is ruled and measured must have a form proportionate to its rule and measure. Now both these conditions are verified of human law, since it is both something ordained to an end and is a rule or measure ruled or measured by a higher measure. And this higher measure is twofold, viz., the divine law and the natural law, as explained above (A. 2; Q. 93, A. 3). Now the end of human law is to be useful to man, as the Jurist states. Wherefore Isidore, in determining the nature of law, lays down, at first, three conditions: viz., that it "foster religion," inasmuch as it is proportionate to the divine law; that it be "helpful to discipline," inasmuch as it is proportionate to the natural law; and that it "further the common weal" inasmuch as it is proportionate to the utility of mankind.

All the other conditions mentioned by him are reduced to these three. For it is called "virtuous" because it fosters religion. And when he goes on to say that it should be "just, possible, in accord with nature, and in accordance with the customs of the country, adapted to place and time," he implies that it should be helpful to discipline. For human discipline depends, first, on the order of reason, to which he refers by saying "just"; secondly, it depends on the capacity of the agent, because discipline must be suitable to each one according to his possibility, taking into account also the possibility of nature (for the same burdens should be not laid on children as on adults), and should be according to human customs, since man cannot live alone in society, paying no heed to others; thirdly, it depends on certain circumstances, in respect of which he says, "adapted to place and time."—The remaining words, "necessary," "useful," etc., mean that law should further the common weal, so that "necessity" refers to the removal of evils, "usefulness" to the attainment of good, "clearness of expression" to the need of preventing any harm ensuing from the law itself.—And since, as stated above (Q. 90, A. 2), law is ordained to the common good this is expressed in the last part of the description.

This suffices for the *Replies* to the *Objections.* . . .

## QUESTION 96
## OF THE POWER OF HUMAN LAW
### (*In Six Articles*)

WE must now consider the power of human law. Under this head there are six points of inquiry: (1) Whether human law should be framed for the community? (2) Whether human law should repress all vices? (3) Whether human law is competent to direct all acts of virtue? (4) Whether it binds man in conscience? (5) Whether all men are subject to human law? (6) Whether those who are under the law may act beside the letter of the law?

### FIRST ARTICLE
### WHETHER HUMAN LAW SHOULD BE FRAMED FOR THE COMMUNITY RATHER THAN FOR THE INDIVIDUAL?

*We proceed thus to the First Article*:

*Objection 1.* It would seem that human law should be framed, not for the community, but rather for the individual. For the Philosopher says that "the legal just . . . includes all particular acts of legislation . . . and all those matters which are the subject of decrees," which are also individual matters, since decrees are framed about individual actions. Therefore law is framed not only for the community, but also for the individual.

*Obj. 2.* Further, law is the director of human acts, as stated above (Q. 90, AA. 1, 2). But human acts are about individual matters. Therefore human laws should be framed, not for the community, but rather for the individual.

*Obj. 3.* Further, law is a rule and measure of human acts, as stated above (Q. 90, AA. 1, 2). But a measure should be most certain, as stated in *Metaphysics* x. Since therefore in human acts no general proposition can be so certain as not to fail in some individual cases, it seems that laws should be framed not in general but for individual cases.

*On the contrary,* The Jurist says that "laws should be made to suit the majority of instances; and they are not framed according to what may possibly happen in an individual case."

*I answer that,* Whatever is for an end should be proportionate to that end. Now the end of law is the common good; because, as Isidore says, "law should be framed, not for any private benefit, but for the common good of all the citizens." Hence human laws should be proportionate to the common good. Now the common good comprises many things. Wherefore law should take account of many things, as to persons, as to activities, and as to times; because the community of the state is composed of many persons and its good is procured by many actions; nor is it established to endure for only a short time, but to last for all time by the citizens succeeding one another, as Augustine says.

*Reply Obj. 1.* The Philosopher divides the "legal just," i.e., positive law, into three parts. For some things are laid down simply in a general way: and these are the general laws. Of these he says that "the legal is that which originally was a matter of indifference, but which, when enacted, is so no longer," as the fixing of the ransom of a captive. Some things affect the community in one respect and individuals in another. These are called "privileges," i.e., "private laws," as it were, because they regard private persons, although their power extends to many matters; and in regard to these, he adds, "and further any regulations enacted for particular cases."—Other matters are legal, not through being laws, but through being applications of general laws to particular cases, such are decrees which have the force of law; and in regard to these, he adds "all matters subject to decrees."

*Reply Obj. 2.* A principle of direction should be applicable to many, wherefore the Philosopher says that all things belonging to one genus are measured by one which is the first in that genus. For if there were as many rules or measures as there are things measured or ruled, they would cease to be of use, since their use consists in being applicable to many things. Hence law would be of no use if it did not extend further than to one single act. Because the decrees of prudent men are made for the purpose of directing individual actions, whereas law is a general precept, as stated above (Q. 92, A. 2, Obj. 2).

*Reply Obj. 3.* "We must not seek the same degree of certainty in all things." Consequently in contingent matters, such as natural and human things, it is enough for a thing to be certain, as being true in the greater number of instances, though at times and less frequently it fail.

## SECOND ARTICLE
## WHETHER IT BELONGS TO HUMAN LAW TO REPRESS ALL VICES?

*We proceed thus to the Second Article:*

*Objection 1.* It would seem that it belongs to human law to repress all vices. For Isidore says that "laws were made in order that, in fear thereof, man's audacity might be held in check." But it would not be held in check sufficiently unless all evils were repressed by law. Therefore human law should repress all evils.

*Obj. 2.* Further, the intention of the lawgiver is to make the citizens virtuous. But a man cannot be virtuous unless he forbear from all kinds of vice. Therefore it belongs to human law to repress all vices.

*Obj. 3.* Further, human law is derived from the natural law, as stated above (Q. 95, A. 2). But all vices are contrary to the law of nature. Therefore human law should repress all vices.

*On the contrary,* We read in *De libero arbitrio* i. 5: "It seems to me that the law which is written for the governing of the people rightly permits these things, and that divine providence punishes them." But divine providence punishes nothing but vices. therefore human law- rightly allows some vices, by not repressing them.

*I answer that,* As stated above (Q. 90, AA. 1, 2), law is framed as a rule or measure of human acts. Now a measure should be homogeneous with that which it measures, as stated in *Metaphysics* x text. 3, 4, since different things are measured by different measures. Wherefore laws imposed on men should also be in keeping with their condition, for, as Isidore says, law should be "possible both according to nature, and according to the customs of the country." Now possibility or faculty of action is due to an interior habit or disposition, since the same thing is not possible to one who has not a virtuous habit as is possible to one who has. Thus the same is not possible to a child as to a full-grown man; for which reason the law for children is not the same as for adults, since many things are permitted to children which in an adult are punished by law or at any rate are open to blame. In like manner many things are permissible to men not perfect in virtue which would be intolerable in a virtuous man.

Now human law is framed for a number of human beings, the majority of whom are not perfect in virtue. Wherefore human laws do not forbid all vices from which the virtuous abstain, but only the more grievous vices from which it is possible for the majority to abstain; and chiefly those that are to the hurt of others, without the prohibition of which human society could not be maintained: thus human law prohibits murder, theft, and suchlike.

*Reply Obj. 1.* Audacity seems to refer to the assailing of others. Consequently it belongs to those sins chiefly whereby one's neighbor is injured; and these sins are forbidden by human law, as stated.

*Reply Obj. 2.* The purpose of human law is to lead men to virtue, not suddenly, but gradually. Wherefore it does not lay upon the multitude of imperfect men the burdens of those who are already virtuous, viz., that they should abstain from all evil. Otherwise these imperfect ones, being unable to bear such precepts, would break out into yet greater evils; thus it is written: "He that violently bloweth his nose, bringeth out blood"; and that if "new wine," i.e., precepts of a perfect life, is "put into old bottles," i.e., into imperfect men, "the bottles break, and the wine runneth out," i.e., the precepts are despised and those men, from contempt, break out into evils worse still.

*Reply Obj. 3.* The natural law is a participation in us of the eternal law, while human law falls short of the eternal law. Now Augustine says: "The law which is framed for the government of states allows and leaves unpunished many things that are punished by divine providence. Nor, if this law does not attempt to do everything, is this a reason why it should be blamed for what it does." Wherefore, too, human law does not prohibit everything that is forbidden by the natural law.

### THIRD ARTICLE
### WHETHER HUMAN LAW PRESCRIBES ACTS OF ALL THE VIRTUES?

*We proceed thus to the Third Article:*

*Objection 1.* It would seem that human law does not prescribe acts of all the virtues. For vicious acts are contrary to acts of virtue. But human law does not prohibit all vices, as stated above (A. 2). Therefore neither does it prescribe all acts of virtue.

*Obj. 2.* Further, a virtuous act proceeds from a virtue. But virtue is the end of law, so that whatever is from a virtue cannot come under a precept of law.

Therefore human law does not prescribe all acts of virtue.

*Obj. 3.* Further, law is ordained to the common good, as stated above (Q. 90, A. 2). But some acts of virtue are ordained, not to the common good, but to private good. Therefore the law does not prescribe all acts of virtue.

*On the contrary,* The Philosopher says that the law "prescribes the performance of the acts of a brave man . . . and the acts of the temperate man . . . and the acts of the meek man; and in like manner as regards the other virtues and vices, prescribing the former, forbidding the latter."

*I answer that,* The species of virtues are distinguished by their objects, as explained above. Now all the objects of virtues can be referred either to the private good of an individual or to the common good of the multitude: thus matters of fortitude may be achieved either for the safety of the state or for upholding the rights of a friend, and in like manner with the other virtues. But law, as stated above (Q. 90, A. 2), is ordained to the common good. Wherefore there is no virtue whose acts cannot be prescribed by the law. Nevertheless human law does not prescribe concerning all the acts of every virtue, but only in regard to those that are ordainable to the common good—either immediately, as when certain things are done directly for the common good, or mediately, as when a lawgiver prescribes certain things pertaining to proper instruction whereby the citizens are directed in the upholding of the common good of justice and peace.

*Reply Obj. 1.* Human law does not forbid all vicious acts by the obligation of a precept, as neither does it prescribe all acts of virtue. But it forbids certain acts of each vice, just as it prescribes some acts of each virtue.

*Reply Obj. 2.* An act is said to be an act of virtue in two ways. First, from the fact that a man does something virtuous; thus the act of justice is to do what is right, and an act of fortitude is to do brave things—and in this way law prescribes certain acts of virtue. Secondly, an act of virtue is when a man does a virtuous thing in a way in which a virtuous man does it. Such an act always proceeds from virtue, and it does not come under a precept of law, but is the end at which every lawgiver aims.

*Reply Obj. 3.* There is no virtue whose act is not ordainable to the common good, as stated above, either mediately or immediately.

FOURTH ARTICLE

WHETHER HUMAN LAW BINDS A MAN IN CONSCIENCE?

*We proceed thus to the Fourth Article:*

*Objection 1.* It would seem that human law does not bind a man in conscience. For an inferior power has no jurisdiction in a court of higher power. But the power of man which frames human law is beneath the divine power. Therefore human law cannot impose its precept in a divine court, such as is the court of conscience.

*Obj. 2.* Further, the judgment of conscience depends chiefly on the commandments of God. But sometimes God's commandments are made void by human laws, according to Matthew xv. 6: "You have made void the commandment of

God for your tradition." Therefore human law does not bind a man in conscience.

*Obj. 3.* Further, human laws often bring loss of character and injury on man, according to Isaias x. 1 ff.: "Woe to them that make wicked laws, and when they write, write injustice; to oppress the poor in judgment, and do violence to the cause of the humble of My people." But it is lawful for anyone to avoid oppression and violence. Therefore human laws do not bind man in conscience.

*On the contrary,* It is written: "This is thanksworthy, if for conscience . . . a man endure sorrows, suffering wrongfully."

*I answer that,* Laws framed by man are either just or unjust. If they be just, they have the power of binding in conscience, from the eternal law whence they are derived, according to Proverbs viii. 15: "By Me kings reign, and lawgivers decree just things." Now laws are said to be just—from the end, when, to wit, they are ordained to the common good—and from their author, that is to say, when the law that is made does not exceed the power of the lawgiver—and from their form, when, to wit, burdens are laid on the subjects, according to an equality of proportion and with a view to the common good. For, since one man is a part of the community, each man, in all that he is and has, belongs to the community, just as a part, in all that it is, belongs to the whole; wherefore nature inflicts a loss on the part in order to save the whole, so that on this account such laws as these which impose proportionate burdens are just and binding in conscience and are legal laws.

On the other hand, laws may be unjust in two ways: first, by being contrary to human good, through being opposed to the things mentioned above—either in respect of the end, as when an authority imposes on his subjects burdensome laws, conducive, not to the common good, but rather to his own cupidity or vainglory; or in respect of the author, as when a man makes a law that goes beyond the power committed to him; or in respect of the form, as when burdens are imposed unequally on the community, although with a view to the common good. The like are acts of violence rather than laws, because, as Augustine says, "A law that is not just, seems to be no law at all." Wherefore such laws do not bind in conscience, except perhaps in order to avoid scandal or disturbance, for which cause a man should even yield his right, according to Matthew v. 40, 41: "If a man . . . take away thy coat, let go thy cloak also unto him; and whosoever will force thee one mile, go with him other two."

Secondly, laws may be unjust through being opposed to the divine good: such are the laws of tyrants inducing to idolatry or to anything else contrary to the divine law; and laws of this kind must nowise be observed because, as stated in Acts v. 29, "we ought to obey God rather than men."

*Reply Obj. 1.* As the Apostle says, all human power is from God . . . "therefore he that resisteth the power" in matters that are within its scope "resisteth the ordinance of God"; so that he becomes guilty according to his conscience.

*Reply Obj. 2.* This argument is true of laws that are contrary to the commandments of God, which is beyond the scope of (human) power. Wherefore in such matters human law should not be obeyed.

*Reply Obj. 3.* This argument is true of a law that inflicts unjust hurt on its subjects. The power that man holds from God does not extend to this, wherefore neither in such matters is man bound to obey the law, provided he avoid giving scandal or inflicting a more grievous hurt.

FIFTH ARTICLE

WHETHER ALL ARE SUBJECT TO THE LAW?

*We proceed thus to the Fifth Article*:

*Objection 1.* It would seem that not all are subject to the law. For those alone are subject to a law for whom a law is made. But the Apostle says: "The law is not made for the just man." Therefore the just are not subject to the law.

*Obj. 2.* Further, Pope Urban says: "He that is guided by a private law need not for any reason be bound by the public law." Now all spiritual men are led by the private law of the Holy Ghost, for they are the sons of God, of whom it is said: "Whosoever are led by the Spirit of God, they are the sons of God." Therefore not all men are subject to human law.

*Obj. 3.* Further, the Jurist says that "the sovereign is exempt from the laws." But he that is exempt from the law is not bound thereby. Therefore not all are subject to the law.

*On the contrary*, The Apostle says: "Let every soul be subject to the higher powers." But subjection to a power seems to imply subjection to the laws framed by that power. Therefore all men should be subject to human law.

*I answer that*, As stated above (Q. 90, AA. 1, 2; A. 3 *ad* 2), the notion of law contains two things: first, that it is a rule of human acts; secondly, that it has coercive power. Wherefore a man may be subject to law in two ways. First, as the regulated is subject to the regulator; and, in this way, whoever is subject to a power is subject to the law framed by that power. But it may happen in two ways that one is not subject to a power. In one way, by being altogether free from its authority; hence the subjects of one city or kingdom are not bound by the laws of the sovereign of another city or kingdom, since they are not subject to his authority. In another way, by being under a yet higher law; thus the subject of a proconsul should be ruled by his command, but not in those matters in which the subject receives his orders from the emperor, for in these matters he is not bound by the mandate of the lower authority, since he is directed by that of a higher. In this way one who is simply subject to a law may not be subject thereto in certain matters in respect of which he is ruled by a higher law.

Secondly, a man is said to be subject to a law as the coerced is subject to the coercer. In this way the virtuous and righteous are not subject to the law, but only the wicked. Because coercion and violence are contrary to the will, but the will of the good is in harmony with the law, whereas the will of the wicked is discordant from it. Wherefore in this sense the good are not subject to the law, but only the wicked.

*Reply Obj. 1.* This argument is true of subjection by way of coercion, for, in this way, "the law is not made for the just men: because they are a law to themselves," since they "show the work of the law written in their hearts," as the Apostle says. Consequently the law does not enforce itself upon them as it does on the wicked.

*Reply Obj. 2.* The law of the Holy Ghost is above all law framed by man; and therefore spiritual men, in so far as they are led by the law of the Holy Ghost, are not subject to the law in those matters that are inconsistent with the guidance of the Holy Ghost. Nevertheless the very fact that spiritual men are subject to law is due to the leading of the Holy Ghost, according to 1 Peter ii. 13: "Be ye subject . . . to every human creature for God's sake."

*Reply Obj. 3.* The sovereign is said to be "exempt from the law," as to its coercive power, since, properly speaking, no man is coerced by himself, and law has no coercive power save from the authority of the sovereign. Thus then is the sovereign said to be exempt from the law, because none is competent to pass sentence on him if he acts against the law. Wherefore on Psalm L. 6: "To Thee only have I sinned," a gloss says that "there is no man who can judge the deeds of a king."—But as to the directive force of law, the sovereign is subject to the law by his own will, according to the statement that "whatever law a man makes for another, he should keep himself." And a wise authority says: "Obey the law that thou makest thyself." Moreover the Lord reproaches those who "say and do not"; and who "bind heavy burdens and lay them on men's shoulders, but with a finger of their own they will not move them." Hence, in the judgment of God, the sovereign is not exempt from the law as to its directive force, but he should fulfill it of his own free will and not of constraint.—Again the sovereign is above the law in so far as, when it is expedient, he can change the law and dispense in it according to time and place. . . .

## QUESTION 97
## OF CHANGE IN LAWS
### (*In Four Articles*)

WE must now consider change in laws, under which head there are four points of inquiry: (1) Whether human law is changeable? (2) Whether it should always be changed whenever something better occurs? (3) Whether it is abolished by custom, and whether custom obtains the force of law? (4) Whether the application of human law should be changed by dispensation of those in authority?

### FIRST ARTICLE
### WHETHER HUMAN LAW SHOULD BE CHANGED IN ANY WAY?

*We proceed thus to the First Article*:

*Objection 1.* It would seem that human law should not be changed in any way at all. Because human law is derived from the natural law, as stated above (Q. 95, A. 2). But the natural law endures unchangeably. Therefore human law should also remain without any change.

*Obj. 2.* Further, as the Philosopher says, a measure should be absolutely stable. But human law is the measure of human acts, as stated above (Q. 90. AA. 1, 2). Therefore it should remain without change.

*Obj. 3.* Further, it is of the essence of law to be just and right, as stated above (Q. 95, A. 2). But that which is right once is right always. Therefore that which is law once should be always law.

*On the contrary,* Augustine says: "A temporal law, however just, may be justly changed in course of time."

*I answer that,* As stated above (Q. 92, A. 3), human law is a dictate of reason whereby human acts are directed. Thus there may be two causes for the just change of human law: one on the part of reason, the other on the part of man whose acts are regulated by law. The cause on the part of reason is that it seems natural to human reason to advance gradually from the imperfect to the perfect. Hence, in speculative sciences, we see that the teaching of the early philosophers was imperfect, and that it was afterward perfected by those who succeeded them. So also in practical matters; for those who first endeavored to discover something useful for the human community, not being able by themselves to take everything into consideration, set up certain institutions which were deficient in many ways, and these were changed by subsequent lawgivers who made institutions that might prove less frequently deficient in respect of the common weal.

On the part of man whose acts are regulated by law the law can be rightly changed on account of the changed condition of man, to whom different things are expedient according to the difference of his condition. An example is proposed by Augustine: "If the people have a sense of moderation and responsibility and are most careful guardians of the common weal, it is right to enact a law allowing such a people to choose their own magistrates for the government of the commonwealth. But if, as time goes on, the same people become so corrupt as to sell their votes and entrust the government to scoundrels and criminals, then the right of appointing their public officials is rightly forfeit to such a people, and the choice devolves to a few good men."

*Reply Obj. 1.* The natural law is a participation of the eternal law, as stated above (Q. 91, A. 2), and therefore endures without change, owing to the unchangeableness and perfection of the divine reason, the Author of nature. But the reason of man is changeable and imperfect wherefore his law is subject to change.—Moreover the natural law contains certain universal precepts which are everlasting, whereas human law contains certain particular precepts, according to various emergencies.

*Reply Obj. 2.* A measure should be as enduring as possible. But nothing can be absolutely unchangeable in things that are subject to change. And therefore human law cannot be altogether unchangeable.

*Reply Obj. 3.* In material things, straight (right) is predicated absolutely and therefore, as far as itself is concerned, always remains right. But right is predicated of law with reference to the common weal, to which one and the same thing is not always adapted, as stated above; wherefore rectitude of this kind is subject to change.

## SECOND ARTICLE
### WHETHER HUMAN LAW SHOULD ALWAYS BE CHANGED WHENEVER SOMETHING BETTER OCCURS?

*We proceed thus to the Second Article*:

*Objection 1.* It would seem that human law should be changed whenever something better occurs. Because human laws are devised by human reason, like other arts. But in the other arts, the tenets of former times give place to others if something better occurs. Therefore the same should apply to human laws.

*Obj. 2.* Further, by taking note of the past we can provide for the future. Now unless human laws had been changed when it was found possible to improve them, considerable inconvenience would have ensued because the laws of old were crude in many points. Therefore it seems that laws should be changed whenever anything better occurs to be enacted.

*Obj. 3.* Further, human laws are enacted about single acts of man. But we cannot acquire perfect knowledge in singular matters except by experience, which "requires time," as stated in *Ethics* ii. Therefore it seems that as time goes on it is possible for something better to occur for legislation.

*On the contrary*, It is stated in the *Decretals*: "It is absurd and a detestable shame that we should suffer those traditions to be changed which we have received from the fathers of old."

*I answer that*, As stated above (A. 1), human law is rightly changed in so far as such change is conducive to the common weal. But, to a certain extent, the mere change of law is of itself prejudicial to the common good because custom avails much for the observance of laws, seeing that what is done contrary to general custom, even in slight matters, is looked upon as grave. Consequently, when a law is changed, the binding power of the law is diminished in so far as custom is abolished. Wherefore human law should never be changed unless, in some way or other, the common weal be compensated according to the extent of the harm done in this respect. Such compensation may arise either from some very great and very evident benefit conferred by the new enactment or from the extreme urgency of the case, due to the fact that either the existing law is clearly unjust or its observance extremely harmful. Wherefore the Jurist says that "in establishing new laws, there should be evidence of the benefit to be derived, before departing from a law which has long been considered just."

*Reply Obj. 1.* Rules of art derive their force from reason alone, and therefore, whenever something better occurs, the rule followed hitherto should be changed. But "laws derive very great force from custom," as the Philosopher states; consequently they should not be quickly changed.

*Reply Obj. 2.* This argument proves that laws ought to be changed, not in view of any improvement, but for the sake of a great benefit or in a case of great urgency, as stated above. This answer applies also to the *Third Objection*.

## WHETHER CUSTOM CAN OBTAIN FORCE OF LAW?

*We proceed thus to the Third Article:*

*Objection 1.* It would seem that custom cannot obtain force of law, nor abolish a law. Because human law is derived from the natural law and from the divine law, as stated above (Q. 93, A. 3; Q. 95, A. 2). But human custom cannot change either the law of nature or the divine law. Therefore neither can it change human law.

*Obj. 2.* Further, many evils cannot make one good. But he who first acted against the law did evil. Therefore by multiplying such acts nothing good is the result. Now a law is something good, since it is a rule of human acts. Therefore law is not abolished by custom, so that the mere custom should obtain force of law.

*Obj. 3.* Further, the framing of laws belongs to those public men whose business it is to govern the community; wherefore private individuals cannot make laws. But custom grows by the acts of private individuals. Therefore custom cannot obtain force of law, so as to abolish the law.

*On the contrary,* Augustine says: "The customs of God's people and the institutions of our ancestors are to be considered as laws. And those who throw contempt on the customs of the Church ought to be punished as those who disobey the law of God."

*I answer that,* All law proceeds from the reason and will of the lawgiver: the divine and natural laws from the reasonable will of God, the human law from the will of man regulated by reason. Now just as human reason and will, in practical matters, may be made manifest by speech, so may they be made known by deeds, since seemingly a man chooses as good that which he carries into execution. But it is evident that by human speech law can be both changed and expounded in so far as it manifests the interior movement and thought of human reason. Wherefore by actions also, especially if they be repeated so as to make a custom, law can be changed and expounded; and also something can be established which obtains force of law in so far as by repeated external actions the inward movement of the will and concepts of reason are most effectually declared, for when a thing is done again and again, it seems to proceed from a deliberate judgment of reason. Accordingly custom has the force of law, abolishes law, and is the interpreter of law.

*Reply Obj. 1.* The natural and divine laws proceed from the divine will, as stated above. Wherefore they cannot be changed by a custom proceeding from the will of man, but only by divine authority. Hence it is that no custom can prevail over the divine or natural laws, for Isidore says: "Let custom yield to authority; evil customs should be eradicated by law and reason."

*Reply Obj. 2.* As stated above (Q. 96, A. 6), human laws fail in some cases, wherefore it is possible sometimes to act beside the law—namely, in a case where the law fails, yet the act will not be evil. And when such cases are multiplied, by reason of some change in man, then custom shows that the law is no longer useful, just as it might be declared by the verbal promulgation of a law to the contrary. If, however, the same reason remains for which the law was useful hitherto, then it is not the custom that prevails against the law, but the law that overcomes the custom, unless perhaps the sole reason for the law seeming useless be that it is not "possible according to the custom of the country," which has been stated to be one of the conditions of law. For it is not easy to set aside the custom of a whole people.

*Reply Obj. 3.* The people among whom a custom is introduced may be of two conditions. For if they are free and able to make their own laws, the consent of the whole people expressed by a custom counts far more in favor of a particular observance than does the authority of the sovereign, who has not the power to frame laws except as representing the people. Wherefore, although a single individual cannot make laws, yet the whole people can. If however the people have not the free power to make their own laws or to abolish a law made by a higher authority, nevertheless with such a people a prevailing custom obtains force of law in so far as it is tolerated by those to whom it belongs to make laws for that people; because by the very fact that they tolerate it they seem to approve of that which is introduced by custom.

FOURTH ARTICLE
## WHETHER THE RULERS OF THE PEOPLE CAN DISPENSE FROM HUMAN LAWS?

*We proceed thus to the Fourth Article*:

*Objection 1.* It would seem that the rulers of the people cannot dispense from human laws. For the law is established for the "common weal," as Isidore says. But the common good should not be set aside for the private convenience of an individual, because, as the Philosopher says, "the good of the nation is more godlike than the good of one man." Therefore it seems that a man should not be dispensed from acting in compliance with the general law.

*Obj. 2.* Further, those who are placed over others are commanded as follows: "You shall hear the little as well as the great; neither shall you respect any man's person, because it is the judgment of God." But to allow one man to do that which is equally forbidden to all seems to be respect of persons. Therefore the rulers of a community cannot grant such dispensations, since this is against a precept of the divine law.

*Obj. 3.* Further, human law, in order to be just, should accord with the natural and divine laws, else it would not *foster religion*, nor be *helpful to discipline* which is a requisite of law, as laid down by Isidore. But no man can dispense from the divine and natural laws. Neither, therefore, can he dispense from the human law.

*On the contrary*, The Apostle says: "A dispensation is committed to me."

*I answer that*, Dispensation, properly speaking, denotes a measuring out to individuals of some common goods: thus the head of a household is called a dispenser because to each member of the household he distributes work and necessaries of life in due weight and measure. Accordingly in every community a man is said to dispense, from the very fact that he directs how some general precept is to be fulfilled by each individual. Now it happens at times that a precept which is conducive to the common weal as a general rule is not good for a particular individual or in some particular case, either because it would hinder some greater good or because it would be the occasion of some evil, as explained above (Q. 96, A. 6). But it would be dangerous to leave this to the discretion of each individual, except perhaps by reason of an evident and sudden emergency, as stated above (*ibid*). Consequently he who is placed over a community is empowered to dispense in a human law that rests upon his authority, so that, when the law fails in its application to persons or circumstances, he may allow the precept of the law not to be observed. If however he grant this permission without any such reason and of his mere will, he will be an unfaithful or an imprudent dispenser: unfaithful, if he has not the common good in view; imprudent, if he ignores the reasons for granting dispensations. Hence our Lord says: "Who, thinkest thou, is the faithful and wise dispenser, whom his lord setteth over his family?"

*Reply Obj. 1.* When a person is dispensed from observing the general law, this should not be done to the prejudice of, but with the intention of benefiting, the common good.

*Reply Obj. 2.* It is not "respect of persons" if unequal measures are served out to those who are themselves unequal. Wherefore when the condition of any person requires that he should reasonably receive special treatment, it is not "respect of persons" if he be the object of special favor.

*Reply Obj. 3.* Natural law, so far as it contains general precepts, which never fail, does not allow of dispensation. In the other precepts, however, which are as conclusions of the general precepts, man sometimes grants a dispensation: for instance, that a loan should not be paid back to the betrayer of his country, or something similar. But to the divine law each man stands as a private person to the public law to which he is subject. Wherefore just as none can dispense from public human law, except the man from whom the law derives its authority, or his delegate, so, in the precepts of the divine law, which are from God, none can dispense but God or the man to whom He may give special power for that purpose.

# 10

# Notes on the Summa Theologica

1. Thomas Aquinas lived from roughly 1225-1274. His major intellectual contribution is sometimes thought to be a fusion of elements of Aristotle's thought into Augustinian and general Judaeo-Christian doctrine. For a brief biography without pretensions to technical scholarship, but which is often provocative and expressive, see G.K. CHESTERTON, SAINT THOMAS AQUINAS: "THE DUMB OX" (1956). In the preceding excerpts from the *Summa Theologica*, Aquinas's references to the "Philosopher" are to Aristotle, and those to the "Apostle" are to Paul. The "Jurist" refers to the third century Roman official Ulpian, whose work substantially influenced the later Roman Emperor Justinian's legal *Digest*.

2. For an understanding of Aquinas on political obligation, it is important to note that late in the *Summa Theologica*, and in particular in what is referred to as the second part of the second part, question 104, article 6, reply to objection 3, Aquinas specifies that "[m]an is bound to obey secular princes in so far as this is required by the order of justice. Wherefore if the prince's authority is not just but usurped, or if he commands what is unjust, his subjects are not bound to obey him, except perhaps accidentally, in order to avoid scandal or danger." See THE POLITICAL IDEAS OF ST. THOMAS AQUINAS 172 (Dino Bigongiari ed. 1953). Note that Aquinas recognizes what the lawyers would call lack of jurisdictional authority, *id.* at article 5, page 170, and that conflicts between what God commands and what the emperor commands must be resolved against the latter, *id.* Aquinas also discusses, with obvious ambivalence, some of the moral and strategic or practical issues associated with the possibility of a popular rebellion against a tyranny in Chapter 6 of his work translated as *On Kingship*. See THE POLITICAL IDEAS OF ST. THOMAS AQUINAS 188-92 (Dino Bigongiari ed. 1953).

3. For a brief discussion of the relationships and distinctions among eternal law, divine law, natural law, and human law according to Aquinas, see Norman Kretzmann, *Lex Iniusta Non Est Lex*, 33 AMERICAN JOURNAL OF JURIS-

PRUDENCE 99, 107 (1988).

4.  Is what Aquinas refers to as the eternal law—the divine order or plan of the universe—a matter of both prescriptive law; that is, what ought to be, as well as law in the sense of sheer regularity of physical behavior? Does Aquinas seem confused on this point, or is this combined concept appropriate? See D.J. O'CONNOR, AQUINAS AND THE NATURAL LAW 59 (1967). For a classic discussion that is similar in drawing upon several senses of the idea of law, see MONTESQUIEU, THE SPIRIT OF THE LAWS 1-3 (Thomas Nugent trans. 1962).

5.  Is Aquinas's principle that good is to be done and pursued and evil avoided really informative, or is it merely an empty truism? For a sense of the opposing views on this point, see RALPH MCINERNEY, ETHICA THOMISTICA 43-44 (1982).

6.  Aquinas seems to believe that something can be law only to the extent that it accords with reason. See Mark R. MacGuigan, *St. Thomas and Legal Obligation*, 35 NEW SCHOLASTICISM 281, 284 (1961). But since statements, commands, or rules can have degrees of reasonableness, this seems to imply that rules can have degrees of lawfulness. Is this a disturbing conclusion?

7.  Mark MacGuigan summarizes Aquinas on legal obligation in this fashion: "[A]n edict clearly at variance with natural law precepts is not law and is not binding in conscience, unless perhaps accidentally for purely extrinsic reasons, viz., the avoidance of scandal or the maintenance of civil peace. On the other hand, . . . every valid human law is binding in conscience, and . . . is thus obligatory primarily because of the natural law which exists within it." Mark R. MacGuigan, *St. Thomas and Legal Obligation*, 35 NEW SCHOLASTICISM 281, 309 (1961). Would anything be lost by conceding that a human law that conflicts with natural law is still, in some obvious senses, a law?

8.  For a sensible discussion of whether, or in what senses, an unjust law can still be said to be a law, see Edward J. Damich, *The Essence of Law According to Thomas Aquinas*, 30 AMERICAN JOURNAL OF JURISPRUDENCE 79 (1985). For responses to Damich, see R.J. Henle, *A Comment on Edward J. Damich's "The Essence of Law According to Thomas Aquinas,"* 33 AMERICAN JOURNAL OF JURISPRUDENCE 161 (1988); Norman Kretzmann, *Lex Iniusta Non Est Lex*, 33 AMERICAN JOURNAL OF JURISPRUDENCE 99, 101-02 n.6 (1988).

9.  Natural law theory is often credited with the resources to explain why a particular positive law can be unjust and in a sense even void. See Charles E. Rice, *Some Reasons For the Restoration of a Natural Law Jurisprudence*,

24 WAKE FOREST LAW REVIEW 539, 567 (1989). Consider whether theories not relying on natural law can give an at least equally satisfactory account in this respect.

10. Charles Rice notes that according to Aquinas, human law is to be framed for the common good of everyone. See Charles E. Rice, *Some Reasons for the Restoration of Natural Law Jurisprudence*, 24 WAKE FOREST LAW REVIEW 539, 564 (1989). Does Aquinas's theory require a richer and more elaborate theory of the common good than contemporary pluralist societies are likely to find plausible? Could a human law merely be just and right, without also promoting a genuinely universal common good more than some alternative law?

11. Could a just law ever benefit one group of people at the expense of another, perhaps in view of relevant past conduct by the latter group? Could such a law be said to promote the common good? See, for background, Norman Kretzmann, *Lex Iniusta Non Est Lex*, 33 AMERICAN JOURNAL OF JURISPRUDENCE 99, 110-11 (1988).

12. Would it be helpful to revise Aquinas's view so that "a just law is one that is enacted by legitimate authority, that is directed at a good end, and that pursues its end by fair means?" ROBERT E. RODES, JR., THE LEGAL ENTERPRISE 55 (1976). Will there be a problem in determining the ends for which laws are adopted? Won't most bad laws aim at, among other things, at least one good end? Consider a compulsory euthanasia law affecting everyone alike at age 80, where the society is poor and medical care expensive. Can it be said that such a law, if universally applied, is unfair, as opposed to being morally wrong?

13. For Aquinas, it has been argued, the obligation of political obedience is based upon the divine and natural order and upon divine and natural law, which, in establishing what is just and unjust, also set moral limits to political obligation. See A.P. D'Entrèves, *Thomas Aquinas*, in ESSAYS IN THE HISTORY OF POLITICAL THOUGHT 97, 104 (Isaac Kramnick ed. 1969).

14. According to Aquinas, do laws have no function other than to lead persons to virtue? See Charles E. Rice, *Some Reasons For the Restoration of a Natural Law Jurisprudence*, 24 WAKE FOREST LAW REVIEW 539, 564 (1989). Is a law requiring that all driving be done on the right side of the road an encouragement to virtue, or is it a more or less arbitrary solution to a social coordination problem?

15. On the co-ordinating function of the law, it has been said that "[a]ccording

to Aquinas, government would be required even if there were no evildoers and even if no one was inclined to break the peace. . . . Even if no one was disposed to infringe the traffic regulations, the latter would still be necessary, and so there must be an authority to settle and prescribe them." F.C. COPLESTON, AQUINAS 237 (1955).

16. As Aquinas describes natural law, are the obligations of the natural law merely externally imposed restraints upon human nature? See Mark R. MacGuigan, *St. Thomas and Legal Obligation*, 35 NEW SCHOLASTICISM 281, 304 (1961).

17. On Aquinas's account, is the role or content of natural law essentially negative, restrictive, or repressive in content? See RALPH MCINERNEY, ETHICA THOMISTICA 50 (1982).

18. Does Aquinas's natural law theory suggest, in contrast, that there are an indefinitely large number of diverse ways in which persons can strive for fulfillment? See RALPH MCINERNEY, ETHICA THOMISTICA 49 (1982).

19. A.P. D'Entrèves writes that Aquinas believed that political institutions can be adequately justified morally without any reference to religious beliefs. See A.P. D'Entrèves, *Thomas Aquinas*, in ESSAYS IN THE HISTORY OF POLITICAL THOUGHT 97, 99 (Isaac Kramnick ed. 1969). Can moral beliefs be genuinely justified independently of any religious beliefs? Does Aquinas adopt this view?

20. Given Aquinas's belief in objective moral standards, can Aquinas plausibly account for the degree of diversity of moral belief, moral uncertainty, and what Aquinas would call moral error displayed by intelligent adults? See D.J. O'CONNOR, AQUINAS AND THE NATURAL LAW 63-64 (1967).

21. If, as Aquinas recognizes, human beings and their societies and cultures change, and human reason is changeable and imperfect, can any theory of moral or legal obligation be objectively true or distinctively rationally defensible? See D.J. O'CONNOR, AQUINAS AND THE NATURAL LAW 78-79 (1967).

22. Could anyone's genuinely conscientious moral disagreement with a positive legal command ever be mistaken, on Aquinas's view? See F.C. COPLESTON, AQUINAS 228 (1955).

23. Can the various principles of the natural law be said to be self-evident? For an influential discussion of what self-evidence means to Aquinas, see

Germain Grisez, *The First Principle of Practical Reason: A Commentary on the Summa Theologica, 1-2, Question 94, Article 2*, 10 NATURAL LAW FORUM 168, 172-75 (1965). On the question of self-evidence, does Aquinas confuse what is logically primitive or underivable with what is psychologically obvious? See D.J. O'CONNOR, AQUINAS AND THE NATURAL LAW 66 (1967).

24. Dino Bigongiari argues that for Aquinas, "[t]he political order is . . . the rule of justice. The prince is expected to govern by laws, and these laws must be just; that is, they cannot be the arbitrary expression of a will, either individual or collective, but rather the rational deduction from principles of justice imparted by God to man. . . ." Dino Bigongiari, *Introduction* to THE POLITICAL IDEAS OF ST. THOMAS AQUINAS xviii (Fathers of the English Dominican Province trans. 1953).

25. As Charles Rice indicates, morally sound human law may be drawn from the natural law, according to Aquinas, in either of two ways: First, "[i]t may be derived by conclusion, as the law that one must not kill is a conclusion from the basic principle that we should do harm to no man." Charles E. Rice, *Some Reasons For a Restoration of Natural Law Jurisprudence*, 24 WAKE FOREST LAW REVIEW 539, 563 (1989). Of course, this conclusion would require the intermediate premise that killing is always harming. Secondly, though, human law may be "derived by determination" from the natural law, as where a human law determines that a convicted criminal should be punished in one particular way, chosen from a range of many legitimate ways. *See id.* at 563-64. Does a human law that is a mere "determination" of the natural law truly constitute a portion of the natural law, or is it merely compatible or consistent with the natural law? Does the idea of a range of permissible "determinations" of the natural law help account for the wide variety and great diversity of styles of life that can be equally accommodated within a natural law framework? More threateningly, though, is natural law ultimately too open and indeterminate to offer useful moral guidance? Could a theory of the exercise of the moral virtues, as Aquinas undertakes elsewhere in the *Summa Theologica*, help to manage the problem of indeterminacy?

26. Ralph McInerney defines natural law as "the view that there are true directives of human action which arise from the very structure of human agency and which anyone can easily formulate for himself. . . ." RALPH MCINERNEY, ETHICA THOMISTICA 40 (1982). Notice that this definition makes no explicit reference to divine will, command, knowledge, or ordering.

27. If we set aside any reference to the divine, what, if anything, can be validly inferred from human nature about how we morally ought to respond to governmental commands, or about the legitimacy of governments? For some

background, see D.J. O'CONNOR, AQUINAS AND THE NATURAL LAW 68-79 (1967).

28. Is Aquinas's view of the nature of political and legal obligation completely dependent for its coherence and plausibility on particular views about the existence and nature of God? If so, how narrowly sectarian are the particular views upon which Aquinas's system depends? See A.P. D'Entrèves, *The Case for Natural Law Re-examined*, 2 NATURAL LAW FORUM 5, 35-37 (1956).

29. Query whether followers of Judaism, Islam, and other major religions must, as a matter of doctrinal principle, take issue with Aquinas on any important aspect of natural law and obligation. If so, at what points?

30. For a further brief discussion of Aquinas's theory of the relationship between law, morality, and reason, see ALAN DONAGAN, HUMAN ENDS AND HUMAN ACTION 14-17 (1985). For a discussion of Aquinas's philosophy of mind and metaphysics, see ANTHONY KENNY, AQUINAS (1980). For a broad discussion of Aquinas's philosophy, see JOSEPH PIEPER, GUIDE TO THOMAS AQUINAS (Richard Winston & Clara Winston trans. 1962).

31. For a valuable collection of essays pursuing, among other matters, some of the natural law themes of Aquinas, see NATURAL LAW THEORY: CONTEMPORARY ESSAYS (Robert P. George ed. 1992).

32. For some of the distinctive original contributions of Robert George to contemporary natural law theory, see Robert P. George, *Human Flourishing As a Criterion of Morality: A Critique of Perry's Naturalism*, 63 TULANE LAW REVIEW 1455 (1989); Robert P. George, *Recent Criticism of Natural Law Theory*, 55 UNIVERSITY OF CHICAGO LAW REVIEW 1371 (1988), as well as his own contribution to NATURAL LAW THEORY: CONTEMPORARY ESSAYS (Robert P. George ed. 1992).

33. Aquinas's most intellectually distinguished predecessor, the fourth and fifth century African bishop St. Augustine, whose life is classically detailed in his *Confessions*, recognizes natural law as distinct from human law or divinely revealed law, as written on the human heart, and as embodying the Golden Rule in its negative formulation. See Herbert A. Deane, *The Political and Social Ideas of St. Augustine*, in ESSAYS IN THE HISTORY OF POLITICAL THOUGHT 85, 85 (Isaac Kramnick ed. 1969).

34. "Men need the state, St. Augustine emphasizes, because they need coercion, in two ways. They need it . . . to keep within proper confines the desires for material goods. And they need it, also, to keep other states from invading the

commonwealth to secure by violence the goods on which they have set their hearts." Dino Bigongiari, *Appendix* to THE POLITICAL IDEAS OF ST. AUGUSTINE 343, 350 (Henry Paolucci ed. 1962).

35. "Augustine is perfectly explicit about the purpose of the earthly state and of the coercion and punishment it employs. The heavy hand of the state and its dreadful instruments of repression are necessary because they are the only methods by which sinful men can be restrained. . . . Only by such means can the wicked be kept from destroying one another as their competing egoisms clash, and discouraged from open assaults upon the minority of good and pious men." Herbert A. Deane, *The Political and Social Ideas of St. Augustine*, in ESSAYS IN THE HISTORY OF POLITICAL THOUGHT 85, 90 (Isaac Kramnick ed. 1969).

36. It has been said that for Augustine, the political order is "reduced to the negative function of maintaining peace, for it merely serves the purpose of enabling the faithful to occupy themselves with the more lasting task of eternal salvation." CARL J. FRIEDRICH, THE PHILOSOPHY OF LAW IN HISTORICAL PERSPECTIVE 37 (rev. 2d ed. 1963).

37. For Augustine, then, "[t]he form of political regime under which Christians are called upon to live is, or ought to be, of little consequence to them." Henry Paolucci, *Introduction* to THE POLITICAL WRITINGS OF ST. AUGUSTINE XX (Henry Paolucci ed. 1962).

38. Augustine himself remarks: "When it is considered how short is the span of human life, does it really matter to a man whose days are numbered what government he must obey, so long as he is not compelled to act against God or his conscience?" ST. AUGUSTINE, CITY OF GOD book V, ch. 17 at 113 (Gerald G. Walsh et al. trans. 1958). How broadly should a conscience-based moral exemption from obedience be interpreted? What sorts of conduct can it justify?

39. Etienne Gilson construes St. Augustine's underlying message as "that the whole world, from its beginning until its final term, has as its unique end the constitution of a holy Society, in view of which everything has been made, even the universe itself." Etienne Gilson, *Foreword* to ST. AUGUSTINE, THE CITY OF GOD 21 (Gerald G. Walsh et al. trans. 1958). Does this central theme effectively unify and account for all of Aquinas's teachings on legal obligation as well?

40. Carl Friedrich draws a contrast between Augustine and Aquinas by suggesting that Augustine tends to emphasize the importance of sinfulness, of command-

ing, and of punishing, whereas Aquinas tends to emphasize the positive, creative, and constructive elements of political society. See CARL J. FRIEDRICH, THE PHILOSOPHY OF LAW IN HISTORICAL PERSPECTIVE 43 (rev. 2d ed. 1963). What would this difference in emphasis imply for the theories of obligation to obey for Augustine and Aquinas?

41. Disagreements between Aquinas and various Reformers, and among Reformers, on other issues should not obscure the essential agreement among Aquinas and the major Reformers on the core of natural law doctrine. See Charles E. Rice, *Some Reasons for a Restoration of Natural Law Jurisprudence*, 24 WAKE FOREST LAW REVIEW 539, 558 (1989). See also John McNeill, *Natural Law in the Teaching of the Reformers*, 26 JOURNAL OF RELIGION 168 (1946).

42. While it is difficult to briefly and uncontroversially summarize the differences between and among Aquinas, Luther, and Calvin on the possibility or scope of permissible disobedience to the temporal authorities, Luther does seem less accommodating to those who wish to disobey or resist a government which is either seeking to set itself in God's rightful place or merely failing to seek the common good. See Thomas L. Shaffer, *Jurisprudence in the Light of the Hebraic Faith*, 1 NOTRE DAME JOURNAL OF LAW, ETHICS & PUBLIC POLICY 77, 81-82 (1984). Calvin, on the other hand, seems somewhat more sympathetic to those who wish to act on the fear that their obedience may risk idolatry. See *id.* at 85.

43. Much of John Calvin's writing that is most directly relevant to the problems of legal and political obligation is contained in JOHN CALVIN, ON POLITICAL DUTY (John McNeill rev. ed. 1956). For discussions of Reformation thought on these issues, see WILLIAM J. BOUWSMA, JOHN CALVIN: A SIXTEENTH CENTURY PORTRAIT 70-75 (1988); JOHN CALVIN, INSTITUTES OF THE CHRISTIAN RELIGION book IV, ch. 20 (Ford L. Battles trans. 1960); HARRO HOPFL, THE CHRISTIAN POLITY OF JOHN CALVIN 172-87 (1982); W.D.J. CARGILL THOMPSON, THE POLITICAL THOUGHT OF MARTIN LUTHER 91-111 (Phillip Broadhead ed. 1984); Edward A. Dowey, *Law in Luther and Calvin*, 41 THEOLOGY TODAY 146 (1984); John T. McNeill, *Calvin and Civil Government*, in READINGS IN CALVIN'S THEOLOGY 260 (Donald McKim ed. 1984); John T. McNeill, *Natural Law in the Teaching of the Reformers*, 26 JOURNAL OF RELIGION 168 (1946); John T. McNeill, *Natural Law in the Thought of Luther*, 10 CHURCH HISTORY 211 (1941).

44. In light of the central importance of the Decalogue for writers such as Aquinas, consider traditional Jewish doctrine regarding the political state. Thomas Shaffer explains that "[i]n the Diaspora, in which Jews have lived in

Gentile nations, the unity of the Mosaic law is broken. The ordinary civil law that binds a Jew, according to the Talmud, is therefore the law of the nation he lives in; that municipal law carries the force of Mosaic law, with this exception—it must not become a god: 'Hebraic society says *no* to society whenever society, in its pride, makes claims to absoluteness. . . .'" Thomas L. Shaffer, *Jurisprudence in the Light of the Hebraic Faith*, 1 NOTRE DAME JOURNAL OF LAW, ETHICS & PUBLIC POLICY 77, 78 (1984) (quoting WILL HERBERG, JUDAISM AND MODERN MAN: AN INTERPRETATION OF JEWISH RELIGION 139 (1980)). See, for background, L.E. GOODMAN, ON JUSTICE: AN ESSAY IN JEWISH PHILOSOPHY (1991).

45. It has been argued that in traditional Jewish thought, the rise of politics in the form of a monarchical ruler is the subject of some ambivalence, reflecting a concession "to human imperfection" undertaken at human, rather than divine, active initiative, and only acquiesced in by God. See Allan Silver, *Kingship and Political Agency in Jewish Thought*, 2 S'VARA 30, 35 (1991).

46. Compare with this summary the following passage from the *Koran*: "Their prophet said to them: 'Allah has appointed Saul to be your king.' But they replied: 'Should he be given the Kingship, when we are more deserving of it than he? Besides, he is not rich at all.' He said: 'Allah has chosen him to rule over you and made him grow in wisdom and stature. Allah gives His sovereignty to whom He will.'" *The Koran* 2:247-248 (N.J. Dawood trans. 1974).

47. More specifically, though, consider in particular the modern European Jewish political experience. Under the relatively favorable circumstances of late eighteenth century Prague under the Emperor Joseph II, for example, Rabbi Ezekiel Landau preached that while Jews must inevitably think of themselves as temporary guests in foreign lands until their return to their collective estate in Israel, Jews owe a recompense, in the form of taxation and general respect, for the relative fairness and protection accorded the Jews by the Emperor. Thus one can be morally obligated to a regime while remaining partially alienated from and not fully free within that society. See 26 YALE JUDAICA SERIES: JEWISH PREACHING 1200-1800 361-64 (Marc Saperstein ed. 1989).

# 11

# From Thomas Hobbes, Leviathan

CHAP. XIII
*Of the* NATURALL CONDITION *of Mankind,*
*as concerning their Felicity,* and *Misery*

NATURE hath made men so equall, in the faculties of body, and mind; as that though there bee found one man sometimes manifestly stronger in body, or of quicker mind then another; yet when all is reckoned together, the difference between man, and man, is not so considerable, as that one man can thereupon claim to himselfe any benefit, to which another may not pretend, as well as he. For as to the strength of body, the weakest has strength enough to kill the strongest, either by secret machination, or by confederacy with others, that are in the same danger with himself.

And as to the faculties of the mind, (setting aside the arts grounded upon words, and especially that skill of proceeding upon generall, and infallible rules, called Science; which very few have, and but in few things; as being not a native faculty, born with us; nor attained, (as Prudence,) while we look after somewhat els,) I find yet a greater equality amongst men, than that of strength. For Prudence, is but Experience; which equall time, equally bestowes on all men, in those things they equally apply themselves unto. That which may perhaps make such equality incredible, is but a vain conceipt of ones owne wisdome, which almost all men think they have in a greater degree, than the Vulgar; that is, than all men but themselves, and a few others, whom by Fame, or for concurring with themselves, they approve. For such is the nature of men, that howsoever they may acknowledge many others to be more witty, or more eloquent, or more learned; Yet they will hardly believe there be many so wise as themselves: For they see their own wit at hand, and other mens at a distance. But this proveth rather that men are in that point equall, than unequall. For there is not ordinarily a greater signe of the equall distribution of any thing, than that every man is contented with his share.

From this equality of ability, ariseth equality of hope in the attaining of our Ends. And therefore if any two men desire the same thing, which neverthelesse they cannot both enjoy, they become enemies; and in the way to their End, (which is principally their owne conservation, and sometimes their delectation only,) endeavour to destroy, or subdue one an other. And from hence it comes to passe, that where an Invader hath no more to feare, than an other mans single power; if one plant, sow, build, or possesse a convenient Seat, others may probably be expected to come prepared with forces united, to dispossesse, and deprive him, not only of the fruit of his labour, but also of his life, or liberty. And the Invader again is in the like danger of another.

And from this diffidence of one another, there is no way for any man to secure himselfe, so reasonable, as Anticipation; that is, by force, or wiles, to master the persons of all men he can, so long, till he see no other power great enough to endanger him: And this is no more than his own conservation requireth, and is generally allowed. Also because there be some, that taking pleasure in contemplating their own power in the acts of conquest, which they pursue farther than their security requires; if others, that otherwise would be glad to be at ease within modest bounds, should not by invasion increase their power, they would not be able, long time, by standing only on their defence, to subsist. And by consequence, such augmentation of dominion over men, being necessary to a mans conservation, it ought to be allowed him.

Againe, men have no pleasure, (but on the contrary a great deale of griefe) in keeping company, where there is no power able to overawe them all. For every man looketh that his companion should value him, at the same rate he sets upon himselfe: And upon all signes of contempt, or undervaluing, naturally endeavours, as far as he dares (which amongst them that have no common power to keep them in quiet, is far enough to make them destroy each other,) to extort a greater value from his contemners, by dommage; and from others, by the example.

So that in the nature of man, we find three principall causes of quarrell. First, Competition; Secondly, Diffidence; Thirdly, Glory.

The first, maketh men invade for Gain; the second, for Safety; and the third, for Reputation. The first use Violence, to make themselves Masters of other mens persons, wives, children, and cattell, the second, to defend them; the third, for trifles, as a word, a smile, a different opinion, and any other signe of undervalue, either direct in their Persons, or by reflexion in their Kindred, their Friends, their Nation, their Profession, or their Name.

Hereby it is manifest, that during the time men live without a common Power to keep them all in awe, they are in that condition which is called Warre; and such a warre, as is of every man against every man. For WARRE, consisteth not in Battell onely, or the act of fighting; but in a tract of time, wherein the Will to contend by Battell is sufficiently known: and therefore the notion of *Time*, is to be considered in the nature of Warre; as it is in the nature of Weather. For as the nature of Foule weather, lyeth not in a showre or two of rain; but in an inclination thereto of many dayes together; So the nature of War, consisteth not in actuall fighting; but in the known disposition thereto, during all the time there is no assurance to the contrary. All other time is PEACE.

Whatsoever therefore is consequent to a time of Warre, where every man is Enemy to every man; the same is consequent to the time, wherein men live without other security, than what their own strength, and their own invention shall furnish them withall. In such condition, there is no place for Industry; because the fruit thereof is uncertain: and consequently no Culture of the Earth, no Navigation, nor use of the commodities that may be imported by Sea; no commodious Building; no Instruments of moving, and removing such things as require much force; no Knowledge of the face of the Earth; no account of Time; no Arts; no Letters; no Society; and which is worst of all, continuall feare, and danger of violent death; And the life of man, solitary, poore, nasty, brutish, and short.

It may seem strange to some man, that has not well weighed these things; that Nature should thus dissociate, and render men apt to invade, and destroy one another: and he may therefore, not trusting to this Inference, made from the Passions, desire perhaps to have the same confirmed by Experience. Let him therefore consider with himselfe, when taking a journey, he armes himselfe, and seeks to go well accompanied; when going to sleep, he locks his dores; when even in his house he locks his chests; and this when he knowes there bee Lawes, and publike Officers, armed, to revenge all injuries shall bee done him; what opinion he has of his fellow subjects, when he rides armed; of his fellow Citizens, when he locks his dores; and of his children, and servants, when he locks his chests. Does he not there as much accuse mankind by his actions, as I do by my words? But neither of us accuse mans nature in it. The Desires, and other Passions of man, are in themselves no Sin. No more are the Actions, that proceed from those Passions, till they know a Law that forbids them: which till Lawes be made they cannot know: nor can any Law be made, till they have agreed upon the Person that shall make it.

It may peradventure be thought, there was never such a time, nor condition of warre as this; and I believe it was never generally so, over all the world: but there are many places, where they live so now. For the savage people in many places of *America*, except the government of small Families, the concord whereof dependeth on naturall lust, have no government at all; and live at this day in that brutish manner, as I said before. Howsoever, it may be perceived what manner of life there would be, where there were no common Power to feare; by the manner of life, which men that have formerly lived under a peacefull government, use to degenerate into, in a civill Warre.

But though there had never been any time, wherein particular men were in a condition of warre one against another; yet in all times, Kings, and Persons of Soveraigne authority, because of their Independency, are in continuall jealousies, and in the state and posture of Gladiators; having their weapons pointing, and their eyes fixed on one another; that is, there Forts, Garrisons, and Guns, upon the Frontiers of their Kingdomes; and continuall Spyes upon their neighbours; which is a posture of War. But because they uphold thereby, the Industry of their

Subjects; there does not follow from it, that misery, which accompanies the Liberty of particular men.

To this warre of every man against every man, this also is consequent; that nothing can be Unjust. The notions of Right and Wrong, Justice and Injustice have there no place. Where there is no common Power, there is no Law: where no Law, no Injustice. Force, and Fraud, are in warre the two Cardinall vertues. Justice, and Injustice are none of the Faculties neither of the Body, nor Mind. If they were, they might be in a man that were alone in the world, as well as his Senses, and Passions. They are Qualities, that relate to men in Society, not in Solitude. It is consequent also to the same condition, that there be no Propriety, no Dominion, no *Mine* and *Thine* distinct; but onely that to be every mans, that he can get; and for so long, as he can keep it. And thus much for the ill condition, which man by meer Nature is actually placed in; though with a possibility to come out of it, consisting partly in the Passions, partly in his Reason.

The Passions that encline men to Peace, are Feare of Death; Desire of such things as are necessary to commodious living; and a Hope by their Industry to obtain them. And Reason suggesteth convenient Articles of Peace, upon which men may be drawn to agreement. These Articles, are they, which otherwise are called the Lawes of Nature: whereof I shall speak more particularly, in the two following Chapters.

## CHAP. XIV
### *Of the first and second* NATURALL LAWES,  *and of* CONTRACTS

THE RIGHT OF NATURE, which Writers commonly call *Jus Naturale*, is the Liberty each man hath, to use his own power, as he will himselfe, for the preservation of his own Nature; that is to say, of his own Life; and consequently, of doing any thing, which in his own Judgement, and Reason, hee shall conceive to be the aptest means thereunto.

By LIBERTY, is understood, according to the proper signification of the word, the absence of externall Impediments: which Impediments, may oft take away part of a mans power to do what hee would; but cannot hinder him from using the power left him, according as his judgement, and reason shall dictate to him.

A LAW OF NATURE, (*Lex Naturalis*,) is a Precept, or generall Rule, found out by Reason, by which a man is forbidden to do, that, which is destructive of his life, or taketh away the means of preserving the same; and to omit, that, by which he thinketh it may be best preserved. For though they that speak of this subject, use to confound *Jus*, and *Lex*, *Right* and *Law*; yet they ought to be distinguished; because RIGHT, consisteth in liberty to do, or to forbeare; Whereas LAW, determineth, and bindeth to one of them: so that Law, and Right, differ as much, as Obligation, and Liberty; which in one and the same matter are inconsistent.

And because the condition of Man, (as hath been declared in the precedent

Chapter) is a condition of Warre of every one against every one; in which case every one is governed by his own Reason; and there is nothing he can make use of, that may not be a help unto him, in preserving his life against his enemyes; It followeth, that in such a condition, every man has a Right to every thing; even to one anothers body. And therefore, as long as this naturall Right of every man to every thing endureth, there can be no security to any man, (how strong or wise soever he be,) of living out the time, which Nature ordinarily alloweth men to live. And consequently it is a precept, or generall rule of Reason, *That every man, ought to endeavour Peace, as farre as he has hope of obtaining it; and when he cannot obtain it, that he may seek, and use, all helps, and advantages of Warre.* The first branch of which Rule, containeth the first, and Fundamentall Law of Nature; which is, *to seek Peace, and follow it.* The Second, the summe of the Right of Nature; which is, *By all means we can, to defend our selves.*

From this Fundamentall Law of Nature, by which men are commanded to endeavour Peace, is derived this second Law; *That a man be willing, when others are so too, as farre-forth, as for Peace, and defence of himselfe he shall think it necessary, to lay down this right to all things; and be contented with so much liberty against other men, as he would allow other men against himselfe.* For as long as every man holdeth this Right, of doing any thing he liketh; so long are all men in the condition of Warre. But if other men will not lay down their Right, as well as he; then there is no Reason for any one, to devest himselfe of his: For that were to expose himselfe to Prey, (which no man is bound to) rather than to dispose himselfe to Peace. This is that Law of the Gospell; *Whatsoever you require that others should do to you, that do ye to them.* And that Law of all men, *Quod tibi fieri non vis, alteri ne feceris.*

To *lay downe* a mans *Right* to any thing, is to *devest* himselfe of the *Liberty,* of hindring another of the benefit of his own Right to the same. For he that renounceth, or passeth away his Right, giveth not to any other man a Right which he had not before; because there is nothing to which every man had not Right by Nature: but onely standeth out of his way, that he may enjoy his own originall Right, without hindrance from him; not without hindrance by another mans defect of Right, is but so much diminution of impediments to the use of his own Right originall.

Right is layd aside, either by simply Renouncing it; or by Transferring it to another. By *Simply* RENOUNCING; when he cares not to whom the benefit thereof redoundeth. By TRANSFERRING; when he intendeth the benefit thereof to some certain person, or persons. And when a man hath in either manner abandoned, or granted away his Right; then is he said to be OBLIGED, or  BOUND, not to hinder those, to whom such Right is granted, or abandoned, from the benefit of it: and that he *Ought,* and it is his DUTY, not to make voyd that voluntary act of his own: and that such hindrance is INJUSTICE, and INJURY, as being *Sine Jure;* the Right being before renounced, or transferred. So that *Injury,* or *Injustice,* in the controversies of the world, is somewhat like to that, which in the disputations of

Scholers is called *Absurdity*. For as it is there called an Absurdity, to contradict what one maintained in the Beginning: so in the world, it is called Injustice, and Injury, voluntarily to undo that, which from the beginning he had voluntarily done. The way by which a man either simply Renounceth, or Transferreth his Right, is a Declaration, or Signification, by some voluntary and sufficient signe, or signes, that he doth so Renounce, or Transferre; or hath so Renounced, or Transferred the same, to him that accepteth it. And these Signes are either Words onely, or Actions onely; or (as it happeneth most often) both Words, and Actions. And the same are the BONDS, by which men are bound, and obliged: Bonds, that have their strength, not from their own Nature, (for nothing is more easily broken then a mans word,) but from Feare of some evill consequence upon the rupture.

Whensoever a man Transferreth his Right, or Renounceth it; it is either in consideration of some Right reciprocally transferred to himselfe; or for some other good he hopeth for thereby. For it is a voluntary act: and of the voluntary acts of every man, the object is some *Good to himselfe*. And therefore there be some Rights, which no man can be understood by any words, or other signes, to have abandoned, or transferred. As first a man cannot lay down the right of resisting them, that assault him by force, to take away his life; because he cannot be understood to ayme thereby, at any Good to himselfe. The same may be sayd of Wounds, and Chayns, and Imprisonment; both because there is no benefit consequent to such patience; as there is to the patience of suffering another to be wounded, or imprisoned: as also because a man cannot tell, when he seeth men proceed against him by violence, whether they intend his death or not. And lastly the motive, and end for which this renouncing, and transferring of Right is introduced, is nothing else but the security of a mans person, in his life, and in the means of so preserving life, as not to be weary of it. And therefore if a man by words, or other signes, seem to despoyle himselfe of the End, for which those signes were intended; he is not to be understood as if he meant it, or that it was his will; but that he was ignorant of how such words and actions were to be interpreted.

The mutuall transferring of Right, is that which men call CONTRACT.

There is difference, between transferring of Right to the Thing; and transferring, or tradition, that is, delivery of the Thing it selfe. For the Thing may be delivered together with the Translation of the Right; as in buying and selling with ready mony; or exchange of goods, or lands: and it may be delivered some time after.

Again, one of the Contractors, may deliver the Thing contracted for on his part, and leave the other to perform his part at some determinate time after, and in the mean time be trusted; and then the Contract on his part, is called PACT, or COVENANT: Or both parts may contract now, to performe hereafter: in which cases, he that is to performe in time to come, being trusted, his performance is called *Keeping of Promise*, or Faith; and the fayling of performance (if it be voluntary) *Violation of Faith*.

When the transferring of Right, is not mutuall; but one of the parties transferreth, in hope to gain thereby friendship, or service from another, or from his friends; or in hope to gain the reputation of Charity, or Magnanimity; or to deliver his mind from the pain of compassion; or in hope of reward in heaven; This is not Contract, but GIFT, FREE-GIFT, GRACE: which words signifie one and the same thing.

Signes of Contract, are either *Expresse*, or *by Inference*. Expresse, are words spoken with understanding of what they signifie: And such words are either of the time *Present* or *Past* as, *I Give, I Grant, I have Given, I have Granted, I will that this be yours*: Or of the future, as *I will Give, I will Grant*: which words of the future, are called PROMISE.

Signes by Inference, are sometimes the consequence of Words; sometimes the consequence of Silence; sometimes the consequence of Actions; sometimes the consequence of Forbearing an Action: and generally a signe by Inference, of any Contract, is whatsoever sufficiently argues the will of the Contractor.

Words alone, if they be of the time to come, and contain a bare promise, are an insufficient signe of a Free-gift and therefore not obligatory. For if they be of the time to Come, as *To morrow I will Give*, they are a signe I have not given yet, and consequently that my right is not transferred, but remaineth till I transferre it by some other Act. But if the words be of the time Present, or Past, as *I have given, or do give to be delivered to morrow*, then is my to morrows Right given away to day; and that by the vertue of the words, though there were no other argument of my will. And there is a great difference in the signification of these words, *Volo hoc tuum esse cras*, and *Cras dabo*; that is, between *I will that this be thine to morrow*, and *I will give it thee to morrow*: For the word *I will*, in the former manner of speech, signifies an act of the will Present; but in the later, it signifies a promise of an act of the will to Come; and therefore the former words, being of the Present, transferre a future right; the later, that be of the Future, transferre nothing. But if there be other signes of the Will to transferre a Right, besides Words; then, though the gift be Free, yet may the Right be understood to passe by words of the future: as if a man propound a Prize to him that comes first to the end of a race, The gift is Free; and though the words be of the Future, yet the Right passeth: for if he would not have his words so be understood he should not have let them runne.

In Contracts, the right passeth, not onely where the words are of the time Present, or Past; but also where they are of the Future: because all Contract is mutuall translation, or change of Right; and therefore he that promiseth onely, because he hath already received the benefit for which he promiseth, is to be understood as if he intended the Right should passe: for unlesse he had been content to have his words so understood, the other would not have performed his part first. And for that cause, in buying, and selling, and other acts of Contract, a Promise is equivalent to a Covenant; and therefore obligatory.

He that performeth first in the case of a Contract, is said to MERIT that which he is to receive by the performance of the other; and he hath it as *Due*. Also when a Prize is propounded to many, which is to be given to him onely that winneth; or mony is thrown amongst many, to be enjoyed by them that catch it; though this be a Free gift; yet so to Win, or so to Catch, is to *Merit*, and to have it as Due. For the Right is transferred in the Propounding of the Prize, and in throwing down the mony; though it be not determined to whom, but by the Event of the contention. But there is between these two sorts of Merit, this difference, that In Contract, I Merit by vertue of my own power, and the Contractors need; but in this case of Free gift, I am enabled to Merit onely by the benignity of the Giver: In Contract, I merit at the Contractors hand that he should depart with his right; In this case of Gift, I Merit not that the giver should part with his right; but that when he has parted with it, it should be mine, rather than anothers. And this I think to be the meaning of that distinction of the Schooles, between *Meritum congrui*, and *Meritum condigni*. For God Almighty, having promised Paradise to those men (hoodwinkt with carnall desires,) that can walk through this world according to the Precepts, and Limits prescribed by him; they say, he that shall so walk, shall Merit Paradise *Ex congruo*. But because no man can demand a right to it, by his own Righteousnesse, or any other power in himselfe, but by the Free Grace of God onely; they say, no man can Merit Paradise *ex condigno*. This I say, I think is the meaning of that distinction; but because Disputers do not agree upon the signification of their own termes of Art, longer than it serves their turn; I will not affirme any thing of their meaning: onely this I say; when a gift is given indefinitely, as a prize to be contended for, he that winneth Meriteth, and may claime the Prize as Due.

If a Covenant be made, wherein neither of the parties performe presently, but trust one another; in the condition of meer Nature, (which is a condition of Warre of every man against every man,) upon any reasonable suspition, it is Voyd: But if there be a common Power set over them both, with right and force sufficient to compell performance; it is not Voyd. For he that performeth first, has no assurance the other will performe after; because the bonds of words are too weak to bridle mens ambition, avarice, anger, and other Passions, without the feare of some coerceive Power; which in the condition of meer Nature, where all men are equall, and judges of the justnesse of their own fears, cannot possibly be supposed. And therefore he which performeth first, does but betray himselfe to his enemy; contrary to the Right (he can never abandon) of defending his life, and means of living.

But in a civill estate, where there is a Power set up to constrain those that would otherwise violate their faith, that feare is no more reasonable; and for that cause, he which by the Covenant is to perform first, is obliged so to do.

The cause of feare, which maketh such a Covenant invalid, must be alwayes something arising after the Covenant made; as some new fact, or other signe of the Will not to performe: else it cannot make the Covenant voyd. For that which would not hinder a man from promising, ought not to be admitted as a hindrance of performing.

He that transferreth any Right, transferreth the Means of enjoying it, as farre as lyeth in his power. As he that selleth Land, is understood to transferre the Herbage, and whatsoever growes upon it; Nor can he that sells a Mill turn away the Stream that drives it. And they that give to a man the Right of government in Soveraignty, are understood to give him the right of levying mony to maintain Souldiers; and of appointing Magistrates for the administration of Justice.

To make Covenants with bruit Beasts, is impossible; because not understanding our speech, they understand not, nor accept of any translation of Right; nor can translate any Right to another: and without mutuall acceptation, there is no Covenant.

To make Covenant with God, is impossible, but by Mediation of such as God speaketh to, either by Revelation supernaturall, or by his Lieutenants that govern under him, and in his Name: For otherwise we know not whether our Covenants be accepted, or not. And therefore they that Vow any thing contrary to any law of Nature, Vow in vain; as being a thing unjust to pay such Vow. And if it be a thing commanded by the Law of Nature, it is not the Vow, but the Law that binds them.

The matter, or subject of a Covenant, is alwayes something that falleth under deliberation; (For to Covenant, is an act of the Will; that is to say an act, and the last act, of deliberation;) and is therefore alwayes understood to be something to come; and which is judged Possible for him that Covenanteth, to performe.

And therefore, to promise that which is known to be Impossible, is no Covenant. But if that prove impossible afterwards, which before was thought possible, the Covenant is valid, and bindeth, (though not to the thing it selfe,) yet to the value; or, if that also be impossible, to the unfeigned endeavour of performing as much as is possible: for to more no man can be obliged.

Men are freed of their Covenants two wayes; by Performing; or by being Forgiven. For Performance, is the naturall end of obligation; and Forgivenesse, the restitution of liberty; as being a re-transferring of that Right, in which the obligation consisted.

Covenants entred into by fear, in the condition of mere Nature, are obligatory. For example, if I Covenant to pay a ransome, or service for my life, to an enemy; I am bound by it. For it is a Contract, wherein one receiveth the benefit of life; the other is to receive mony, or service for it; and consequently, where no other Law (as in the condition, of meer nature) forbiddeth the performance, the Covenant is valid. Therefore Prisoners of warre, if trusted with the payment of their Ransome, are obliged to pay it: And if a weaker Prince, make a disadvantageous peace with a stronger, for feare; he is bound to keep it; unlesse (as hath been sayd before) there ariseth some new, and just cause to feare, to renew the war. And even in Common-wealths, if I be forced to redeem my selfe from a Theefe by promising him mony, I am bound to pay it, till the Civill Law discharge me. For whatsoever I may lawfully do without Obligation, the same I may lawfully Covenant to do through feare: and what I lawfully Covenant, I cannot lawfully break.

A former Covenant makes voyd a later. For a man that hath passed away his Right to one man to day, hath it not to passe to morrow to another: and therefore the later promise passeth no Right, but is null.

A Covenant not to defend my selfe from force, by force, is alwayes voyd. For (as I have shewed before) no man can transferre, or lay down his Right to save himselfe from Death, Wounds, and Imprisonment, (the avoyding whereof is the onely End of laying down any Right, and therefore the promise of not resisting force, in no Covenant transferreth any right; nor is obliging. For though a man may Covenant thus, *Unlesse I do so, or so, kill me*; he cannot Covenant thus, *Unlesse I do so, or so, I will not resist you, when you come to kill me*. For man by nature chooseth the lesser evill, which is danger of death in resisting; rather than the greater, which is certain and present death in not resisting. And this is granted to be true by all men, in that they lead Criminals to Execution, and Prison, with armed men, notwithstanding that such Criminals have consented to the Law, by which they are condemned.

A Covenant to accuse ones selfe, without assurance of pardon, is likewise invalide. For in the condition of Nature, where every man is Judge, there is no place for Accusation: and in the Civill State, the Accusation is followed with Punishment; which being Force, a man is not obliged not to resist. The same is also true, of the Accusation of those by whose Condemnation a man falls into misery; as of a Father, Wife, or Benefactor.

For the Testimony of such an Accuser, if it be not willingly given, is præsumed to be corrupted by Nature; and therefore not to be received: and where a mans Testimony is not to be credited, he is not bound to give it. Also Accusations upon Torture, are not to be reputed as Testimonies. For Torture is to be used but as means of conjecture, and light, in the further examination, and search of truth: and what is in that case confessed, tendeth to the ease of him that is Tortured; not to the informing of the Torturers: and therefore ought not to have the credit of a sufficient Testimony: for whether he deliver himselfe by true, or false Accusation, he does it by the Right of preserving his own life.

The force of Words, being (as I have formerly noted) too weak to hold men to the performance of their Covenants; there are in mans nature, but two imaginable helps to strengthen it. And those are either a Feare of the consequence of breaking their word; or a Glory, or Pride in appearing not to breake it. This later is a Generosity too rarely found to be presumed on, especially in the pursuers of Wealth, Command, or sensuall Pleasure; which are the greatest part of Mankind. The Passion to be reckoned upon, is Fear; whereof there be two very generall Objects: one, The Power of Spirits Invisible; the other, The Power of those men they shall therein Offend. Of these two, though the former be the greater Power, yet the feare of the later is commonly the greater Feare. The Feare of the former is in every man, his own Religion, which hath place in the nature of man before Civill Society. The later hath not so; at least not place enough, to keep men to their promises; because in the condition of meer Nature, the inequality of Power is not discerned, but by the event of Battell. So that before the time of Civill Society, or in the interruption thereof by Warre, there is nothing can strengthen a Covenant of Peace agreed on, against the temptations of Avarice, Ambition, Lust, or other strong desire, but the feare of that Invisible Power, which they every one Worship as God; and Feare as a Revenger of their perfidy. All therefore that can be done between two men not subject to Civill Power, is to put one another to swear by the God he feareth: Which *Swearing*, or OATH, is a *Forme of Speech, added to a Promise; by which he that promiseth, signifieth, that unlesse he performe, he renounceth the mercy of his God, or calleth to him for vengeance on himselfe*. Such was the Heathen Forme, *Let* Jupiter *kill me else, as I kill this Beast*. So is our Forme, *I shall do thus, and thus, so help me God*. And this, with the Rites and Ceremonies, which every one useth in his own Religion, that the feare of breaking faith might be the greater.

By this it appears, that an Oath taken according to any other Forme, or Rite, then his, that sweareth, is in vain; and no Oath: And that there is no Swearing by any thing which the Swearer thinks not God. For though men have sometimes used to swear by their Kings, for feare, or flattery; yet they would have it thereby understood, they attributed to them Divine honour. And that Swearing unnecessarily by God, is but prophaning of his name: and Swearing by other things, as men do in common discourse, is not Swearing, but an impious Custome, gotten by too much vehemence of talking.

It appears also, that the Oath addes nothing to the Obligation. For a Covenant, if lawful, binds in the sight of God, without the Oath, as much as with it: if unlawfull, bindeth not at all; though it be confirmed with an Oath. . . .

## CHAP. XVII
### *Of the Causes, Generation, and Definition*
### *of a* COMMON-WEALTH

The finall Cause, End, or Designe of men, (who naturally love Liberty, and Dominion over others,) in the introduction of that restraint upon themselves, (in which wee see them live in Common-wealths,) is the foresight of their own preservation, and of a more contented live thereby; that is to say, of getting themselves out from that miserable condition of Warre, which is necessarily consequent (as hath been shewn) to the naturall Passions of men, when there is no visible Power to keep them in awe, and tye them by feare of punishment to the performance of their Covenants. . . .

[T]herefore it is no wonder if there be somewhat else required (besides Covenant) to make their Agreement constant and lasting; which is a Common Power, to keep them in awe, and to direct their actions to the Common Benefit.

The only way to erect such a Common Power, as may be able to defend them from the invasion of Forraigners, and the injuries of one another, and thereby to secure them in such sort, as that by their owne industrie, and by the fruites of the Earth, they may nourish themselves and live contentedly; is, to conferre all their power and strength upon one Man, or upon one Assembly of men, that may reduce all their Wills, by plurality of voices, unto one Will: which is as much as to say, to appoint one Man, or Assembly of men, to beare their Person; and every one to owne, and acknowledge himselfe to be Author of whatsoever he that so beareth their Person, shall Act, or cause to be Acted, in those things which concerne the Common Peace and Safetie; and therein to submit their Wills, every one to his Will, and their Judgements, to his Judgement. This is more than Consent, or Concord; it is a reall Unitie of them all, in one and the same Person, made by Covenant of every man with every man, in such manner, as if every man should say to every man, *I Authorise and give up my Right of Governing my selfe, to this Man, or to this Assembly of men, on this condition, that thou give up thy Right to him, and Authorise all his Actions in like manner*. This done, the Multitude so united in one Person, is called a COMMON-WEALTH, in latine CIVITAS. This is the Generation of that great LEVIATHAN, or rather (to speake more reverently) of that *Mortall God*, to which wee owe under the *Immortall God*, our peace and defence. For by this Authoritie, given him by every particular man in the Common-Wealth, he hath the use of so much Power and Strength conferred on him, that by terror thereof, he is inabled to forme the wills of them all, to Peace at home, and mutuall ayd against their enemies abroad. And in him consisteth the Essence of the Common-wealth; which (to define it,) is *One Person, of whose Acts a great Multitude, by mutuall Covenants one with another, have made themselves every one the Author, to the end he may use the strength and means of them all, as he shall think expedient, for their Peace and Common Defence.*

And he that carryeth this Person, is called SOVERAIGNE, and said to have *Soveraigne Power*; and every one besides, his SUBJECT.

The attaining to this Soveraigne Power, is by two wayes. One, by Naturall force; as when a man maketh his children, to submit themselves, and their children to his government, as being able to destroy them if they refuse; or by Warre subdueth his enemies to his will, giving them their lives on that condition. The other, is when men agree amongst themselves, to submit to some Man, or Assembly of men, voluntarily, on confidence to be protected by him against all others. This later, may be called a Politicall Common-wealth, or Common-wealth by *Institution* and the former, a Common-wealth by *Acquisition*. . . .

# 12

# Notes on the Leviathan

1. Legendarily, in 1588, Thomas Hobbes entered the world when his mother went into premature labor at the news of the imminent threat posed by the Spanish Armada. This allowed Hobbes to later report that fear and he were born twins. While Hobbes does not neglect higher values, it is fair to say that physical safety is never far removed from his philosophical concerns. He was able to navigate the dangers of English secular and religious politics well enough to die in retirement at the age of ninety.

2. Does Hobbes believe that all equally stable governments are equally just and equally legitimate? See ANDRZEJ RAPACZYNSKI, NATURE AND POLITICS 102 (1987). Does he believe in general that in politics, might makes right? See *id.* at 99-100.

3. Can Hobbes's sovereign ruler ordinarily rely, for effective government, solely upon sheer physical power, threats, intimidation, coercion, and punishment? See HOWARD WARRENDER, THE POLITICAL PHILOSOPHY OF HOBBES 318 (1957).

4. Brian Barry argues that one's obligation to obey the Hobbesian sovereign has a three-part structure: First, violating one's agreement to obey would ordinarily be unjust. Second, the sovereign is one's authorized agent, acting on one's behalf and with one's consent. Third, prudence and self-interest dictate, under appropriate circumstances, the establishment of and obedience to the sovereign. See Brian Barry, *Warrender and His Critics*, in HOBBES AND ROUSSEAU: A COLLECTION OF CRITICAL ESSAYS 57 (Maurice Cranston & Richard S. Peters eds. 1972).

5. Consider the role of coerced agreements in Hobbes. For an exposition of Hobbes's view on why compelled but voluntary agreements may be binding, see HOWARD WARRENDER, THE POLITICAL PHILOSOPHY OF HOBBES 313-14 (1957). Would a voluntary agreement by a drowning sailor to exchange a house for the use of a lifebuoy ordinarily be thought morally or legally binding?

6. John Simmons declares in this context that "Hobbes is wrong. There is a significant moral difference between cases of coerced consent and cases when consent results from difficult choice." A. John Simmons, *Consent, Free Choice, and Democratic Government*, 18 GEORGIA LAW REVIEW 791, 812 (1984). See also HADLEY ARKES, FIRST THINGS 218-19 (1986).

7. Gregory Kavka argues that coerced promises cannot be morally binding, where coercion involves the promisee's creating fear of undesirable consequences precisely for the purpose of moving the potential promisor to make the promise in question. See GREGORY S. KAVKA, HOBBESIAN MORAL AND POLITICAL THEORY 396 (1986). Do we ordinarily adopt this view with regard to, say, labor-management agreements? Note also that a person might be coerced to do what they already have a separate binding moral obligation to do anyway, however unwilling they may be to fulfill that obligation.

8. On the relationship among fear, freedom, and obligation, Michael Oakeshott has written that "fear, even if it is fear of being thwarted by the power of another man, is . . . a reason for acting or refraining from a particular action, not an external restraint upon conduct." MICHAEL OAKESHOTT, HOBBES ON CIVIL ASSOCIATION 65 (1975). But does our acting as we do only in fear of a tyrant's wrath reflect only our balance of reasons for acting, without also reflecting any lack of freedom on our part?

9. For an argument that some coerced agreements, particularly those involving no use or threat of force, fraud, or illegality, such as some coerced labor-management work agreements, are and ought to be legally binding, see generally Michael Phillips, *Are Coerced Agreements Involuntary?*, 3 LAW & PHILOSOPHY 133 (1984).

10. For further discussions of the problem of consent, fear, force, duress, coercion, voluntarity, and bindingness, see ALAN WERTHEMIER, COERCION (1987) as well as Jeffrie G. Murphy, *Consent, Coercion, and Hard Choices*, 67 VIRGINIA LAW REVIEW 79 (1981). See also LEONARD T. HOBHOUSE, LIBERALISM 50 (1964).

11. Gregory Kavka concludes that "Hobbes's tacit consent theory of political obligation is a dismal failure. It does not solve the voluntariness problem, and insofar as it has any plausibility or arguments behind it, the notion of tacit consent is merely a proxy for other moral notions, such as gratitude, fair play, and hypothetical consent." Is this sound? GREGORY S. KAVKA, HOBBESIAN MORAL AND POLITICAL THEORY 398 (1986). Note that Kavka links fair play and gratitude to Hobbes's second and fourth laws of nature. *See id.* at 414. Hobbes's fourth law of nature, gratitude, involves giving one who has bestowed a free gift

upon us no reason to regret that gift.

12. Does Hobbes rely at any point not upon actual express contracting, or even upon "tacit," symbolically understood contracting, but instead upon merely hypothetical contracting—i.e., that if persons had been placed into certain specified circumstances, with certain interests and motives, they *would have* contracted with one another or with a sovereign ruler? See Alan Zaitchik, *Hobbes's Reply To the Fool*, 10 POLITICAL THEORY 245, 249 (1982).

13. C.B. Macpherson suggests that "Hobbes was not asking his contemporaries to make a contract, but only to acknowledge the same obligation they would have had if they had made such a contract." C.B. Macpherson, *Introduction to* THOMAS HOBBES, LEVIATHAN 45 (C.B. Macpherson ed. 1968). If so, is it possible to simplify hypothetical contract theory by simply eliminating its reference to contract?

14. Patrick Riley has raised the following problem: If Hobbes thinks of the will, as he appears to do elsewhere in the *Leviathan*, as merely what turns out to be the last "appetite" or impulse before our acting, can our "willing" to obey a ruler really manifest the choice of a stable, continuing, integrated moral personality in such a way as to bind us morally to that choice? See PATRICK RILEY, WILL AND POLITICAL LEGITIMACY 26 (1982).

15. Would it be accurate to say that for Hobbes, the sovereign's first crucial act is, by standing ready to enforce agreements between persons, to alleviate the otherwise reasonable suspicion that the first persons to disarm themselves are disadvantaged and vulnerable? See Steve Beackon & Andrew Reeve, *The Benefits of Reasonable Conduct*, 4 POLITICAL THEORY 423, 434 (1976).

16. Brian Barry contends that "Hobbes does not argue that the covenant obliges you because 'there is a power set up to constrain' *you*; he says that the covenant obliges you because 'there is a power set up to constrain' the *other* parties to it, thus taking away the 'reasonable suspicion' of being double-crossed that would otherwise invalidate such a covenant." Brian Barry, *Warrender and His Critics*, in HOBBES AND ROUSSEAU: A COLLECTION OF CRITICAL ESSAYS 54 (Maurice Cranston & Richard S. Peters eds. 1972) (emphasis in the original). On such a view, the legal obligation to one's sovereign ruler would not be simply a mystification of the ruler's ability to enforce compliance.

17. For an argument that the crucial feature of the transition out of a Hobbesian state of nature is not a general contract either among individual persons or between a ruler and the subjects generally, but the fulfillment of contracts between the ruler and a few subjects building the ruler's enforcement powers,

see JEAN HAMPTON, HOBBES AND THE SOCIAL CONTRACT TRADITION 187 (1986).

18. In Hobbes's scheme of things, are the laws of nature in society best understood as divine moral commandments, or as practical, hypothetical imperatives that might be compared to a doctor's orders that assume the patient wishes to get well? See J.W.M. WATKINS, HOBBES' SYSTEM OF IDEAS 87 (1965).

19. Carl Friedrich argues that Hobbes's theory strongly emphasizes considerations of utility, and of the recognized usefulness of peace and order in accounting for peoples' willingness to obey the law. See CARL FRIEDRICH, THE PHILOSOPHY OF LAW IN HISTORICAL PERSPECTIVE 87 (rev. 2d ed. 1963). Does this view understate the independent importance of natural law or natural right?

20. Howard Warrender suggests that there are really two conceptions of the law of nature at work in Hobbes's theory. First is the law of nature as interpreted by each person's conscience regarding her inner disposition to obey, where the sovereign supposedly cannot reach and has no power. Second is the law of nature as authoritatively interpreted by the sovereign, so as to reduce social conflict. See HOWARD WARRENDER, THE POLITICAL PHILOSOPHY OF HOBBES 324-29 (1952).

21. What relationship is there between the ideas of Aquinas and Hobbes on natural law and law-giving? For a brief discussion of the relationship between divine law-giving authority and that of the Hobbesian civil authority, see MICHAEL OAKESHOTT, HOBBES ON CIVIL ASSOCIATION 67-69 (1975).

22. It has been argued that Augustine would agree with Hobbes that legitimizing any resistance to the established government invites chaos and anarchy. See Herbert A. Deane, *The Political and Social Ideas of St. Augustine*, in ESSAYS IN THE HISTORY OF POLITICAL THOUGHT 85, 93 (Isaac Kramnick ed. 1969). Note Augustine's exception, though, for "laws or commands that run contrary to God's commands." *Id.* at 94. Will the scope or applicability of this exception generally be clear? Is Augustine here contributing to the foundation of the theory of civil disobedience and conscientious nonperformance?

23. Richard Peters argues that for Hobbes, "[t]he sovereign must be the final arbiter in all matters of law, morals and religion. . . . The liberty of the subject consisted only in those things which were not forbidden by law, law being simply the command of the sovereign. To say that a law was unjust could mean nothing except that it had been abrogated by another law." Richard S. Peters, *Introduction* to THOMAS HOBBES, LEVIATHAN 11 (Michael Oakeshott ed. 1962). Does this formulation leave room for the natural right

of self-preservation apparently recognized by Hobbes?

24. Is it both helpful, and a fair reading of Hobbes, to conclude that when we enter into civil society, we surrender only a portion of our right of private judgment and of our right to defend ourselves from danger? Specifically, do we surrender only our right of judgment or of self-defense in close, borderline cases where questions of danger may have no clear right or wrong answers? See RICHARD TUCK, HOBBES 64-65 (1989). Could the sovereign ruler and subjects differ precisely over whether a particular case is in fact a close or borderline case? Is the ruler typically the best judge of how much danger a given individual faces? For further discussion of Hobbes's inability to establish a moral obligation to obey life-threatening commands of the sovereign in circumstances less grave than total war, see HADLEY ARKES, FIRST THINGS ch. X (1986).

25. On Richard Tuck's formulation of Hobbes's theory, "where it is absolutely clear to an individual citizen that his life is in danger . . . then of course he must defend it himself, whatever the sovereign might say. . . ." RICHARD TUCK, HOBBES 66 (1989). Would Hobbes therefore fall into the general category of those contemporary theorists who reject the idea of a truly general prima facie moral obligation to obey the law?

26. Can it fairly be said of Hobbes's theory that "[u]ltimately obedience depends, not on a covenant or promise to obey, but on the continuance of protection. . . ?" J.W. GOUGH, THE SOCIAL CONTRACT 111 (2d ed. 1957).

27. Do Hobbes's subjects have any obligation to the sovereign ruler to continue their authorization or allegiance to the ruler? Or do the subjects have such an obligation to one another to continue their allegiance to the ruler? See DAVID GAUTHIER, THE LOGIC OF LEVIATHAN 159 (1969).

28. For a brief summary of David Gauthier's reconstruction of the logic of Hobbes's argument on political obligation, emphasizing the role of the idea of authorization of the sovereign's actions by the subjects, see DAVID GAUTHIER, THE LOGIC OF LEVIATHAN 150-51 (1969).

29. In connection with Gauthier's *The Logic of Leviathan*, see DAVID GAUTHIER, MORALS BY AGREEMENT 158-65 (1986). For responses to Gauthier's own independent moral theory, see THE NEW SOCIAL CONTRACT: ESSAYS ON GAUTHIER (Ellen Frankel Paul et· al. eds. 1988).

30. Is Hobbes's central focus on the political obligation of the mass of isolated, abstract individuals? Is Hobbes a methodological individualist? For criticism

of these assumptions, see DEBORAH BAUMGOLD, HOBBES'S POLITICAL THEORY 1-2, 14-15 (1988).

31. Is Hobbes's theory of political obligation an early attempt to apply the methods of what we would now call rational choice theory to political problems? See ANDRZEJ RAPACZYNSKI, NATURE AND POLITICS 101 (1987).

32. Quentin Skinner concludes that Hobbes's contemporary critics agreed that the foundation of political obligation for Hobbes is the calculation of individual self-interest. See Quentin Skinner, *The Context of Hobbes' Theory of Political Obligation*, in HOBBES AND ROUSSEAU: A COLLECTION OF CRITICAL ESSAYS 139 (Maurice Cranston & Richard S. Peters eds. 1972). Is rational self-interest really as closely and overwhelmingly tied to the fear of violent death as Hobbes imagines?

33. C.B. Macpherson asks: "If the obligation of individuals to the state is based only on their calculation of their own self-interest, how can it be sufficient to hold a society together, since the same self-interest can be expected to dictate a breach of that obligation whenever changed circumstances would seem to make that profitable?" C.B. Macpherson, *Introduction* to THOMAS HOBBES, LEVIATHAN 61 (C.B. Macpherson ed. 1968). Does economic class interest help to supply the otherwise missing stability? *See id.* at 63.

34. How would Hobbes react to the suggestion that in many cases, obedience to the law is not really necessary to protect society's interests? For David Gauthier's view of Hobbes's response, see DAVID GAUTHIER, THE LOGIC OF LEVIATHAN 152 (1969). Is part of the answer that the cost of obeying either necessary or unnecessary laws on, for example, traffic stoplights, or the consumption of recreational drugs, is usually quite low, that the risk of underestimating the value of general habits or patterns of obedience is at least minimal, and that the cost of falsely assuming that certain kinds of disobedience are harmless may potentially be high?

35. How helpful in explaining Hobbes's theory is it to notice that saying "I promise" under the proper circumstances not only conveys an idea, but performs the very act of promising itself? See generally Geraint Parry, *Performative Utterances and Obligation in Hobbes*, 17 PHILOSOPHICAL QUARTERLY 246 (1967).

36. Note that the classical Chinese philosopher Mo Tzu presents what is in substance a social contract theory bearing some close and important resemblances to that of Hobbes. See FUNG YU-LAN, 1 A HISTORY OF CHINESE PHILOSOPHY 100-03 (Derk Bodde trans. 1952). For further discussion of what

might be called a classical Chinese account of the transition between an ordered, regulated society and its lack, see Antonio S. Cua, *The Concept of Li in Confucian Moral Theory*, in UNDERSTANDING THE CHINESE MIND 209, 221 (Robert E. Allinson ed. 1989).

37. For a republican turn on some of Hobbes's basic themes and methods, see BENEDICT DE SPINOZA, A THEOLOGICO-POLITICAL TREATISE AND A POLITICAL TREATISE (R.H.M. Elwes trans. 1951). For general commentary on Spinoza's theory, see ROBERT J. MCSHEA, THE POLITICAL PHILOSOPHY OF SPINOZA (1968). For two brief accounts of Spinoza's political thought in relation to the developing Jewish tradition, see JEWISH PHILOSOPHERS 145-46 (Steven T. Katz ed. 1975); NORBERT M. SAMUELSON, AN INTRODUCTION TO MODERN JEWISH PHILOSOPHY 130-35 (1989).

38. Note that according to Montesquieu's account, Hobbes errs in failing to recognize that in a true state of nature, humans are naturally fearful rather than aggressive. See MONTESQUIEU, THE SPIRIT OF THE LAWS 4 (Thomas Nugent trans. 1962). But as soon as persons enter society, encouraged in part by their recognition of the shared nature of their fear, a state of war develops which gives rise to political authority and positive human law. *See id.* at 5-6.

39. For a detailed comparison of the theories of legal obligation of Hobbes and the contemporary theorist H.L.A. Hart, see Roger Shiner, *Hart and Hobbes*, 22 WILLIAM & MARY LAW REVIEW 201 (1980).

40. Those interested in further pursuit of the interpretation of Hobbes's political philosophy are encouraged to consult HOBBES STUDIES (K.C. Brown ed. 1965) and LEO STRAUSS, THE POLITICAL PHILOSOPHY OF HOBBES (Elsa M. Sinclair trans. 1952).

# 13

# From John Locke,
# Second Treatise of Government

... 4. To understand political power aright, and derive it from its original, we must consider what estate all men are naturally in, and that is, a state of perfect freedom to order their actions, and dispose of their possessions and persons as they think fit, within the bounds of the law of Nature, without asking leave or depending upon the will of any other man.

A state also of equality, wherein all the power and jurisdiction is reciprocal, no one having more than another, there being nothing more evident than that creatures of the same species and rank, promiscuously born to all the same advantages of Nature, and the use of the same faculties, should also be equal one amongst another, without subordination or subjection, unless the lord and master of them all should, by any manifest declaration of his will, set one above another, and confer on him, by an evident and clear appointment, an undoubted right to dominion and sovereignty.

5. This equality of men by Nature, the judicious Hooker looks upon as so evident in itself, and beyond all question, that he makes it the foundation of that obligation to mutual love amongst men on which he builds the duties they owe one another, and from whence he derives the great maxims of justice and charity. His words are:

> The like natural inducement hath brought men to know that it is no less their duty to love others than themselves, for seeing those things which are equal, must needs all have one measure; if I cannot but wish to receive good, even as much at every man's hands, as any man can wish unto his own soul, how should I look to have any part of my desire herein satisfied, unless myself be careful to satisfy the like desire, which is undoubtedly in other men weak, being of one and the same nature: to have anything offered them repugnant to this desire must needs, in all respects, grieve them as much as me; so that if I do harm, I must look to suffer, there being no reason that others should show greater measure of love to me than they have by me showed unto them; my desire, therefore, to be loved of my equals in Nature, as much as possible may be, imposeth upon me a natural duty of bearing to themward fully the like affection. From which relation of equality between ourselves and them

that are as ourselves, what several rules and canons natural reason hath drawn for direction of life no man is ignorant. (*Eccl. Pol.* i.)

6. But though this be a state of liberty, yet it is not a state of license; though man in that state have an uncontrollable liberty to dispose of his person or possessions, yet he has not liberty to destroy himself, or so much as any creature in his possession, but where some nobler use than its bare preservation calls for it. The state of Nature has a law of Nature to govern it, which obliges every one, and reason, which is that law, teaches all mankind who will but consult it, that being all equal and independent, no one ought to harm another in his life, health, liberty or possessions; for men being all the workmanship of one omnipotent and infinitely wise Maker; all the servants of one sovereign Master, sent into the world by His order and about His business; they are His property, whose workmanship they are made to last during His, not one another's pleasure. And, being furnished with like faculties, sharing all in one community of Nature, there cannot be supposed any such subordination among us that may authorise us to destroy one another, as if we were made for one another's uses, as the inferior ranks of creatures are for ours. Every one as he is bound to preserve himself, and not to quit his station wilfully, so by the like reason, when his own preservation comes not in competition, ought he as much as he can to preserve the rest of mankind, and not unless it be to do justice on an offender, take away or impair the life, or what tends to the preservation of the life, the liberty, health, limb, or goods of another.

7. And that all men may be restrained from invading others' rights, and from doing hurt to one another, and the law of Nature be observed, which willeth the peace and preservation of all mankind, the execution of the law of Nature is in that state put into everyman's hands, whereby every one has a right to punish the transgressors of that law to such a degree as may hinder its violation. For the law of Nature would, as all other laws that concern men in this world, be in vain if there were nobody that in the state of Nature had a power to execute that law, and thereby preserve the innocent and restrain offenders; and if any one in the state of Nature may punish another for any evil he has done, every one may do so. For in that state of perfect equality, where naturally there is no superiority or jurisdiction of one over another, what any may do in prosecution of that law, every one must needs have a right to do.

8. And thus, in the state of Nature, one man comes by a power over another; but yet no absolute or arbitrary power, to use a criminal, when he has got him in his hands, according to the passionate heats or boundless extravagancy of his own will, but only to retribute to him so far as calm reason and conscience dictate, what is proportionate to his transgression, which is so much as may serve for reparation and restraint. For these two are the only reasons why one man may lawfully do harm to another, which is that we call punishment. In transgressing the law of Nature, the offender declares himself to live by another rule than that of reason and common equity, which is that measure God has set to actions of

men for their mutual security, and so he becomes dangerous to mankind; the tie which is to secure them from injury and violence being slighted and broken by him, which being a trespass against the whole species, and the peace and safety of it, provided for by the law of Nature, every man upon this score, by the right he hath to preserve mankind in general, may restrain, or where it is necessary, destroy things noxious to them, and so may bring such evil on any one who hath transgressed that law, as may make him repent the doing of it, and thereby deter him, and, by his example, others from doing the like mischief. And in this case, and upon this ground, every man hath a right to punish the offender, and be executioner of the law of Nature.

9. I doubt not but this will seem a very strange doctrine to some men; but before they condemn it, I desire them to resolve me by what right any prince or state can put to death or punish an alien for any crime he commits in their country? It is certain their laws, by virtue of any sanction they receive from the promulgated will of the legislature, reach not a stranger. They speak not to him, nor, if they did, is he bound to hearken to them. The legislative authority by which they are in force over the subjects of that commonwealth hath no power over him. Those who have the supreme power of making laws in England, France, or Holland are, to an Indian, but like the rest of the world—men without authority. And therefore, if by the law of Nature every man hath not a power to punish offences against it, as he soberly judges the case to require, I see not how the magistrates of any community can punish an alien of another country, since, in reference to him, they can have no more power than what every man naturally may have over another.

10. Besides the crime which consists in violating the laws, and varying from the right rule of reason, whereby a man so far becomes degenerate, and declares himself to quit the principles of human nature and to be a noxious creature, there is commonly injury done, and some person or other, some other man, receives damage by his transgression; in which case, he who hath received any damage has (besides the right of punishment common to him, with other men) a particular right to seek reparation from him that hath done it. And any other person who finds it just may also join with him that is injured, and assist him in recovering from the offender so much as may make satisfaction for the harm he hath suffered.

11. From these two distinct rights (the one of punishing the crime, for restraint and preventing the like offence, which right of punishing is in everybody, the other of taking reparation, which belongs only to the injured party) comes it to pass that the magistrate, who by being magistrate hath the common right of punishing put into his hands, can often, where the public good demands not the execution of the law, remit the punishment of criminal offences by his own authority, but yet cannot remit the satisfaction due to any private man for the damage he has received. That he who hath suffered the damage has a right to demand in his own name, and he alone can remit. The damnified person has this

power of appropriating to himself the goods or service of the offender by right of
self-preservation, as every man has a power to punish the crime to prevent its
being committed again, by the right he has of preserving all mankind, and doing
all reasonable things he can in order to that end. And thus it is that every man in
the state of Nature has a power to kill a murderer, both to deter others from doing
the like injury (which no reparation can compensate) by the example of the
punishment that attends it from everybody, and also to secure men from the
attempts of a criminal who, having renounced reason, the common rule and
measure God hath given to mankind, hath, by the unjust violence and slaughter
he hath committed upon one, declared war against all mankind, and therefore may
be destroyed as a lion or a tiger, one of those wild savage beasts with whom men
can have no society nor security. And upon this is grounded that great law of
Nature, "Whoso sheddeth man's blood, by man shall his blood be shed." And Cain
was so fully convinced that every one had a right to destroy such a criminal, that,
after the murder of his brother, he cries out, "Every one that findeth me shall slay
me," so plain was it writ in the hearts of all mankind.

12. By the same reason may a man in the state of Nature punish the lesser
breaches of that law, it will, perhaps, be demanded, with death? I answer: Each
transgression may be punished to that degree, and with so much severity, as will
suffice to make it an ill bargain to the offender, give him cause to repent, and
terrify others from doing the like. Every offence that can be committed in the state
of Nature may, in the state of Nature, be also punished equally, and as far forth,
as it may, in a commonwealth. For though it would be beside my present purpose
to enter here into the particulars of the law of Nature, or its measures of
punishment, yet it is certain there is such a law, and that too as intelligible and
plain to a rational creature and a studier of that law as the positive laws of
commonwealths, nay, possibly plainer; as much as reason is easier to be
understood than the fancies and intricate contrivances of men, following contrary
and hidden interests put into words; for truly so are a great part of the municipal
laws of countries, which are only so far right as they are founded on the law of
Nature, by which they are to be regulated and interpreted.

13. To this strange doctrine—viz., That in the state of Nature every one has
the executive power of the law of Nature—I doubt not but it will be objected that
it is unreasonable for men to be judges in their own cases, that self-love will make
men partial to themselves and their friends; and, on the other side, ill-nature,
passion, and revenge will carry them too far in punishing others, and hence
nothing but confusion and disorder will follow, and that therefore God hath
certainly appointed government to restrain the partiality and violence of men. I
easily grant that civil government is the proper remedy for the inconveniences of
the state of Nature, which must certainly be great where men may be judges in
their own case, since it is easy to be imagined that he who was so unjust as to do
his brother an injury will scarce be so just as to condemn himself for it. But I
shall desire those who make this objection to remember that absolute monarchs

are but men; and if government is to be the remedy of those evils which necessarily follow from men being judges in their own cases, and the state of Nature is therefore not to be endured, I desire to know what kind of government that is, and how much better it is than the state of Nature, where one man commanding a multitude has the liberty to be judge in his own case, and may do to all his subjects whatever he pleases without the least question or control of those who execute his pleasure? And in whatsoever he doth, whether led by reason, mistake, or passion, must be submitted to? Which men in the state of Nature are not bound to do one to another. And if he that judges, judges amiss in his own or any other case, he is answerable for it to the rest of mankind.

14. It is often asked as a mighty objection, where are, or ever were, there any men in such a state of Nature? To which it may suffice as an answer at present, that since all princes and rulers of "independent" governments all through the world are in a state of Nature, it is plain the world never was, nor never will be, without numbers of men in that state. I have named all governors of "independent" communities, whether they are, or are not, in league with others; for it is not every compact that puts an end to the state of Nature between men, but only this one of agreeing together mutually to enter into one community, and make one body politic; other promises and compacts men may make one with another, and yet still be in the state of Nature. The promises and bargains for truck, etc., between the two men in Soldania, in or between a Swiss and an Indian, in the woods of America, are binding to them, though they are perfectly in a state of Nature in reference to one another for truth, and keeping of faith belongs to men as men, and not as members of society.

15. To those that say there were never any men in the state of Nature, I will not only oppose the authority of the judicious Hooker (*Eccl. Pol.* i. 10), where he says, "the laws which have been hitherto mentioned"—*i.e.*, the laws of Nature—"do bind men absolutely, even as they are men, although they have never any settled fellowship, never any solemn agreement amongst themselves what to do or not to do; but for as much as we are not by ourselves sufficient to furnish ourselves with competent store of things needful for such a life as our Nature doth desire, a life fit for the dignity of man, therefore to supply those defects and imperfections which are in us, as living single and solely by ourselves, we are naturally induced to seek communion and fellowship with others; this was the cause of men uniting themselves as first in politic societies." But I, moreover, affirm that all men are naturally in that state, and remain so till, by their own consents, they make themselves members of some politic society, and I doubt not, in the sequel of this discourse, to make it very clear.

16. THE state of war is a state of enmity and destruction; and therefore declaring by word or action, not a passionate and hasty, but a sedate, settled design upon another man's life puts him in a state of war with him against whom he has declared such an intention, and so has exposed his life to the other's power to be taken away by him, or any one that joins with him in his defence, and

espouses his quarrel; it being reasonable and just I should have a right to destroy that which threatens me with destruction; for by the fundamental law of Nature, man being to be preserved as much as possible, when all cannot be preserved, the safety of the innocent is to be preferred, and one may destroy a man who makes war upon him, or has discovered an enmity to his being, for the same reason that he may kill a wolf or a lion, because they are not under the ties of the common law of reason, have no other rule but that of force and violence, and so may be treated as a beast of prey, those dangerous and noxious creatures that will be sure to destroy him whenever he falls into their power.

17. And hence it is that he who attempts to get another man into his absolute power does thereby put himself into a state of war with him; it being to be understood as a declaration of a design upon his life. For I have reason to conclude that he who would get me into his power without my consent would use me as he pleased when he had got me there, and destroy me too when he had a fancy to it; for nobody can desire to have me in his absolute power unless it be to compel me by force to that which is against the right of my freedom—*i.e.* make me a slave. To be free from such force is the only security of my preservation, and reason bids me look on him as an enemy to my preservation who would take away that freedom which is the fence to it; so that he who makes an attempt to enslave me thereby puts himself into a state of war with me. He that in the state of Nature would take away the freedom that belongs to any one in that state must necessarily be supposed to have a design to take away everything else, that freedom being the foundation of all the rest; as he that in the state of society would take away the freedom belonging to those of that society or commonwealth must be supposed to design to take away from them everything else, and so be looked on as in a state of war.

18. This makes it lawful for a man to kill a thief who has not in the least hurt him, nor declared any design upon his life, any farther than by the use of force, so to get him in his power as to take away his money, or what he pleases, from him; because using force, where he has no right to get me into his power, let his pretence be what it will, I have no reason to suppose that he who would take away my liberty would not, when he had me in his power, take away everything else. And, therefore, it is lawful for me to treat him as one who has put himself into a state of war with me—*i.e.*, kill him if I can; for to that hazard does he justly expose himself, whoever introduces a state of war, and is aggressor in it.

19. And here we have the plain difference between the state of Nature and the state of war, which however some men have confounded, are as far distant as a state of peace, goodwill, mutual assistance, and preservation; and a state of enmity, malice, violence and mutual destruction are one from another. Men living together according to reason without a common superior on earth, with authority to judge between them, is properly the state of Nature. But force, or a declared design of force upon the person of another, where there is no common superior on earth to appeal to for relief, is the state of war; and it is the want of such an

appeal gives a man the right of war even against an aggressor, though he be in society and a fellow-subject. Thus, a thief whom I cannot harm, but by appeal to the law, for having stolen all that I am worth, I may kill when he sets on me to rob me but of my horse or coat, because the law, which was made for my preservation, where it cannot interpose to secure my life from present force, which if lost is capable of no reparation, permits me my own defence and the right of war, a liberty to kill the aggressor, because the aggressor allows not time to appeal to our common judge, nor the decision of the law, for remedy in a case where the mischief may be irreparable. Want of a common judge with authority puts all men in a state of Nature; force without right upon a man's person makes a state of war both where there is, and is not, a common judge.

20. But when the actual force is over, the state of war ceases between those that are in society and are equally on both sides subject to the judge; and, therefore, in such controversies, where the question is put, "Who shall be judge?" it cannot be meant who shall decide the controversy; every one knows what Jephtha here tells us, that "the Lord the Judge" shall judge. Where there is no judge on earth the appeal lies to God in Heaven. That question then cannot mean who shall judge, whether another hath put himself in a state of war with me, and whether I may, as Jephtha did, appeal to Heaven in it? Of that I myself can only judge in my own conscience, as I will answer it at the great day to the Supreme Judge of all men. . . .

95. MEN being, as has been said, by nature all free, equal, and independent, no one can be put out of this estate and subjected to the political power of another without his own consent, which is done by agreeing with other men, to join and unite into a community for their comfortable, safe, and peaceable living, one amongst another, in a secure enjoyment of their properties, and a greater security against any that are not of it. This any number of men may do, because it injures not the freedom of the rest; they are left, as they were, in the liberty of the state of Nature. When any number of men have so consented to make one community or government, they are thereby presently incorporated, and make one body politic, wherein the majority have a right to act and conclude the rest.

96. For, when any number of men have, by the consent of every individual, made a community, they have thereby made that community one body, with a power to act as one body, which is only by the will and determination of the majority. For that which acts any community, being only the consent of the individuals of it, and it being one body, must move one way, it is necessary the body should move that way whither the greater force carries it, which is the consent of the majority, or else it is impossible it should act or continue one body, one community, which the consent of every individual that united into it agreed that it should; and so every one is bound by that consent to be concluded by the majority. And therefore we see that in assemblies empowered to act by positive laws where no number is set by that positive law which empowers them, the act of the majority passes for the act of the whole, and of course determines as

having, by the law of Nature and reason, the power of the whole.

97. And thus every man, by consenting with others to make one body politic under one government, puts himself under an obligation to every one of that society to submit to the determination of the majority, and to be concluded by it; or else this original compact, whereby he with others incorporates into one society, would signify nothing, and be no compact if he be left free and under no other ties than he was in before in the state of Nature. For what appearance would there be of any compact? What new engagement if he were no farther tied by any decrees of the society than he himself thought fit and did actually consent to? This would be still as great a liberty as he himself had before his compact, or any one else in the state of Nature, who may submit himself and consent to any acts of it if he thinks fit.

98. For if the consent of the majority shall not in reason be received as the act of the whole, and conclude every individual, nothing but the consent of every individual can make anything to be the act of the whole, which, considering the infirmities of health and avocations of business, which in a number though much less than that of a commonwealth, will necessarily keep many away from the public assembly; and the variety of opinions and contrariety of interests which unavoidably happen in all collections of men, it is next impossible ever to be had. And, therefore, if coming into society be upon such terms, it will be only like Cato's coming into the theatre, *tantum ut exiret*. Such a constitution as this would make the mighty Leviathan of a shorter duration than the feeblest creatures, and not let it outlast the day it was born in, which cannot be supposed till we can think that rational creatures should desire and constitute societies only to be dissolved. For where the majority cannot conclude the rest, there they cannot act as one body, and consequently will be immediately dissolved again.

99. Whosoever, therefore, out of a state of Nature unite into a community, must be understood to give up all the power necessary to the ends for which they unite into society to the majority of the community, unless they expressly agreed in any number greater than the majority. And this is done by barely agreeing to unite into one political society, which is all the compact that is, or needs be, between the individuals that enter into or make up a commonwealth. And thus, that which begins and actually constitutes any political society is nothing but the consent of any number of freemen capable of majority, to unite and incorporate into such a society. And this is that, and that only, which did or could give beginning to any lawful government in the world. . . .

119. Every man being, as has been showed, naturally free, and nothing being able to put him into subjection to any earthly power, but only his own consent, it is to be considered what shall be understood to be a sufficient declaration of a man's consent to make him subject to the laws of any government. There is a common distinction of an express and a tacit consent, which will concern our present case. Nobody doubts but an express consent of any man, entering into any society, makes him a perfect member of that society, a subject of that government.

The difficulty is, what ought to be looked upon as a tacit consent, and how far it binds—*i.e.*, how far any one shall be looked on to have consented, and thereby submitted to any government, where he has made no expressions of it at all. And to this I say, that every man that hath any possession or enjoyment of any part of the dominions of any government doth thereby give his tacit consent, and is as far forth obliged to obedience to the laws of that government, during such enjoyment, as any one under it, whether this his possession be of land to him and his heirs for ever, or a lodging only for a week; or whether it be barely travelling freely on the highway; and, in effect, it reaches as far as the very being of any one within the territories of that government.

120. To understand this the better, it is fit to consider that every man when he at first incorporates himself into any commonwealth, he, by his uniting himself thereunto, annexes also, and submits to the community those possessions which he has, or shall acquire, that do not already belong to any other government. For it would be a direct contradiction for any one to enter into society with others for the securing and regulating of property, and yet to suppose his land, whose property is to be regulated by the laws of the society, should be exempt from the jurisdiction of that government to which he himself, and the property of the land, is a subject. By the same act, therefore, whereby any one unites his person, which was before free, to any commonwealth, by the same he unites his possessions, which were before free, to it also; and they become, both of them, person and possession, subject to the government and dominion of that commonwealth as long as it hath a being. Whoever therefore, from thenceforth, by inheritance, purchases, permission, or otherwise enjoys any part of the land so annexed to, and under the government of that commonweal, must take it with the condition it is under—that is, of submitting to the government of the commonwealth, under whose jurisdiction it is, as far forth as any subject of it.

121. But since the government has a direct jurisdiction only over the land and reaches the possessor of it (before he has actually incorporated himself in the society) only as he dwells upon and enjoys that, the obligation any one is under by virtue of such enjoyment to submit to the government begins and ends with the enjoyment; so that whenever the owner, who has given nothing but such a tacit consent to the government will, by donation, sale or otherwise, quit the said possession, he is at liberty to go and incorporate himself into any other commonwealth, or agree with others to begin a new one *in vacuis locis*, in any part of the world they can find free and unpossessed; whereas he that has once, by actual agreement and any express declaration, given his consent to be of any commonweal, is perpetually and indispensably obliged to be, and remain unalterably a subject to it, and can never be again in the liberty of the state of Nature, unless by any calamity the government he was under comes to be dissolved.

122. But submitting to the laws of any country, living quietly and enjoying privileges and protection under them, makes not a man a member of that society;

it is only a local protection and homage due to and from all those who, not being in a state of war, come within the territories belonging to any government, to all parts whereof the force of its law extends. But this no more makes a man a member of that society, a perpetual subject of that commonwealth, than it would make a man a subject to another in whose family he found it convenient to abide for some time, though, whilst he continued in it, he were obliged to comply with the laws and submit to the government he found there. And thus we see that foreigners, by living all their lives under another government, and enjoying the privileges and protection of it, though they are bound, even in conscience, to submit to its administration as far forth as any denizen, yet do not thereby come to be subjects or members of that commonwealth. Nothing can make any man so but his actually entering into it by positive engagement and express promise and compact. This is that which I think, concerning the beginning of political societies, and that consent which makes any one a member of any commonwealth. . . .

123. IF man in the state of Nature be so free as has been said, if he be absolute lord of his own person and possessions, equal to the greatest and subject to nobody, why will he part with his freedom, this empire, and subject himself to the dominion and control of any other power? To which it is obvious to answer, that though in the state of Nature he hath such a right, yet the enjoyment of it is very uncertain and constantly exposed to the invasion of others; for all being kings as much as he, every man his equal, and the greater part no strict observers of equity and justice, the enjoyment of the property he has in this state is very unsafe, very insecure. This makes him willing to quit this condition which, however free, is full of fears and continual dangers; and it is not without reason that he seeks out and is willing to join in society with others who are already united, or have a mind to unite for the mutual preservation of their lives, liberties and estates, which I call by the general name—property.

124. The great and chief end, therefore, of men uniting into commonwealths, and putting themselves under government, is the preservation of their property; to which in the state of Nature there are many things wanting.

Firstly, there wants an established, settled, known law, received and allowed by common consent to be the standard of right and wrong, and the common measure to decide all controversies between them. For though the law of Nature be plain and intelligible to all rational creatures, yet men, being biased by their interest, as well as ignorant for want of study of it, are not apt to allow of it as a law binding to them in the application of it to their particular cases.

125. Secondly, in the state of Nature there wants a known and indifferent judge, with authority to determine all differences according to the established law. For every one in that state being both judge and executioner of the law of Nature, men being partial to themselves, passion and revenge is very apt to carry them too far, and with too much heat in their own cases, as well as negligence and unconcernedness, make them too remiss in other men's.

126. Thirdly, in the state of Nature there often wants power to back and

support the sentence when right, and to give it due execution. They who by any injustice offended will seldom fail where they are able by force to make good their injustice. Such resistance many times makes the punishment dangerous, and frequently destructive to those who attempt it.

127. Thus mankind, notwithstanding all the privileges of the state of Nature, being but in an ill condition while they remain in it are quickly driven into society. Hence it comes to pass, that we seldom find any number of men live any time together in this state. The inconveniencies that they are therein exposed to by the irregular and uncertain exercise of the power every man has of punishing the transgressions of others, make them take sanctuary under the established laws of government, and therein seek the preservation of their property. It is this makes them so willingly give up every one his single power of punishing to be exercised by such alone as shall be appointed to it amongst them, and by such rules as the community, or those authorised by them to that purpose, shall agree on. And in this we have the original right and rise of both the legislative and executive power as well as of the governments and societies themselves.

128. For in the state of Nature, to omit the liberty he has of innocent delights, a man has two powers. The first is to do whatsoever he thinks fit for the preservation of himself and others within the permission of the law of Nature; by which law, common to them all, he and all the rest of mankind are one community, make up one society distinct from all other creatures, and were it not for the corruption and viciousness of degenerate men, there would be no need of any other, no necessity that men should separate from this great and natural community, and associate into lesser combinations. The other power a man has in the state of Nature is the power to punish the crimes committed against that law. Both these he gives up when he joins in a private, if I may so call it, or particular political society, and incorporates into any commonwealth separate from the rest of mankind.

129. The first power—viz., of doing whatsoever he thought fit for the preservation of himself and the rest of mankind, he gives up to be regulated by laws made by the society, so far forth as the preservation of himself and the rest of that society shall require; which laws of the society in many things confine the liberty he had by the law of Nature.

130. Secondly, the power of punishing he wholly gives up, and engages his natural force, which he might before employ in the execution of the law of Nature, by his own single authority, as he thought fit, to assist the executive power of the society as the law thereof shall require. For being now in a new state, wherein he is to enjoy many conveniencies from the labour, assistance, and society of others in the same community, as well as protection from its whole strength, he is to part also with as much of his natural liberty, in providing for himself, as the good, prosperity, and safety of the society shall require, which is not only necessary but just, since the other members of the society do the like.

131. But though men when they enter into society give up the equality,

liberty, and executive power they had in the state of Nature in the hands of the society, to be so far disposed of by the legislative as the good of the society shall require, yet it being only with an intention in every one the better to preserve himself, his liberty and property (for no rational creature can be supposed to change his condition with an intention to be worse), the power of the society or legislative constituted by them can never be supposed to extend farther than the common good, but is obliged to secure every one's property by providing against those three defects above mentioned that made the state of Nature so unsafe and uneasy. And so, whoever has the legislative or supreme power of any commonwealth, is bound to govern by established standing laws, promulgated and known to the people, and not by extemporary decrees, by indifferent and upright judges, who are to decide controversies by those laws; and to employ the force of the community at home only in the execution of such laws, or abroad to prevent or redress foreign injuries and secure the community from inroads and invasion. And all this to be directed to no other end but the peace, safety, and public good of the people. . . .

134. THE great end of men's entering into society being the enjoyment of their properties in peace and safety, and the great instrument and means of that being the laws established in that society, the first and fundamental positive law of all commonwealths is the establishing of the legislative power, as the first and fundamental natural law which is to govern even the legislative. Itself is the preservation of the society and (as far as will consist with the public good) of every person in it. This legislative is not only the supreme power of the commonwealth, but sacred and unalterable in the hands where the community have once placed it. Nor can any edict of anybody else, in what form soever conceived, or by what power soever backed, have the force and obligation of a law which has not its sanction from that legislative which the public has chosen and appointed; for without this the law could not have that which is absolutely necessary to its being a law, the consent of the society, over whom nobody can have a power to make laws but by their own consent and by authority received from them; and therefore all the obedience, which by the most solemn ties any one can be obliged to pay, ultimately terminates in this supreme power, and is directed by those laws which it enacts. Nor can any oaths to any foreign power whatsoever, or any domestic subordinate power, discharge any member of the society from his obedience to the legislative, acting pursuant to their trust, nor oblige him to any obedience contrary to the laws so enacted or farther than they do allow, it being ridiculous to imagine one can be tied ultimately to obey any power in the society which is not the supreme.

135. Though the legislative, whether placed in one or more, whether it be always in being or only by intervals, though it be the supreme power in every commonwealth, yet, first, it is not, nor can possibly be, absolutely arbitrary over the lives and fortunes of the people. For it being but the joint power of every member of the society given up to that person or assembly which is legislator, it

can be no more than those persons had in a state of Nature before they entered into society, and gave it up to the community. For nobody can transfer to another more power than he has in himself, and nobody has an absolute arbitrary power over himself, or over any other, to destroy his own life, or take away the life or property of another. A man, as has been proved, cannot subject himself to the arbitrary power of another; and having, in the state of Nature, no arbitrary power over the life, liberty, or possession of another, but only so much as the law of Nature gave him for the preservation of himself and the rest of mankind, this is all he doth, or can give up to the commonwealth, and by it to the legislative power, so that the legislative can have no more than this. Their power in the utmost bounds of it is limited to the public good of the society. It is a power that hath no other end but preservation and therefore can never have a right to destroy, enslave, or designedly to impoverish the subjects; the obligations of the law of Nature cease not in society, but only in many cases are drawn closer, and have, by human laws, known penalties annexed to them to enforce their observation. Thus the law of Nature stands as an eternal rule to all men, legislators as well as others. The rules that they make for other men's actions must, as well as their own and other men's actions, be conformable to the law of Nature—*i.e.*, to the will of God, of which that is a declaration, and the fundamental law of Nature being the preservation of mankind, no human sanction can be good or valid against it.

136. Secondly, the legislative or supreme authority cannot assume to itself a power to rule by extemporary arbitrary decrees, but is bound to dispense justice and decide the rights of the subject by promulgated standing laws, and known authorised judges. For the law of Nature being unwritten, and so nowhere to be found but in the minds of men, they who, through passion or interest, shall miscite or misapply it, cannot so easily be convinced of their mistake where there is no established judge; and so it serves not as it aught, to determine the rights and fence the properties of those that live under it, especially where every one is judge, interpreter, and executioner of it too, and that in his own case; and he that has right on his side, having ordinarily but his own single strength, hath not force enough to defend himself from injuries or punish delinquents. To avoid these inconveniencies which disorder men's properties in the state of Nature, men unite into societies that they may have the united strength of the whole society to secure and defend their properties, and may have standing rules to bound it by which every one may know what is his. To this end it is that men give up all their natural power to the society they enter into, and the community put the legislative power into such hands as they think fit, with this trust, that they shall be governed by declared laws, or else their peace, quiet, and property will still be at the same uncertainty as it was in the state of Nature.

137. Absolute arbitrary power, or governing without settled standing laws, can neither of them consist with the ends of society and government, which men would not quit the freedom of the state of Nature for, and tie themselves up under,

were it not to preserve their lives, liberties, and fortunes, and by stated rules of
right and property to secure their peace and quiet. It cannot be supposed that they
should intend, had they a power so to do, to give any one or more an absolute
arbitrary power over their persons and estates, and put a force into the magistrate's
nand to execute his unlimited will arbitrarily upon them; this were to put
themselves into a worse condition than the state of Nature, wherein they had a
liberty to defend their right against the injuries of others, and were upon equal
terms of force to maintain it, whether invaded by a single man or many in
combination. Whereas by supposing they have given up themselves to the absolute
arbitrary power and will of a legislator, they have disarmed themselves, and armed
him to make a prey of them when he pleases; he being in a much worse condition
that is exposed to the arbitrary power of one man who has the command of a
hundred thousand than he that is exposed to the arbitrary power of a hundred
thousand single men, nobody being secure, that his will who has such a command
is better than that of other men, though his force be a hundred thousand times
stronger. And, therefore, whatever form the commonwealth is under, the ruling
power ought to govern by declared and received laws, and not by extemporary
dictates and undetermined resolutions, for then mankind will be in a far worse
condition than in the state of Nature if they shall have armed one or a few men
with the joint power of a multitude, to force them to obey at pleasure the
exorbitant and unlimited decrees of their sudden thoughts, or unrestrained, and till
that moment, unknown wills, without having any measures set down which may
guide and justify their actions. For all the power the government has, being only
for the good of the society, as it ought not to be arbitrary and at pleasure, so it
ought to be exercised by established and promulgated laws, that both the people
may know their duty, and be safe and secure within the limits of the law, and the
rulers, too, kept within their due bounds, and not be tempted by the power they
have in their hands to employ it to purposes, and by such measures as they would
not have known, and own not willingly.

138. Thirdly, the supreme power cannot take from any man any part of his
property without his own consent. For the preservation of property being the end
of government, and that for which men enter into society, it necessarily supposes
and requires that the people should have property, without which they must be
supposed to lose that by entering into society which was the end for which they
entered into it; too gross an absurdity for any man to own. Men, therefore, in
society having property, they have such a right to the goods, which by the law of
the community are theirs, that nobody hath a right to take them, or any part of
them, from them without their own consent; without this they have no property
at all. For I have truly no property in that which another can by right take from
me when he pleases against my consent. Hence it is a mistake to think that the
supreme or legislative power of any commonwealth can do what it will, and
dispose of the estates of the subject arbitrarily, or take any part of them at
pleasure. This is not much to be feared in governments where the legislative

consists wholly or in part in assemblies which are variable, whose members upon the dissolution of the assembly are subjects under the common laws of their country, equally with the rest. But in governments where the legislative is in one lasting assembly, always in being, or in one man as in absolute monarchies, there is danger still, that they will think themselves to have a distinct interest from the rest of the community, and so will be apt to increase their own riches and power by taking what they think fit from the people. For a man's property is not at all secure, though there be good and equitable laws to set the bounds of it between him and his fellow-subjects, if he who commands those subjects have power to take from any private man what part he pleases of his property, and use and dispose of it as he thinks good.

139. But government, into whosesoever hands it is put, being as I have before showed, entrusted with this condition, and for this end, that men might have and secure their properties, the prince or senate, however it may have power to make laws for the regulating of property between the subjects one amongst another, yet can never have a power to take to themselves the whole, or any part of the subjects' property, without their own consent; for this would be in effect to leave them no property at all. And to let us see that even absolute power, where it is necessary, is not arbitrary by being absolute, but is still limited by that reason, and confined to those ends which required it in some cases to be absolute, we need look no farther than the common practice of martial discipline. For the preservation of the army, and in it of the whole commonwealth, requires an absolute obedience to the command of every superior officer, and it is justly death to disobey or dispute the most dangerous or unreasonable of them; but yet we see that neither the sergeant that could command a soldier to march up to the mouth of a cannon, or stand in a breach where he is almost sure to perish, can command that soldier to give him one penny of his money; nor the general that can condemn him to death for deserting his post, or not obeying the most desperate orders, cannot yet with all his absolute power of life and death dispose of one farthing of that soldier's estate, or seize one jot of his goods; whom yet he can command anything, and hang for the least disobedience. Because such a blind obedience is necessary to that end for which the commander has his power—viz., the preservation of the rest, but the disposing of his goods has nothing to do with it.

140. It is true governments cannot be supported without great charge, and it is fit every one who enjoys his share of the protection should pay out of his estate his proportion for the maintenance of it. But still it must be with his own consent—i.e., the consent of the majority, giving it either by themselves or their representatives chosen by them; for if any one shall claim a power to lay and levy taxes on the people by his own authority, and without such consent of the people, he thereby invades the fundamental law of property, and subverts the end of government. For what property have I in that which another may by right take when he pleases to himself?

141. Fourthly. The legislative cannot transfer the power of making laws to any other hands, for it being but a delegated power from the people, they who have it cannot pass it over to others. The people alone can appoint the form of the commonwealth, which is by constituting the legislative, and appointing in whose hands that shall be. And when the people have said, "We will submit, and be governed by laws made by such men, and in such forms," nobody else can say other men shall make laws for them, nor can they be bound by any laws but such as are enacted by those whom they have chosen and authorised to make laws for them.

142. These are the bounds which the trust that is put in them by the society and the law of God and Nature have set to the legislative power of every commonwealth, in all forms of government. First: They are to govern by promulgated established laws, not to be varied in particular cases, but to have one rule for rich and poor, for the favourite at Court, and the countryman at plough. Secondly: These laws also ought to be designed for no other end ultimately but the good of the people. Thirdly: They must not raise taxes on the property of the people without the consent of the people given by themselves or their deputies. And this properly concerns only such governments where the legislative is always in being, or at least where the people have not reserved any part of the legislative to deputies, to be from time to time chosen by themselves. Fourthly: the Legislative neither must nor can transfer the power of making laws to anybody else, or place it anywhere but where the people have. . . .

211. HE that will, with any clearness, speak of the dissolution of government, ought in the first place to distinguish between the dissolution of the society and the dissolution of the government. That which makes the community, and brings men out of the loose state of Nature into one politic society, is the agreement which every one has with the rest to incorporate and act as one body, and so be one distinct commonwealth. The usual, and almost only way whereby this union is dissolved, is the inroad of foreign force making a conquest upon them. For in that case (not being able to maintain and support themselves as one entire and independent body) the union belonging to that body, which consisted therein, must necessarily cease, and so every one return to the state he was in before, with a liberty to shift for himself and provide for his own safety, as he thinks fit, in some other society. Whenever the society is dissolved, it is certain the government of that society cannot remain. Thus conquerors' swords often cut up governments by the roots, and mangle societies to pieces, separating the subdued or scattered multitude from the protection of and dependence on that society which ought to have preserved them from violence. The world is too well-instructed in, and too forward to allow of this way of dissolving of governments, to need any more to be said of it; and there wants not much argument to prove that where the society is dissolved, the government cannot remain; that being as impossible as for the frame of a house to subsist when the materials of it are scattered and displaced by a whirlwind, or jumbled into a confused heap by an earthquake.

212. Besides this overturning from without, governments are dissolved from within:

First. When the legislative is altered, civil society being a state of peace amongst those who are of it, from whom the state of war is excluded by the umpirage which they have provided in their legislative for the ending all differences that may arise amongst any of them; it is in their legislative that the members of a commonwealth are united and combined together into one coherent living body. This is the soul that gives form, life, and unity to the commonwealth; from hence the several members have their mutual influence, sympathy, and connection; and therefore when the legislative is broken, or dissolved, dissolution and death follows. For the essence and union of the society consisting in having one will, the legislative, when once established by the majority, has the declaring and, as it were, keeping of that will. The constitution of the legislative is the first and fundamental act of society, whereby provision is made for the continuation of their union under the direction of persons and bonds of laws, made by persons authorised thereunto, by the consent and appointment of the people, without which no one man, or number of men, amongst them can have authority of making laws that shall be binding to the rest. When any one, or more, shall take upon them to make laws whom the people have not appointed so to do, they make laws without authority, which the people are not therefore bound to obey; by which means they come again to be out of subjection, and may constitute to themselves a new legislative, as they think best, being in full liberty to resist the force of those who, without authority, would impose anything upon them. Every one is at the disposure of his own will, when those who had, by the delegation of the society, the declaring of the public will, are excluded from it, and others usurp the place who have no such authority or delegation.

213. This being usually brought about by such in the commonwealth, who misuse the power they have, it is hard to consider it aright, and know at whose door to lay it, without knowing the form of government in which it happens. Let us suppose, then, the legislative placed in the concurrence of three distinct persons:—First, a single hereditary person having the constant, supreme, executive power, and with it the power of convoking and dissolving the other two within certain periods of time. Secondly, an assembly of hereditary nobility. Thirdly, an assembly of representatives chosen, *pro tempore*, by the people. Such a form of government supposed, it is evident:

214. First, that when such a single person or prince sets up his own arbitrary will in place of the laws which are the will of the society declared by the legislative, then the legislative is changed. For that being, in effect, the legislative whose rules and laws are put in execution, and required to be obeyed, when other laws are set up, and other rules pretended and enforced than what the legislative, constituted by the society, have enacted, it is plain that the legislative is changed. Whoever introduces new laws, not being thereunto authorised, by the fundamental appointment of the society, or subverts the old, disowns and overturns the power

by which they were made, and so sets up a new legislative.

215. Secondly, when the prince hinders the legislative from assembling in its due time, or from acting freely, pursuant to those ends for which it was constituted, the legislative is altered. For it is not a certain number of men—no, nor their meeting, unless they have also freedom of debating and leisure of perfecting what is for the good of the society, wherein the legislative consists; when these are taken away, or altered, so as to deprive the society of the due exercise of their power, the legislative is truly altered. For it is not names that constitute governments, but the use and exercise of those powers that were intended to accompany them; so that he who takes away the freedom, or hinders the acting of the legislative in its due seasons, in effect takes away the legislative, and puts an end to the government.

216. Thirdly, when, by the arbitrary power of the prince, the electors or ways of election are altered without the consent and contrary to the common interest of the people, there also the legislative is altered. For if others than those whom the society hath authorised thereunto do choose, or in another way than what the society hath prescribed, those chosen are not the legislative appointed by the people.

217. Fourthly, the delivery also of the people into the subjection of a foreign power, either by the prince or by the legislative, is certainly a change of the legislative, and so a dissolution of the government. For the end why people entered into society being to be preserved one entire, free, independent society, to be governed by its own laws, this is lost whenever they are given up into the power of another.

218. Why, in such a constitution as this, the dissolution of the government in these cases is to be imputed to the prince is evident, because he, having the force, treasure, and offices of the State to employ, and often persuading himself or being flattered by others, that, as supreme magistrate, he is incapable of control; he alone is in a condition to make great advances towards such changes under pretence of lawful authority, and has it in his hands to terrify or suppress opposers as factious, seditious, and enemies to the government; whereas no other part of the legislative, or people, is capable by themselves to attempt any alteration of the legislative without open and visible rebellion, apt enough to be taken notice of, which, when it prevails, produces effects very little different from foreign conquest. Besides, the prince, in such a form of government, having the power of dissolving the other parts of the legislative, and thereby rendering them private persons, they can never, in opposition to him, or without his concurrence, alter the legislative by a law, his consent being necessary to give any of their decrees that sanction. But yet so far as the other parts of the legislative any way contribute to any attempt upon the government, and do either promote, or not, what lies in them, hinder such designs, they are guilty, and partake in this, which is certainly the greatest crime men can be guilty of one towards another.

219. There is one way more whereby such a government may be dissolved,

and that is: When he who has the supreme executive power neglects and abandons that charge, so that the laws already made can no longer be put in execution; this is demonstratively to reduce all to anarchy, and so effectively to dissolve the government. For laws not being made for themselves, but to be, by their execution, the bonds of the society to keep every part of the body politic in its due place and function. When that totally ceases, the government visibly ceases, and the people become a confused multitude without order or connection. Where there is no longer the administration of justice for the securing of men's rights, nor any remaining power within the community to direct the force, or provide for the necessities of the public, there certainly is no government left. Where the laws cannot be executed it is all one as if there were no laws, and a government without laws is, I suppose, a mystery in politics inconceivable to human capacity, and inconsistent with human society.

220. In these, and the like cases, when the government is dissolved, the people are at liberty to provide for themselves by erecting a new legislative differing from the other by the change of persons, or form, or both, as they shall find it most for their safety and good. For the society can never, by the fault of another, lose the native and original right it has to preserve itself, which can only be done by a settled legislative and a fair and impartial execution of the laws made by it. But the state of mankind is not so miserable that they are not capable of using this remedy till it be too late to look for any. To tell people they may provide for themselves by erecting a new legislative, when, by oppression, artifice, or being delivered over to a foreign power, their old one is gone, is only to tell them they may expect relief when it is too late, and the evil is past cure. This is, in effect, no more than to bid them first be slaves, and then to take care of their liberty, and, when their chains are on, tell them they may act like free men. This, if barely so, is rather mockery than relief, and men can never be secure from tyranny if there be no means to escape it till they are perfectly under it; and, therefore, it is that they have not only a right to get out of it, but to prevent it.

221. There is, therefore, secondly, another way whereby governments are dissolved, and that is, when the legislative, or the prince, either of them act contrary to their trust.

For the legislative acts against the trust reposed in them when they endeavour to invade the property of the subject, and to make themselves, or any part of the community, masters or arbitrary disposers of the lives, liberties, or fortunes of the people.

222. The reason why men enter into society is the preservation of their property; and the end why they choose and authorise a legislative is that there may be laws made, and rules set, as guards and fences to the properties of all the society, to limit the power and moderate the dominion of every part and member of the society. For since it can never be supposed to be the will of the society that the legislative should have a power to destroy that which every one designs to secure by entering into society, and for which the people submitted themselves to

legislators of their own making: whenever the legislators endeavour to take away and destroy the property of the people, or to reduce them to slavery under arbitrary power, they put themselves into a state of war with the people, who are thereupon absolved from any farther obedience, and are left to the common refuge which God hath provided for all men against force and violence. Whensoever, therefore, the legislative shall transgress this fundamental rule of society, and either by ambition, fear, folly, or corruption, endeavour to grasp themselves, or put into the hands of any other, an absolute power over the lives, liberties, and estates of the people, by this breach of trust they forfeit the power the people had put into their hands for quite contrary ends, and it devolves to the people, who have a right to resume their original liberty, and by the establishment of a new legislative (such as they shall think fit), provide for their own safety and security, which is the end for which they are in society. What I have said here concerning the legislative in general holds true also concerning the supreme executor, who having a double trust put in him, both to have a part in the legislative and the supreme execution of the law, acts against both, when he goes about to set up his own arbitrary will as the law of the society. He acts also contrary to his trust when he employs the force, treasure, and offices of the society to corrupt the representatives and gain them to his purposes, when he openly pre-engages the electors, and prescribes, to their choice, such whom he has, by solicitation, threats, promises, or otherwise, won to his designs, and employs them to bring in such who have promised beforehand what to vote and what to enact. Thus to regulate candidates and electors, and new model the ways of election, what is it but to cut up the government by the roots, and poison the very fountain of public security? For the people having reserved to themselves the choice of their representatives as the fence to their properties, could do it for no other end but that they might always be freely chosen, and so chosen, freely act and advise as the necessity of the commonwealth and the public good should, upon examination and mature debate, be judged to require. This, those who give their votes before they hear the debate, and have weighed the reasons on all sides, are not capable of doing. To prepare such an assembly as this, and endeavour to set up the declared abettors of his own will, for the true representatives of the people, and the law makers of the society, is certainly as great a breach of trust, and as perfect a declaration of a design to subvert the government, as is possible to be met with. To which, if one shall add rewards and punishments visibly employed to the same end, and all the arts of perverted law made use of to take off and destroy all that stand in the way of such a design, and will not comply and consent to betray the liberties of their country, it will be past doubt what is doing. What power they ought to have in the society who thus employ it contrary to the trust went along with it in its first institution, is easy to determine; and one cannot but see that he who has once attempted any such thing as this cannot any longer be trusted.

223. To this, perhaps, it will be said that the people being ignorant and always discontented, to lay the foundation of government in the unsteady opinion and

uncertain humour of the people, is to expose it to certain ruin; and no government will be able long to subsist if the people may set up a new legislative whenever they take offence at the old one. To this I answer, quite the contrary. People are not so easily got out of their old forms as some are apt to suggest. They are hardly to be prevailed with to amend the acknowledged faults in the frame they have been accustomed to. And if there be any original defects, or adventitious ones introduced by time or corruption, it is not an easy thing to get them changed, even when all the world sees there is an opportunity for it. This slowness and aversion in the people to quit their old constitutions has in the many revolutions which have been seen in this kingdom, in this and former ages, still kept us to, or after some interval of fruitless attempts, still brought us back again to our old legislative of king, lords and commons; and whatever provocations have made the crown be taken from some of our princes' heads, they never carried the people so far as to place it in another line.

224. But it will be said this hypothesis lays a ferment for frequent rebellion. To which I answer:

First: no more than any other hypothesis. For when the people are made miserable, and find themselves exposed to the ill usage of arbitrary power, cry up their governors as much as you will for sons of Jupiter, let them be sacred and divine, descended or authorised from Heaven; give them out for whom or what you please, the same will happen. The people generally ill treated, and contrary to right, will be ready upon any occasion to ease themselves of a burden that sits heavy upon them. They will wish and seek for the opportunity, which in the change, weakness, and accidents of human affairs, seldom delays long to offer itself. He must have lived but a little while in the world, who has not seen examples of this in his time; and he must have read very little who cannot produce examples of it in all sorts of governments in the world.

225. Secondly: I answer, such revolutions happen not upon every little mismanagement in public affairs. Great mistakes in the ruling part, many wrong and inconvenient laws, and all the slips of human frailty will be borne by the people without mutiny or murmur. But if a long train of abuses, prevarications, and artifices, all tending the same way, make the design visible to the people, and they cannot but feel what they lie under, and see whither they are going, it is not to be wondered that they should then rouse themselves, and endeavour to put the rule into such hands which may secure to them the ends for which government was at first erected, and without which, ancient names and specious forms are so far from being better, that they are much worse than the state of Nature or pure anarchy; the inconveniencies being all as great and as near, but the remedy farther off and more difficult.

226. Thirdly: I answer, that this power in the people of providing for their safety anew by a new legislative when their legislators have acted contrary to their trust by invading their property, is the best fence against rebellion, and the probablest means to hinder it. For rebellion being an opposition, not to persons,

but authority, which is founded only in the constitutions and laws of the government: those, whoever they be, who, by force, break through, and, by force, justify their violation of them, are truly and properly rebels. For when men, by entering into society and civil government, have excluded force, and introduced laws for the preservation of property, peace, and unity amongst themselves, those who set up force again in opposition to the laws, do *rebellare*—that is, bring back again the state of war, and are properly rebels, which they who are in power, by the pretence they have to authority, the temptation of force they have in their hands, and the flattery of those about them being likeliest to do, the properest way to prevent the evil is to show them the danger and injustice of it who are under the greatest temptation to run into it.

# 14

# Notes on the
# Second Treatise of Government

1. John Locke was a participant in English secular and religious politics in the late seventeenth century, out of which arose not only his *Two Treatises of Government*, but his *Letter Concerning Toleration*. Locke was initially trained in science and medicine, wrote the highly influential work of empiricist epistemology entitled *Essay Concerning Human Understanding*, and eventually turned to religious, economic, and commercial subjects. His direct or indirect influence on the American Revolution and the Constitution was substantial.

2. Is Locke right in concluding that persons in Hobbes's state of nature will be less, and not more, secure upon establishing the Hobbesian sovereign ruler? See DAVID GAUTHIER, THE LOGIC OF LEVIATHAN 163 (1969). For a useful comparison of Hobbes and Locke regarding the use of the idea of the state of nature, see generally A. John Simmons, *Locke's State of Nature*, 17 POLITICAL THEORY 449 (1989).

3. Jeremy Waldron argues that "[t]he contract story is not intended as a historical description; it is intended rather as a moral tool for historical understanding. . . . [Locke's] general strategy is to suggest that, with the growth of political authority, those subject to it indicated by their implicit acquiescence at each step that it was made with their consent, and on conditions of trust rather than abject prostration." Jeremy Waldron, *John Locke: Social Contract Versus Political Anthropology*, 51 REVIEW OF POLITICS 3, 17-18 (1989). But could a reasonable person give consent to each separate stage or step in an evolving, somewhat mysterious historical process, without consenting to the final overall result? Compare Jeremy Waldron's discussion of Locke with Gordon J. Schochet, *The Family and the Origins of the State in Locke's Political Philosophy* in JOHN LOCKE: PROBLEMS AND PERSPECTIVES 81 (John W. Yolton ed. 1969). See also Richard Ashcraft, *Locke's State of*

*Nature: Historical Fact or Moral Fiction*, 62 AMERICAN POLITICAL SCIENCE REVIEW 898, 898 (1968) ("Locke regards the state of nature as both an historical and a moral description of human existence").

4. Consider Locke's discussion of consent, and in particular the idea of tacit or implied consent. As against Locke, it is suggested that "traveling on a highway and being within the territories of a government simply are not forms of consent, nor do they imply a willingness to give consent should an appropriate occasion arise." Charles R. Beitz, *Tacit Consent and Property Rights*, 8 POLITICAL THEORY 487, 488 (1980). In particular, problems of lack of notice of the terms of obedience, lack of awareness of what will be taken as a sign of consent, lack of intention to give consent, and lack of reasonable alternative courses of action loom large. *See id.*

5. Should it therefore be concluded, as against Locke, that "[t]here is simply no good reason to understand . . . continued residence as a sign of binding consent, in the absence of appropriate conventions?" A. John Simmons, *Consent, Free Choice, and Democratic Government*, 18 GEORGIA LAW REVIEW 791, 819 (1984) (footnote omitted).

6. Can persons who choose to leave Locke's civil society also take rights to control the use of their land with them? Paul Russell argues that "Locke regards possession of land as a paradigm case of tacit consent. As such it obliges the owner to recognize . . . the jurisdiction of the government over his or her property and . . . over him- or herself while he or she dwells upon that property." Paul Russell, *Locke On Express and Tacit Consent*, 14 POLITICAL THEORY 291, 296-97 (1986).

7. For a broader account of Locke's tacit consent argument that relies upon the law of land ownership and trespass, see John G. Bennett, *A Note On Locke's Theory of Tacit Consent*, 88 PHILOSOPHICAL REVIEW 224, 230 (1979). *See also* Charles R. Beitz, *Tacit Consent and Property Rights*, 8 POLITICAL THEORY 487 (1980).

8. Can we reconcile Locke's comments on residence as indicating consent with the idea that only some governments are morally owed obedience by concluding that for Locke, consent is a necessary condition for political obligation, but is not by itself a sufficient condition? See A. JOHN SIMMONS, MORAL PRINCIPLES AND POLITICAL OBLIGATIONS 86-87 (1979).

9. It is sometimes argued that the idea of the political legitimacy or authority of a government should be kept separate from the question of who, if anyone, is obligated to obey that government. Charles R. Beitz has written that "[t]he legitimacy of a government—that is, its conformity to principles respecting natural rights that all rational persons would accept—is at best a necessary condition for political obligation; another necessary condition, [Locke] reiterates time and again, is consent." Charles R. Beitz, *Tacit Consent and Property Rights*, 8 POLITICAL THEORY 487, 489 (1980).

10. Can we make Locke's argument that mere residence in a country involves tacit consent more plausible by insisting that the consent thereby given is not to whatever the government does, but only to the terms of the original governmental contract, which reserve the right of revolution where the government acts tyrannically? See Hanna Pitkin, *Obligation and Consent—I*, 59 AMERICAN POLITICAL SCIENCE REVIEW 990, 995-96 (1965).

11. On John Simmons's view, "[i]t seems that tacit consent need not really be expressed in the strict sense at all for Locke. Tacit consent can be understood or inferred by the observer, quite independent of the consentor's intentions or awareness that he is consenting." A. JOHN SIMMONS, MORAL PRINCIPLES AND POLITICAL OBLIGATIONS 83 (1979). If so, does Locke really have a theory of tacit consent?

12. Would it be accurate to say that ultimately, Locke's discussion of personal consent is irrelevant, in the sense that one's obligation to obey depends not on one's own consent, but on the character of the regime itself—on whether it respects natural rights and the purposes for which it was instituted? See Hanna Pitkin, *Obligation and Consent—I*, 59 AMERICAN POLITICAL SCIENCE REVIEW 990, 996 (1965). Could Locke's approach be called one of "hypothetical" or "deserved" consent? *See id.* at 999.

13. Is it helpful to think of the ordinary native-born English citizen's consent "as a hypothetical event, like the express consent of the propertied, as the answer they would give if asked the question, 'Are you an Englishman, a subject of the King of England?'" John Dunn, *Consent in the Political Theory of John Locke*, in LIFE, LIBERTY, AND PROPERTY: ESSAYS ON LOCKE'S POLITICAL IDEAS 145 (Gordon J. Schochet ed. 1971).

14. Leslie Green observes that "[w]ith increasing frequency it is argued that Locke is not a consent theorist at all." Leslie Green, *Consent and Community*, in ON POLITICAL OBLIGATION 89, 103 (Paul Harris ed. 1990). On such an approach, human nature, human interests, social circumstances, and rationality would combine, according to Locke, to virtually dictate the broad outlines,

substance, and limits of the legitimate scope of government. Is this a faithful reading of Locke?

15. Is there a sense in which Locke's approach to political obligation may really be said to rest ultimately upon divine ordering of the world? See JOHN DUNN, THE POLITICAL THOUGHT OF JOHN LOCKE 127 (1969).

16. According to Peter Laslett, for Locke "[n]atural law . . . was at one and the same time a command of God, a rule of reason, and a law in the very nature of things as they are, by which they work and we work too." Peter Laslett, *Introduction* to JOHN LOCKE, TWO TREATISES OF GOVERNMENT 95 (Peter Laslett rev. ed. 1963). In this respect, is Locke much different from Aquinas?

17. For an argument that Locke's doctrine of consent or contract cannot be understood apart from Locke's reliance upon concepts such as natural law and natural right, see Patrick Riley, *Locke On "Voluntary Agreement" and Political Power*, 29 WESTERN POLITICAL QUARTERLY 136, 136-37 (1976).

18. Can it be said that for Locke, people know the law of nature by means of the light of reason and nature? Would that imply that our knowledge of the law of nature is in any sense inborn or innate, rather than learned? How much difference is there between Aquinas and Locke on how we know the natural law? For discussion, see Hans Aarsleff, *The State of Nature and the Nature of Man in Locke* in JOHN LOCKE: PROBLEMS AND PERSPECTIVES 99, 129-31 (John W. Yolton ed. 1969).

19. What is the precise "legal" relationship between the people and the government, according to Locke? J.W. Gough suggests that "while the people agree by compact to establish a 'civil government,' they do not enter into a contract with their rulers, but . . . make the government trustees on their behalf." J.W. GOUGH, THE SOCIAL CONTRACT 135 (2d ed. 1957). On this view, the people are both the creators and beneficiaries of a trust on their behalf, with the government having only the minimal rights, and the substantial duties, of a trustee.

20. If the people are the sole judge of whether the government has violated their rights in such a way as to undermine the legitimate authority of that government, can the relationship between the people and the government really be said to involve any sort of "contract?" See Willmoore Kendall, *John Locke and the Doctrine of Majority-Rule*, in ESSAYS IN THE HISTORY OF POLITICAL THOUGHT 201, 210 (Isaac Kramnick ed. 1969).

21. Note that it has been argued that on Locke's approach, "[a]lthough

contractually related to each other, the people are not contractually obliged to government, and governors benefit from governing only as fellow members of the 'Politick Body'. . . . They are merely deputies for the people, trustees who can be discarded if they fail in their trust. . . ." Peter Laslett, *Introduction* to JOHN LOCKE, TWO TREATISES OF GOVERNMENT 127 (Peter Laslett rev. ed. 1963).

22. In the United States Supreme Court case of Calder v. Bull, 3 U.S. (3 Dall.) 386 (1798), Justice Chase argued that "[t]he purposes for which men enter into society will determine the nature and terms of the social compact; and as they are the foundation of the legislative power, they will decide what are the proper objects of it." *Id.* at 388. Is this view consistent with that of Locke?

23. Is Locke's focus perhaps not so much on legitimizing any particular kind of government, through consent or otherwise, but on defending the legitimacy of resistance to vicious behavior by any kind of governmental regime? See JOHN DUNN, THE POLITICAL THOUGHT OF JOHN LOCKE 142-43 (1969).

24. More broadly, it has been argued that "[c]ontractarianism has critical as well as legitimating resources. The strength of the theory is that it provides a set of categories by which events like oppression and subjugation can be evaluated negatively, and with which attempts to draw doctrines of obligation, allegiance, and legitimacy out of such a history can be resisted." Jeremy Waldron, *John Locke: Social Contract Versus Political Anthropology*, 52 REVIEW OF POLITICS 3, 26 (1989).

25. John Kilcullen argues that according to Locke, political obligation "cannot be unlimited. There are three rights which a person must exercise on his own judgment without deferring to the judgment of the community's representative, namely, not to do anything contrary to natural law, to defend oneself and others against serious injury which the community cannot or will not repair; and to rebel against a corrupt government." John Kilcullen, *Locke On Political Obligation*, 45 REVIEW OF POLITICS 323, 325 (1983) (footnote omitted). What if the typical democratic government's judgment on these sorts of questions tends, by consensus, to be better than the judgment of the citizens affected? Should private citizens then defer to the government on such questions? If Kilcullen is right, could it be said that Locke does not believe in a *general* moral obligation to obey?

26. Precisely who holds the right to rebel, according to Locke? Carole Pateman's conclusion is that "[a]t times Locke seems to suggest that a single individual has the right to resist arbitrary and unjust treatment from his government, but

he usually refers to the right of the majority to do so. It is not really clear whether Locke here means the 'majority' of the politically relevant members of the community." CAROLE PATEMAN, THE PROBLEM OF POLITICAL OBLIGATION 76-77 (1979) (1985). Ian Shapiro writes similarly that "Locke has no institutional mechanism for dealing with what would come to be known . . . as tyrannous majorities, or for preventing the systematic violation of the rights of minorities by the king or his magistrates. In such circumstances all these groups can do is resort to (presumably unsuccessful) force; in so doing the moral status of their actions remains deeply ambiguous." IAN SHAPIRO, THE EVOLUTION OF RIGHTS IN LIBERAL THEORY 116 (1986).

27. Is Willmoore Kendall correct in his interpretation that "[e]ven the individual's right to life is valid only to the extent that it is compatible with the good (= preservation) of his community, and it is the people, not the individual, to whom Locke has clearly imputed the power to make the necessary judgments as to what is compatible with its preservation?" Willmoore Kendall, *John Locke and the Doctrine of Majority Rule*, in ESSAYS IN THE HISTORY OF POLITICAL THOUGHT 201, 215 (Isaac Kramnick ed. 1969). Is Kendall further correct in concluding that "Locke's right of revolution is, in effect, a right on the part of the bulk of the community to treat as non-members those who take exception to its opinions," *id.* at 218, and in his general conclusion that "the inalienable rights of the individual prove to be merely those which the majority of the people have not yet seen fit to withdraw," *id.* at 221?

28. By way of comparison with Locke, consider the limited right of the ruler's relatives to depose a ruler who persists in failing to promote the welfare of the people, as argued for by Confucius's great successor Mencius. See HARLEE G. GREEN, CHINESE THOUGHT FROM CONFUCIUS TO MAO TSE-TUNG 80, 83 (1953). Would such an approach both limit the threat of unjustified revolution, while in some small part providing a way around the problem of a tyranny of the majority?

29. Consider the problem of individualism and individual development in Locke. C.B. Macpherson concludes that "Locke, by carrying into his postulates the implicit assumptions of class differential rationality and rights . . ., reached an ambiguous theory of differential membership in civil society, a theory which justified a class state from postulates of equal individual natural rights. Ambiguity about membership concealed from Locke himself the contradiction in his individualism, which produced full individuality for some by consuming the individuality of others." C.B. Macpherson, *The Social Bearing of Locke's Political Theory*, in ESSAYS IN THE HISTORY OF POLITICAL THOUGHT 183, 201 (Isaac Kramnick ed. 1969).

30. John W. Yolton argues that for Locke, "[t]he move into a civil society is a move from individualism to corporatism. . . . This corporatism of the body politic, of the will of the community, of the living organism which is the total society, is Locke's way of protecting that aspect of individualism which is most important for him: the person and the extension of the person, all his property. . . ." JOHN W. YOLTON, LOCKE: AN INTRODUCTION 72 (1985). Does Locke really think of the society as a living organism in any meaningful sense?

31. Is it accurate to say that "Locke's theoretical perspective enabled him to distinguish, as Hobbes could not, between the 'dissolution' of a government and the destruction of a community?" CAROLE PATEMAN, THE PROBLEM OF POLITICAL OBLIGATION 76 (1979) (1985).

32. Consider the relationship between Locke's theory and the value of democracy. Ian Shapiro notes that "there is nothing in Locke's writings remotely approaching a doctrine of democratic participation. . . . There is no notion of the people participating in government as being intrinsically good or right, as there was to be for Rousseau." IAN SHAPIRO, THE EVOLUTION OF RIGHTS IN LIBERAL THEORY 117 (1986).

33. Locke seems to clearly envision a common scenario of obedience to a rights-respecting government, and a less common scenario of outright revolution against a government that has forfeited its authority to rule. Does Locke have, or could he consistently develop, a theory of what would today be called civil disobedience? See CAROLE PATEMAN, THE PROBLEM OF POLITICAL OBLIGATION 77-78 (1979) (1985).

34. John Ladd argues intriguingly that "[i]f, as Locke would presumably hold, our political obligation is valid only as long as it requires nothing contrary to the natural law and does not exceed the bounds of the powers delegated by the contract, then no great moral issues can arise within the political framework." John Ladd, *Legal and Moral Obligation*, in 12 NOMOS: POLITICAL AND LEGAL OBLIGATION 30 (J. Roland Pennock & John Chapman eds. 1970). Is this so? If no one is challenging the legitimacy of the government, can no great moral issue arise regarding, say, the proper use of our guaranteed liberties?

35. For a detailed and extended discussion of Locke's political ideas in the historical context of the political movements and debates of his day, see RICHARD ASHCRAFT, REVOLUTIONARY POLITICS & LOCKE'S TWO TREATISES OF GOVERNMENT (1986).

# 15

# From David Hume, A Treatise of Human Nature, Book III, Part II

### SECT. VII
*Of the origin of government*

NOTHING is more certain, than that men are, in a great measure, govern'd by interest, and that even when they extend their concern beyond themselves, 'tis not to any great distance; nor is it usual for them, in common life, to look farther than their nearest friends and acquaintance. 'Tis no less certain, that 'tis impossible for men to consult their interest in so effectual a manner, as by an universal and inflexible observance of the rules of justice, by which alone they can preserve society, and keep themselves from falling into that wretched and savage condition, which is commonly represented as the *state of nature*. And as this interest, which all men have in the upholding of society, and the observation of the rules of justice, is great, so is it palpable and evident, even to the most rude and uncultivated of human race; and 'tis almost impossible for any one, who has had experience of society, to be mistaken in this particular. Since, therefore, men are so sincerely attach'd to their interest, and their interest is so much concern'd in the observance of justice, and this interest is so certain and avow'd; it may be ask'd, how any disorder can ever arise in society, and what principle there is in human nature so *powerful* as to overcome so strong a passion, or so *violent* as to obscure so clear a knowledge?

It has been observ'd, in treating of the passions, that men are mightily govern'd by the imagination, and proportion their affections more to the light, under which any object appears to them, than to its real and intrinsic value. What strikes upon them with a strong and lively idea commonly prevails above what lies in a more obscure light; and it must be a great superiority of value, that is able to compensate this advantage. Now as every thing, that is contiguous to us, either in space or time, strikes upon us with such an idea, it has a proportional effect on the will and passions, and commonly operates with more force than any object, that lies in a more distant and obscure light. Tho' we may be fully convinc'd, that the latter object excels the former, we are not able to regulate our actions by this judgment; but yield to the solicitations of our passions, which always plead in favour of whatever is near and contiguous.

This is the reason why men so often act in contradiction to their known interest; and in particular why they prefer any trivial advantage, that is present, to the maintenance of order in society, which so much depends on the observance of justice. The consequences of every breach of equity seem to lie very remote, and are not able to counter-ballance any immediate advantage, that may be reap'd from it. They are, however, never the less real for being remote; and as all men are, in some degree, subject to the same weakness, it necessarily happens, that the violations of equity must become very frequent in society, and the commerce of men, by that means, be render'd very dangerous and uncertain. You have the same propension, that I have, in favour of what is contiguous above what is remote. You are, therefore, naturally carried to commit acts of injustice as well as me. Your example both pushes me forward in this way by imitation, and also affords me a new reason for any breach of equity, by shewing me, that I should be the cully of my integrity, if I alone shou'd impose on myself a severe restraint amidst the licentiousness of others.

This quality, therefore, of human nature, not only is very dangerous to society, but also seems, on a cursory view, to be incapable of any remedy. The remedy can only come from the consent of men; and if men be incapable of themselves to prefer remote to contiguous, they will never consent to any thing, which wou'd oblige them to such a choice, and contradict, in so sensible a manner, their natural principles and propensities. Whoever chuses the means, chuses also the end; and if it be impossible for us to prefer what is remote, 'tis equally impossible for us to submit to any necessity, which wou'd oblige us to such a method of acting.

But here 'tis observable, that this infirmity of human nature becomes a remedy to itself, and that we provide against our negligence about remote objects, merely because we are naturally inclin'd to that negligence. When we consider any objects at a distance, all their minute distinctions vanish, and we always give the preference to whatever is in itself preferable, without considering its situation and circumstances. This gives rise to what in an improper sense we call *reason*, which is a principle, that is often contradictory to those propensities that display themselves upon the approach of the object. In reflecting on any action, which I am to perform a twelve-month hence, I always resolve to prefer the greater good, whether at that time it will be more contiguous or remote; nor does any difference in that particular make a difference in my present intentions and resolutions. My distance from the final determination makes all those minute differences vanish, nor am I affected by any thing, but the general and more discernible qualities of good and evil. But on my nearer approach, those circumstances, which I at first over-look'd, begin to appear, and have an influence on my conduct and affections. A new inclination to the present good springs up, and makes it difficult for me to adhere inflexibly to my first purpose and resolution. This natural infirmity I may very much regret, and I may endeavour, by all possible means, to free my self from it. I may have recourse to study and reflection within myself; to the advice of friends; to frequent meditation, and repeated resolution: And having experienc'd how ineffectual all these are, I may embrace with pleasure any other expedient, by which I may impose a restraint upon myself, and guard against this weakness.

The only difficulty, therefore, is to find out this expedient, by which men cure their natural weakness, and lay themselves under the necessity of observing the laws of justice and equity, notwithstanding their violent propension to prefer contiguous to remote. 'Tis evident such a remedy can never be effectual without correcting this propensity; and as 'tis impossible to change or correct any thing material in our nature, the utmost we can do is to change our circumstances and situation, and render the observance of the laws of justice our nearest interest, and their violation our most remote. But this being impracticable with respect to all mankind, it can only take place with respect to a few, whom we thus immediately interest in the execution of justice. There are the persons, whom we call civil magistrates, kings and their ministers, our governors and rulers, who being indifferent persons to the greatest part of the state, have no interest, or but a remote one, in any act of injustice; and being satisfied with their present condition, and with their part in society, have an immediate interest in every execution of justice, which is so necessary to the upholding of society. Here then is the origin of civil government and society. Men are not able radically to cure, either in themselves or others, that narrowness of soul, which makes them prefer the present to the remote. They cannot change their natures. All they can do is to change their situation, and render the observance of justice the immediate interest of some particular persons, and its violation their more remote. These persons, then, are not only induc'd to observe those rules in their own conduct, but also to constrain others to a like regularity, and inforce the dictates of equity thro' the whole society. And if it be necessary, they may also interest others more immediately in the execution of justice, and create a number of officers, civil and military, to assist them in their government.

But this execution of justice, tho' the principal, is not the only advantage of government. As violent passion hinders men from seeing distinctly the interest they have in an equitable behaviour towards others; so it hinders them from seeing that equity itself, and gives them a remarkable partiality in their own favours. This inconvenience is corrected in the same manner as that above-mention'd. The same persons, who execute the laws of justice, will also decide all controversies concerning them; and being indifferent to the greatest part of the society, will decide them more equitably than every one wou'd in his own case.

By means of these two advantages, in the *execution* and *decision* of justice, men acquire a security against each others weakness and passion, as well as against their own, and under the shelter of their governors, begin to taste at ease the sweets of society and mutual assistance. But government extends farther its beneficial influence; and not contented to protect men in those conventions they make for their mutual interest, it often obliges them to make such conventions, and forces them to seek their own advantage, by a concurrence in some common end or purpose. There is no quality in human nature, which causes more fatal errors in our conduct, than that which leads us to prefer whatever is present to the distant and remote, and makes us desire objects more according to their situation than their intrinsic value. Two neighbours may agree to drain a meadow, which they possess in common; because 'tis easy for them to know each others mind; and each must perceive, that the immediate consequence of his failing in his part, is, the abandoning the whole project. But 'tis very difficult, and indeed impossible, that a thousand persons shou'd agree in any such action; it being difficult for them to concert so complicated a design, and still more difficult for them to execute it; while each seeks a pretext to free himself of the trouble and expence, and wou'd lay the whole burden on others. Political society easily remedies both these inconveniences. Magistrates find an immediate interest in the interest of any considerable part of their subjects. They need consult no body but themselves to form any scheme for the promoting of that interest. And as the failure of any one piece in the execution is connected, tho' not immediately, with the failure of the whole, they prevent that failure, because they find no interest in it, either immediate or remote. Thus bridges are built; harbours open'd; ramparts rais'd; canals form'd; fleets equip'd; and armies disciplin'd every where, by the care of government, which, tho' compos'd of men subject to all human infirmities, becomes, by one of the finest and most subtle inventions imaginable, a composition, which is, in some measure, exempted from all these infirmities.

## Sect. VIII
### Of the source of allegiance

. . . When men have once perceiv'd the necessity of government to maintain peace, and execute justice, they wou'd naturally assemble together, wou'd chuse magistrates, determine power, and *promise* them obedience. As a promise is suppos'd to be a bond or security already in use, and attended with a moral obligation, 'tis to be consider'd as the original sanction of government, and as the source of the first obligation to obedience. This reasoning appears so natural, that it has become the foundation of our fashionable system of politics, and is in a manner the creed of a party amongst us, who pride themselves, with reason, on the soundness of their philosophy, and their liberty of thought. *All men*, say they, *are born free and equal: Government and superiority can only be establish'd by consent: The consent of men, in establishing government, imposes on them a new obligation, unknown to the laws of nature. Men, therefore, are bound to obey their magistrates, only because they promise it; and if they had not given their word, either expressly or tacitly, to preserve allegiance, it would never have become a part of their moral duty.* This conclusion, however, when carried so far as to comprehend government in all its ages and situations, is entirely erroneous; and I maintain, that tho' the duty of allegiance be at first grafted on the obligation of promises, and be for some time supported by that obligation, yet it quickly takes root of itself, and has an original obligation and authority, independent of all contracts. This is a principle of moment, which we must examine with care and attention, before we proceed any farther.

'Tis reasonable for those philosophers, who assert justice to be a natural virtue, and antecedent to human conventions, to resolve all civil allegiance into the obligation of a promise, and assert that 'tis our own consent alone, which binds us to any submission to magistracy. For as all government is plainly an invention of men, and the origin of most governments is known in history, 'tis necessary to mount higher, in order to find the source of our political duties, if we wou'd assert them to have any *natural* obligation of morality. These philosophers, therefore, quickly observe, that society is as antient as the human species, and those three fundamental laws of nature as antient as society: So that taking advantage of the antiquity, and obscure origin of these laws, they first deny them to be artificial and voluntary inventions of men, and then seek to ingraft on them those other duties, which are more plainly artificial. But being once undeceiv'd in this particular, and having found that *natural*, as well as *civil* justice, derives its origin from human conventions, we shall quickly perceive, how fruitless it is to resolve the one into the other, and seek, in the laws of nature, a stronger foundation for our political duties than interest, and human conventions; while these laws themselves are built on the very same foundation. On which ever side we turn this subject, we shall find, that these two kinds of duty are exactly on the same footing, and have the same source both of their *first invention* and *moral obligation*. They are contriv'd to remedy like inconveniences, and acquire their moral sanction in the same manner, from their remedying those inconveniences. These are two points, which we shall endeavour to prove as distinctly as possible.

We have already shewn, that men *invented* the three fundamental laws of nature, when they observ'd the necessity of society to their mutual subsistance, and found, that 'twas impossible to maintain any correspondence together, without some restraint on their natural appetites. The same self-love, therefore, which renders men so incommodious to each other, taking a new and more convenient direction, produces the rules of justice, and is the *first* motive of their observance. But when men have observ'd, that tho' the rules of justice be sufficient to maintain any society, yet 'tis impossible for them, of themselves, to observe those rules, in large and polish'd societies; they establish government, as a new invention to attain their ends, and preserve the old, or procure new advantages, by a more strict execution of justice. So far, therefore, our *civil* duties are connected with our *natural*, that the former are invented chiefly for the sake of the latter; and that the principal object of government is to constrain men to observe the laws of nature. In this respect, however, that law of nature, concerning the performance of promises, is only compriz'd along with the rest; and its exact observance is to be consider'd as an effect of the institution of government, and not the obedience to government as an effect of the obligation of a promise. Tho' the object of our civil duties be the enforcing of our natural, yet the *first* motive of the invention, as well as performance of both, is nothing but self-interest: And since there is a separate interest in the obedience to government, from that in the performance of promises, we must also allow of a separate obligation. To obey the civil magistrate is requisite to preserve order and concord in society. To perform promises is requisite to beget mutual trust and confidence in the common offices of life. The ends, as well as the means, are perfectly distinct; nor is the one subordinate to the other.

To make this more evident, let us consider, that men will often bind themselves by promises to the performance of what it wou'd have been their interest to perform, independent of these promises; as when they wou'd give others a fuller security, by super-adding a new obligation of interest to that which they formerly lay under. The interest in the performance of promises, besides its moral obligation, is general, avow'd, and of the last consequence in life. Other interests may be more particular and doubtful; and we are apt to entertain a greater suspicion, that men may indulge their humour, or passion, in acting contrary to them. Here, therefore, promises come naturally in play, and are often requir'd for fuller satisfaction and security. But supposing those other interests to be as general and avow'd as the interest in the performance of a promise, they will be regarded as on the same footing, and men will begin to repose the same confidence in them. Now this is exactly the case with regard to our civil duties, or obedience to the magistrate; without which no government cou'd subsist, nor any peace or order be maintain'd in large societies, where there are so many possessions on the one hand, and so many wants, real or imaginary, on the other. Our civil duties, therefore, must soon detach themselves from our promises, and acquire a separate force and influence. The interest in both is of the very same kind: 'Tis general, avow'd, and prevails in all times and places. There is, then, no pretext of reason for founding the one upon the other; while each of them has a foundation peculiar to itself. We might as well resolve the obligation to abstain from the possessions of others, into the obligation of a promise, as that of allegiance. The interests are not more distinct in the one case than the other. A regard to property is not more necessary to natural society, than obedience is to civil society or government; nor is the former society more necessary to the being of mankind, than the latter to their well-being and happiness. In short, if the performance of promises be advantageous, so is obedience to government: If the former interest be general, so is the latter: If the one interest be obvious and avow'd, so is the other. And as these two rules are founded on like obligations of interest, each of them must have a peculiar authority, independent of the other.

But 'tis not only the *natural* obligations of interest, which are distinct in promises and allegiance; but also the *moral* obligations of honour and conscience: Nor does the merit or demerit of the one depend in the least upon that of the other. And indeed, if we consider the close connexion there is betwixt the natural and moral obligations, we shall find this conclusion to be entirely unavoidable.

Our interest is always engag'd on the side of obedience to magistracy; and there is nothing but a great present advantage, that can lead us to rebellion, by making us over-look the remote interest, which we have in the preserving of peace and order in society. But tho' a present interest may thus blind us with regard to our own actions, it takes not place with regard to those of others; nor hinders them from appearing in their true colours, as highly prejudicial to public interest, and to our own in particular. This naturally gives us an uneasiness, in considering such seditious and disloyal actions, and makes us attach to them the idea of vice and moral deformity. 'Tis the same principle, which causes us to disapprove of all kinds of private injustice, and in particular of the breach of promises. We blame all treachery and breach of faith; because we consider, that the freedom and extent of human commerce depend entirely on a fidelity with regard to promises. We blame all disloyalty to magistrates; because we perceive, that the execution of justice, in the stability of possession, its translation by consent, and the performance of promises, is impossible, without submission to government. As there are here two interests entirely distinct from each other, they must give rise to two moral obligations, equally separate and independent. Tho' there was no such thing as a promise in the world, government wou'd still be necessary in all large and civiliz'd societies; and if promises had only their own proper obligation, without the separate sanction of government, they wou'd have but little efficacy in such societies. This separates the boundaries of our public and private duties, and shews that the latter are more dependent on the former, than the former on the latter. *Education*, and *the artifice of politicians*, concur to bestow a farther morality on loyalty, and to brand all rebellion with a greater degree of guilt and infamy. Nor is it a wonder, that politicians shou'd be very industrious in inculcating such notions, where their interest is so particularly concern'd.

Lest those arguments shou'd not appear entirely conclusive (as I think they are) I shall have recourse to authority, and shall prove, from the universal consent of mankind, that the obligation of submission to government is not deriv'd from any promise of the subjects. Nor need any one wonder, that tho' I have all along endeavour'd to establish my system on pure reason, and have scarce ever cited the judgment even of philosophers or historians on any article, I shou'd now appeal to popular authority, and oppose the sentiments of the rabble to any philosophical reasoning. For it must be observ'd, that the opinions of men, in this case, carry with them a peculiar authority, and are, in a great measure, infallible. The distinction of moral good and evil is founded on the pleasure or pain, which results from the view of any sentiment, or character; and as that pleasure or pain cannot be unknown to the person who feels it, it follows, that there is just so much vice or virtue in any character, as every one places in it, and that 'tis impossible in this particular we can ever be mistaken. And tho' our judgments concerning the *origin* of any vice or virtue, be not so certain as those concerning their *degrees*; yet, since the question in this case regards not any philosophical origin of an obligation, but a plain matter of fact, 'tis not easily conceiv'd how we can fall into an error. A man, who acknowledges himself to be bound to another, for a certain sum, must certainly know whether it be by his own bond, or that of his father, whether it be of his mere good will, or for money lent him; and under what conditions, and for what purposes he has bound himself. In like manner, it being certain, that there is a moral obligation to submit to government, because every one thinks so; it must be as certain, that this obligation arises not from a promise; since no one, whose judgment has not been led astray by too strict adherence to a system of philosophy, has ever yet dreamt of ascribing it to that origin. Neither magistrates nor subjects have form'd this idea of our civil duties.

We find, that magistrates are so far from deriving their authority, and the obligation to obedience in their subjects, from the foundation of a promise or original contract, that they conceal, as far as possible, from their people, especially from the vulgar, that they have their origin from thence. Were this the sanction of government, our rulers wou'd never receive it tacitly, which is the utmost that can be pretended; since what is given tacitly and insensibly can never have such influence on mankind, as what is perform'd expressly and openly. A tacit promise is, where the will is signified by other more diffuse signs than those of speech; but a will there must certainly be in the case, and that can never escape the person's notice, who exerted it, however silent or tacit. But were you to ask the far greatest part of the nation, whether they had ever consented to the authority of their rulers, or promis'd to obey them, they wou'd certainly reply, that the affair depended not on their consent, but that they were born to such an obedience. In consequence of this opinion, we frequently see them imagine such persons to be their natural rulers, as are at that time depriv'd of all power and authority, and whom no man, however foolish, wou'd voluntarily chuse; and this merely because they are in that line, which rul'd before, and in that degree of it, which us'd to succeed; tho' perhaps in so distant a period, that scarce any man alive cou'd ever have given any promise of obedience. Has a government, then, no authority over such as these, because they never consented to it, and wou'd esteem the very attempt of such a free choice a piece of arrogance and impiety? We find by experience, that it punishes them very freely for what it calls treason and rebellion, which, it seems, according to this system, reduces itself to common injustice. If you say, that by dwelling in its dominions, they in effect consented to the establish'd government; I answer, that this can only be, where they think the affair depends on their choice, which few or none, beside those philosophers, have ever yet imagin'd. It never was pleaded as an excuse for a rebel, that the first act he perform'd, after he came to years of discretion, was to levy war against the sovereign of the state; and that while he was a child he cou'd not bind himself by his own consent, and having become a man, show'd plainly, by the first act he perform'd, that he had no design to impose on himself any obligation to obedience. We find, on the contrary, that civil laws punish this crime at the same age as any other, which is criminal, of itself, without our consent; that is, when the person is come to the full use of reason: Whereas to this crime they ought in justice to allow some intermediate time, in which a tacit consent at least might be suppos'd. To which we may add, that a man living under an absolute government, wou'd owe it no allegiance; since, by its very nature, it depends not on consent. But as that is as *natural* and *common* a government as any, it must certainly occasion some obligation; and 'tis plain from experience, that men, who are subjected to it, do always think so. This is a clear proof, that when our promise is upon any account expressly engag'd, we always distinguish exactly betwixt the two obligations, and believe the one to add more force to the other, than in a repetition of the same promise. Where no promise is given, a man looks not on his faith as broken in private matters, upon account of rebellion; but keeps those two duties of honour and allegiance perfectly distinct and separate. As the uniting of them was thought by these philosophers a very subtle invention, this is a convincing proof, that 'tis not a true one; since no man can either give a promise, or be restrain'd by its sanction and obligation unknown to himself. . . .

SECT. X

*Of the objects of allegiance*

BUT tho', on some occasions, it may be justifiable, both in sound politics and morality, to resist supreme power, 'tis certain, that in the ordinary course of human affairs nothing can be more pernicious and criminal; and that besides the convulsions, which always attend revolutions, such a practice tends directly to the subversion of all government, and the causing an universal anarchy and confusion among mankind. As numerous and civiliz'd societies cannot subsist without government, so government is entirely useless without an exact obedience. We ought always to weigh the advantages, which we reap from authority, against the disadvantages; and by this means we shall become more scrupulous of putting in practice the doctrine of resistance. The common rule requires submission; and 'tis only in cases of grievous tyranny and oppression, that the exception can take place.

Since then such a blind submission is commonly due to magistracy, the next question is, *to whom it is due, and whom we are to regard as our lawful magistrates?* In order to answer this question, let us recollect what we have already establish'd concerning the origin of government and political society. When men have once experienc'd the impossibility of preserving any steady order in society, while every one is his own master, and violates or observes the laws of society, according to his present interest or pleasure, they naturally run into the invention of government, and put it out of their own power, as far as possible, to transgress the laws of society. Government, therefore, arises from the same voluntary conversation of men; and 'tis evident, that the same convention, which establishes government, will also determine the persons who are to govern, and will remove all doubt and ambiguity in this particular. And the voluntary consent of men must here have the greater efficacy, that the authority of the magistrate does *at first* stand upon the foundation of a promise of the subjects, by which they bind themselves to obedience; as in every other contract or engagement. The same promise, then, which binds them to obedience, ties them down to a particular person, and makes him the object of their allegiance.

But when government has been establish'd on this footing for some considerable time, and the separate interest, which we have in submission, has produc'd a separate sentiment of morality, the case is entirely alter'd, and a promise is no longer able to determine the particular magistrate; since it is no longer consider'd as the foundation of government. We naturally suppose ourselves born to submission; and imagine, that such particular persons have a right to command, as we on our part are bound to obey. These notions of right and obligation are deriv'd from nothing but the *advantage* we reap from government, which gives us a repugnance to practise resistance ourselves, and makes us displeas'd with any instance of it in others. But here 'tis remarkable, that in this new state of affairs, the original sanction of government, which is *interest*, is not admitted to determine the persons, whom we are to obey, as the original sanction did at first, when affairs were on the footing of a *promise*. A *promise* fixes and determines the persons, without any uncertainty: But 'tis evident, that if men were to regulate their conduct in this particular, by the view of a peculiar *interest*, either public or private, they wou'd involve themselves in endless confusion, and wou'd render all government, in a great measure, ineffectual. The private interest of every one is different; and tho' the public interest in itself be always one and the same, yet it becomes the source of as great dissentions, by reason of the different opinions of particular persons concerning it. The same interest, therefore, which causes us to submit to magistracy, makes us renounce itself in the choice of our magistrates, and binds us down to a certain form of government, and to particular persons, without allowing us to aspire to the utmost perfection in either. The case is here the same as in that law of nature concerning the stability of possession. 'Tis highly advantageous, and even absolutely necessary to society, that possession shou'd be stable; and this leads us to the establishment of such a rule: But we find, that were we to follow the same advantage, in assigning particular possessions to particular persons, we shou'd disappoint our end, and perpetuate the confusion, which that rule is intended to prevent. We must, therefore, proceed by general rules, and regulate ourselves by general interests, in modifying the law of nature concerning the stability of possession. Nor need we fear, that our attachment to this law will diminish upon account of the seeming frivolousness of those interests, by which it is determin'd. The impulse of the mind is deriv'd from a very strong interest; and those other more minute interests serve only to direct the motion, without adding any thing to it, or diminishing from it. 'Tis the same case with government. Nothing is more advantageous to society than such an invention; and this interest is sufficient to make us embrace it with ardour and alacrity; tho' we are oblig'd afterwards to regulate and direct our devotion to government by several considerations, which are not of the same importance, and to chuse our magistrates without having in view any particular advantage from the choice.

The *first* of those principles I shall take notice of, as a foundation of the right of magistracy, is that which gives authority to all the most establish'd governments of the world without exception: I mean, *long possession* in any one form of government, or succession of princes. 'Tis certain, that if we remount to the first origin of every nation, we shall find, that there scarce is any race of kings, or form of a commonwealth, that is not primarily founded on usurpation and rebellion, and whose title is not at first worse than doubtful and uncertain. Time alone gives solidity to their right; and operating gradually on the minds of men, reconciles them to any authority, and makes it seem just and reasonable. Nothing causes any sentiment to have a greater influence upon us than custom, or turns our imagination more strongly to any object. When we have been long accustom'd to obey any set of men, that general instinct or tendency, which we have to suppose a moral obligation attending loyalty, takes easily this direction, and chuses that set of men for its objects. 'Tis interest which gives the general instinct; but 'tis custom which gives the particular direction.

And here 'tis observable, that the same length of time has a different influence on our sentiments of morality, according to its different influence on the mind. We naturally judge of every thing by comparison; and since in considering the fate of kingdoms and republics, we embrace a long extent of time, a small duration has not in this case a like influence on our sentiments, as when we consider any other object. One thinks he acquires a right to a horse, or a suit of cloaths, in a very short time; but a century is scarce sufficient to establish any new government, or remove all scruples in the minds of the subjects concerning it. Add to this, that a shorter period of time will suffice to give a prince a title to any additional power he may usurp, than will serve to fix his right, where the whole is an usurpation. The kings of *France* have not been possess'd of absolute power for above two reigns; and yet nothing will appear more extravagant to *Frenchmen* than to talk of their liberties. If we consider what has been said concerning *accession*, we shall easily account for this phaenomenon.

When there is no form of government establish'd by *long* possession, the *present* possession is sufficient to supply its place, and may be regarded as the *second* source of all public authority. Right to authority is nothing but the constant possession of authority, maintain'd by the laws of society and the interests of mankind; and nothing can be more natural than to join this constant possession to the present one, according to the principles above-mention'd. If the same principles did not take place with regard to the property of private persons, 'twas because these principles were counter-ballanc'd by very strong considerations of interest; when we observ'd, that all restitution wou'd by that means be prevented, and every violence be authoriz'd and protected. And tho' the same motives may seem to have force, with regard to public authority, yet they are oppos'd by a contrary interest; which consists in the preservation of peace, and the avoiding of all changes, which, however they may be easily produc'd in private affairs, are unavoidably attended with bloodshed and confusion, where the public is interested.

Any one, who finding the impossibility of accounting for the right of the present possessor, by any receiv'd system of ethics, shou'd resolve to deny absolutely that right, and assert, that it is not authoriz'd by morality, wou'd be justly thought to maintain a very extravagant paradox, and to shock the common sense and judgment of mankind. No maxim is more conformable, both to prudence and morals, than to submit quietly to the government, which we find establish'd in the country where we happen to live, without enquiring too curiously into its origin and first establishment. Few governments will bear being examin'd so rigorously. How many kingdoms are there at present in the world, and how many more do we find in history, whose governors have no better foundation for their authority than that of present possession? To confine ourselves to the *Roman* and *Grecian* empire; is it not evident, that the long succession of emperors, from the dissolution of the *Roman* liberty, to the final extinction of that empire by the *Turks*, cou'd not so much as pretend to any other title to the empire? The election of the senate was a mere form, which always follow'd the choice of the legions; and these were almost always divided in the different provinces, and nothing but the sword was able to terminate the difference. 'Twas by the sword, therefore, that every emperor acquir'd, as well as defended his right; and we must either say that all the known world, for so many ages, had no government, and ow'd no allegiance to any one, or must allow, that the right of the stronger, in public affairs, is to be receiv'd as legitimate, and authoriz'd by morality, when not oppos'd by any other title.

The right of *conquest* may be consider'd as a *third* source of the title of sovereigns. This right resembles very much that of present possession; but has rather a superior force, being seconded by the notions of glory and honour, which we ascribe to *conquerors*, instead of the sentiments of hatred and detestation, which attend *usurpers*. Men naturally favour those they love; and therefore are more apt to ascribe a right to successful violence, betwixt one sovereign and another, than to the successful rebellion of a subject against his sovereign. . . .

# 16

# Notes on the Treatise of Human Nature

1. David Hume was born in Edinburgh, Scotland in 1711, at about the same time as Rousseau. While in a sense he developed the empiricist approach of John Locke, he was perhaps the most powerful skeptical or critical intellect of the modern era. His most important philosophical work is his *Treatise of Human Nature*. He wrote political and economic essays as well as his *Dialogues of Natural Religion*. While the popular reception of *Treatise of Human Nature* may not have met Hume's expectations, his contemporary intellectual influence is very substantial indeed.

2. Does Hume believe that the ideas of utility or promotion of human interest are all that is necessary to explain political obligation. Would that mean that a citizen who has promised to obey a government that promotes the public well-being has two moral reasons for obeying, or one? See DAVID MILLER, PHILOSOPHY AND IDEOLOGY IN HUME'S POLITICAL THOUGHT 80 (1981). What if someone has promised to obey a government that does not promote the public good as well as an alternative government would?

3. Does Hume's theory focus on maximizing the happiness or utility of individual persons, or on promoting shared interests and the common good? If the latter, is Hume's theory vulnerable to skeptical accounts of the common good? See Leslie Green, *Authority and Convention*, 35 PHILOSOPHICAL QUARTERLY 329, 333-34 (1985). That is, our real common interests may be too narrow, as in the case of the coordination provided by traffic rules. Or they may be too unspecified and indeterminate, as in the need for some sort of stable distribution of rights. In either case, it may be difficult to justify or disqualify almost any actual political regime. See *id.* at 334.

4. David Miller contends that "[i]n Hume's story we set up governors to compel us to follow those rules of justice which we can see we have an interest in following when we consider each case in its true perspective, from a distance." DAVID MILLER, PHILOSOPHY AND IDEOLOGY IN HUME'S POLITICAL THOUGHT

Thought 82 (1981). Is the essential function of law and government really to restrain us from actions that may be tempting to us in the short term or under stress, but which we recognize to be against our settled interests in the long term, like indulging in an extra slice of high-calorie pie?

5.   Is it Hume's view that social contracts or promises to obey are merely a needless intervening step between the real source of political obligation, our moral duty to promote utility, the public welfare, or the common good, and the conclusion that we are obligated to obey a government that promotes these ends? See Paul Brownsey, *Hume and the Social Contract*, 28 PHILOSOPHICAL QUARTERLY 132, 144 (1978). Is it possible that we could be morally obligated to obey an illegitimate usurper government, based on reasons of utility, without that government holding rightful authority over its subjects? See *id.* at 144-45.

6.   Harry Beran criticizes Hume's argument that contracts or promises of obedience have no special force because the obligation to keep such promises and the obligation to obey the government itself are both based on their sheer practical necessity for civilized life. Beran argues that this does not make the contract or promise of obedience redundant. He draws an analogy to family life: "Married people have an obligation to love and support each other because they promise to do so in the marriage ceremony. I hope no one would want to challenge this 'consent theory of marital obligation' on the ground that marital obligation can be derived directly from the necessity of the family for civilized life." Harry Beran, *In Defense of the Consent Theory of Political Obligation and Authority*, 87 ETHICS 260, 264 (1977). Beran goes on to endorse the idea that consent is a necessary condition of political obligation, whether it is sufficient by itself or not. See *id.* at 216, 270-71.

7.   Consider the case of a long-established constitutional regime that has recently been conquered by a foreign power. Does Hume offer sufficiently clear guidance on whom we ought to acknowledge as the authoritative government? See DAVID MILLER, PHILOSOPHY AND IDEOLOGY IN HUME'S POLITICAL THOUGHT 86 (1981). How does one commensurate the greater effectiveness of one government against the greater legitimacy of a rival government in any objective way?

8.   Does Hume believe that it is a strike against social contract theories that they often imply that most governments do not possess rightful authority to rule? Is this a defect in social contract theory? See Paul Brownsey, *Hume and the Social Contract*, 28 PHILOSOPHICAL QUARTERLY 132, 135 (1978).

9.   Does Hume believe that social contract theories can be criticized on the

grounds that most people do not believe that only government by consent can be legitimate? Do most people in fact have an opinion one way or another on this? See Paul Brownsey, *Hume and the Social Contract*, 28 PHILOSOPHICAL QUARTERLY 132, 140 (1978).

10. How loose or stringent are Hume's standards for governmental performance? Would it be accurate to say that Hume would allow for rebellion against an established, otherwise legitimate government if the government seriously infringes property rights, engages in grievous tyranny, or promotes the public ruin? See DAVID MILLER, PHILOSOPHY AND IDEOLOGY IN HUME'S POLITICAL THOUGHT 92 (1981). Is a right of rebellion of this scope too limited?

11. A.J. Ayer interprets Hume as concluding that "the habit of civil obedience leads men to put up with tyranny for longer than would be the case if they strictly attended to their interest." A.J. AYER, HUME 92 (1980). What other factors might account for an apparently irrational public passivity in the face of tyranny?

12. John Mackie notes that Hume's view seems to be that "[t]o be lastingly viable, a government must make it a large part of its business to enforce the same rules that sufficient prudence would have led its subjects to observe, even left to themselves. To do this, it will not need absolute power." JOHN L. MACKIE, HUME'S MORAL THEORY 108 (1980). To the extent that government merely helps all of us overcome our own short-sightedness and excessive concern for the short term, does this point toward, or away from, democracy as a viable form of government?

13. Leslie Green writes that "Hume thought that 'exact obedience' to the magistrate is a necessary condition for the existence of the political system, and grounded his view in common sense. Yet common sense actually supports only a much weaker conclusion: there must be general, but not perfect, obedience." LESLIE GREEN, THE AUTHORITY OF THE STATE 229 (1988). Is Hume committed to the view that any act of disobeying the law, from ordinary criminality to conscientious objection, removes a necessary condition for a viable political system?

14. Mendel Cohen argues interestingly that Hume's attempt to base obligation in feeling rather than reason lands him in an uncomfortable spot. According to Cohen, Hume believed that a person can have a moral obligation only if everyone would have similar feelings if they were in a similar situation. This would mean that if Hume wants to conclude that people in similar circumstances have similar moral obligations, they must have uniformly shared moral feelings. See Mendel F. Cohen, *Obligation and Human Nature*

*in Hume's Philosophy*, 40 PHILOSOPHICAL QUARTERLY 316, 333, 340 (1990).
Do people in fact display a great deal of uniformity of moral feeling? For a
skeptical answer in the context of discussing Hume, see STUART HAMPSHIRE,
MORALITY AND CONFLICT 163 (1983).

15. Alasdair MacIntyre concludes that Hume's "appeal to a universal verdict by
    mankind turns out to be the mask worn by an appeal to those who
    physiologically and socially share Hume's attitudes. . . . The passions of some
    are to be preferred to the passions of others. Whose preferences reign? The
    preferences of those . . . who believe that the passage of time confers
    legitimacy upon what was originally acquired by violence and aggression.
    What Hume identifies as the standpoint of universal human nature turns out
    in fact to be that of the prejudices of the Hanoverian ruling elite." ALASDAIR
    MACINTYRE, AFTER VIRTUE 231 (2d ed. 1984). Would it be possible to
    construct a more genuinely universal or objective defense of any of the key
    elements of Hume's theory of political obligation?

16. It should be emphasized that for Hume, the role of reason in ethics is limited.
    Hume famously concludes that ['t]is not contrary to reason to prefer the
    destruction of the whole world to the scratching of my finger." DAVID HUME,
    A TREATISE OF HUMAN NATURE book II, Part III, section III at 416 (L.A.
    Selby-Bigge ed. 1968). On J.L. Mackie's interpretation, denying this claim by
    Hume simply means that we are speaking only within a particular kind of
    prescriptive institution or convention, but there is no objective or intrinsic
    reason for adopting any such convention. See J.L. MACKIE, ETHICS:
    INVENTING RIGHT AND WRONG 79-80 (1977) and, more fully, J.L. MACKIE,
    HUME'S MORAL THEORY (1980).

17. For further discussion of Hume on political obligation and other related
    matters, see DUNCAN FORBES, HUME'S PHILOSOPHICAL POLITICS ch. 3 (1975)
    and FREDERICK G. WHALEN, ORDER AND ARTIFICE IN HUME'S POLITICAL
    PHILOSOPHY (1985). For a broadranging general discussion of Hume's social
    philosophy, see F.A. Hayek, *The Legal and Political Philosophy of David
    Hume*, in HUME 335 (V.C. Chappell ed. 1968). For a background discussion
    of Hume's theory of the concept of obligation itself, see Bernard Wand,
    *Hume's Account of Obligation*, in *id.* at 308.

# 17

# Notes on Utilitarian, Anarchist, and Conservative Approaches

1. Jeremy Bentham's utilitarianism famously begins with the principle that "[n]ature has placed mankind under the governance of two sovereign masters, pain and pleasure. It is for them alone to point out what we ought to do, as well as to determine what we shall do." JEREMY BENTHAM, PRINCIPLES OF MORALS AND LEGISLATION ch. 1, sec. I at 17 (1961). In an idealized case, moral or legal decisionmaking involves considering various dimensions of pain and pleasure. These include the intensity, duration, uncertainty, remoteness, fecundity, and purity of each of the pains and pleasures affecting each of the persons involved. Bentham, though, does not otherwise characterize pleasures as morally "higher" or "lower," or as legitimate or illegitimate. See *id.* at ch. IV, secs. IV-VII at 38-39. Government or law is simply one institution among many affecting both the schedule of pains and pleasures we face and our capacity or enthusiasm for each sort of pain or pleasure, *id.* at ch. VI, sec. XLI at 66-67. Government and law aim ideally at maximizing, in some sense, the net balance of pleasure over pain, in the community, see *id.* at ch. I, either as a total sum, or on the basis of an average per person.

2. Elie Halévy expounds Bentham's view that the social contract is redundant: "Instead of saying that the People owe obedience to the King because they ought to obey the contract in which the King undertook to govern for his subjects' happiness, why not say that the People obey the King because, and just insofar as, he governs for their happiness?" ELIE HALÉVY, THE GROWTH OF PHILOSOPHIC RADICALISM 134-35 (Mary Morris trans. 1972). Note Bentham's echoing of Hume in this respect. One might reply to Bentham that a breach of promise may be more accurately detectable than whether an act of the King has led to public unhappiness. But this would provide no advantage for a social contract theory that in turn depends upon whether the government has satisfactorily promoted happiness as a term of the contract.

3.  John Plamenatz notes that Bentham concluded "that democracy, direct or
    indirect, would necessarily promote the greatest happiness of the greatest
    number," but Plamenatz goes on to argue that "the problem cannot be solved
    by *a priori* arguments, for it is essentially empirical." JOHN P. PLAMENATZ,
    CONSENT, FREEDOM AND POLITICAL OBLIGATION 157 (2d ed. 1968). Whether
    some form of democracy really best promotes happiness must therefore be
    worked out in practice.

4.  For a concise discussion of some of the alleged incoherencies, indeter-
    minacies, and problems of incommensurability in Bentham's utilitarianism,
    see John Finnis, *The Authority of Law In the Predicament of Contemporary
    Social Theory*, 1 NOTRE DAME JOURNAL OF LAW, ETHICS AND PUBLIC
    POLICY 115, 123 (1984); Germain Grisez, *Against Consequentialism*, 23
    AMERICAN JOURNAL OF JURISPRUDENCE 21-72 (1978). Generally, a problem
    of incommensurability arises when we try to objectively weigh or balance two
    things, such as pleasure and some other moral value, in a way that cannot
    succeed—as when we say that one cannot compare apples and oranges.

5.  John Austin's utilitarian jurisprudence begins with a linkage between natural
    law and utility: "Inasmuch as the goodness of God is boundless and impartial,
    he designs the greatest happiness of all of his sentient creatures. From the
    tendency of human actions to increase or diminish the aggregate of human
    enjoyments, we may infer the laws which he has given, but has not expressed
    or revealed." JOHN AUSTIN, LECTURES ON JURISPRUDENCE lecture II, part 1,
    § 1 at 23 (abridged ed. 1913). General public obedience to the law or the
    government is partly a reflection of habit, but partly due to considerations of
    utility. JOHN AUSTIN, THE PROVINCE OF JURISPRUDENCE DETERMINED 321
    (1984). Focusing on the consent of the people, though, is misleading in
    accounting for governmental legitimacy, in that a people might for some
    reason consent to a government that plainly ignores the public welfare. See
    *id.* at 326, 338.

6.  James Mill, the father of John Stuart Mill, observed that "[t]he end of
    government has been described in a great variety of expressions. By Locke
    it was said to be 'the public good,' by others it has been described as being
    'the greatest happiness of the greatest number.' These, and other equivalent
    expressions, are just; but they are defective inasmuch as the particular ideas
    which they embrace are indistinctly announced. . . ." JAMES MILL, AN ESSAY
    ON GOVERNMENT 47 (Currin V. Shields ed. 1955). Are the two formulas
    James Mill cites really equivalent? How should the idea of the greatest
    happiness, or least unhappiness, of the greatest number be interpreted?

7.  John Stuart Mill argued in turn that "the most important point of excellence

which any government can possess is to promote the virtue and intelligence of the people themselves." JOHN STUART MILL, CONSIDERATIONS ON REPRESENTATIVE GOVERNMENT 25 (Currin V. Shields ed. 1958). Mill concluded further that the best form of government involved a degree of active democratic participation. See *id.* at 42. Can John Stuart Mill's aims in both of these respects really be described as utilitarian?

8. For an expression of John Stuart Mill's sympathy for the idea of disobedience to unjust laws under at least certain circumstances, see JOHN STUART MILL, UTILITARIANISM ch. V, at 43 (Samuel Gorovitz ed. 1971).

9. Kent Greenawalt has criticized utilitarian accounts of moral and legal obligation along the following lines: "Most people are not capable of according the same weight to the interests of strangers as they do the interests of themselves and those they love. Nor do most people, in their nonperfectionist moments, feel they have failed morally when they pursue interests of their own at the cost of the much stronger interests of strangers." Kent Greenawalt, *Promise, Benefit, and Need: Ties That Bind Us to the Law*, 18 GEORGIA LAW REVIEW 727, 753 (1984) (citations omitted). Is this incompatible with utilitarianism? Or does it merely make utilitarianism difficult for us to practice? Can preference for oneself and those close to us be justified as somehow maximizing utility? For an extensive discussion of related issues, see JAMES S. FISHKIN, THE LIMITS OF OBLIGATION (1982).

10. Charles Fried argues that "[t]he obligation to keep a promise is grounded not in arguments of utility but in respect for individual autonomy and trust. . . . A liar and a promise-breaker each *use* another person. In both speech and promising there is an invitation to the other to trust, to make himself vulnerable; the liar and the promise-breaker then abuse that trust." CHARLES FRIED, CONTRACT AS PROMISE 16 (1981) (emphasis in the original). Could considerations of utility enter in as one factor in determining whether, in light of the circumstances, one ought to keep one's promise?

11. Do both utilitarian and social contract theories depend upon a theory of a choosing self that is somehow abstracted away from the social roles, institutions, and commitments that help supply the choosing self's own identity, basic values, and sense of what is possible, in the first place? In a word, is the individualized choosing self unrealistic? See ROBERTO M. UNGER, THE CRITICAL LEGAL STUDIES MOVEMENT 99 (1986).

12. For a discussion of what might be called utilitarian elements within the classical political and moral thought of Confucius, Mo Tzu, and Mencius, see HARRLEE G. GREEN, CHINESE THOUGHT FROM CONFUCIUS TO MAO TSE-

TUNG 86-87 (1953).

13. For a mere sampling of book-length discussions, critiques, and defenses of numerous forms of utilitarianism, one might start with RICHARD B. BRANDT, A THEORY OF THE GOOD AND THE RIGHT (1979); D.H. HODGSON, CONSE-QUENCES OF UTILITARIANISM (1967); DAVID LYONS, FORMS AND LIMITS OF UTILITARIANISM (1965); H.J. MCCLOSKEY, METAETHICS AND NORMATIVE ETHICS (1969); JOHN STUART MILL, UTILITARIANISM: TEXT WITH CRITICAL ESSAYS (Samuel Gorovitz ed. 1971); JAN NARVESON, MORALITY AND UTILITY (1967); DONALD REGAN, UTILITARIANISM AND COOPERATION (1980); ROLF SARTORIUS, INDIVIDUAL CONDUCT AND SOCIAL NORMS (1975); J.J.C. SMART & BERNARD WILLIAMS, UTILITARIANISM: FOR AND AGAINST (1973); STEPHEN E. TOULMIN, AN EXAMINATION OF THE PLACE OF REASON IN ETHICS (1950); UTILITARIANISM AND BEYOND (Amartya K. Sen & Bernard Williams eds. 1982).

14. Utilitarianism tended in the direction of philosophical anarchism in the late eighteenth and early nineteenth century writer William Godwin. Godwin wrote that "[i]n proportion as weakness and ignorance shall diminish, the basis of government will also decay." WILLIAM GODWIN, ENQUIRY CONCERN-ING POLITICAL JUSTICE 125 (K. Codell Carter ed. 1971). Godwin argued that "where I make the voluntary surrender of my understanding, and commit my conscience to another man's keeping, . . . I become the most mischievous and pernicious of animals." *Id.* at 122. As for obedience to governmental enactments, Godwin concludes that "in those measures which have the concurrence of my judgment, I may reasonably be expected to co-operate with willingness and zeal; but, for the rest, my only justified ground of obedience is, that I will not disturb the repose of the community, or that I do not perceive the question to be of sufficient magnitude to authorize me in incurring the penalty." *Id.* at 118. Note that Godwin puts emphasis on the potential harm to others of the surrender of one's autonomy, as opposed to viewing the surrender of autonomy as a merely personal denial of one's capacities. For further discussion of Godwin's political views, see MARK PHILP, GODWIN'S POLITICAL JUSTICE (1986).

15. The essential logic of Robert Paul Wolff's contemporary philosophical anarchist position runs as follows: "The defining mark of the state is authority, the right to rule. The primary obligation of man is autonomy, the refusal to be ruled. . . . Insofar as a man fulfills his obligation to make himself the author of his decisions, he will . . . deny that he has a duty to obey the laws of the state *simply because they are the laws.* In that sense, it would seem that anarchism is the only political doctrine consistent with the virtue of autonomy." ROBERT PAUL WOLFF, IN DEFENSE OF ANARCHISM 18

(1970) (emphasis in the original). Has any leading theorist really held that there is a general moral obligation to obey the laws "simply because they are the laws?" Can a case be made that autonomy is a genuine possibility, that autonomy is indeed morally central, and that autonomy requires what Wolff says it requires?

16. For a critique of the anarchist theories of William Godwin and Robert Paul Wolff, see David A.J. Richards, *Conscience, Human Rights, and the Anarchist Challenge to the Obligation to Obey the Law*, 18 GEORGIA LAW REVIEW 771, 776-80 (1984).

17. Bentley LeBaron criticizes Wolff's philosophical anarchism on the grounds that Wolff's categorization of all governments as illegitimate makes it difficult to distinguish governments worthy of support from those "so corrupt or oppressive that they should be overthrown." Bentley LeBaron, *Three Components of Political Obligation*, 6 CANADIAN JOURNAL OF POLITICAL SCIENCE 478, 492 (1973). To what extent does the broad judgment of illegitimacy really impair our ability to draw important moral distinctions among, say, benevolent, responsive states as opposed to repressive, totalitarian regimes? For a further response to Wolff, see JEFFREY REIMAN, IN DEFENSE OF POLITICAL PHILOSOPHY (1972).

18. Against a variety of philosophical anarchists, Joseph Raz argues that at least in some cases, "[o]ne way of wisely exercising one's autonomy is to realize that in certain matters one would do best to abide by the authority of another." Joseph Raz, *Government by Consent*, in 29 NOMOS: AUTHORITY REVISITED 76, 83 (J. Roland Pennock & John W. Chapman eds. 1987).

19. Could it be argued that protecting some of our moral rights, or the bases of those rights, such as autonomy, requires that we all recognize a general moral obligation to obey the law? For a critique of such a theory, see James W. Nickel, *Does Basing Rights on Autonomy Imply Obligations of Political Allegiance?*, 28 DIALOGUE 531 (1989). Nickel claims, interestingly, that many people are best able to promote the social conditions supporting autonomy in countries other than the one in which they reside. See *id.* at 542. This raises the broader question of why we are usually supposed to obey the "local" government in power over us, rather than a distant, but morally better government.

20. For an argument for the rationality of altruists' obeying the law even where the chances that one's disobedience will lead to a descent into a "state of nature" are extremely small, see Christopher McMahon, *Autonomy and Authority*, 16 PHILOSOPHY & PUBLIC AFFAIRS 303, 317-19 (1987).

21. For a mere introduction to some of the leading historical writings representative of the anarchist movement generally, see PIERRE-JOSEPH PROUDHON, SELECTED WRITINGS OF PIERRE-JOSEPH PROUDHON (Stewart Edwards ed. 1970); MICHAEL BAKUNIN, ON ANARCHY (Sam Dolgoff ed. 1971); MAX STIRNER, THE EGO AND HIS OWN: THE CASE OF THE INDIVIDUAL AGAINST AUTHORITY (J. Carroll ed. 1971); PETER KROPOTKIN, KROPOTKIN: SELECTED WRITINGS ON ANARCHISM AND REVOLUTION (Martin Miller ed. 1970); LEO TOLSTOY, THE LAW OF VIOLENCE AND THE LAW OF LOVE (1971). See also 19 NOMOS: ANARCHISM (J. Roland Pennock & John W. Chapman eds. 1978).

22. For a brief discussion of the anarchist elements of classical Chinese Taoist thought, see HARRLEE G. GREEN, CHINESE THOUGHT FROM CONFUCIUS TO MAO TSE-TUNG 107-08 (1953). See also FUNG YU-LAN, 1 A HISTORY OF CHINESE PHILOSOPHY 186 (Derk Bodde trans. 1952). Taoism also bears some similarity to Rousseau's thought in emphasizing the virtues of small, simple, non-commercialized society. See id. at 190-91.

23. Consider the traditional conservative view of Edmund Burke that society "is a partnership in all science, a partnership in all art; a partnership in every virtue, and in all perfection. As the ends of such a partnership cannot be obtained in many generations, it becomes a partnership not only between those who are living, but between those who are living, those who are dead, and those who are to be born. Each contract of each particular state is but a clause in the great primeval contract of eternal society, linking the lower with the higher natures, connecting the visible with the invisible world, according to a fixed compact sanctioned by the inviolable oath which holds all physical and all moral natures, each in their appointed place. This law is not subject to the will of those, who by an obligation above them, and infinitely superior, are bound to submit their will to that law." EDMUND BURKE, REFLECTIONS ON THE REVOLUTION IN FRANCE 110 (1961).

24. For representative further book-length discussions of Burke's political views, see ISAAC KRAMNICK, THE RAGE OF EDMUND BURKE (1977); FRANK O'GORMAN, EDMUND BURKE: HIS POLITICAL PHILOSOPHY (1973); BURLEIGH TAYLOR WILKINS, THE PROBLEM OF BURKE'S POLITICAL PHILOSOPHY (1967).

25. With Burke, compare the late eighteenth and early nineteenth century conservative Joseph de Maistre, who argued that "laws come from God in the sense that he wills that there should be laws and that they should be obeyed. Yet these laws also come from men in that they are made by men. In the same way, sovereignty comes from God, since he is . . . the author of society, which could not exist without sovereignty. However, this same sovereignty comes also from men in a certain sense, . . . insofar as particular forms of

government are established and declared by human consent." Joseph de Maistre, *Study on Sovereignty* book one, ch. I, in THE WORKS OF JOSEPH DE MAISTRE 94 (Jack Lively trans. 1971).

26. The mid-nineteenth century liberal philosopher T.H. Green writes as follows: "To ask why I am to submit to the power of the state, is to ask why I am to allow my life to be regulated by that complex of institutions without which I literally should not have a life to call my own, nor should be able to ask for a justification of what I am called on to do. For that I may have a life which I can call my own, I must not only be conscious of myself; I must be able to reckon on a certain freedom of action and acquisition for the attainment of those ends, and this can only be secured through common recognition of this freedom on the part of each other by members of a society, as being for a common good." *T.H. Green, The Principles of Political Obligation* § 114, in THE POLITICAL THEORY OF T.H. GREEN: SELECTED WRITINGS 118-19 (John R. Rodman ed. 1984). Is the question of an obligation to obey the government a mistaken project undertaken only by those in the grip of a false and abstract individualism? How could Green's view best be developed to distinguish between regimes that are more and less worthy of obedience? *Cf. id.* at 51-52 on "positive" or developmental freedom as our true political end.

# 18

# From Jean-Jacques Rousseau, The Social Contract

## I
### SUBJECT OF THE FIRST BOOK

Man is born free; and everywhere he is in chains. One thinks himself the master of others, and still remains a greater slave than they. How did this change come about? I do not know. What can make it legitimate? That question I think I can answer.

If I took into account only force, and the effects derived from it, I should say: "As long as a people is compelled to obey, and obeys, it does well; as soon as it can shake off the yoke, and shakes it off, it does still better; for, regaining its liberty by the same right as took it away, either it is justified in resuming it, or there was no justification for those who took it away." But the social order is a sacred right which is the basis of all other rights. Nevertheless, this right does not come from nature, and must therefore be founded on conventions. Before coming to that, I have to prove what I have just asserted.
. . .

## VI
### THE SOCIAL COMPACT

I suppose men to have reached the point at which the obstacles in the way of their preservation in the state of nature show their power of resistance to be greater than the resources at the disposal of each individual for his maintenance in that state. That primitive condition can then subsist no longer, and the human race would perish unless it changed its manner of existence.

But, as men cannot engender new forces, but only unite and direct existing ones, they have no other means of preserving themselves than the formation, by aggregation, of a sum of forces great enough to overcome the resistance. These they have to bring into play by means of a single motive power, and cause to act in concert.

This sum of forces can arise only where several persons come together: but, as the force and liberty of each man are the chief instruments of his self-preservation, how can he pledge them without harming his own interests, and neglecting the care he owes to himself? This difficulty, in its bearing on my present subject, may be stated in the following terms:

"The problem is to find a form of association which will defend and protect with the whole common force the person and goods of each associate, and in which each, while uniting himself with all, may still obey himself alone, and remain as free as before." This is the fundamental problem of which the *Social Contract* provides the solution.

The clauses of this contract are so determined by the nature of the act that the slightest modification would make them vain and ineffective; so that, although they have perhaps never been formally set forth, they are everywhere the same and everywhere tacitly admitted and recognized, until, on the violation of the social compact, each regains his original rights and resumes his natural liberty, while losing the conventional liberty in favor of which he renounced it.

These clauses, properly understood, may be reduced to one—the total alienation of each associate, together with all his rights, to the whole community; for, in the first place, as each gives himself absolutely, the conditions are the same for all; and, this being so, no one has any interest in making them burdensome to others.

Moreover, the alienation being without reserve, the union is as perfect as it can be, and no associate has anything more to demand: for, if the individuals retained certain rights, as there would be no common superior to decide between them and the public, each, being on one point his own judge, would ask to be so on all; the state of nature would thus continue, and the association would necessarily become inoperative or tyrannical.

Finally, each man, in giving himself to all, gives himself to nobody; and as there is no associate over which he does not acquire the same right as he yields others over himself, he gains an equivalent for everything he loses, and an increase of force for the preservation of what he has.

If then we discard from the social compact what is not of its essence, we shall find that it reduces itself to the following terms:

"*Each of us puts his person and all his power in common under the supreme direction of the general will, and, in our corporate capacity, we receive each member as an indivisible part of the whole.*"

At once, in place of the individual personality of each contracting party, this act of association creates a moral and collective body composed of as many members as the assembly contains voters, and receiving from this act its unity, its common identity, its life, and its will. . . .

## VII
## THE SOVEREIGN

This formula shows us that the act of association comprises a mutual undertaking between the public and the individuals, and that each individual, in making a contract, as we may say, with himself, is bound in a double capacity;

as a member of the Sovereign he is bound to the individuals, and as a member of the State to the Sovereign. But the maxim of civil right, that no one is bound by undertakings made to himself does not apply in this case; for there is a great difference between incurring an obligation to yourself and incurring one to a whole of which you form a part.

Attention must further be called to the fact that public deliberation, while competent to bind all the subjects to the Sovereign, because of the two different capacities in which each of them may be regarded, cannot, for the opposite reason, bind the Sovereign to itself; and that it is consequently against the nature of the body politic for the Sovereign to impose on itself a law which it cannot infringe. Being able to regard itself in only one capacity, it is in the position of an individual who makes a contract with himself; and this makes it clear that there neither is nor can be any kind of fundamental law binding on the body of the people—not even the social contract itself. This does not mean that the body politic cannot enter into undertakings with others, provided the contract is not infringed by them; for in relation to what is external to it, it becomes a simple being, an individual.

But the body politic or the Sovereign, drawing its being wholly from the sanctity of the contract, can never bind itself, even to an outsider, to do anything derogatory to the original act, for instance, to alienate any part of itself, or to submit to another Sovereign. Violation of the act by which it exists would be self-annihilation; and that which is itself nothing can create nothing.

As soon as this multitude is so united in one body, it is impossible to offend against one of the members without attacking the body, and still more to offend against the body without the members resenting it. Duty and interest therefore equally oblige the two contracting parties to give each other help; and the same men should seek to combine, in their double capacity, all the advantages dependent upon that capacity.

Again, the Sovereign, being formed wholly of the individuals who compose it, neither has nor can have any interest contrary to theirs; and consequently the sovereign power need give no guarantee to its subjects, because it is impossible for the body to wish to hurt all its members. We shall also see later on that it cannot hurt any in particular. The Sovereign, merely by virtue of what it is, is always what it should be.

This, however, is not the case with the relation of the subjects to the Sovereign, which, despite the common interest, would have no security that they would fulfil their undertakings, unless it found means to assure itself of their fidelity.

In fact, each individual, as a man, may have a particular will contrary or dissimilar to the general will which he has as a citizen. His particular interest may speak to him quite differently from the common interest: his absolute and naturally independent existence may make him look upon what he owes to the common cause as a gratuitous contribution, the loss of which will do no less harm to others than the payment of it is burdensome to himself; and, regarding the moral person which constitutes the State as a *persona ficta*, because not a man, he may wish to enjoy the rights of citizenship without being ready to fulfil the duties of a subject. The continuance of such an injustice could not but prove the undoing of the body politic.

In order then that the social compact may not be an empty formula, it tacitly includes the undertaking, which alone can give force to the rest, that whoever refuses to obey the general will shall be compelled to do so by the whole body. This means nothing less than that he will be forced to be free; for this is the condition which, by giving each citizen to his country, secures him against all personal dependence. In this lies the key to the working of the political machine; this alone legitimizes civil undertakings, which, without it, would be absurd, tyrannical, and liable to the most frightful abuses.

## VIII
## THE CIVIL STATE

The passage from the state of nature to the civil state produces a very remarkable change in man, by substituting justice for instinct in his conduct, and giving his actions the morality they had formerly lacked. Then only, when the voice of duty takes the place of physical impulses and right of appetite, does man, who so far had considered only himself, find that he is forced to act on different principles, and to consult his reason before listening to his inclinations. Although, in this state, he deprives himself of some advantages which he got from nature, he gains in return others so great, his faculties are so stimulated and developed, his ideas so extended, his feelings so ennobled, and his whole soul so uplifted, that, did not the abuses of this new condition often degrade him below that which he left, he would be bound to bless continually the happy moment which took him from it for ever, and, instead of a stupid and unimaginative animal, made him an intelligent being and a man.

Let us draw up the whole account in terms easily commensurable. What man loses by the social contract is his natural liberty and an unlimited right to everything he tries to get and succeeds in getting; what he gains is civil liberty and the proprietorship of all he possesses. If we are to avoid mistake in weighing one against the other, we must clearly distinguish natural liberty, which is bounded only by the strength of the individual, from civil liberty, which is limited by the general will, and possession, which is merely the effect of force or the right of the first occupier, from property, which can be founded only on a positive title.

We might, over and above all this, add, to what man acquires in the civil state, moral liberty, which alone makes him truly master of himself; for the mere impulse of appetite is slavery, while obedience to a law which we prescribe to ourselves is liberty. But I have already said too much on this head, and the philosophical meaning of the word liberty does not now concern us. . . .

## BOOK II

### I
### THAT SOVEREIGNTY IS INALIENABLE

The first and most important deduction from the principles we have so far laid down is that the general will alone can direct the State according to the object for which it was instituted, i.e. the common good: for if the clashing of particular interests made the establishment of societies necessary, the agreement of these very interests made it possible. The common element in these different interests is what forms the social tie; and, were there no point of agreement between them all, no society could exist. It is solely on the basis of this common interest that every society should be governed.

I hold then that Sovereignty, being nothing less than the exercise of the general will, can never be alienated, and that the Sovereign, who is no less than a collective being, cannot be represented except by himself: the power indeed may be transmitted but not the will.

In reality, if it is not impossible for a particular will to agree on some point with the general will, it is at least impossible for the agreement to be lasting and constant; for the particular will tends, by its very nature, to partiality, while the general will tends to equality. It is even more impossible to have any guarantee of this agreement; for even if it should always exist, it would be the effect not of art, but of chance. The Sovereign may indeed say: "I now will actually what this man wills, or at least what he says he wills"; but it cannot say: "What he wills to-morrow, I too shall will" because it is absurd for the will to bind itself for the future, nor is it incumbent on any will to consent to anything that is not for the good of the being who wills. If then the people promises simply to obey, by that very act it dissolves itself and loses what makes it a people; the moment a master exists, there is no longer a Sovereign, and from that moment the body politic has ceased to exist.

This does not mean that the commands of the rulers cannot pass for general wills, so long as the Sovereign, being free to oppose them, offers no opposition. In such a case, universal silence is taken to imply the consent of the people. This will be explained later on.

### II
### THAT SOVEREIGNTY IS INDIVISIBLE

Sovereignty, for the same reason as makes it inalienable, is indivisible; for will either is, or is not general;[1] it is the will either of the body of the people, or only of a part of it. In the first case, the will, when declared, is an act of Sovereignty and constitutes law: in the second, it is merely a particular will, or act of magistracy—at the most a decree. . . .

### III
### WHETHER THE GENERAL WILL IS FALLIBLE

It follows from what has gone before that the general will is always right and tends to the public advantage; but it does not follow that the deliberations of the people are always equally correct. Our will is always for our own good, but we do not always see what that is; the people is never corrupted, but it is often deceived, and on such occasions only does it seem to will what is bad.

There is often a great deal of difference between the will of all and the general will; the latter considers only the common interest, while the former takes private interest into account, and is no more than a sum of particular wills: but take away from these same wills the pluses and minuses that cancel one another, and the general will remains as the sum of the difference.

If, when the people, being furnished with adequate information, held its deliberations, the citizens had no communication one with another, the grand total of the small differences would always give the general will, and the decision would always be good. But when factions arise, and partial associations are formed at the expense of the great association, the will of each of these associations becomes general in relation to its members, while it remains particular in relation to the State: it may then be said that there are no longer as many votes as there are men, but only as many as there are associations. The differences become less numerous and give a less general result. Lastly, when one of these associations is so great as to prevail over all the rest, the result is no longer a sum of small differences, but a single difference; in this case there is no longer a general will, and the opinion which prevails is purely particular.

It is therefore essential, if the general will is to be able to express itself, that there should be no partial society within the State, and that each citizen should think only his own thoughts: which was indeed the sublime and unique system established by the great Lycurgus. But if there are partial societies, it is best to have as many as possible and to prevent them from being unequal, as was done by Solon, Numa and Servius. These precautions are the only ones that can guarantee that the general will shall be always enlightened, and that the people shall in no way deceive itself.

## IV
## THE LIMITS OF THE SOVEREIGN POWER

If the State is a moral person whose life is in the union of its members, and if the most important of its cares is the care for its own preservation, it must have a universal and compelling force, in order to move and dispose each part as may be most advantageous to the whole. As nature gives each man absolute power over all his members, the social compact gives the body politic absolute power over all its members also; and it is this power which, under the direction of the general will, bears, as I have said, the name of Sovereignty.

But, besides the public person, we have to consider the private persons composing it, whose life and liberty are naturally independent of it. We are bound then to distinguish clearly between the respective rights of the citizens and the Sovereign, and between the duties the former have to fulfil as subjects, and the natural rights they should enjoy as men.

Each man alienates, I admit, by the social compact, only such part of his powers, goods, and liberty as it is important for the community to control; but it must also be granted that the sovereign is sole judge of what is important.

Every service a citizen can render the State he ought to render as soon as the Sovereign demands it; but the Sovereign, for its part, cannot impose upon its subjects any fetters that are useless to the community, nor can it even wish to do so; for no more by the law of reason than by the law of nature can anything occur without a cause.

The undertakings which bind us to the social body are obligatory only because they are mutual; and their nature is such that in fulfilling them we cannot work for others without working for ourselves. Why is it that the general will is always in the right, and that all continually will the happiness of each one, unless it is because there is not a man who does not think of 'each' as meaning him, and consider himself in voting for all? This proves that equality of rights and the idea of justice which such equality creates originate in the preference each man gives to himself, and accordingly in the very nature of man. It proves that the general will, to be really such, must be general in its object as well as its essence; that it must both come from all and apply to all; and that it loses its natural rectitude when it is directed to some particular and determinate object, because in such a case we are judging of something foreign to us, and have no true principle of equity to guide us.

Indeed, as soon as a question of particular fact or right arises on a point not previously regulated by a general convention, the matter becomes contentious. It is a case in which the individuals concerned are one party, and the public the other, but in which I can see neither the law that ought to be followed nor the judge who ought to give the decision. In such a case, it would be absurd to propose to refer the question to an express decision of the general will, which can be only the conclusion reached by one of the parties and in consequence will be, for the other party, merely an external and particular will, inclined on this occasion to injustice and subject to error. Thus, just as a particular will cannot stand for the general will, the general will, in turn, changes its nature, when its object is particular, and, as general, cannot pronounce on a man or a fact. When, for instance, the people of Athens nominated or displaced its rulers, decreed honors to one, and imposed penalties on another, and, by a multitude of particular decrees, exercised all the functions of government indiscriminately, it had in such cases no longer a general will in the strict sense; it was acting no longer as Sovereign, but as magistrate. This will seem contrary to current views; but I must be given time to expound my own.

It should be seen from the foregoing that what makes the will general is less the number of voters than the common interest uniting them; for, under this system, each necessarily submits to the conditions he imposes on others: and this admirable agreement between interest and justice gives to the common deliberations an equitable character which at once vanishes when any particular question is discussed, in the absence of a common interest to unite and identify the ruling of the judge with that of the party.

From whatever side we approach our principle, we reach the same conclusion, that the social compact sets up among the citizens an equality of such a kind, that they all bind themselves to observe the same conditions and should therefore all enjoy the same rights. Thus, from the very nature of the compact, every act of Sovereignty, i.e. every authentic act of the general will, binds or favors all the citizens equally; so that the Sovereign recognizes only the body of the nation, and draws no distinctions between those of whom it is made up. What, then, strictly speaking, is an act of Sovereignty? It is not a convention between a superior and an inferior, but a convention between the body and each of its members. It is legitimate, because based on the social contract, and equitable, because common to all; useful, because it can have no other object than the general good, and stable because guaranteed by the public force and the supreme power. So long as the subjects have to submit only to conventions of this sort, they obey no one but their own will; and to ask how far the respective rights of the Sovereign and the citizens extend, is to ask up to what point the latter can enter into undertakings with themselves, each with all, and all with each.

We can see from this that the sovereign power, absolute, sacred, and inviolable as it is, does not and cannot exceed the limits of general conventions, and that every man may dispose at will of such goods and liberty as these conventions leave him; so that the Sovereign never has a right to lay more charges on one subject than on another, because, in that case, the question becomes particular, and ceases to be within its competency.

When these distinctions have once been admitted, it is seen to be so untrue that there is, in the social contract, any real renunciation on the part of the individuals, that the position in which they find themselves as a result of the contract is really preferable to that in which they were before. Instead of a renunciation, they have made an advantageous exchange: instead of an uncertain and precarious way of living they have got one that is better and more secure; instead of natural independence they have got liberty, instead of the power to harm others security for themselves, and instead of their strength, which others might overcome, a right which social union makes invincible. Their very life, which they have devoted to the State, is by it constantly protected; and when they risk it in the State's defense, what more are they doing than giving back what they have received from it? What are they doing that they would not do more often and with greater danger in the state of nature, in which they would inevitably have to fight battles at the peril of their lives in defense of that which is the means of their preservation? All have indeed to fight when their country needs them; but then no one has ever to fight for himself. Do we not gain something by running, on behalf of what gives us our security, only some of the risks we should have to run for ourselves, as soon as we lost it?

# NOTE TO THE SOCIAL CONTRACT

1. To be general, a will need not always be unanimous; but every vote must be counted; any exclusion is a breach of generality.

# 19

# Notes on the Social Contract

1.  Jean-Jacques Rousseau was born in 1712 at Geneva. Rousseau's colorful life is memorably recounted in his *Confessions*. Those interested in Rousseau's social thought will want to examine his *Discourse on the Origin of Inequality* and his treatise on education, *Emile*, as well as his other social works. His influence on modern democratic thought and on Romanticism have been substantial, though it has been claimed that Rousseau's writing has given some inspiration to modern totalitarianism as well.

2.  G.D.H. Cole summarizes one crucial difference between Hobbes and Rousseau on popular sovereignty in the following terms: "Rousseau regards as inalienable a supreme power which Hobbes makes the people alienate in its first corporate action." G.D.H. Cole, *Introduction* to JEAN-JACQUES ROUSSEAU, THE SOCIAL CONTRACT AND DISCOURSES xxx (G.D.H. Cole trans. 1950).

3.  T.H. Green compares Locke and Rousseau in this fashion: "That 'sovereignty of the people,' which Locke looks upon as held in reserve after its original exercise in the establishment of government, only to be asserted in the event of a legislature proving false to its trust, Rousseau supposes to be in constant exercise." T.H. GREEN, LECTURES ON THE PRINCIPLES OF POLITICAL OBLIGATION 80 (1950).

4.  According to Ronald Grimsley, "the general will lifts the individual above selfish petty interests and enables him to identify himself with the common good, which is also his own higher good. It emerges from the social setting, but it expresses itself through a collective action based on a rational and moral principle." RONALD GRIMSLEY, JEAN-JACQUES ROUSSEAU 105-06 (1983).

5.  Consider T.H. Green's account of the concept of the general will: "[I]n the assembly of the whole people, if they had sufficient information, and if no

minor combinations of particular interests were formed within the entire body, the difference between the wills of individuals would neutralize each other, and the vote of the whole body would express the true general will." T.H. GREEN, LECTURES ON THE PRINCIPLES OF POLITICAL OBLIGATION 87 (1950).

6. Philip J. Kain has recently made the intriguing argument that Rousseau's general will can, in principle, deliver justice, equality, and the common good given certain specified conditions. First, all citizens must directly vote in person on all issues, and in the absence of faction or association. Second, the general will can exist only with respect to a general or abstract and universal question, without reference to individual persons or facts. Third, the question must be posed in such a way as to call not for the individual interests of each voter, but for each person's judgment as to what is in the common interest, or promotes the common good. Finally, all voters must know at the time of voting that all laws will be rigorously and equally enforced. Kain concludes that Rousseau assumed that those voters who are unable to set aside their own selfish interests will either not form a majority, or that their votes will be divided in several directions and tend to cancel one another out. See Philip J. Kain, *Rousseau, the General Will and Individual Liberty*, 7 HISTORY OF PHILOSOPHY QUARTERLY 315, 316-19 (1990).

7. Roger Masters argues that "[t]he general will, which is to say an 'act of sovereignty' or any 'law,' must fulfill two formal or definitional requirements: it must be willed by all members of the society, and it must apply to all members of the society." ROGER D. MASTERS, THE POLITICAL PHILOSOPHY OF ROUSSEAU 328 (1968). Note that while Masters's formulation is generally less stringent than that of Philip J. Kain, *supra*, it is in one respect more stringent in denying that the general will can be willed by a majority of, but less than all, voters.

8. Hilail Gildin notes that Rousseau rejects sheer majoritarianism: "Rousseau believes . . . that a decision can be unjust even though it enjoys majority support. When this happens, it no longer embodies the general will." HILAIL GILDIN, ROUSSEAU'S SOCIAL CONTRACT 58 (1983).

9. If the general will, in order to be general, must make no implied or express reference to any distinct class or person, does this not imply that much of the legislation with which we are familiar in modern representative democracies cannot, however generously intended, reflect the general will? See G.D.H. Cole, *Introduction* to JEAN-JACQUES ROUSSEAU, THE SOCIAL CONTRACT AND DISCOURSES xxxiii (G.D.H. Cole trans. 1950).

10. Patrick Riley argues that "[w]ill . . . is characteristically a concept of individuality, of particularity; it is only metaphorically that will can be spoken

of as general. . . . What . . . Rousseau admired in ancient society, is not really a general will but a political morality of the common good in which individual will is not suppressed but simply does not appear in contradistinction to, or with claims against, society." PATRICK RILEY, WILL AND POLITICAL LEGITIMACY 112-13 (1982). Could we fairly omit the idea of a "general will" in Rousseau and focus instead on morality, democracy, socialization and so forth? Would this simplify matters?

11. For discussions, some rather skeptical, of the idea of a rich public interest or common good, see RICHARD FLATHMAN, THE PUBLIC INTEREST 13 (1966) (the idea of the public interest as indispensable); VIRGINIA HELD, THE PUBLIC INTEREST AND INDIVIDUAL INTERESTS 18 (1970) (the concept of the public interest as in a "state of confusion"); 5 NOMOS: THE PUBLIC INTEREST (Carl J. Friedrich ed. 1962); GLENDON SCHUBERT, THE PUBLIC INTEREST 223 (1960) (arguing that "there is no public-interest theory worthy of the name").

12. On Ronald Grimsley's interpretation of Rousseau, "[o]bedience to the community will . . . be regarded by each member as obedience to principles freely chosen by himself. . . ." RONALD GRIMSLEY, JEAN-JACQUES ROUSSEAU 101 (1983).

13. Can we accurately summarize Rousseau's view of political obligation in the following fashion?: "Rousseau tells us that the citizen who is not excluded from the sovereign assembly, nor exposed inside it to pressures and intrigues which make his opinions and votes count for nothing, is bound by the laws made by the assembly." John Plamenatz, "Ce Qui Ne Signifie Autre Chose Sinon Qu'on Le Forçera D'Etre Libre," in HOBBES AND ROUSSEAU: A COLLECTION OF CRITICAL ESSAYS 318 (Maurice Cranston & Richard S. Peters eds. 1972). Is no one else morally bound to obey the law, if these conditions are only imperfectly met?

14. On the question of being forced to be free, John Plamenatz has written that we speak of being restrained by rules, but enslaved by appetites, and that we may feel frustrated by rules, but wish to follow them insofar as we are moral. See John Plamenatz, "Ce Qui Ne Signifie Autre Chose Sinon Qu'on Le Forçera D'Etre Libre," in HOBBES AND ROUSSEAU: A COLLECTION OF CRITICAL ESSAYS 331-32 (Maurice Cranston & Richard S. Peters eds. 1972). Can all political selfishness really be thought of as a form of enslavement?

15. George Kateb interprets Rousseau as maintaining that disobedience to a law risks returning to the state of nature, where literal enslavement for that disobedient actor is possible. See George Kateb, Aspects of Rousseau's Political Thought, in ESSAYS IN THE HISTORY OF POLITICAL THOUGHT 244, 256 (Isaac Kramnick ed. 1969). Does this idea help account for Rousseau's idea

of forcing one to be free? Does it matter that the realistic likelihood of one's disobedience ending up in slavery for anyone is small?

16. Rousseau speaks of "forcing" a citizen who has given her morally binding consent to the law to be "free" by denying her the ability to selfishly and immorally withdraw that consent. See JULES STEINBERG, LOCKE, ROUSSEAU, AND THE IDEA OF CONSENT 87-88 (1978). Does Rousseau's idea of freedom here focus not on the absence of some externally or socially imposed restraint, but on engaging in rationally and morally justified behavior based on one's own nature, the nature of one's political society, and one's own established commitments? The former is sometimes referred to as "negative" freedom, and the latter as "positive" freedom. See ISAIAH BERLIN, FOUR ESSAYS ON LIBERTY 118-72 (1969).

17. Ronald Grimsley argues that, in the context of his ideal society, "Rousseau considers that any individual who behaves in an irresponsible, anti-social way is either wicked or insane and has to be restrained from harming the community and himself. By 'forcing him to be free' the community will (it is hoped) make him heed the demands of his own true self." RONALD GRIMSLEY, JEAN-JACQUES ROUSSEAU 102 (1983). Is Rousseau here merely building on well-established psychology and philosophy, or is he leaving his theory of "positive" freedom open to abuse by totalitarian majorities? See Lester G. Crocker, *Introduction* to JEAN-JACQUES ROUSSEAU, THE SOCIAL CONTRACT AND DISCOURSE ON THE ORIGIN OF INEQUALITY xx-xxiii (Lester G. Crocker trans. 1967). See also J.L. TALMON, THE RISE OF TOTALITARIAN DEMOCRACY (1952).

18. For a brief portrayal of Rousseau's theory as posing a "threat to individual liberty," with citations to some of the relevant literature, see Larry M. Preston, *Freedom and Authority: Beyond the Precepts of Liberalism*, 77 AMERICAN POLITICAL SCIENCE REVIEW 666, 667 (1983).

19. Ernst Cassirer has characterized Rousseau's approach in the following way: "Liberty implies an obligation to an inviolable law which every individual enacts for himself. Not in license, but in the free acknowledgment of law, lies the true character of liberty." ERNST CASSIRER, THE PHILOSOPHY OF THE ENLIGHTENMENT 261 (Fritz C.A. Koelln & James P. Pettegrove trans. 1951).

20. Ramon Lemos interprets Rousseau along the following lines: "Given the existence of the laws, I can come to obey myself alone simply through willing my good in ways compatible with the attainment of the good of other members of the association. . . . [L]iberty, as distinct from license, is possible only insofar as each man acts compatibly with the good of every person affected by his action." RAMON M. LEMOS, ROUSSEAU'S POLITICAL PHILOSOPHY

115 (1977). Does Rousseau finally mean that liberty, as he uses the term, is the same as liberty put to a morally proper use? Would it be fair to say that Rousseau's citizen is not really free, but may well not notice or feel that lack of freedom?

21. Judith Shklar concludes that for Rousseau, the real conflict is not between authority and freedom, but between authority and equality. Authority promotes freedom through assisting in the process of building an integrated, independent, psychologically liberated self. See Judith N. Shklar, *Rousseau's Images of Authority*, in HOBBES AND ROUSSEAU: A COLLECTION OF CRITICAL ESSAYS 333, 362 (Maurice Cranston & Richard S. Peters eds. 1972). Should any political authority that consciously undertakes as its task the therapy of the public psyche be trusted?

22. Stephen Ellenburg writes that for Rousseau, "[l]iberty is permanent and unmediated participation in legislation. Liberty is literal self-government." STEPHEN ELLENBURG, ROUSSEAU'S POLITICAL PHILOSOPHY 160 (1976). Are these two formulas equivalent? Could we say instead that Rousseau aims at a society in which permanent and unmediated participation in legislation in fact involves genuine self-government?

23. Would it be fair to say that "Rousseau's conclusion is that self-government is the only legitimate form of government?" HILAIL GILDIN, ROUSSEAU'S SOCIAL CONTRACT 31 (1983).

24. According to Jules Steinberg, Rousseau's view is that "it is improper to speak of citizens having a moral obligation to obey the law in any state where the laws express only the selfish interests of a ruling class." JULES STEINBERG, LOCKE, ROUSSEAU, AND THE IDEA OF CONSENT 83 (1978) (footnote omitted). Is it possible that some degree of either absolute poverty, or inequality and dependence, could undermine the "consent" given by the poor? What implications might this have for our own society?

25. Carl Friedrich holds that in Rousseau's work, autonomy requires that for law to be genuinely binding and legitimate, it must have been established through the free participation of those bound by that law. See CARL J. FRIEDRICH, THE PHILOSOPHY OF LAW IN HISTORICAL PERSPECTIVE 122 (rev. 2d ed. 1963). Does this formulation, if faithful to Rousseau, reject the possibility of a person's being morally bound by laws in the making of which they have not participated?

26. Note that for political generations after the first, Rousseau apparently simply adopts Locke's mere residency-based approach to imposing a binding obligation to obey. See T.H. GREEN, LECTURES ON POLITICAL OBLIGATION 89 (1950). Is such an approach any more convincing as part of Rousseau's

theory than as part of Locke's?

27. Hilail Gildin writes that Rousseau "makes his preference for small and free republics clear . . . but does not wish to encourage men whose societies cannot be of this character to overthrow the societies in which they *do* live merely because those societies are not small and free." HILAIL GILDIN, ROUSSEAU'S SOCIAL CONTRACT 40 (1983) (emphasis in the original). Does Rousseau's theory imply that essentially all modern governments, including representative democracies, are in some sense illegitimate? Could such governments be illegitimate, on Rousseau's theory, without this fact's morally licensing widespread disobedience of even controversial, politically-charged laws?

28. Stephen Ellenburg observes that for Rousseau, "[l]iberty is possible only in small communities where all citizens know one another and are able to gather together in the public square for legislative assemblies." STEPHEN ELLENBURG, ROUSSEAU'S POLITICAL PHILOSOPHY 163 (1976). Is it possible, though, that small, homogeneous communities also tend to suffocate liberty in another sense, via enforced conformance to narrow standard norms, through continuous high personal public visibility, and subtle public intrusiveness?

29. J.W. Gough has concluded that "the ultimate significance of Rousseau in the history of political thought is as a precursor of a collectivist attitude to man's place in society rather than as a vindicator of individual liberty." J.W. GOUGH, THE SOCIAL CONTRACT 173 (2d ed. 1957). Does Rousseau's theory lose its appeal on the grounds that freedom as we normally use the term requires more pluralism, diversity, and tolerance of difference than Rousseau is willing to allow?

30. How thoroughly does Rousseau reject all forms of moral diversity and pluralism in his ideal community? Does this rejection suggest that we dismiss Rousseau's ideal as undesirable or unattainable? See JULES STEINBERG, LOCKE, ROUSSEAU, AND THE IDEA OF CONSENT 82 (1978).

31. Ronald Grimsley argues that for Rousseau, equality is "an essential concomitant of freedom since freedom must be for all." RONALD GRIMSLEY, JEAN-JACQUES ROUSSEAU 101 (1983). Is Rousseau suggesting merely that if some citizens are deprived of liberty, those citizens are in a significant sense not politically equals? Or is he perhaps suggesting that if some citizens are not free, or equal, then no citizen can really be free?

32. For a discussion of the extent to which even the relatively democratic consent theory of Rousseau excludes and minimizes the capacities of women, see Carole Pateman, *Women and Consent*, 8 POLITICAL THEORY 149, 153-54 (1980).

Susan Moller Okin has concluded that "Rousseau's ideal republic of free and equal heads of patriarchal families is necessarily built on the political exclusion, total confinement and repression of women." SUSAN MOLLER OKIN, WOMEN IN WESTERN POLITICAL THOUGHT 144 (1979). Okin observes that "Rousseau never envisaged that women should be enfranchised citizens whose voices contribute to the formulation of the general will." *Id.* Could Rousseau's theory be simply reformulated to include women, or do the problems with Rousseau's theory run deeper than that?

# 20

# Notes on Immanuel Kant

1. Immanuel Kant was born in 1724 and died in 1804, having led his life within the geographic compass of Koenigsberg. His work stands as the culmination of Enlightenment Rationalism. Among his most important general philosophical and social philosophical works are the *Foundations of the Metaphysics of Morals, The Critique of Pure Reason, The Critique of Judgment, Perpetual Peace, Religion Within the Limits of Reason Alone*, and his work on theory and practice. Some of Kant's most directly political work has been translated as *The Metaphysical Elements of Justice.*

2. Michael Sandel has compared Locke and Kant in the following terms: "Where Locke backs up the original contract with the law of God and Nature, Kant backs it up with a principle of right given not by nature but by pure reason." MICHAEL J. SANDEL, LIBERALISM AND THE LIMITS OF JUSTICE 119 (1982). Might not this comparison be extended to Kant's differences with Hobbes as well? For Kant's own discussion of Hobbes's theory, see THE PHILOSOPHY OF KANT: IMMANUEL KANT'S MORAL AND POLITICAL WRITINGS 415-22 (Carl J. Friedrich ed. 1949).

3. Carl Friedrich has written that for Kant, force, freedom, and law must all be combined in order to realize a worthy political order. In the absence of any of these elements, anarchism, despotism, or barbarism must result. See Carl J. Friedrich, *Introduction* to THE PHILOSOPHY OF KANT: IMMANUEL KANT'S MORAL AND POLITICAL WRITINGS xliii (Carl J. Friedrich ed. 1949).

4. As interpreted by George Fletcher, Kant conceives of law and morality as occupying separate spheres. Law expresses and preserves one's contingent, perhaps morally questionable choices from external restraint. Morality, on the other hand, is the sphere of internal freedom, where reason and universal principle triumph over mere emotion, sensual impulse, and appetite. See George P. Fletcher, *Law and Morality: A Kantian Perspective*, 87 COLUMBIA LAW REVIEW 533, 534, 542-43 (1987). In the legal realm, mere compliance

with the law, from whatever motive, is generally enough. But a desire merely to avoid legal punishment does not constitute a good will, which is alone of moral value. See *id.* at 542-43. For a brief discussion of Fletcher's interpretation of Kant, see David S. Stern, *Autonomy and Political Obligation in Kant,* 29 SOUTHERN JOURNAL OF PHILOSOPHY 127, 132-34 (1991).

5.  In part one of the *Metaphysics of Morals,* Kant argues that "[t]here can be no legitimate resistance of the people to the legislative state. . . . Accordingly, there is no . . . right of revolution. . . . It is the people's duty to endure even the most intolerable abuse of supreme authority. The reason for this is that resistance to the supreme legislation can itself only be unlawful; indeed it must be conceived as destroying the entire lawful constitution, because, in order for it to be authorized, there would have to be a public law that would permit the resistance. . . . The self-contradiction involved here is immediately evident if we ask who would act as judge in this controversy between the people and the sovereign." IMMANUEL KANT, THE METAPHYSICAL ELEMENTS OF JUSTICE 86 (John Ladd trans. 1965). Kant continues at a later point to the effect that unauthorized rebellion against the government proceeds from the "arbitrary will," and that following a rebellion, "a good constitution would come into being only as a matter of chance." *Id.* at 140. Is Kant here simply emphasizing the inevitable confusions, uncontrollability, and uncertainties of revolution, along with the fear that the costs of revolution may exceed its likely benefits? Note that Kant does allow that "[a] limited constitution permits . . . a negative resistance, that is, a refusal by the people (in parliament) to accede always to the demands of the executive authority. . . ." *Id.* at 89. Could the latter provision possibly be expanded to allow for "passive" resistance or civil disobedience? How wide does Kant then open the door to disobedience, if not rebellion, by imposing a general moral requirement to obey authority, but with the qualification that obedience is owed only "in everything that does not conflict with internal morality?" *Id.* at 139.

6.  Roger Sullivan argues that "Kant does allow the possible legitimacy, within a limited constitutional state, of passive resistance to unjust laws when obedience to them would be morally corrupting; we may not obey civil laws that command what the moral law forbids." ROGER J. SULLIVAN, IMMANUEL KANT'S MORAL THEORY 224 (1989). Is Kant's view in this respect compatible with his apparent denial of any right of revolution? *See id.*; LESLIE A. MULHOLLAND, KANT'S SYSTEM OF RIGHTS 338-46 (1990).

7.  Carl Friedrich presents as Kant's view that injustice involves the absence of freedom in accordance with general laws, and that removing obstacles to such freedom is just. See CARL J. FRIEDRICH, THE PHILOSOPHY OF LAW IN HISTORICAL PERSPECTIVE 127 (rev. 2d ed. 1963). While Kant doubtless intends this

principle to justify state coercion against unjust actions by individuals, might not the same idea be used to justify individual disobedience to unjust positive law?

8. Kant offers the following test for the justice of individual laws, or at least for the public duty to consider such laws just: "[I]f a law were such that it was impossible for an entire people to give consent to it (as for example a law that a certain class of subjects, by inheritance, should have the privilege of the *status of lords*), then such a law is unjust. On the other hand, if there is a mere *possibility* that a people might consent to a (certain) law, then it is a duty to consider that the law is just, even though at the moment the people might . . . refus[e] to give their consent to it if asked." THE PHILOSOPHY OF KANT: IMMANUEL KANT'S MORAL AND POLITICAL WRITINGS 411 (Carl J. Friedrich ed. 1949) (emphasis in the original). Can laws really be separated into these two categories? Couldn't an heredity nobility even possibly be popularly consented to? Is Kant's test too lenient in allowing too many unjust, deservedly unpopular (but facially neutral) laws to pass as just?

9. Patrick Riley similarly interprets Kant as holding that legitimate laws are those framed such that they could have been generated by and agreed to by the whole united public. PATRICK RILEY, WILL AND POLITICAL LEGITIMACY 126 (1982). Can we therefore call Kant a hypothetical social contractarian? See *id.* at 125-27. Note that while we might call both Kant and, say, John Rawls hypothetical contract theorists, Kant does not offer a full and crisply determinate set of just fundamental political and legal principles. Kant is often compared to Rousseau, whose work Kant greatly admired. Can Rousseau be called a merely hypothetical social contract theorist?

10. For a brief discussion of Patrick Riley's interpretation of Kant, see David S. Stern, *Autonomy and Political Obligation in Kant*, 29 SOUTHERN JOURNAL OF PHILOSOPHY 127, 137 (1991). David Stern interprets Kant's position to be that "obligatory laws are those which are rationally legislated laws of willing." *Id.* Might this view suggest that to the extent that individuals are really capable of the difficult act of formulating universal moral principles to act upon, they should do so, but that to the extent that they cannot, individuals should defer to apparently sound moral principle embodied in duly enacted governmental decrees?

11. Patrick Riley concludes that according to Kant, law and politics should operate instrumentally to remove obstacles to the development and expression of the only unqualifiedly good thing, the morally good will, which is determined by reason and aims to respect persons as ends in themselves. PATRICK RILEY, WILL AND POLITICAL LEGITIMACY 128-29 (1982). What are the

practical limits to which states should be permitted to encourage the expression of a morally good will among the citizenry? Can the state reliably tell with what motive a given person's action has been performed?

12. Could Kant's moral and legal philosophy be developed in such a way as to establish the distinctive moral value of a regime that recognized public as well as private moral obligations to protect every potentially rational agent from those unfulfilled needs, of whatever sort, that threaten the development of that person's capacity for rational agency or autonomy? See ONORA O'NEILL, CONSTRUCTIONS OF REASON 232-33 (1989). Should a government seek to maximize everyone's moral autonomy, or establish the basis for everyone's exercising at least a minimum of moral autonomy, or some third possibility?

13. Robert Paul Wolff's examination of Kant's moral philosophy concludes, intriguingly, in this fashion: "My own view is that Kant's analysis of rational agency, autonomy, and moral principles entails the doctrine which in political philosophy is known as anarchism." ROBERT PAUL WOLFF, THE AUTONOMY OF REASON 129 n.12 (1973). For a statement of Wolff's philosophical anarchism, see ROBERT PAUL WOLFF, IN DEFENSE OF ANARCHISM (1970).

14. For a brief but suggestive discussion by Kant of the relationships among autonomy, consent, and equality, see IMMANUEL KANT, PERPETUAL PEACE 11-12 n.2 (Lewis White Beck trans. 1957).

15. For an argument to the effect that Kant's theory should be considered as within the natural law tradition, as opposed to the classical social contract or consent-based approach to political obligation, see LESLIE A. MULHOLLAND, KANT'S SYSTEM OF RIGHTS 346-47 (1990).

16. For further relevant discussion of Kant, see HANNAH ARENDT, LECTURES ON KANT'S POLITICAL PHILOSOPHY (Ronald Beiner ed. 1982); HANS SANER, KANT'S POLITICAL THOUGHT: ITS ORIGINS AND DEVELOPMENT (E.B. Ashton trans. 1973). For Kant's moral philosophy, see HENRY E. ALLISON, KANT'S THEORY OF FREEDOM (1990); H.J. PATON, THE CATEGORICAL IMPERATIVE (1948).

# 21

# Notes on Hegel

1. Hegel was born in Stuttgart in 1770. Perhaps his most important practical impact on the world has been through Marx and Engels, who were influenced by Hegel's thinking even as they largely recast it. On its own merits, Hegel's work richly repays the necessary effortful reading. The beginner might start with what has been translated as *Reason In History*. For the student of political and legal philosophy, his *Philosophy of Right* and *Phenomenology of Spirit* are of central importance. Among the major influences on Hegel were Kant and Schelling. On the latter influence, see Michael H. Hoffheimer, *Schelling's Philosophy of Natural Law*, 64 TEMPLE LAW REVIEW 1 (1991).

2. What we would ordinarily refer to as the state has distinctive moral value for Hegel just insofar as it contributes to a gradually unfolding historical process of realizing freedom in the world, understood not as the expression of arbitrary will, but as genuinely rational self-conscious self-determination. See CARL J. FRIEDRICH, THE PHILOSOPHY OF LAW IN HISTORICAL PERSPECTIVE 136-38 (rev. 2d ed. 1963); Richard L. Schacht, *Hegel On Freedom*, in HEGEL: A COLLECTION OF CRITICAL ESSAYS 289, 300 (Alasdair MacIntyre ed. 1972). For a discussion of Hegel's difficulties in accommodating women and the poor into this conception, see CAROLE PATEMAN, THE PROBLEM OF POLITICAL OBLIGATION 111-12 (1979) (1985).

3. As Patrick Riley observes, for Hegel, "some things are too important to be seen as contractual, and therefore merely legal—among them marriage and the state. . . . To conceive of the state as a bargain was as offensive to Hegel as it had been to Burke." PATRICK RILEY, WILL AND POLITICAL LEGITIMACY 194 (1982).

4. It has similarly been said that "Hegel's criticism of bourgeois society is directed against the liberal conception of the state as a mere means to an end." KARL LÖWITH, FROM HEGEL TO NIETZSCHE 239 (David E. Green trans. 1967).

5.  For Hegel, the nature of the state thus transcends, and cannot be explained on the basis of, any arbitrary giving of consent or denial of consent by individuals, or of the arbitrary willing of parties to a contract. See G.W.F. HEGEL, PHILOSOPHY OF RIGHT 59, 71, 157 (T.M. Knox trans. 1952).

6.  As to the pointed question of the precise circumstances in which citizens ought to obey the law, John Plamenatz finds Hegel's answer to be equivocal. On Plamenatz's reading, Hegel implies that "in the fully rational or fully developed State, the citizen really wills what the law requires of him and is therefore free when he obeys the law," but Hegel is "unclear what the citizen should do when the State is not fully rational." JOHN P. PLAMENATZ, CONSENT, FREEDOM AND POLITICAL OBLIGATION 165 (2d ed. 1968). Carole Pateman notes that while Hegel celebrated the French Revolution, it is far from clear that Hegel would have endorsed rebellion against any modern government. See CAROLE PATEMAN, THE PROBLEM OF POLITICAL OBLIGATION 112-13 (1979) (1985). To take it upon oneself to pronounce the modern state ethically inadequate may, for Hegel, be to fall into abstract individualism. See id.

7.  For other worthy contributions to the secondary literature on Hegel's extraordinarily valuable political thought, see SHLOMO AVINERI, HEGEL'S THEORY OF THE MODERN STATE (1972); J.N. FINDLAY, HEGEL: A RE-EXAMINATION (1958); JEAN HYPPOLITE, STUDIES ON MARX AND HEGEL (John O'Neill trans. 1969); WALTER KAUFMANN, HEGEL: A REINTERPRETATION (1965); HERBERT MARCUSE, REASON AND REVOLUTION: HEGEL AND THE RISE OF SOCIAL THEORY (1941); WERNER MARX, HEGEL'S PHENOMENOLOGY OF SPIRIT: A COMMENTARY ON THE PREFACE AND INTRODUCTION (Peter Heath trans. 1975); G.R.G. MURE, THE PHILOSOPHY OF HEGEL (1965); ROBERT C. SOLOMON, IN THE SPIRIT OF HEGEL (1983); W.T. STACE, THE PHILOSOPHY OF HEGEL (1924) (1955); CHARLES TAYLOR, HEGEL (1975); *Hegel and Legal Theory Symposium*, 10 CARDOZO LAW REVIEW 847 (1989).

# 22

# Notes on Some
# General Critiques and Defenses of
# Social Contract and Consent Theory

1. As a concise expression of consent theory in early American constitutional jurisprudence, consider the declaration by Justice Wilson of the Supreme Court that "[t]he only reason, I believe, why a free man is bound by human laws, is, that he binds himself." Chisholm v. Georgia, 2 U.S. (2 Dall.) 419, 455 (1793).

2. Don Herzog argues that "[a] world of masterless individuals, recognized by others as having the right to make their own decisions, is a world of dignified agents: that is the most profound justification of consent theory, the deepest vindication of modern society against its critics." DON HERZOG, HAPPY SLAVES: A CRITIQUE OF CONSENT THEORY 225 (1989).

3. For Sigmund Freud's version of social contract theory, in which a majority of persons somehow unite and politically proclaim what they take to be right, on the basis of a partial renunciation of their selfish instincts, see SIGMUND FREUD, CIVILIZATION AND ITS DISCONTENTS 41-42 (James Strachey trans. 1961).

4. Joseph Tussman reluctantly concludes that "[w]hen we reflect upon what we mean when we describe ourselves as members of a body politic I think we come to accept the fact that it means we have agreed to something, that we are parties to a social contract. But we must accept it as a plain fact that many native 'citizens' have in no meaningful sense agreed to anything. . . . Non-consenting adult citizens are, in effect, like minors who are governed without their own consent. The period of tutelage and dependence is unduly prolonged. And this . . . is a failure of political education." JOSEPH TUSSMAN, OBLIGATION AND THE BODY POLITIC 36-37 (1960). If we are sure that such non-consenting adults ought to consent, and of the reasons why they ought to

consent, why can't those reasons, rather than consent theory, explain why the state exercises legitimate authority?

5. For a discussion exploring possible approaches to why merely hypothetical consent, under specified conditions, to a particular government might be thought to create binding moral obligations, see David Zimmerman, *The Force of Hypothetical Consent*, 93 ETHICS 467 (1983).

6. Is it possible that while consent theory by itself may not be a satisfactory theory of political or legal obligation, consent theory might be a useful or even a necessary part of some broader, more satisfactory theory? See Jeffrey Paul, *Substantive Social Contracts and the Legitimate Basis of Political Authority*, 66 MONIST 517, 517 (1983).

7. Does a promise to obey a government create a morally binding obligation because the act of promising itself conveys an intention to undertake that obligation, or because such a promise may induce reliance by other persons on that promise, perhaps regardless of the promisor's intentions? For discussion, see Christopher McMahon, *Promising and Coordination*, 26 AMERICAN PHILOSOPHICAL QUARTERLY 239 (1989).

8. Suppose we found a case of either express or tacit, but vague, consent by a citizen. Would that simply raise the question of to what policies, rules, or laws the citizen has consented? Does a voluntary act of consent to a government necessarily involve consent to each of that government's present and future policies, at all levels of detail, whether the consenting party knows or approves of them or not? See DON HERZOG, HAPPY SLAVES: A CRITIQUE OF CONSENT THEORY 232 (1989).

9. Leslie Green assumes that in order for consent to be morally binding, it must be given freely and under conditions of full information. Leslie Green, *Consent and Community*, in ON POLITICAL OBLIGATION 89, 92 (Paul Harris ed. 1990). Does morally binding consent require full information, or perhaps only a reasonable amount of information, or even the mere reasonable availability of information, in the absence of fraud?

10. Are we under any sort of moral obligation if we have consented to perform an immoral act? Thomas McPherson has said: "It would be odd to say that I am *obliged* to carry out an immoral act, however strong my consent to it may have been." THOMAS MCPHERSON, POLITICAL OBLIGATION 24 (1967) (emphasis in the original). Similarly, Joseph Raz has argued that: "[t]hose who consent to perform atrocities are not bound by their consent." Joseph Raz, *Government by Consent*, in 29 NOMOS: AUTHORITY REVISITED 76, 85

(J. Roland Pennock & John W. Chapman eds. 1987). Finally, John Charvet argues that "the mere fact of expressly consenting to the absolute dictatorship of some ruler cannot create a political obligation, if, as seems reasonable to hold, absolute dictatorship is not a morally acceptable form of rule." John Charvet, *Political Obligation: Individualism and Communitarianism*, in ON POLITICAL OBLIGATION 65, 67 (Paul Harris ed. 1990). In contrast, though, note that Jeffrie Murphy argues that "[o]bligations quite clearly can bind us to the immoral or the moral." Jeffrie Murphy, *In Defense of Obligation*, in 12 NOMOS: POLITICAL AND LEGAL OBLIGATION 39 (J. Roland Pennock & John W. Chapman eds. 1970). George Klosko may be recognizing a middle ground on this issue in concluding that "the content of the obligation affects its force. If Jack promises to do something that is morally wrong, under many circumstances his promise should not be complied with." George Klosko, *The Moral Force of Political Obligations*, 84 AMERICAN POLITICAL SCIENCE REVIEW 1235, 1238 (1990).

11. Consider Jeremy Waldron's critique of social contract theory: "We all think promise-breaking is wrong, no doubt, but is it so conclusively and momentously wrong that people should be prepared to put up with hardship, oppression, mortal danger, and even death (in the story of Socrates) just because they promised to obey?" Jeremy Waldron, *Theoretical Foundations of Liberalism*, 37 PHILOSOPHICAL QUARTERLY 127, 136 (1987). No doubt people may rely on promises, but the weight of their reliance interests may depend on how much moral weight those interests, such as life, liberty, or property have in themselves.

12. Does social contract theory inevitably find itself caught between building controversial conclusions into its own basic assumptions, or else being unable to generate sufficiently clear and determinate conclusions to be useful? See ROBERTO M. UNGER, THE CRITICAL LEGAL STUDIES MOVEMENT 101 (1986).

13. Does consent theory go wrong in assuming that political obligations, unlike some obligations among members of a family, must be voluntarily undertaken? Could we think of legitimate governments as principled, egalitarian, fraternal communities transcending the relationships that might exist among mere strangers? See RONALD DWORKIN, LAW'S EMPIRE 106-16 (1986).

14. Nancy Hirschmann has described traditional consent theory as distinctively and unfortunately masculine in character, insofar as it assumes, contrary to women's experience, that all binding moral obligations must be taken on voluntarily, and that persons have no inherent social connectedness, but are best thought of for purposes of a theory of obligation as separate and isolated individuals who merely happen to choose to associate and thereby assume

responsibility. See Nancy J. Hirschmann, *Freedom, Recognition, and Obligation: A Feminist Approach to Political Theory*, 83 AMERICAN POLITICAL SCIENCE REVIEW 1227, 1229, 1231, 1238, 1241 (1989). Note that this critique implies that consent theory is not only biased against women in, for example, not taking seriously women's consent or failure to consent, but is fundamentally untrue to women's experience. See *id.* at 1229, 1231.

15. Can we say that the typical function of consent theory is to legitimize the established political authority? See CAROLE PATEMAN, THE PROBLEM OF POLITICAL OBLIGATION (1979) (1985). Does consent theory in practice serve also "to check and influence government authority?" Fred M. Frohock, *Liberal Maps of Consent*, 22 POLITY 231, 248 n.20 (1989).

16. Is the subordination of women merely a recurring element of traditional consent theories, or does such subordination point to an inherent problem within consent theory generally? See CAROLE PATEMAN, THE PROBLEM OF POLITICAL OBLIGATION 189-94 (1979) (1985). Carole Pateman has written that "[w]omen exemplify the individuals who consent theorists have declared are incapable of consenting. Yet, simultaneously, women have been presented as always consenting, and their explicit nonconsent has been treated as irrelevant or has been reinterpreted as 'consent.'" Carole Pateman, *Women and Consent*, 8 POLITICAL THEORY 149, 150 (1980). See also SUSAN MOLLER OKIN, WOMEN IN WESTERN POLITICAL THOUGHT 286 (1979) (concluding that "it is by no means a simple matter to integrate the female half of the human race into a tradition of political theory which has been based, almost without exception, upon the belief that women must be defined exclusively by their role within the family, and which has defined them, and intrafamilial relationships, as outside the scope of the political").

17. Consider the possible role of elections in consent theory. For a discussion of the role of elections in conferring legitimacy through popular consent, see James A. Gardner, *Consent, Legitimacy and Elections: Implementing Popular Sovereignty Under the Lockean Constitution*, 52 UNIVERSITY OF PITTSBURGH LAW REVIEW 189 (1990).

18. For criticism of the argument that the act of voting or other political participation ordinarily involves giving consent and assuming political obligation, see John Kilcullen, *Locke On Political Obligation*, 48 REVIEW OF POLITICS 323, 344 n.41 (1983). John Simmons contends, though, that "voting is often a way not of consenting to something, but merely of *expressing a preference*." A. John Simmons, *Consent, Free Choice, and Democratic Government*, 18 GEORGIA LAW REVIEW 791, 800 (1984) (emphasis in the original) (footnote deleted).

19. In response to John Simmons's broad rejection of consent theory, is has been argued that "for Simmons's objection to undermine consent theory, it has to be the case that the high cost of emigration invalidates the consent even of those who wish to consent to obey their government. This claim is neither stated nor argued for by Simmons." Harry Beran, *What Is the Basis of Political Authority?*, 66 MONIST 487, 495 (1983). Beran goes on to argue that even in the case of persons who do wish to emigrate, but who find the cost of doing so prohibitively high, it may be inappropriate to say that anyone, including the government, is coercing them to remain. See *id.* at 496. Could a person remain within a country without coercion, yet not give consent by remaining?

20. For a brief sketch of a model of political obligation building upon the idea of membership in the community and concern for the common good without adopting a voluntarist or consent-based theory, see Karen Johnson, *Political Obligation and the Voluntary Association Model of the State*, 86 ETHICS 17 (1975).

# 23

# Notes on Marx and Engels

1. Karl Marx (1818-1883) and Friedrich Engels (1820-1895), writing separately and in collaboration, produced a number of works in political economy, history, sociology, and philosophy. Their dramatic influence on twentieth century history is clear, though it is open to doubt how they would have reacted to many of those who have ruled in their name. While many of the economic and historical predictions of scientific inevitability made by Marx and Engels have fared poorly, their thinking will remain important as long as economic relations crucially affect culture and politics, as long as economic class remains an important category, and as long as alienation in work remains a theme of economic life.

2. Consider the character of law for Marx and Engels. Carl Friedrich writes that: "Law is seen by Marx and Engels . . . essentially as a part of the ideological superstructure which rises above the material reality of the control of the means of production. . . . Law is therefore not oriented to the idea of justice but is a means of dominance and a tool of the exploiters who use it in the interest of their class. It is the task of the critic of the existing legal system, as of the existing society, to unmask it as a facade and to recognize its role as part of the ideology of a class." CARL J. FRIEDRICH, THE PHILOSOPHY OF LAW IN HISTORICAL PERSPECTIVE 143-44 (rev. 2d ed. 1963).

3. For a characterization by Marx and Engels of the law as a reflection of the economic conditions and interests of the dominant bourgeoisie, see PAUL PHILLIPS, MARX AND ENGELS ON LAW AND LAWS 34 (1980).

4. Harold Laski writes that in the *Communist Manifesto*, Marx and Engels hold that the economic class legally owning the means of economic production uses the power of the state to establish and legitimize a distribution of that economic product in that class's interests. See Harold J. Laski, *The Communist Manifesto*, in ESSAYS IN THE HISTORY OF POLITICAL THOUGHT 323, 335 (Isaac Kramnick ed. 1969).

5. There is, of course, good evidence that Marx and Engels recognized some reciprocal influence between the law and economic production. Legal forms and rules may feed back to modify modes of production. See Mark Tushnet, *Is There a Marxist Theory of Law?*, in 26 NOMOS: MARXISM 171, 181 (J. Roland Pennock & John W. Chapman eds. 1983).

6. Hugh Collins argues that "[s]ince legal rules can inhibit the arbitrary exercise of power, even if their control is precarious, law can contribute an important dimension to political philosophies seeking to explain or justify the existing structures of domination on the ground that the powerful are constrained by the demands of due process of law." HUGH COLLINS, MARXISM AND LAW 13-14 (1982). Would all those faithful to Marx agree that the law, however that term is conceived, can in fact genuinely constrain the exercise of arbitrary power?

7. Note the possibility, on a Marxist analysis, of the law's serving to disguise, consolidate, and legitimize ruling class power by limiting ruling class options for suppression, and by allowing limited conflicts of class interests to be played out judicially with unpredictable results. See E.P. Thompson, *The Rule of Law*, in MARXISM AND LAW 130, 134-35 (Piers Beirne & Richard Quinney eds. 1982).

8. Nicos Poulantzas writes that "faced with working-class struggle on the political plane, law organizes the structure of the compromise political equilibrium" under which "the capitalist legal system . . . takes the dominated classes into account in regulating the exercise of power." Nicos Poulantzas, *Law*, in MARXISM AND LAW 185, 195 (Piers Beirne & Richard Quinney eds. 1982).

9. Poulantzas has argued that although "law plays an important (positive and negative) role in organizing repression, its efficacy is just as great in the devices of creating consent. . . . [L]aw is an important factor in organizing the consent of the dominated classes. . . ." Nicos Poulantzas, *Law*, in MARXISM AND LAW 185, 189-90 (Piers Beirne & Richard Quinney eds. 1982).

10. For an interpretation of Marx in which law, in the sense in which individuals are governed by general rules, will be unnecessary in the higher phase of communism, see STEVEN LUKES, MARXISM AND MORALITY 56-59 (1985).

11. For Hans Kelsen's discussion of conflicting approaches to the necessity or usefulness of law under a fully developed communist society, see HANS KELSEN, THE COMMUNIST THEORY OF LAW 34 (1955) (reprinted 1988).

12. Consider Marx and Engels on the concept of social justice. A.M. Shandro notes the elements in Marx and Engels suggesting that the idea of justice in

distribution may at some historical stage be transcended, but Shandro asks whether there may always be scarcity in the material instruments that are required for self-realization, and hence a continuing need for the idea of justice. See A.M. Shandro, *A Marxist Theory of Justice?*, 22 CANADIAN JOURNAL OF POLITICAL SCIENCE 27, 29 (1989). For a survey of the conflicting analyses by contemporary interpreters of Marx, see Kai Nielsen, *Arguing About Justice: Marxist Immoralism and Marxist Moralism*, 17 PHILOSOPHY AND PUBLIC AFFAIRS 212 (1988).

13. For a discussion of the tension in Marx and Engels's thought between empirical scientific and predictive analysis of historical stages, reductionism, and moral relativism on the one hand, and more straightforward moral realist condemnation of injustice on the other, see ALAN GILBERT, DEMOCRATIC INDIVIDUALITY 206-38 (1990). See also JON ELSTER, MAKING SENSE OF MARX 196-233 (1985).

14. For an attempt by Hans Kelsen to analogize Marx's doctrine of the state to traditional natural law theory, see HANS KELSEN, THE COMMUNIST THEORY OF LAW 20 (1955) (reprinted 1988).

# 24

# From Kai Nielsen,
# State Authority and Legitimation*

. . . I shall argue that, given the development of the productive forces, *de jure* legitimation of state authority cannot be attained in capitalist societies, even the most benign liberal welfare-state societies. I do not say this because like an anarchist I believe no state can have *de jure* legitimate authority. Whatever might be said about the withering away of the state in developed communism, the state, at least for the foreseeable future, is a necessity and some of these states can—or so at least I shall argue—have *de jure* legitimate authority. My argument is rather that capitalist states lack that legitimacy in our historical period in developed capitalist societies where there is a feasible alternative mode of production that would, if it were to come into existence, answer more adequately to the needs of people in those societies and make possible a more extensive respect for their rights. A socialist mode of production, I shall argue, is such an alternative mode of production, and a democratic socialism would be such a society. My thesis is the relatively strong one that not only does no capitalist state have that legitimacy, but that, given what a capitalist system is, no capitalist state in our period could have legitimacy. . . .

Where once people such as T. H. Green and L. T. Hobhouse talked of political obligation—namely, the question of the conditions under which we are obligated to obey the state and the limits of our obligation—contemporary thinkers tend to talk of a legitimation crisis. How (if at all) can the contemporary state or the contemporary social order establish its legitimacy? Whatever we might say of actually existing states, is it even possible that some empirically feasible future state or future society could have legitimacy?

Much of this new attitude, at least for many of those who extensively discuss it, is tied up with discussions of what they call 'modernity' and 'post-modernity'. These terms, as they occur in current discussion, are not clearly characterized, but I think that they mean something like this: modernity is the set of beliefs and characteristic attitudes to life that have grown up in reaction to traditionalism and with the rise of science as a more dominant factor in our lives. It is the set of attitudes and beliefs that go with the Enlightenment. It is a secular attitude, or at least an attitude tending towards secularism. (Hume was an atheist, Kant was not, but towards a good bit of the world, as Georg Hammann saw, Kant's attitudes were thoroughly secular. He is a very different person from Augustine.) Instead of taking God's providence as something given, and with it a set of divinely sanctioned hierarchies in both the social world and the natural world, God—even for the religious—retreats from the world. Kierkegaard's God, and indeed even Luther's God, is much more removed from the world than Augustine's or Aquinas's God. Science and everyday life get along in such a modern world-view, as do the practices that go with them, without God's help. There is an increasing secularization of our pictures of nature and of humankind, and as the effects of the Enlightenment deepen in the nineteenth and twentieth centuries, we get an increasingly more extensive demystification of the world. If we contrast Rousseau, writing in the mid eighteenth century, with a medieval writer like Aquinas, we find Rousseau seeing the established norms as customs or conventions in need of justification, whereas for Aquinas they were natural laws ordained by God. For Rousseau, by contrast, they are taken as the result, directly or indirectly, of human will rather than as divine ordinances for the good of humankind of which human beings, if they are not utterly corrupted by sin, are aware.

These characteristic attitudes and beliefs of modernity have become more and more pervasive and ever more thoroughly secularized in Western societies. A distinctively modern question, which has come to the forefront since Rousseau, Hobbes, Locke, and Hume, is how we can discern, or at least forge, a plausible set of conventions that will merit our reflective allegiance and will serve to govern our social lives together. This is a question—which has arisen since the emergence of Protestantism, the French Revolution, and the ascent of capitalism—to which modernists seek an answer, though by now often with a considerable lack of confidence over being able to give one that is objective. (If there is no objective answer, is it not plain that there is no answer at all? A 'subjective answer' is hardly an answer.)

If we say, in looking for an answer, that a social order is legitimate because it expresses the moral will or the moral will through the general will—a Rousseauian or Kantian answer—it becomes important to discover or forge that moral will. People committed to modernity can no longer simply take it as something given by God or something obvious to 'natural reason' as God's ordinances for human beings. There is an increasing awareness that in some way or other there are problems about the relativity of norms as the attitudes of modernity dig deeper into our cultural life. There is a sense that moral beliefs, or at least many of the beliefs that have been taken to be moral beliefs, may be little more than customs or conventions. However, if they really are customs or conventions, then they could be otherwise, and this means, plainly, that questions of their validation or legitimacy arise. We come to ask: do our existing customs or conventions deserve our allegiance, and if they do not what set of customs or conventions would? Can we get to any norms that deserve our allegiance that are not just customs or conventions, or where the customary or conventional element is not ineradicable?

Post-modernity and post-modernists look on the Enlightenment commitments of modernity with deep suspicion, often with thorough disbelief and, frequently, with irony. Yet Post-modernists are not, even in some indirect way, returning to traditionalism. Rather, they are out to debunk what they take to be the mystifications of the Enlightenment, in a way comparable with the Enlightenment's debunking of traditionalism. They are out to show that the whole Enlightenment project rests on a mistake.

Friedrich Nietzsche, writing in the late nineteenth century during a high tide of modernity, brought the spirit of post-modernity to life in a powerful and perceptive form. He argued—or at least he often was taken to have argued—that the secularizing world of the Enlightenment brought with it not emancipation but nihilism. In our time Michel Foucault takes a similar turn. Indeed, as Nietzsche is to Mill, so Foucault is to Habermas or Rawls, Mill and Rawls being paradigmatic representatives of modernity from the nineteenth century and twentieth century respectively. Earlier theorists of modernity (Rousseau, Holbach, Hobbes, Locke, and Hume) 'demolished old standards to establish new ones; but the nihilism Nietzsche discerns at the centre of modernity dissolves old standards without bringing new and convincing ones into being'. The Enlightenment, Nietzsche contends and Foucault reiterates, is really a destroyer rather than a creator of a new and more rational basis for social life. If we see what is involved in the Enlightenment through to the bitter end, we will come to see that modernity will reveal the arbitrary character of Enlightenment ideas about agency, truth, and legitimacy. Post-modernity—or so the standard post-modernist tale goes—takes us across the abyss that modernity deceives itself out of crossing. It faces without evasion the realization that even the best thought out fundamental standards cannot but be ungrounded and arbitrary. Unlike modernity, post-modernity sheds all belief in progress, social evolution, or emancipation, and recognizes, or at least thinks it recognizes, that there is and can be no ground beneath modernity's basic constructions. There is no way that we can attain any kind of legitimate centring of our lives. Modernity undermined traditionalism and its appeal to something like the natural moral law. Post-modernity, as post-modernists see it, undermines modernity with its secular replacements of traditional values. Post-modernists really do believe that if God is dead, then nothing matters. . . .

Let us now see, in the teeth of post-modernism, if we can plausibly articulate what *de jure* legitimate state authority would look like. What, given the large-scale, highly industrialized societies that are, for good or for ill, our lot, would our states have to be like to have such legitimacy, if they can have it at all? What conditions would have to be satisfied for a state in contemporary conditions to have such legitimacy? The post-modernists are right in recognizing that to see, if that is at all possible, what paradise regained would be like, we would need to have a good understanding of paradise lost. We must first see what is wrong with our societies; we must see the depth of the illness and the needless frustration of needs, human aspirations, and potentialities that seem to be endemic to our societies to see how far they are from being *de jure* legitimate societies and to be aware of the distance and direction they must travel to gain such legitimacy.

In trying to articulate what a legitimate social order with a legitimate state would look like, I want to rely rather heavily on some cues from Jürgen Habermas. His characterization of the difference between distorted discourse and the undistorted discourse of the ideal speech situation, excised of its needless pedantry and over-elaboration, provides us with the abstract characterization of the type of situation in which state power would be exercised legitimately if it were exercised under such conditions and restraints. . . .

Habermas observes that in important respects in modern industrial societies, both capitalist and state socialist, we are living an unfree, one-dimensional existence. There is in our societies an undermining of perfectly realizable human possibilities for emancipation. Important needs are unnecessarily going unmet, and there is a considerable amount of unnecessary, identifiable suffering. Here, with that stress, Habermas is a loyal follower of the Frankfurt School.

Moving away from a stress more typical of Marxism, Habermas contends that the restrictions we suffer are not primarily imposed on us by external forces. Rather, they are restrictions we, as a people, under conditions of an extensive imposed consciousness, impose on ourselves. Our ideological bafflement is such, Habermas claims, that we do not understand the prevailing mechanisms and relationships of power and control in our society and how they manage to retain an ascendancy over us, often in rather subtle ways. He thinks this malaise has cut so deeply in advanced capitalist societies, and is causing such alienation, that we have, in diverse ways, problems of what he calls 'a legitimation crisis'.

We have in the fabric of our social life and embedded in our life-world, a cluster of distorted legitimating beliefs which, taken in clusters, provide us with legitimating myths. These false beliefs and their associated mistaken attitudes are the norms and attitudes that go to make up our world-picture and our social consciousness, and they prompt us to commend as legitimate, or at least to accept as necessary, a network of institutions and practices of a highly repressive character, including political attitudes and the acceptance of an authoritarian work discipline. These very central ideologically distorted beliefs underwrite our repressive and coercive social system.

It is because of the pervasiveness and subterranean power of these legitimating beliefs—in a normative sense, these *ersatz* legitimating beliefs—that a critique of ideology is so important. In doing this, it is incumbent upon us (so that the unmaskers can be seen not to be donning a few masks themselves) to be able to understand and to state with reasonable clarity what it would be like to have a set of non-ideological legitimating beliefs. We need to know what really would make for our well-being, what our distinctive human needs are, the scheduling of their importance (what comparative weight we would give to them), and what stable social conditions there would have to be to sustain and to increase that need satisfaction. Seeing the world correctly is something that is vital to us here. We need, that is, to understand the nature and conditions of human flourishing and what would make for an equitable achievement of that flourishing in—if these conditions are obtained—a world of just institutions. People who had a good grasp of these things would be people who had escaped the beguilements of ideology. They would not be people who are led to uphold and to participate in a gratuitously restrictive set of social arrangements, mistakenly believing they were indispensable to human well-being. They would not be imprisoned by a false consciousness that would help stabilize them into leading frustrated lives where they are deprived—indeed, in a way, self-deprived—of many important human potentialities. . . .

What are these circumstances—the counterfactual states of affairs—of the ideal speech situation which would give us a correct picture of undistorted discourse? Like a good liberal in the Millian tradition, but also in a way that a Marxist should not disavow, Habermas argues that an ideal speech situation requires that our legitimating beliefs (including, of course, our central normative beliefs) must be formed in conditions of absolutely free and unlimited debate in which all parties to the institutions and practices being set up must be capable of recognizing that they are freely consenting to their establishment under conditions in which the only constraints on their acceptance derive from the force of the better argument. In communication, simply in virtue of what communication is, we seek to reach *understanding*, indeed a mutual understanding. In an ideal speech situation, the speaker and hearer aim not only at consensus but at a *rational* consensus in which the only accepted motive for discoursing is that of a co-operative search for truth. What will be taken as a rational consensus is the consensus that is rooted in whatever has the force of the better argument. . . .

A number of objections can and have been made to such an ideal speech conception of undistorted discourse. Firstly, it has been thought to be far too utopian and unrealistic. People will never get within a country mile of achieving a consensus rooted in the force of the better argument or the better deliberation. Particularly where what is to be done is at stake, it will seldom, if ever, be the case that the sole or even the decisive motive for discoursing will be the co-operative search for truth. Our *consensus* will be rooted in many other things than the force of the better argument or deliberation. We will not be equal partners in an absolutely free and unlimited debate. The institutions we create in the future, like the institutions created in the past, will not be created under conditions of freedom and equality. We are not and never will be such autonomous and ideally rational characters; we are just not wired that way.

Secondly, it has been thought that such a conception suffers from defects analogous to Kantian formalism. In speaking of the beliefs that would be the outcome of absolutely free and unlimited debate, and in taking those beliefs, whatever they are, to be genuinely legitimating beliefs, we have beliefs with too little content to give us anything with much substance. What is legitimate is what comes from following certain procedures no matter what their content. However, we need something more robust which would tell us what beliefs are ideological and what beliefs are not. The Habermasian conception is just liberal formalism all over again in a Teutonic guise.

Thirdly, and even more fundamentally, it could be maintained, such a conception—when carefully inspected—turns out to be incoherent, or at least so problematic as to be without determinable sense.

Fourthly, and finally, even assuming that people could so consent, or come to approximate such consent, why should people—particularly members of the dominant class in a securely situated class society—so consent or accept that conception of rationality rather than accept a purely instrumental rationality where they reason as utility maximizers, or perhaps as what David Gauthier calls 'constrained utility maximizers'?

The first criticism, that ideal speech theory is too utopian, does not have much force. Habermas repeatedly talks about counterfactuals here: it is not that people act that way, or even that they will be expected to act that way, but that we have a model for how people are to act such that if they did act that way we would have undistorted discourse. Even if the construction turns out to be a mere heuristic device, it would still be of considerable value in showing what we would have to approximate to have the kind of societal understanding required to free us from ideological fetters. Moreover, there is no good reason to think that human nature is so firmly fixed that we cannot move in the direction of this heuristic ideal, and that the closer we come to it the closer we come to a morally attractive social order with a state to which we clear-headedly can give allegiance. Of course, if we could not move anywhere at all in that direction—if we were incapable of becoming more enlightened, more autonomous, if we were utterly unable to create greater equality and a further understanding of our situation, and if a concern for a co-operative and impartial search for truth would have no weight with us at all—we could hardly treat the model of undistorted discourse as even a heuristic device. Indeed, we would be in something that was even worse than the post-modernist swamp. However, that is not something that a hard, non-evasive look at the situation justifies; it may in reality be a convenient and helpful ideological myth in the struggle to secure late capitalism. A deep scepticism making Hamlets of us all has its power in quieting down intellectuals so that they will willingly accept the *status quo*.

The second criticism has more force. As Rawls realized at the outset, if we just rely on procedures without appealing to any antecedent substantive moral beliefs at all, then we will never, with a *purely* communicative ethic, be able to make any choices at all, even under conditions of freedom and equality. We will indeed ask ourselves what we would choose if we were free agents reasoning together co-operatively with full knowledge of our situation. However, if there were nothing at all antecedent to that deliberation that we wanted, that we thought answered to our interests, that we thought we needed, or that we believed to be good, we would not know what to choose when we deliberated together in those ideal situations. Indeed, we would not even be able to choose. We would not have even a tentative basis for plumping one way or the other. Hence the need for Rawls's primary social and natural goods, or (to take a somewhat different conception) what I have elsewhere called 'our moral truisms'—for example, the belief that health is good, that autonomy is good, that the institution of promise-keeping is vital to our lives, that human consideration and concern for each other are good, that suffering is bad, that isolation and alienation are bad, that domination and torturing of others are evil, or (to take another somewhat different conception) that we have some tolerably objective conception of human needs, and that our firm and reasonable belief in the desirability of the satisfaction of these needs is warranted. We need some such conception, or perhaps a combination of such conceptions, to give some content to what otherwise would be too formalistic and too procedural an approach. However, there is no good reason to believe that this could not be added to a basically Habermasian conception without undermining its basic structure.

However, we also need the Habermasian procedure to winnow out in a critical way what would otherwise be a motley of goods. (Something like wide reflective equilibrium could be put to work here.) We need an index of the primary social and natural goods; we also need a much more nuanced statement of moral truisms, nuanced in such ways that they will cease to be mere truisms and become critical moral beliefs, and we need some way of weighing them when they conflict. The procedures mandated by the ways we should reason in ideal speech situations are indispensable to gaining these.

The third criticism, that the conception of undistorted discourse as specified by the ideal speech situation is itself incoherent, or at least utterly problematic, seems to me to be itself problematic. Just why—if indeed at all—is it incoherent or thoroughly problematic to speak of beliefs, even of legitimating beliefs, formed in conditions of absolutely free and unlimited debate? It is not at all evident to me that it is. Perhaps it will be said that when we try to imagine or conceive in concrete detail a consensus being forged under freedom and equality, we will come to see that that very idea is incoherent. As we have already seen, it is unrealistic, but it does not follow that it is incoherent or even conceptually problematic. It is unrealistic for you, at our present time, to believe that you will live to be 150 years old, but it is not at all incoherent or problematic. We know perfectly well what it would be like for it to be true, and in future years, for good or for ill, it may well come to pass that people will routinely, or at least not infrequently, live to that age. Conceptually speaking, beliefs being forged under conditions of freedom and equality are roughly parallel. There is no more reason to conclude that they are incoherent or problematic than to conclude that about a belief in doubled life expectancy.

The fourth objection seems to me the most powerful. Consider those people who are members of the *haute bourgeoisie* or their well-paid facilitators. Why should they (at least where the 'should' is prudential) seek a consensus rooted in undistorted discourse? It is not in the interests of the *haute bourgeoisie*, and probably of many of their highly-placed facilitators, to have a working class that is not manipulated by ruling-class ideology. They are hardly being irrational in the straightforward sense in which instrumental rationality is its opposite if they do not seek such a consensus based on undistorted discourse. They might also say, as Bertrand Russell did, that an instrumental conception of rationality is the only coherent sense of rationality. But even if in good Habermasian fashion they claimed there to be a richer sense of 'rationality' linked with an interest in achieving truth, and that an optimal search for truth requires the commitment to co-operative communication that goes with seeking to achieve and sustain undistorted discourse so that it is after all evident enough that there is an interest in truth, that interest is still only one strategic and central interest among others. Given the associated power and domination with its manifest advantages, a member of the *haute bourgeoisie* might very well find that such a passionate concern to make an optimal achievement of truth is not, everything considered, in that person's best interests and in the best interests of the person's class, and that he or she and his or her class as a whole could clear-headedly not have any commitment to the reign of an order of undistorted discourse, though for moral reasons it is not something either the person or they could publicly oppose. In addition, this would even more evidently be so when the person and his or her class peers stick together. They need moral *ideology* but not morality.

However, this indicates what on other grounds is manifestly true—namely, that the *haute bourgeoisie* could not but, *morally speaking*, accept the reign of an order of undistorted discourse. Impartiality and fairness require it, where it is attainable; and morality, just in virtue of what a morality is, requires a commitment to impartiality and fairness. To this it could be replied that the ways of ideology are protean. If the *haute bourgeoisie* reason strictly in accordance with their own enlightened interests, when they are firmly in control, they should become (though not as matters of public pronouncement) classist amoralists—people of good morals but not morally good people—using ideology, as I hinted above, to make it appear that they are committed to an impartial concern for the interests of everyone alike, and that they are in favour of conditions of clarity in social relations, while in reality, though necessarily in a surreptitious way, supporting their class position with the obfuscations that support requires. There is nothing irrational about the *haute bourgeoisie* and its well-placed and well-rewarded facilitators supporting classist amoralism when the modes of production are such that capitalist domination is secure. For it to be secure requires, among other things, that the consciousness industry be firmly in their hands. In such a situation there appears at least to be nothing irrational about the *haute bourgeoisie* and its well-placed facilitators being classist amoralists—a position that is immoral, but not, for all of that, irrational.

The beginning of a response should start like this: with the rise of bourgeois democracies, democratic ideas get firmly entrenched (as they are by now in industrial capitalist societies). This will inescapably and persistently give rise to Habermasian and Rawlsian claims about autonomy for all, equality, conditions of undistorted discourse, and the like. The very general thrust of these ideas, as distinct from the details of particular conceptions of them (as in some philosopher or other), cannot be morally, and thus publicly resisted. This being so, they will in a democratic ethos become ever more firmly the accepted norms. There is a certain sociological irreversibility here, such that it will become increasingly difficult for a class committed to preserving its privileges to do so. More and more complicated obfuscation will have to be used—the tides of ideology will run even higher—but in the long run it will fail.

We have seen that the *haute bourgeoisie* cannot publicly avow classist amoralism. They will have to commit themselves, as even writers like Hayek and Nozick do, to what Thomas Nagel calls 'moral equality', the belief that the life of everyone matters and matters equally. In anything even remotely like normal circumstances, one cannot *publicly* reject morality and get away with it. In present conditions, however, a clear-headed commitment to morality leads to something that bears some reasonable similarity to this Habermasian commitment to undistorted discourse as well as to moral equality. Moreover, given the way the productive forces will predictably develop, it is not unreasonable to hope that conditions of life cannot in the long run undermine this increasingly clear-headed grasp of the situation. Obfuscation for privilege is, sociologically and historically speaking, on the losing side.

Even if matters do not take this happy turn, and the continued development of the productive forces do not require such a democratic ethos, it is still the case that one is at odds with a modern understanding of morality by not being committed to what people reasoning from positions of equality and equal autonomy, and motivated to acceptance only by the force of the better argument, would accept. However, a social order at odds with morality could not have *de jure* legitimacy, and a state monopolizing force for that social order could only have *de facto* authority, that is, effective power. It could not also have *de jure* legitimate authority. A social order in which undistorted discourse obtains is not a conceptually incoherent possibility, and where it comes into being (if indeed it ever comes into being) with a matching state, that state will have *de jure* legitimate authority as well as *de facto* authority. To the extent that societies approximate those conditions, their states will approach being states with *de jure* legitimate authority. . . .

I turn now to an examination and defence of . . . the thesis that no state in a capitalist society under modern conditions can have such authority. One short general way to argue for that contention is to point out that a capitalist society is inescapably a class-divided society, with extensive domination of one class over another, where a capitalist class owns and controls the means of production, and where a working class must sell its labour power as a commodity. It is, moreover, a society in which the working class owns and controls no significant means of production, if indeed it owns or controls any means of production at all. (In some of the old sweat shops in the clothing industry, a worker had to own his or her own sewing machine to get a job, and thus had to own some means of production. That did not, of course, make that person a capitalist or any the less a wage slave. It shows, if anything, that the worker's domination by the capitalist class was even more complete.) Such a society cannot, while remaining capitalist, avoid relations of domination and control by one class over another, and this state of affairs is plainly incompatible with the conditions of freedom and equality necessary for legitimacy. . . .

Our societies are hardly societies where there is anything like popular sovereignty, or the rule of the people, or even much in the way of respect for persons. (Forty thousand homeless people in New York City provide good evidence for the latter.) Indeed, not a few theorists in modern democracies would sneer at the very idea of the rule of the people, though usually not very loudly, for they do not take it as a matter for wide public consumption. However, a *de jure* legitimate state authority must also be the protector of a society committed to equality of condition, autonomy for everyone alike, and to a world in which the interests and rights of everyone alike are equally the object of societal concern. In a capitalist society, however, even in a welfare state capitalist society, such equality, autonomy and justice do not and cannot obtain. . . .

Where some own and control the means of production and others must sell their labour power as a commodity, power differentials and influence differentials will remain sufficient such that representative members of each class cannot compete fairly. There must be a greater equality of condition than capitalism, even welfare-state capitalism, could possibly accommodate for there to be fair equality of opportunity.

Defenders of capitalism will reply that even rough equality of condition will undermine an even more fundamental value in our societies than equality—namely, autonomy. Letting that comparative ranking stand for the sake of this discussion, it needs to be asked whether equality of condition does undermine autonomy, and why? The standard answer is that, given normal interactions, such as people trading things, making gifts, or bestowing things, there would have to be a constant interference—presumably state interference—with people's lives to keep anything like even a rough equality of condition in existence. However, such repeated interference would undermine autonomy—namely, people's being able to control their own lives, being able to be self-directed.

However, the kind of interference in the lives of people that the prohibition of capitalist acts licenses has to do with freedoms to buy and sell, to invest, to bestow *productive* property, and the like. Prohibiting such acts cannot realistically be thought to keep people's lives from being self-directed or from their having control over their own lives. A world in which people are so interfered with can still be a world in which people are self-directed. . . .

Even if I am mistaken in the above argument and such interference does limit people's autonomy somewhat, it can and should be pointed out that any society whatsoever, in virtue of having norms, will in some way interfere with some things that people do or want to do; this may or may not affect their autonomy, but it certainly does affect their negative liberty. However, there being some interference of some kind is simply the price of having a society, any society at all: the real question is whether the interference is justified and whether it affects their autonomy. Granting for the sake of discussion what I have not granted in fact—namely, that there is some limitation on people's autonomy by a prohibition of capitalist acts—it should be said in reply that, if it is an interfering in such a way that affects the autonomy of some, it is a justified interference, for by that limitation of autonomy a more extensive autonomy, more widely distributed, is protected or made possible. By prohibiting capitalism we prohibit wage labour, and with the adoption of democratic socialism we bring in industrial democracy. . . .

In capitalism there cannot be an industrial democracy: social ownership and control of the means of production would violate the very prerogatives of capitalism. Thus, the workers under capitalism do not, and indeed cannot, no matter how benign the capitalism, co-operatively own the means of life. They do not, except perhaps for little bits, own or control the means of life. Rather they must sell their labour power if they can. Whether they work, on what they work, in what ways they work, and what is done with what they produce, is not determined by them. Under such conditions, work cannot but be alienating; it is not an autonomous life activity. Under a democratic socialism, by contrast, there must be public ownership and control of the workplace, and that means just what it says; ownership and control of the workplace by the public. Where we have that in any genuine form, we have industrial democracy, and this would take the form of the workers in their different workplaces having a very considerable control over their particular workplaces. (They would not have complete control for the public at large is also involved.)

In a world in which every able-bodied person is, was, or will be (in a broad sense) a worker, people would decide democratically what work would be done, what would be produced, how it would be produced, what would be done with what was produced, the conditions under which it would be produced, the working hours, and the like. This would give workers a far greater control over the conditions of their lives, a far greater self-direction in their work, than is possible under capitalism. They would also in a socialist society have a *right* to the means of life in the way they could not have under capitalism, for in a socialist society there is public ownership of the means of production and this, of course, would mean that they have a right to work and would also, collectively, have a control over their work in the way they do not have and cannot have under capitalism. In this very vital way, their lives would have more autonomy than they could have in a capitalist society.

In addition to being an industrial democracy, a democratic socialism would also be a political democracy. It would keep in place, and in all likelihood enhance, the autonomy that goes with political democracy: majority vote, protection of individual rights, civil liberties, and the like. All the basic liberties—those that Rawls speaks of, for example—possible under capitalism would also be available under democratic socialism. And, as Rosa Luxemburg argued, these rights would no longer be merely formal rights, as they so often are under capitalism: democratic socialism would provide the conditions for their being a concrete reality. Furthermore, its commitment to equality, including a rough equality of condition, would make not only for autonomy but for social *conditions* conducive to making equal autonomy a genuine possibility. (That people would actually be equally autonomous is another issue again. That, while remaining a heuristic ideal, is not to be expected. There is too much complicated and differentiated wiring for that.) A society that was *both* more autonomous and more egalitarian could not fail to be a better society and, indeed, more just than a society that was not as autonomous and as egalitarian. However, democratic socialism comes out better than capitalism (any capitalism you like) in exactly this way. Given this, to stand in the way of the move to democratic socialism from capitalism is neither morally justifiable nor morally acceptable where we can do something about it. Thus, where socialism is a feasible possibility, as it now is, a capitalist state and a capitalist society (any capitalist society) standing in such a relation to socialism, could not have *de jure* legitimate authority.

## NOTE ON FROM KAI NIELSEN, STATE AUTHORITY AND LEGITIMATION

* For further discussion by Nielsen of some basic problems of authority, legitimacy, and political obligation, see Kai Nielsen, *Why Is There a Problem About Political Obligation?*, 24 JOURNAL OF VALUE INQUIRY 235 (1990).

# Notes on Fair Play or Reciprocity Theories

1. The initial development of a fairness-based or reciprocity-based theory of obligation is sometimes traced to H.L.A. Hart, *Are There Any Natural Rights*, 64 PHILOSOPHICAL REVIEW 175, 185 (1955) (reprinted in POLITICAL PHILOSOPHY 53-63 (Anthony Quinton ed. 1967)).

2. John Rawls contends that there is a "natural duty . . . to support and further just institutions" including a duty "to comply with and do our share in just institutions when they exist and apply to us . . . ." JOHN RAWLS, A THEORY OF JUSTICE 334 (1971). Does such a view build too much into its assumptions? We will of course need to know what it is for an institution to "apply" to us more than other institutions. But on a natural understanding, if an institution applies to us and is indeed conceded to be just, it seems difficult to object to it on moral grounds, or to see our participation in or acceptance of it as morally optional. Rawls's view in this respect seems to push the issue back, crucially, to how we know that an institution is just. Much of the *Theory of Justice* can be taken as an answer to this question, or at least as an answer that simply presumes the truth of a broad sort of liberal individualism. But Rawls's conclusions have, it is fair to say, not been universally concurred in. See, as representative of the massive literature, READING RAWLS (Norman Daniels ed. n.d.).

3. For a brief discussion of the ambiguities associated with whether, as in Rawls's fair play-based theory, a just institution can be said to "apply" to us, see LESLIE GREEN, THE AUTHORITY OF THE STATE 227-28 (1988).

4. Rawls elaborates his "principle of fairness" as holding that "a person is under an obligation to do his part as specified by the rules of an institution whenever he has voluntarily accepted the benefits of the scheme or has taken advantage of the opportunities it offers to advance his interests, provided the

institution is just or fair, that is, satisfies the two principles of justice. . . . [T]he intuitive idea here is that when a number of persons engage in a mutually advantageous cooperative venture according to certain rules and thus voluntarily restrict their liberty, those who have submitted to these restrictions have a right to a similar acquiescence on the part of those who have benefitted from their submission. We are not to gain from the cooperative efforts of others without doing our fair share." JOHN RAWLS, A THEORY OF JUSTICE 342-43 (1971) (footnote omitted). Rawls specifies that "[a]cquiescence in, or even consent to, clearly unjust institutions does not give rise to obligations." *Id.* at 343. Again, the problem of political obligation becomes largely a broad problem of political justice. One wonders as well whether Rawls means to deny that we have any obligations to clearly unjust institutions in general, or only in the respects in which they are unjust. Under a fascist regime, should we feel free to ignore neutral traffic laws?

5.   Is it possible, apparently contrary to Rawls, that "we may sometimes have obligations of fair play to cooperate within unjust schemes?" A. John Simmons, *The Principle of Fair Play*, 8 PHILOSOPHY & PUBLIC AFFAIRS 307, 317 (1979).

6.   Anthony D'Amato has raised several intriguing objections to Rawls's fair play or reciprocity theory. He asks first whether there is "such a thing as an objective benefit, or is one man's benefit another man's burden?" Anthony D'Amato, *Obligation to Obey the Law: A Study of the Death of Socrates*, 49 SOUTHERN CALIFORNIA LAW REVIEW 1079, 1104 (1976). As well, could society ask too much of anyone in exchange for its benefits? Could a general obligation to obey the law be "too much" to ask? For a variant of this question, see *id.* at 1104-05. Finally, is it legitimate to offer to repay the benefits conferred on one not through one's obedience to a law, but through some other means? See *id.* at 1105.

7.   For Robert Nozick's entertaining and thought-provoking, if not independently decisive, objection to Rawls's argument from fair play and reciprocity, see his discussion of the hypothetical neighborhood public address system in ROBERT NOZICK, ANARCHY, STATE AND UTOPIA 93-95 (1974).

8.   Do "fair share" or "reciprocity" theories of political or legal obligation really depend upon the voluntariness of the receipt of benefits? Kent Greenawalt has argued that "[i]f someone is delighted to receive a benefit, understands the cooperative scheme by which it is supplied, and believes that his required contribution is a fair share, then he may be in the same position as someone who has genuinely chosen to receive a benefit he could freely refuse." Kent Greenawalt, *Promise, Benefit, and Need: Ties That Bind Us to the Law*, 18 GEORGIA LAW REVIEW 727, 757 (1984). See also George Klosko,

*Presumptive Benefit, Fairness, and Political Obligation,* 16 PHILOSOPHY AND PUBLIC AFFAIRS 241, 249 (1987). Could a beneficiary be bound by such a scheme even if the beneficiary does not consider the scheme just, if it really is just?

9. George Klosko has endorsed a principle of obligation based on fair play where the goods provided are worth the average recipient's effort in providing them, if not every recipient's such effort, and are also what Klosko refers to as "presumptively beneficial" goods from which it is impossible or unduly costly to exclude some potential recipients while including others. See George Klosko, *The Principle of Fairness and Political Obligation,* 97 ETHICS 353, 354-55 (1987). Public goods such as societal defense or environmental protection will typically count as nonexcludable goods. Klosko then explains what he means by "presumptively beneficial" goods as follows: "Basically, such goods must be necessary for a minimally acceptable life. In other words, they must be desired by rational individuals regardless of whatever else they desire, though even this account presupposes a background of generally accepted values and beliefs." *Id.* at 355. Klosko denies that his fairness theory amounts to a form of express or tacit consent theory, despite his reliance on desire for the goods by the actors in question. *See id.* at 356.

Even if we set aside people who, for example, care only about their eternal salvation, and not about environmental protection, does Klosko face a problem of "level of generality?" National defense in the abstract may qualify as a nonexcludable presumptive good. But citizens are not called upon to decide whether the general minimal idea of defense is sound. The question citizens face is whether they have an obligation to support an army of a certain size, to help fight a particular war, to pay taxes sufficient to support a certain level of defense expenditure, or to cooperate with a compulsory military draft. What does fairness require of us in such cases? Note that Klosko seeks to place the burden of proof on those who deny that the presumed goods are worth the costs. *Id.* at 355 n.9. If the state proposes to coerce cooperation, is this placement of the burden of proof morally sound?

10. For a brief discussion of the logic of a hypothetical person who may accept the legitimacy of some level of national defense, but who objects on principle to the purported "benefits" of particular military operations, see A. John Simmons, *The Principle of Fair Play,* 8 PHILOSOPHY & PUBLIC AFFAIRS 307, 335 (1979).

11. For further development of Klosko's overall theory of political obligation, see George Klosko, *Parfit's Moral Arithmetic and the Obligation to Obey the Law,* 20 CANADIAN JOURNAL OF PHILOSOPHY 191 (1990).

12. John Simmons has criticized Klosko's argument for a fairness or reciprocity-

based theory of obligation on the grounds that whatever moral obligation we have to, say, not injure peoples' health by selfishly refusing to curtail our pollution, can be accounted for simply in terms of basic moral duties to avoid injuring others, with no need for any theory involving cooperation in a collective scheme of sacrifice for a public good. See A. John Simmons, *The Anarchist Position: A Reply to Klosko and Senor*, 16 PHILOSOPHY AND PUBLIC AFFAIRS 269, 272-73 (1987). Does Simmons's proposed simplification work as well in the case of national defense, where a person's refusal to fight may not seem to unjustly injure or violate the moral rights of others in the way that intentionally putting dangerous chemicals in the air might?

13. For a further critique of the fairness or reciprocity-based theory of obligation generally along the lines sketched by John Simmons, see DEREK L. PHILLIPS, TOWARD A JUST SOCIAL ORDER 308-11 (1986).

14. For a formulation of a fairness-based approach to legal obligation emphasizing the variety of benefits flowing from the law as a seamless web, see John Finnis, *The Authority of Law In the Predicament of Contemporary Social Theory*, 1 NOTRE DAME JOURNAL OF LAW, ETHICS AND PUBLIC POLICY 115, 119-20 (1984).

15. M.B.E. Smith adopts the view that "[c]onsiderations of fairness apparently do show that, when cooperation is perfect and when each member has benefitted from the submission of every other, each member of an enterprise has a prima facie obligation to obey its rules when obedience benefits some other member or when disobedience harms the enterprise." M.B.E. Smith, *Is There a Prima Facie Obligation to Obey the Law?*, 82 YALE LAW JOURNAL 950, 956 (1973). How easily resolved are typical questions of whether a particular instance of law violating genuinely harms the overall ongoing enterprise?

16. With regard to fairness-based theories of political obligation, Gregory Kavka asks: "What is the *baseline of comparison* against which the citizen's position is to be judged in determining whether he really benefits from a system of mutual constraint and obedience to civil law? To generate obligations under the principle of fair play, must the political system in question be a *just* one that distributes benefits and burdens fairly?" GREGORY S. KAVKA, HOBBESIAN MORAL AND POLITICAL THEORY 410 (1986) (emphasis in the original). Do fairness-based theories of obligation simply postpone the tough issues until it is asked what fairness or justice requires? Can the unwilling receipt of unwanted or lightly valued benefits morally obligate those who receive them? *See id.* at 410-12.

# 26

# Notes on "Necessity" Arguments

1. Philip Soper has argued for a prima facie obligation to obey based on the view that governments are necessary as a practical matter and that we have such an obligation in recognition of such good faith effort to promote justice and the common good as is undertaken by the government. See Philip Soper, *The Moral Value of Law*, 84 MICHIGAN LAW REVIEW 63, 64 (1985). What percentage of governmental acts are directly related to goals or activities that can be described as "necessary?" Does "necessity" merely mean "necessary *if* we are to maximize some value or achieve some goal we have chosen?"

2. For discussion of the recurring idea that the basis of legitimate authority may be the necessity, in some sense, of completing a task for which general obedience may be required, see G.E.M. Anscombe, *On the Source of the Authority of the State*, in 3 THE COLLECTED PHILOSOPHICAL PAPERS OF G.E.M. ANSCOMBE: ETHICS, RELIGION, AND POLITICS 130, 134-35 (1981). Does this approach simply push back the question of obligation to one of the practical or moral inescapability of those of our goals for which government may be required? Are we obligated to obey any government that minimally pursues those goals, or must the government achieve some moderate level of success in order to be worthy of obedience?

3. Is there really any distinctive "necessity" theory of political obligation? Can Hobbes, for example, be described as a necessity theorist, in that he argues that without general obedience, life is solitary, poor, nasty, brutish and short? Can Locke be read, similarly, as arguing that general obedience is necessary if there is to be effective respect for life, liberty, and property? Who, among the classical writers, is not a necessity theorist?

4. Tony Honore argues that "man never is and never can be free of the claims of his fellows. He is bound to them not by chance but by necessity." Tony Honore, *Must We Obey? Necessity As a Ground of Obligation*, 67 VIRGINIA LAW REVIEW 39, 61 (1981). Why does this kind of necessity create a binding

moral obligation to obey, rather than simply removing the question from the realm of morality entirely? Is it that we can choose to pretend that we are not inescapably bound to our fellows? How do we know that other people have moral claims on us?

5.  For a critique of Joseph Raz's denial of the moral authority of the law, based on the idea that the law, insofar as it is necessary or uniquely suited to attain morally binding aims, must itself be morally binding, see John Finnis, *The Authority of Law In the Predicament of Contemporary Social Theory*, 1 NOTRE DAME JOURNAL OF LAW, ETHICS AND PUBLIC POLICY 115, 117 (1984).

6.  To what extent can or do we have moral obligations to the broader community that are best understood not as genuinely voluntary undertakings, but as loyalties or allegiances that significantly help to establish one's very identity as a person? See MICHAEL J. SANDEL, LIBERALISM AND THE LIMITS OF JUSTICE 179 (1982). Could this approach be developed into a "necessity" theory of legal or political obligation?

7.  William Galston argues that "the net social value of a law is equal to the social benefits it engenders minus the social costs of enforcing it. As the individual propensity to obey the law diminishes, so does a society's ability to pursue collective goals through the law. Law-abidingness is therefore a core social virtue, in liberal communities and elsewhere." William A. Galston, *Liberal Virtues*, 82 AMERICAN POLITICAL SCIENCE REVIEW 1278, 1281 (1988). Can we infer from this the beginnings of a theory that unless we at least act as if the law were generally morally binding, we impair the society's ability to effectively promote whatever widely shared goals it may have?

8.  Rolf Sartorius raises the interesting idea that there may be a mismatch between the grounds of governmental authority and of political obligation, such that the former might exist without the latter. This could be so, Sartorius argues, if governmental authority is based on the practical necessity of relying on broadly coercive means to promote the benefits of social cooperation, while obligation is based on voluntary acceptance of benefits from or consent to government. Thus governmental authority might be based on necessity, but in the absence of any sort of consent, political obligation might not exist. See Rolf Sartorius, *Political Authority and Political Obligation*, 67 VIRGINIA LAW REVIEW 3, 4 (1981). Note that on Sartorius's theory, we must still explain why the government is morally entitled to coerce those who dissent on the benefits of social cooperation, generally or in particular cases.

# 27

# Notes on the Contemporary Denial of a General Prima Facie Moral Obligation to Obey

1. Many contemporary writers deny that there is a general prima facie moral obligation to obey the law. The term "prima facie" moral obligation usually refers to the idea that a moral obligation may be overcome, trumped, or outweighed in particular cases by other moral considerations. For example, the moral obligation to return what we have borrowed, on demand, is only a prima facie moral obligation, as it might be morally permissible or right not to immediately return a sword to a person who is in a drunken rage. The idea of a "general" obligation to obey usually refers to a duty with regard to all relevant laws, whatever their character, and not just some laws of the government in question.

2. Philip Soper has observed that "the currently fashionable conclusion seems to be that there is no general obligation to obey the law," despite the enduring conviction of government actors that the law does morally obligate. See Philip Soper, *Legal Theory and the Claim of Authority*, 18 PHILOSOPHY AND PUBLIC AFFAIRS 209, 211 (1989).

3. What are the practical differences between contemporary writers who recognize a moral obligation to obey the law and those who do not? Sometimes, those rejecting the idea of a moral obligation to obey the law hold that the law can influence the way we ought to think about our moral beliefs, that we ought to act as if legal rules were morally binding, and even that we ought morally to teach that legal decisions are morally binding. See Larry Alexander, *Law and Exclusionary Reasons*, 18 PHILOSOPHICAL TOPICS 5, 12, 19-20 (1990).

4. Donald H. Regan grants that "[e]ven among people (such as myself) who deny that there is a moral obligation to comply with the law, all would admit

that many acts the law requires are acts we have a moral obligation to do, on some other ground." Donald H. Regan, *Reasons, Authority, and the Meaning of 'Obey': Further Thoughts on Raz and Obedience to Law*, 3 CANADIAN JOURNAL OF LAW AND JURISPRUDENCE 3, 18 (1990). H.L.A. Hart observes that "[i]n all communities there is a partial overlap in content between legal and moral obligation. . . ." H.L.A. HART, THE CONCEPT OF LAW 166 (1961).

5.   Tom Campbell concludes that "law as such has no moral authority," but that within any particular legal system, "there are a number of putatively good reasons for conforming to the law's meager obligations that turn them into material obligations for the person who accepts those reasons. . . ." Tom Campbell, *Obligation: Societal, Political, and Legal*, in ON POLITICAL OBLIGATION 120, 148 (Paul Harris ed. 1990).

6.   Similarly, Donald Regan elsewhere reiterates that "[l]ike many people these days, I believe there is no general moral obligation to obey the law." Donald H. Regan, *Law's Halo*, 4 SOCIAL PHILOSOPHY & POLICY 15, 15 (1986). Regan then not surprisingly commends the law as creating moral obligations and as a good in itself. See *id.* at 16. Thus some might say that we should do what the law requires, without "obeying" the law in a strict sense.

7.   John Simmons is also among those who deny any general political obligation while minimizing the practical import of this claim. Simmons notes that "from a conclusion that no one in a state has political obligations, nothing follows immediately concerning a justification of disobedience. . . . There are, even in the absence of political obligations, still strong reasons for supporting at least certain types of government and for obeying the law." A. JOHN SIMMONS, MORAL PRINCIPLES AND POLITICAL OBLIGATIONS 193 (1979).

8.   As John Charvet has concisely pointed out, Simmons believes both that few persons are under a political obligation, as few persons have consented to their government, and that everyone, in view of the natural duty to act justly, owes a duty to support just states and obey just laws. John Charvet, *Political Obligation: Individualism and Communitarianism*, in ON POLITICAL OBLIGATION 65, 65 (Paul Harris ed. 1990). Should not our interest then shift drastically in the direction of trying to discover what we can about just and unjust laws and states?

9.   Professor Heidi Hurd writes that "[t]he central question in political theory has been the question of whether the law obligates: does law compel obedience just because it is the law?" Heidi M. Hurd, *Challenging Authority*, 100 YALE LAW JOURNAL 1611, 1677 (1991). Professor Hurd's answer is in the negative, but she goes on to discuss how law or government can function as a merely theoretical or advisory authority, in the sense of providing recognizably

superior judgments of the preexisting balance of moral reasons made by citizens who do not look to government in its capacity as theoretical authority. See id. at 1613, 1615-16, 1667-77.

10. Joseph Raz notes that "because of the bureaucratic necessity to generalize and disregard distinctions too fine for large scale enforcement and administration, some people are able to do better [in judging well] if they refuse to acknowledge the authority of [even a just] law." JOSEPH RAZ, THE MORALITY OF FREEDOM 78 (1986). As accurate as this may be, does a healthy regard for human fallibility, egocentrism, and pride suggest that the scope for its desirable practical application will be limited? See id. at 100 for Raz's discussion of the partial authority for certain purposes of just governments. For further relevant discussion of Raz's theory of obligation by writers including Leslie Green, Michael Moore, Yasumoto Morïgiwa, Stephen Perry, and Donald Regan, together with a response by Raz, see Symposium: The Works of Joseph Raz in 62 SOUTHERN CALIFORNIA LAW REVIEW 731 (1989). For a further critique of Raz's theory, see Roger A. Shiner, Law and Authority, 2 CANADIAN JOURNAL OF LAW AND JURISPRUDENCE 3 (1989).

11. John Mackie argues sweepingly that "[t]here is . . . no objectively prescriptive obligation to obey the law, for the simple reason that there are no objectively prescriptive obligations at all." J.L. Mackie, Obligations to Obey the Law, 67 VIRGINIA LAW REVIEW 143, 143 (1981). Mackie then goes on to recommend that we "invent" an underived prima facie moral obligation, of a strength varying according to circumstances, to obey the law. See id. at 151-52. If we can invent the wheel and the microchip, can we also invent a reasonably stable and effective morality? Is Mackie's project logically coherent and practically feasible? Would we be better off, on the whole, if we de-moralized the idea of governmental authority, and stopped looking for moral reasons to do or not do what governments ask us to do? On such a view, governments in particular, and government in general, might be seen as merely useful or desirable, but as neither objectively morally sound nor morally objectionable. This would presumably be part of a broader process of debunking and abandoning moral evaluation, as ordinarily conceived, generally. See JOHN L. MACKIE, HUME'S MORAL THEORY 155 (1980). Compare much of the contemporary work of Richard Rorty, including, for example, RICHARD RORTY, CONTINGENCY, IRONY, AND SOLIDARITY (1989); RICHARD RORTY, CONSEQUENCES OF PRAGMATISM (1982); Richard Rorty, Postmodernist Bourgeoise Liberalism, 80 JOURNAL OF PHILOSOPHY 583 (1983).

12. Kent Greenawalt argues for a "natural duty" to obey with "enough power to override marginal and correctible impairments of moral rights" in at least some cases. Kent Greenawalt, The Natural Duty to Obey the Law, 84 MICHIGAN LAW REVIEW 1, 61 (1985). Greenawalt limits the scope of this

natural duty even with respect to laws that are conceded to be just: "given the many trivial, foolish, and overbroad laws and the many circumstances in which disobedience, even if widespread, will not undermine the serious aims behind laws, a natural duty to obey does not apply on every occasion of application of just laws." *Id.* at 44. All in all, then, how much practical difference is there between writers who reject, and those who accept, a prima facie general moral obligation to obey the law?

13. Kurt Baier poses the issue of political obligation as "whether one ought, prima facie, to obey any and every government actually having political authority," or whether we instead "should consider each directive of such a government on its own merits. . . ." Kurt Baier, *Obligation: Political and Moral*, in 12 NOMOS: POLITICAL AND LEGAL OBLIGATION 117 (J. Roland Pennock & John W. Chapman eds. 1970). Isn't this set of alternatives too stark? Once we have decided the Nazi regime is unworthy of obedience, must we consider every traffic law in a generally just society solely on its apparent merits, with no presumption that it deserves obedience?

14. Joseph Raz reports: "I would feel insulted if it were suggested that I refrain from murder and rape because I recognize a moral obligation to obey the law." Joseph Raz, *The Obligation to Obey: Revision and Tradition*, 1 NOTRE DAME JOURNAL OF LAW, ETHICS AND PUBLIC POLICY 139, 141 (1984). Isn't it possible, though, that this reflects the fact that of the several moral reasons for not killing or raping, the general moral obligation to obey the law is a relatively trivial, though not utterly unreal, such reason? Doesn't the insult stem from the implication that Raz would be unpersuaded by those more important reasons? Does this argument really help show that there is no general moral obligation, of any strength, to obey the law?

15. Does morally binding authority reside in the law's status as a solution, promoting the common good, to various social coordination problems? Many standard traffic laws are thought of as solutions to coordination problems. See JOHN FINNIS, NATURAL LAW AND NATURAL RIGHTS 245-52 (1980). How might the law claim moral authority over matters other than coordination problems, such as issues involving strong conflicts of basic interests?

16. James Fishkin argues that four conditions are jointly sufficient to establish that practices of government are genuinely legitimate. The four conditions are, roughly, as follows: First, that the practices are widely agreed upon, at least at the level of how they are to be procedurally arrived at, if not at the level of the substantive content of policy. Second, that exit from the system should be unimpeded. Third, that the practices provide the social bases for full membership in the political system. Fourth, that the practices in question be subject to continuing genuinely free debate. See James Fishkin, *Towards a*

*New Social Contract*, 24 NOUS 217, 221 (1990). Is the "exit" condition any more realistic today than in Locke's time? What does the third or "full membership" condition really require? *See id.* at 223.

17. William Boardman argues that "[o]ne important reason why existing legal standards are relevant to morality is that they create expectations which, like those created by promises, are relied upon and expected to be relied upon." William S. Boardman, *Coordination and the Moral Obligation to Obey the Law*, 97 ETHICS 546, 548 (1987). Of course, we will normally have to pass independent judgment on the moral worthiness of the expectation or reliance interest—an expectation that fugitive slaves will be returned is presumably entitled to no moral weight.

18. Paul Harris argues that no moral claim to obedience can be made by repressive, intolerant societies, or by "by a legal system that has a role in producing or maintaining poverty, racism, inadequate health care, poor education, or substandard housing, for these conditions are certain to detract from the ability of individuals and groups disadvantaged by the law in these ways to live a moral life in conditions of respect and autonomy." Paul Harris, *The Moral Obligation to Obey the Law*, in ON POLITICAL OBLIGATION 151, 173 (Paul Harris ed. 1989) Is respect for one's personhood by the government a necessary condition if one is to act morally or develop the ability to adhere to rational universal moral principles one formulates for oneself? Is the idea of autonomy, as ordinarily understood, simply an unrealistic individualist abstraction? Or is Harris close to a deep understanding of why governments, at least in advanced industrial societies, are legitimate or illegitimate?

19. As against Paul Harris's expansive view of what a government must undertake in order to be legitimate, contrast for example the libertarian approach to legitimate government articulated by Ellen Frankel Paul, in *On Three "Inherent Powers of Government*," 66 MONIST 529, 530 (1983).

20. Tony Honore argues that if skepticism about a general prima facie obligation to obey took effect on the public mind, "there would be a great deal more disobedience, especially in cases in which obedience is burdensome to the citizen and its advantage to others is debatable. This increase in disobedience might be a desirable thing, and skeptics are entitled to argue that it would be. But surely they are wrong to minimize the likely impact of their ideas on the legal system." Tony Honore, *Must We Obey? Necessity As a Ground of Obligation*, 67 VIRGINIA LAW REVIEW 39, 42-43 (1981). Is this so? What percentage of any increased disobedience would be genuinely justified? Note that what might be called the conscientious, but covert, evasion of taxes might fall into the category Honore describes.

21. For some survey evidence suggesting that obedience to law is indeed linked to the perceived moral legitimacy of the legal system and its procedures, see TOM R. TYLER, WHY PEOPLE OBEY THE LAW 161-69, 178 (1990). For contrast, though, consider the classic experimentally-based study of the potential horrifying consequences of abandoning moral responsibility to the judgment of authority figures, STANLEY MILGRAM, OBEDIENCE TO AUTHORITY (1975). Consider also Natan Sharansky's account of the former Soviet regime: "The state was maintained not by tanks and missiles, or even by camps and prisons. These were necessary, of course, but only for strengthening the *real* base of the regime—the consciousness of the slave who looks for guidance to the good czar, the leader, the teacher." NATAN SHARANSKY, FEAR NO EVIL xiv-xv (Stefani Hoffman trans. 1988) (emphasis in the original).

22. Joseph Raz concludes that "[a]ny conditional or qualified recognition of legitimacy will deny the law the authority it claims for itself. If you say, 'one has an obligation to obey any law which does not violate fundamental human rights' you have denied that the law has the authority it claims for itself." JOSEPH RAZ, THE MORALITY OF FREEDOM 76-77 (1986). How far is Raz's view from, say, that of John Locke in this respect?

23. David Lyons argues that "the reasons that might be given in support of the claim that there is a general moral obligation to obey the law do not apply generally enough. They refer to conditions that can, but do not always, exist." DAVID LYONS, ETHICS AND THE RULE OF LAW 211 (1984). Would any of the classic theorists of obligation, including Hobbes, disagree with this claim?

24. In practical effect, most of the contemporary writers denying a general prima facie moral obligation to obey the law thus restore to the law with the left hand much of what they have taken away with the right. In fact, there may thus be less to the "no general moral obligation" thesis than meets the eye. As the thesis is usually formulated, couldn't someone with views much like, say, John Locke or Aquinas accept the thesis calmly? Why not even an Hobbesian? Why couldn't an Hobbesian argue that any strong prima facie obligation we may have to obey the sovereign takes hold only after we have independently determined whether our obeying the law at issue would involve a substantial threat to our safety, or whether the sovereign, even if we were to obey, would have the power to protect us? Couldn't the Hobbesian say that if obeying would threaten our life, we have a legal, but no moral, reason to obey? Compare Donald H. Regan, *Law's Halo*, 4 SOCIAL PHILOSOPHY & POLICY 15, 19 (1986).

25. George Christie interestingly concludes that many writers find a general

obligation to obey specified moral rules, but no general moral obligation to obey the law, only because they impose different standards in the two cases. Such writers assume that there is a general obligation to keep one's promises, for example, without considering the effect of the various kinds of exceptions or counterexamples in particular cases or circumstances of promising. Some promises should not morally be kept. But those writers often reject the idea of a general, even prima facie, duty to obey the law, based precisely on considering the various possible circumstances in which obeying the law seems morally optional or objectionable. See George Christie, *On the Moral Obligation to Obey the Law*, 1990 DUKE LAW JOURNAL 1311, 1331-32.

26. Rex Martin helpfully notes that as long as we look to any sort of justification external to the law itself, such as divine command, or utility, or a categorical imperative, as the moral grounds for obeying the law, our obligation or loyalty is really to divine command, utility, or the categorical imperative themselves, and not to the law or legal system as such. See Rex Martin, *The Character of Political Allegiance in a System of Rights*, in ON POLITICAL OBLIGATION 184, 187 (Paul Harris ed. 1990).

27. Is there any sort of genuinely meaningful "legal" obligation to obey the law? For a denial that there is some sort of non-moral "legal" obligation to observe and adhere to the laws, see Rodger Beehler, *The Concept of Law and the Obligation to Obey*, 23 AMERICAN JOURNAL OF JURISPRUDENCE 120 (1978).

# Index